John Stuart Mackenzie

**An Introduction to Social Philosophy**

John Stuart Mackenzie

**An Introduction to Social Philosophy**

ISBN/EAN: 9783337073596

Printed in Europe, USA, Canada, Australia, Japan

Cover: Foto ©Thomas Meinert / pixelio.de

More available books at **www.hansebooks.com**

# INTRODUCTION TO
# SOCIAL PHILOSOPHY.

PUBLISHED BY

JAMES MACLEHOSE AND SONS, GLASGOW,

Publishers to the University.

———

MACMILLAN AND CO., LONDON AND NEW YORK.

London, - - Simpkin, Hamilton and Co.
Cambridge, - Macmillan and Bowes.
Edinburgh, - Douglas and Foulis.

———

MDCCCXCV.

# AN
# INTRODUCTION TO
# SOCIAL PHILOSOPHY

BY

## JOHN S. MACKENZIE

M.A., FELLOW OF TRINITY COLLEGE, CAMBRIDGE; PROFESSOR OF LOGIC AND PHILO-
SOPHY IN THE UNIVERSITY COLLEGE OF SOUTH WALES AND MONMOUTHSHIRE

*SECOND EDITION*
*REVISED AND SLIGHTLY ENLARGED*

GLASGOW
JAMES MACLEHOSE & SONS
Publishers to the University
1895

„Die Zukunft decket
Schmerzen und Glücke.
Schrittweis dem Blicke,
Doch ungeschrecket,
Dringen wir vorwärts."

GOETHE.

# PREFACE.

THE substance of this book was contained in outline in a series of Lectures, delivered, in accordance with the conditions of the Shaw Fellowship, at the University of Edinburgh, in January, 1889. Since that time, however, it has been very considerably altered and enlarged; and I have followed the example of my predecessor, Professor W. R. Sorley, in not retaining the Lecture form. As the work is not meant to be used as a text-book, I have not thought it necessary to introduce minute subdivisions of chapters, but have preferred to leave it in the form of six continuous essays.

With a subject requiring so much care and deliberation, the process of correction and improvement is an endless one. In several places I am still conscious of serious deficiencies and imperfections; but it would have been hardly possible to introduce much further change, without such an entire reconstruction as would have involved the labour of many years—if, indeed, it could ever have been completed. On the whole it seemed best to issue the book as it stands; especially as it is expected that the substance of the Shaw Lectures should be printed as soon as possible after the time appointed for their delivery. I can only trust that the faults which it contains may prove, for the most part, to be such as will be hurtful rather to the author than to the reader.

Little, if anything, of what is now published can be claimed as original. I have indicated in the footnotes most of the sources from which suggestions have been taken; but it has not always been possible definitely to recall them. I have also given several references to books in which fuller statements of particular points may be found. The help which I have received, however, has not come exclusively from books. I have naturally derived much assistance from the various teachers of Philosophy and Social Science in Glasgow, Berlin, and Cambridge, whose Lectures I have had the benefit of attending. My deepest obligations are, in particular, due to the Master of Balliol, who added to the immeasurable debt which I already owed him, by reading the whole book in manuscript and suggesting many improvements. For the statements which it contains, however, I am alone responsible.

It is scarcely necessary to add, that this work is not intended as a systematic treatise on the subject with which it deals, but only as a slight contribution to the discussion of it. It is, indeed, not so much a book as an indication of the lines on which a book might be written.   The only merit which I can hope it may be found to possess, is that it has brought into close relation to each other a number of questions which are usually, at least in England, treated in a more disconnected way.

In bringing out a second edition, I have not been able to do much more than try to correct a few of the most obvious deficiencies of statement, and add a few references to the recent literature of the subject.   A Note on the Theory of Value has, however, been added at the end of Chapter IV. ; there are a few additional paragraphs in Chapter VI. ; and numerous smaller changes, chiefly in the form of footnotes, will be found at various points throughout the book.   I am not without hope that I may at some time be able to deal with the whole material in a more thorough and satisfactory way.   But the prospect is a distant one.

I have to thank Mr. W. F. Trotter, of Trinity College, Cambridge, for his valuable assistance in reading the proofs.

J. S. M.

UNIVERSITY COLLEGE,
   CARDIFF, *April*, 1895.

# CONTENTS.

## CHAPTER III.

### THE SOCIAL ORGANISM.

## CHAPTER IV.

### THE SOCIAL AIM.

## CHAPTER V.

### THE SOCIAL IDEAL.

## CHAPTER VI.

### THE ELEMENTS OF SOCIAL PROGRESS.

# CHAPTER VII.

## SUMMARY AND CONCLUSION.

# SOCIAL PHILOSOPHY.

## CHAPTER I.

*3ᵈ class hours*
*omit this*
*chapter*
*Go to p—.*

### THE SCOPE OF SOCIAL PHILOSOPHY.

IT is my object in this essay to define, in a broad and general way, the scope and limits of the application of philosophical principles to social questions. I wish to ascertain in what respects we may hope for light and guidance from philosophy in dealing with such questions, and in what respects it is necessary that we should look for light and guidance elsewhere.

The importance of such an inquiry at the present time will hardly be denied. Most of the leaders of social reform in our own and recent generations who have had a profound influence on the thought of their time, as distinguished from those who have had a merely transitory interest, have avowedly based their teaching on philosophical ideas;[1] and even in the case of those who have

---

[1] We cannot go far, for instance, in the writings of such men as Adam Smith, Comte, Carlyle, J. S. Mill, Herbert Spencer, without finding that their theories of social progress are dependent on certain views with regard to the nature of the world as a whole. In the case of such writers as Proudhon, Karl Marx, and some other Anarchists and Socialists, the intimate relation to the philosophy of Hegel is perhaps more apparent than real; but at least the avowal of such

A

not so based it, we find continually that the discussion of their doctrines leads us into philosophical questions. Whether we are or are not in sympathy with their theories, therefore, it can scarcely fail to be of profit to us to investigate the foundations on which principles that have been so influential rest. It is true that there are many difficulties in the way of such a study: for not only is it, like all philosophical inquiries, one of considerable intricacy in itself, but it is one which it is very hard to disentangle from the multitude of particular interests with which it is in danger of being confused. The reason which is applied to the problems of life, even by those who appeal explicitly to the principles of thought, is rarely a quite pure reason; and the conclusions to which particular thinkers are led can seldom be regarded as only the logical outcome of the "dry light" from which they profess to start. When reason is made the handmaid of conduct, the logic which is expressed will in most cases be found to have been subjected to a more subtle logic which is concealed; and the premises of the former, which slip in as a matter of course, are often only the unconscious conclusions of the latter. In dealing with a philosophy of life which is (in Bacon's phrase) so "drenched and blooded," it is hard to decide how much is observation and how much is hope, and whether the life is more determined by the philosophy or the philosophy by the life.

Thought which is thus characterised cannot easily be made an object of scientific study. When we think we are refuting the argument on which a particular doctrine

a relationship is significant, and cannot be altogether ignored. Cf. Bonar's *Philosophy and Political Economy*, Book v., chap. i., and *passim.* Some recent books on social science rest rather on biology than on philosophy; but in the effort to interpret the biological data philosophical principles are, explicitly or implicitly, involved.

rests, we may discover that that argument is in fact only a part of the scaffolding that has been used in the erection of the structure, the true foundation of which is to be found in some entirely different principle. How little, for instance, would the doctrines of Proudhon or of Karl Marx be affected by the withdrawal of the Hegelian dialectic ! If that were removed, the form of the doctrines would no doubt require to be modified ; but the substance of them would in most cases be found to depend on considerations that are completely different, and that have indeed but little reference to philosophy at all. The philosophic basis is in such instances little more than a casual weapon which has been snatched up to defend a foregone conclusion. If, therefore, our study of Social Philosophy is to be of any real profit, it will be necessary that we should not only discuss principles which *may* be applied to social problems—for almost any principles may be so applied—but that we should ascertain precisely to what extent such principles furnish the ultimate and only valid basis on which our method of dealing with these problems must rest, and to what extent they serve no higher purpose than that of a convenient handle. In the effort to ascertain this, the fact that philosophical ideas have been widely made use of in the discussion of social questions will be apt to prove rather a hindrance than a help; and we must exercise some caution if we are not to be misled by irrelevant issues.

There is one consideration which may naturally deter us even at the threshold of this inquiry—the fact, namely, that it belongs rather to the end than to the beginning of philosophic study. It ought rather to occupy the concluding volume of a system than to be the theme of a first essay. This is an objection which, in the interest of exact science, I am certainly not disposed to overlook. Philosophy is nothing if not systematic; and few things are more prejudicial to the advance of knowledge than the effort to attain the results before we have mastered the elements. At the same time, such an effort is less dangerous in philosophy than in some other studies; and indeed it is almost unavoidable if we are to make progress at all. To find the true beginning of philosophy is one of the most difficult of philosophical questions, and must perhaps—paradoxical though it may seem—be postponed to the end of the study. Philosophy, indeed, may be compared to a serpent of eternity. It has neither beginning, middle, nor end. Every road in it leads us to the end of the world; and there is often as much hope of penetrating into the heart of the subject from the point that seems last as from the point that seems first. In a science whose chief aim and glory is to see things as a whole, or *sub specie aeternitatis*, it is necessary to observe where we are going as well as where we ought to start; and indeed in such a study we can hardly be said to know anything until we know everything, since to know anything truly is to know it in the light of the whole. There must consequently always be a certain objection to *any* starting point.

It must be allowed, indeed, that there is a special danger in any attempt to work at what may be called the edifying side of philosophic study, before the more purely theoretical parts of the subject have been placed on a secure foundation. Questions in which our sympathies and hopes are directly concerned can scarcely be treated without bias; and there is a risk that if we begin with these, our whole subsequent speculations may take their colour from our personal aims and wishes.[1] But there is an opposite danger which is scarcely less fatal to the

---

[1] Hence the point of Fichte's saying—"Tell me what a man's character is, and I will tell you the kind of philosophy which he will adopt."

interests of philosophic study. Philosophy is not likely to be exhausted in the lifetime of any one individual or in the course of any one generation, and yet it is of the very essence of philosophy that it aims at being complete and systematic, and the chief interest of the pursuit is that it helps us to "see life steadily and see it whole." Hence philosophy is always exposed to this twofold peril, that it may grasp too hastily at the results which it wishes to secure, or that it may cease to be philosophy at all by losing sight of its end; and in the history of the subject we may observe a continual oscillation between the Scylla and Charybdis of these opposite abstractions. When philosophy is treated from the purely analytic or scientific side, without any reference to the guidance which it supplies for conduct, it is apt to sink into the position of "a virgin consecrated to God," which is entirely barren as regards all the particular concerns of mankind; and then all but a few of its most ardent devotees begin to think that, however true it may be that it can "give us God, Freedom, and Immortality"—and even this may appear doubtful— it is at least certain that it "bakes no bread." Thus divorced from life, its purely scientific interest becomes so impalpable and evanescent that it is soon crowded out of the serious employments of mankind, as a study that has not body enough, to command attention.

Hence, though it is necessary to make a careful investigation of the first principles of philosophic truth before we can have a secure possession of any results that will help us in life, though it is perfectly true that philosophy must be light-bearing before it can be fruit-bearing, yet we may sometimes with advantage look forwards as well as backwards, in order that we m   se   if not the results that have actually been reached, at least the results for which we hope, and the hope of which constitutes the main interest of our search. If it is true that

" Two desires toss about
    The poet's feverish blood ;
  One drives him to the world without,
    And one to solitude,"

it may also be said of the philosopher that he finds himself
constrained at once to beat back into the region of the
thinnest abstractions, and to move forward to the region
of concrete fact, which these abstractions are to help him
to understand.

In a sense, no doubt, it must be acknowledged that we
can never find in philosophy any direct assistance in dealing
with the particular problems of life. When we have devoted ourselves to this study, we must content ourselves
with the pursuit of truth for its own sake, and must be
so far from expecting any other reward, that we may not
even hope to attain that which is the immediate object
of our pursuit, but must find our profit in the search.
But it is none the less true that in the search for ultimate
truth we are stimulated by the hope that we shall gain
also a certain degree of light on the meaning of our
everyday existence. He who " seeks first the kingdom of
God " does so always with a certain latent conviction that
" these other things will be added unto him,"—that, as
he gains glimpses of what is universal and absolute, he
will also see more clearly the relation of the particular to
it. And thus, though it is dangerous to attempt to make
philosophy edifying before 'we have made it precise, it is
yet inevitable that we should glance sometimes at the
methods in which the principles of philosophy may be
applied to life, as well as at the methods in which these
principles, themselves may be deduced and established.
While we glance at the former, however, it will be necessary to keep the latter steadily in view, in order that we
may not report the verdicts of philosophy on cases that
have never been brought within her jurisdiction.

It happens that such a glance is especially important just at the present time. There is a certain broad sense in which it is always true that "the proper study of mankind is man," and that if we are not in some way or other helping to advance human well-being, we are doing nothing. There is a certain broad sense also in which it is always true, as Aristotle put it,[1] that the well-being of a society is "a larger and more perfect" end than that of any single individual. Hence the science which deals with social welfare may always be regarded as a master-science in human studies, not indeed in the sense that, like Logic, it regulates their principles, but in the sense that it determines their worth. It is worth while to know Social Philosophy, because, until we know that, we do not know what else it is worth while to know. But there are, besides, a number of special circumstances which have caused social questions to assume a peculiar prominence in recent times, and have made it more than ever necessary to have clear ideas with regard to the principles on which their solution depends. Into the nature of these we shall shortly have occasion to inquire. In the meantime we may regard them simply as part of the general intellectual unrest by which our time is characterised. In an "age of criticism" social questions are almost sure to come to the front, because they are the questions with respect to which criticism can be most directly appreciated and carried into act; and, accordingly, in our own time,— as in the time of the Sophists in Athens,—it is into this channel that much of our recent criticism has run. Many of the ideas and principles of conduct by which men were formerly guided in dealing with the great questions of the life and welfare of human beings in societies have been discredited or swept away. We are now engaged in groping our way to something new; and whether the new light is

[1] *Ethics*, I. ii. 8.

to be better than the old, will depend mainly on the thoroughness with which we set ourselves to discover what is ultimately true and what is ultimately desirable with reference to social affairs.

One of the most evident signs of this intellectual unrest in our time with reference to the subject of social well-being may be found in the discontent which is felt with regard to the study of Political Economy, as hitherto pursued.  To some extent, no doubt, this discontent has expressed itself in a somewhat unreasonable form, in sneers at Economics as "the dismal science," or in the representation of its students as men whose interests in life are sordid and mean.  But beneath such ineptitudes as these[1] it can hardly be denied that there has been in recent times a growing consciousness of the inadequacy of the older methods of economic study, a perception that the factors of social well-being are more numerous and more subtle than men had formerly supposed, and that for the right analysis and evaluation of them it is necessary to take a broader survey of the nature and history of human society than had in earlier times been found possible or convenient.

Not only has there been a tendency to subordinate the study of Economics to the larger science of Sociology, but there has also been a demand—largely through the influence of such writers as Carlyle and Ruskin—for a more distinct recognition of the bearing of ethical considerations on the economic aspects of life.[2]  There are indeed still some who hold that the discussion of that

---

[1] Which, however, are not entirely without point.  Cf. *infra*, p. 55.  For an excellent statement of the deficiencies of the older economists, see Toynbee's *Industrial Revolution*, pp. 1-26.

[2] On this point it may be sufficient to refer to the article on "Political Economy" in the *Encyclopaedia Britannica* (vol. xix.) *passim*.  See also Devas's *Political Economy*, and cf. *infra*, p. 64.

which lies beyond what may be called the external or mechanical means of welfare belongs rather to Ethics than to Economics, and that the economist has done all that can reasonably be expected of him if he has dealt with the means of material production and with the general laws of distribution in society as he finds it, and has at the same time indicated generally the points at which his subject touches Ethics.[1] But such an attitude cannot ultimately prove satisfactory. The division between the two sciences of Ethics and Economics cannot be thus sharply drawn; and if the attempt is persistently made so to draw it, there is a large department of life—and that one of the most important—which remains untouched by either. For in reality the two subjects do not touch, with a rigid boundary at their point of contact; they may rather be said to overlap, with a kind of No-Man's Land within their common section. And the result is that, when we pass from Economics to Ethics, instead of finding that the latter science deals with those questions which are relegated to it by the former, we find rather that Ethics throw them back again to Economics, and that they are consequently never dealt with at all. For, while the economist is naturally concerned almost exclusively with the fact that human well-being involves a certain mastery over material conditions, and that in the effort to obtain this mastery men are led to associate themselves together in quasi-mechanical combinations, and to act in

---

[1] The extent to which moral considerations have tended to be forgotten altogether not only in the stress of actual business competition, but even in the writings of theoretical economists, is often very striking. Wagner quotes the following from Emminghaus—"An elastic conscience helps a man to many a victory. Overscrupulousness is, rightly enough, at a discount in trade." As Wagner adds, "Wenn das schon die graue Theorie sagt, was wird erst die grüne Praxis leisten!"—*Lehrbuch der politischen Oekonomie*, I. 233.

conformity with quasi-mechanical laws; the ethical philosopher, on the other hand, is concerned almost exclusively
with the fact that human well-being involves the subjection
of the individual will to universal principles of conduct,
which are independent, or almost independent, of such
material conditions. And ·thus it happens that neither
the economist nor the moralist, as such, concerns himself
directly with the problems which arise from the fact that
human well-being depends on *both* these conditions. The
absence of any adequate treatment of such problems has,
for many reasons, become especially conspicuous at the
present time. Now, whether such a limitation of the
provinces of Economics and Ethics implies a false abstraction in our modes of thought, is a question which
we cannot now consider: but when we have said that
it is at least a part of the business of Social Philosophy to deal with the debatable territory which is
thus omitted, we have said enough to show that Social
Philosophy is a subject which at present will repay a
careful study.

A science, however, which is to deal with the general
conditions of social well-being, in such a way as to connect
Economics with Ethics, must, even if this were its only
function, be not only a great but a large subject; one,
moreover, to which the saying "ardua quae pulchra" is
clearly applicable. In such an essay as this we cannot
hope to do more than indicate broadly the nature of the
problem, the general method on which it ought to be dealt
with, and a few of the most important results which such a
method discloses.

We must first try to define the nature and scope of our
inquiry. Although a full understanding of the aims and
limits of a subject is often the very last thing that we reach
in our study of it, yet it is important at the beginning to
mark out its boundaries as carefully as we can; since

otherwise we are in constant danger of confusing our discussion by the introduction of matter which is irrelevant to our line of thought. Mrs. Carlyle said once that "mixing things up is the great Bad," and in philosophical investigations this has certainly an element of truth.

Probably most people, when they hear Social Philosophy mentioned, will think of one or other of three methods of inquiry; and a few words on the nature and limitations of these methods may serve to introduce us to that conception of its scope, and of its position among other sciences, which I regard as most correct.

I. The simplest sense of the term is that in which philosophy means nothing more than reflective thinking. Any effort to get below the facts revealed to us by observation and simple analysis, may be said to be a philosophising about them: and such philosophising may be conducted with regard to the facts of social life, as well as with regard to any others. In the case of human life, moreover, it is particularly easy—indeed, inevitable for anyone who thinks at all—to philosophise in this sense: because in this case we are dealing not merely with facts and classes of facts, but with ends and aspirations. The consideration of the ends which human beings set before themselves, of the motives by which they are led to conceive of such ends, and of the methods by which means are made subservient to them, carries us at once beyond the mere observation and analysis of facts, and introduces us into the region of what may, in a certain sense, be fairly described as philosophy. Such philosophy as this is that which may most properly be characterised as common-sense philosophy. Some of the best examples of such philosophy may be found in Aristotle, in those passages in which he takes up the ἔνδοξα, or ordinary views of human beings with regard to life, and endeavours to fit them together and give them a certain

coherence.[1]   Illustrations of such a philosophy are also to
be found in the works of many modern writers—*e.g.* in most
of the popular treatises on history and economics.   Experience, however, soon teaches us the inadequacy of such a
philosophy of life.   We find that but few of the ἔνδοξα of
human beings remain quite constant from age to age, and
that even those which co-exist at any one period are seldom
capable of being shaped into a harmonious whole.   Our
ordinary views and aims in life are acquired by partial
glances.   They may be compared to photographic scenes,
which may be admirable at the focus where the main
interest centres, but beyond that fade away into indistinct-
ness and confusion.   Each of them singly may be excellent
for its purpose, but they cannot, without a certain absurdity,
be combined into a picture.   Even whole peoples and
generations live only from hand to mouth, and the wisdom
which is embodied in their common-sense is generally, as
Emerson said of the styles of men of genius, "good for
this trip only."   It serves its time, but is not intended to
be perpetuated and combined with alien intuitions.   It is
that kind of knowledge which we have only when we are
not asked.

> " Wer *nicht* denkt,
>     Dem wird sie geschenkt ;
>     Er hat sie ohne Sorgen " ;

but he who deliberates on it is lost.

II. The second sense in which Social Philosophy may
be understood is one which is at the present time regarded
with more favour.   It is the sense in which the now
familiar term Sociology is commonly accepted, which may
be described as the study of society as the object of an
empirical science.   It is evident that human society may

---

[1] Aristotle, however, always aims at something more than this.   In
giving a statement of current opinions he is not simply seeking to give
them coherence, but rather to teach a deeper view by means of them.

be made the object of such a study, just as any other
collection of facts may; and the utility of such a study,
within its own limits, is hardly now in danger of being
overlooked. But its unsatisfactoriness, so long as it
remains merely empirical, must also be sufficiently apparent.
The rôle of the mere observer must always be a humble
one, even in the case of those sciences which offer him
the most abundant scope. The true "seer," indeed, is
the rarest of all discoverers: but the true seer is one who
brings to his observation more than he finds in it. The
drudgery of the patient interrogator of nature is made
divine only when it is inspired by ideas which are not
objects of observation. And if this is the case even with
regard to those sciences which are directed most entirely
to phenomena that are capable of being externally perceived, it must hold to a much greater extent where the
object is not any collection of facts, but rather a stream
of tendency and aspiration. And when to this it is added
that we who observe the stream are ourselves a portion
of it, and that our observation of it may become a factor
in the modification of its course;[1] it becomes clear that
a merely empirical study of society, however useful and
even indispensable it may be as an adjunct to other
inquiries, cannot of itself be made a satisfactory basis for
a philosophy of life.

III. We are thus led to notice the third sense in which
the term "Social Philosophy" might naturally be interpreted; and this is indeed in some respects the most
obvious sense of all. It may be understood to mean a
systematic effort to deduce the laws of social life from
certain primary principles, which are ascertained by
philosophical analysis. The pursuit of such a "high
*priori* road" has in modern times fallen somewhat into
discredit, especially with regard to questions which have

[1] Cf. Venn's *Empirical Logic*, p. 576 *seq.*

a distinctly practical bearing. And indeed it is evident that the application of philosophical principles to such questions must be expected to be among the latest results of philosophic study, and that it will be dangerous to attempt to apply them before we have succeeded in making our first principles thoroughly clear and certain. This we can hardly hope to see immediately accomplished; and consequently it would seem that our method of investigation must for the present be somewhat more tentative in its character. Yet it seems equally evident that, until we can secure such a systematic method of study as has now been indicated, there cannot be, in any proper sense of the word, a Social Philosophy. We cannot be satisfied with a mere aggregate of ἔνδοξα or with a mere effort to analyse facts.

Τί οὖν ποιήσομεν φιλοσοφίας πέρι; We might, no doubt, effect a compromise by combining two or more of the methods of study to which reference has been made. As a matter of fact, this is what has usually been done in the systematic study of social questions; and since there are such serious difficulties in the way of the adoption of any single method, it might certainly seem to be the wisest course to pursue. But if this were all that we had to offer, it would scarcely merit the title of a Social Philosophy. It would, at the best, be only a struggling with materials out of which we might hope that a Social Philosophy would some day be evolved. And indeed it would come perilously near to a selling of ourselves to "the great Bad," if we were to content ourselves with the simple attitude of a compromise, accepting a little of this and a little of that, and mixing them up to suit our fancy. There would be no means of determining which of the elements in the compound should be allowed to *draw* most powerfully; and this could be decided only by the caprice of the individual writer or by the spirit of the particular age.

A sense of the uncertainty as to the correct method of procedure in inquiries of this kind has frequently led even those who are otherwise "friends of ideas" to regard the philosophic treatment of social questions as a somewhat unprofitable ideology, and to believe that such problems may be better trusted for their solution to the practical sagacity which comes of experience. Writers like Carlyle have hoped that when the Augean stables of social difficulty become too foul a Hercules will arise to cleanse them, and have thought that unless we are aided by some such heroic intervention there is little else than confusion to be gained by philosophic study. Perhaps this may prove to be the case; but at any rate we need not despair of our study till we have made an effort to ascertain the value and scope of the various methods of inquiry, so as to see what kind of light and how much of it may be expected from each. In order to ascertain this, however, it will be necessary to consider with some care what the general nature of philosophic study is. We may then hope to be able to understand how it may be applied to social problems.

There is a distinction as old as Aristotle between the different methods of explanation which may be adopted in scientific inquiry—a distinction which has not yet lost its force, and which, with some slight modification, will be serviceable to us here. Aristotle points out,[1] that with reference to every object of our investigation there are four different kinds of explanation (αἰτίαι) of which it is possible to make use. We may ask what it is, and analyse it into the particular elements of which it is composed: we may ask what makes it what it is, and investigate the laws or principles by which its nature is determined: we may inquire into its history, and trace its development back to the earliest origin of its changes: or

---

[1] *Metaphysics*, I. iii. 1. Cf. *Physics*, II. iii. 1 *seq.*

we may endeavour to discover the <u>ideal at which it aims,</u> or the end for which it has been formed, and by the effort after which its progress is guided. This is scarcely the way in which the distinction would be drawn in modern times[1]: but it is at least an exhaustive summary of the various questions that may be asked; and the attempt to answer some or all of them with respect to particular classes of objects is the aim of every human science. The attempt to answer the first question is the aim of Natural Science, in its more restricted sense: the attempt to answer the second is the aim of Mathematical Science, and of what are called the exact sciences generally: the attempt to answer the third is the aim of Historical Science, in the broadest sense of that term: the attempt to answer the fourth is the aim of Teleological Science, in so far as there is any such. To justify these divisions would carry us beyond the limits of the present subject; but what we have now to ask is—What is the attitude of philosophy with regard to these various inquiries?

Now it might seem at first that along the line of each of these inquiries we must be led ultimately to a distinct philosophic problem—*i.e.* to a problem which we recognise as fundamental when we try to think things out.[2] For an analysis of the material with which we are dealing would lead us on to the question of its ultimate constitution, and would thus land us in the problem with which the earliest of the Greek philosophers started. An investigation of the laws or principles by which the material is determined would lead us on to an inquiry into the nature and relations of the categories—*i.e.* of the necessary forms which give determination to all thought and being. So too the attempt to trace the history of the material which is the

---

[1] Cf. *infra*, p. 24.

[2] That this is what we understand by a philosophic problem, may, I suppose, be taken for granted.

object of our study would force us back upon the question
as to the ultimate origin[1] of the world of our experience;
and the search for the end to which the material is adapted
would force us forward to the Platonic problem as to the
nature of the Good, or of the ideal "to which the whole
creation moves." Philosophic research would thus be a
kind of square, with four separate sides.

But further consideration will lead us to a different
conclusion, and will make it apparent that these four
inquiries (so far as they are ultimate or fundamental) are,
in the last resort, but one; and that philosophy is rather
to be compared to a circle than a square. For, in truth,
neither the first, the third, nor the fourth of the methods
of explanation which have now been mentioned, leads to
any ultimate philosophical problem, except in so far as it
becomes coincident with the second method; and the
problem with which that method deals is, consequently,
the centre round which all philosophy revolves. That
this is so may become evident by a brief consideration
of the ways in which the other three methods or αἰτίαι
lead us into philosophical questions.

Let us ask, first, how it is that the analysis of any given
material leads us back to a philosophical problem. It is
clear at once that it leads us to no such problem so long
as we are able simply to take to pieces the material which
is presented to us, and to find in the pieces which we thus
reach a new material which is similarly presented. When
we analyse water into oxygen and hydrogen, there is no
problem raised by the components, as such, which is not
equally raised by the compound substance with which we
start. So long as we merely see before our eyes that one
object has certain other objects as its constituents, we are
still in the region of simple observation, and are not led

---

[1] *Ultimate origin* sounds like a *contradictio in adjectis.* But, of course,
*ultimate* is here used simply in the sense of *terminal.*

to any problem with regard to what is ultimate or fundamental—which is what we understand by a philosophical
problem.    Such a problem arises only when we ask such
questions as these : What are the *ultimate* constituents
of the object before us? or, By what *laws* is the formation
of the object out of certain constituents governed? or,
By what *process* does the object as it is now presented
arise out of such constituents; or, For what *end* is the
object formed out of these constituents?    Such questions
carry us behind the facts that are presented to us into an
investigation of the fundamental principles involved in
their presentation.    Now it is clear that the last three
of these questions belong to the other αἰτίαι or methods
which are to be considered.    So long as we confine ourselves to the first method, the only philosophical problem
which arises is with reference to the *ultimate* constitution
of our given material.    But this question, again, is a
philosophical one only in so far as it leads us on to our
second class of inquiries—*i.e.* to an inquiry into the laws
or categories or ultimate principles of determination.    For
if it could be ascertained by direct inspection that a certain
analysis of our material is ultimate, the problem involved
in this discovery would not be any more philosophical than
that which is already implied in the observation of the
material itself.    Nor indeed could any philosophical problem
be raised if the ultimate constitution of our material were
discoverable by a train of inference proceeding from the
known to the unknown, except in so far as such a train
of inference presupposes the application of certain universal principles of the connection of facts or events.
But, in truth, it is inconceivable that any analysis of our
material should be known to be ultimate merely by inspection or merely by a direct train of inference.    Such
inspection or such inference could only tell us that the
analysis which we have made is the last which we at

present see our way to make, or that it is the last which the present state of our knowledge entitles us to assume as possible.[1] The discovery that such an analysis is ultimate could be made only by the application of certain principles of inference, the validity of which is not given along with our given material; and the validity of such principles could be established only by an investigation of the general laws of knowledge or of being, or of particular kinds of knowledge or of being as such—*i.e.* only by the introduction of our second method of explanation.

Similarly, an investigation of the nature of the process by which a given object *arises* would lead us to a philosophical problem only in so far as the tracing of that process involves the application of certain universal principles by which events are determined. The tracing of a process from one point of time to another, except in so far as we are guided in the act of following it out by the consciousness of a law of causality or continuity in change, is not of a more distinctly philosophical character than the observation of a single event. Now the application of such a law of continuity can be vindicated only by an analysis of the principles of determination of events in general. Indeed, an inquiry into a process of development differs from an investigation of the constitution of a compound material only as a time-series differs from a series of co-existent phenomena; and it must, therefore, be as clear in the former case as in the latter that no philosophical question can be raised, except in so far as we are led into a consideration of the ultimate principles involved in the determination of our material.

With respect to an inquiry into ends or ideals, the case is somewhat different. Here the whole question is from the very first a philosophical one. The analysis of the

[1] We might be aware that we are brought to a *stand*, but not that we are brought to an *end*.

constitution of a given object, or the tracing of the process of its development, leads us to no ultimate problem;
because each element in the analysis and each stage in
the process is similar to every other element or stage,
and raises no new question, but only carries the old
questions farther back. An end, on the other hand, is,
by its very nature, thought of as something terminal. If
we have discovered what the end of a thing is, we have
gone as far as we can go in one particular direction in
ascertaining what the meaning of that thing is. It might
be thought, indeed, that when an end is externally imposed
on a material to which it does not essentially belong, there
is no philosophical problem raised. When the end is, so
far as the material to which it relates is concerned, capriciously chosen, it might seem that such an end can be
nothing more than a matter for observation, and cannot
give rise to any speculative inquiry. It merely enables us
to say: "Here is a given object and here is a given
end," and the one of these facts is no more enlightening
than the other. But it must be remembered that, in the
last resort, no end is capriciously selected. At least, the
caprice which chooses any end can be reckoned caprice
only with reference to certain other ends·; but it must
itself, in every case, find its determination in the presentation of an end which is not capricious,[1] and the inquiry
into this end leads us at once to a philosophical question.
For we are forced to inquire whence it is that this particular end derives its determining power; and this is a
question to which no answer can be given until we have
analysed the nature of the Good. Consequently, whenever there is an end or ideal presented to us, there is, at

---

[1] Unless, of course, there is an ultimate inexplicability in the choice
of ends—in which case the investigation of them would be an unprofitable inquiry. But we may assume that this view is out of court.
See the remarks on this point near the beginning of Chap. IV.

least *primâ facie*, a philosophical problem raised. And if the question which is thus raised be essentially different from that which is raised by our second method of explanation, then it must be admitted that the roots of philosophy are two-fold. But that this is not the case is apparent on a little further reflection. For it is clear that the presentation of an end or ideal must be either an empirical datum or the result of a reflective study of the object for which the ideal is proposed. Now, if it be merely an empirical datum—if, for instance, we find the explanation of the end or ideal in the fact of a certain pleasure or satisfaction which arises in the being to whom the ideal is presented—then there ceases to be any philosophical problem at all. The ideal or end is then a fact which may be observed like any other fact, and the inquiry into its nature will be conducted according to the first or third method,—neither of which, as we have seen, leads to any ultimate problem. There is a philosophical problem involved only if it be the case that the empirical datum in question—*e.g.* the pleasure or satisfaction—is itself capable of explanation by reference to some deeper principle. And such a deeper principle of explanation can hardly be looked for anywhere else than in an analysis of the laws or principles which underlie all being and knowledge, or at any rate of those which underlie the particular kind of being and knowledge which is concerned in the individual instance under discussion. Consequently it would seem that the consideration of an end or ideal either leads to no ultimate philosophical problem at all— carrying us back simply to an empirical datum—or else it leads to a problem which is identical with that of our second method.

We are thus led to consider in what sense it may be held that that second method leads us to an ultimate philosophical problem. It might seem that even an examination of the principles of determination of the existence of an object would not lead us to any problem which could be regarded as terminal. For it might be thought that an examination of such principles is precisely on a par with an analysis of the constitution of an object or of the process by which it is developed; and that in the one case, as in the others, we should simply be led back from point to point, without reaching any ultimate problem in which thought could rest. But there is an important difference between the three cases. Two of them are simply analyses of *fact*: the other is an analysis of *meaning* or explanation. Now the analysis of fact leads simply to other facts which may equally well be made objects of a further analysis.[1] Indeed, by analysing a single fact into a number of separate elements, we are in general only multiplying our problems. An analysis of meaning or explanation, on the other hand, simplifies our problem, by leading us to broader principles under which a number of particular cases may be brought; and such a method may at last lead us to that which explains itself and carries us no farther. It is, at any rate, on the possibility of reaching such a self-explanatory system of principles in which the wheel of our investigations may " come full circle," that the hopes of philosophy rest.

Further, it is not difficult to see how such a method of explanation connects itself with the idea of an end: since a deeper insight into the meaning of being and knowledge —*i.e.* into the principles by which their nature is determined—can hardly fail to give rise to a demand for a fuller

---

[1] There may, no doubt, be an ultimate limit to such a process of analysis. But we cannot know the limit to be ultimate by merely finding that we cannot go farther in such a process. To know that it is ultimate we must have an *explanation* of the fact that it is ultimate— *i.e.* we must go beyond the mere analysis of facts.

expression of that meaning than we can find in being and knowledge as they are actually presented to us.   To discover what an object means is usually to discover that it does not mean it with perfect clearness ; and thus to gain *ideas* of the principles by which objects are determined is at the same time to gain *ideals* of their further determination.   On this point, however, we need not now insist.   It is sufficient for our present purpose to have indicated the steps by which we are led to the conviction that philosophy is concerned with the analysis of the principles involved in knowledge and being, and, by means of that analysis, with the consideration of an end or ideal.

But if philosophy is thus to appropriate the second and fourth of our methods of explanation, the question remains how it is to relate itself to the first and third.   The consideration of this question may help us to understand the relation of philosophy to the various particular sciences. It has already been pointed out that each of the four methods of explanation may give rise to a special department of science.   It might be truer, however, to say rather that in the subject-matter of every concrete science there are elements which require all the four methods for their adequate discussion.   Every concrete material may be considered with reference to its constitution, its development, or its meaning—including in this last expression at once its essential nature [1] and its end.   If, therefore, the consideration of the meaning of things is to be regarded as the province of philosophy, it might seem that we are left with two departments of science in addition—viz., the consideration of the constitution of things and the consideration of their development.   But if we reflect on the distinction between these two departments, we shall, I think,

---

[1] *I.e.* its *reality*, as distinct from its mere *existence* or appearance. Cf. Bradley's *Appearance and Reality.*

be led to draw the line of demarcation in a somewhat different way.

For wherein does the essential difference between the *constitution* and the *development* of a thing consist? So far as the tracing of its development is merely the sketch of the series of its successive states, while the analysis of its constitution is simply the unfolding of its present condition, there is no fundamental difference between these two things. The one exhibits the nature of the object at a particular moment: the other exhibits the same nature as it presents itself through a series of successive moments. Between these there is no difference but that of time; and there is no particular dignity about a series in time, any more than about a series in space, which should cause the observation of the former to give rise to a higher kind of science. The real difference is to be found rather in this, that in the case of a historical study we are led to investigate the laws of change as well as the mere disposition of facts or elements. The observation of the oak as it stands is the same in kind as the tracing of its growth from the acorn to the completed tree: a higher kind of knowledge is implied only when we are able to "look into the seeds of time, and say which grain will grow, and which will not," or when we are able to explain why from a given grain the growth took place in one particular direction rather than in any other. It is, in short, not a *historical* but a *prophetic* science which is higher than an observational one. For this reason, indeed, the observational sciences themselves are properly enough described as Natural History. It is only when we are able so far to disentangle the elements in the process of growth as to be able to calculate the various lines of tendency, that we are elevated into a higher region of knowledge. Consequently, if we were asked to make a broad classification of the concrete sciences, we should be led to arrange them thus: (1) The science of *Facts and Events*;[1] (2) The science of *Tendencies*. The tendencies, however, which are present in any particular collection of facts at any particular moment are infinitely varied; and the treatment of them can consequently become scientific only in so far as they are clearly distinguished from each other, and their relative forces estimated. In so far as they are merely observed as a set of existing tendencies, we are still only in the region of the observational sciences. Now the clear definition and estimation of tendencies is the work of the exact sciences: and thus our distinction between the two levels of concrete science comes to be identical with the old distinction between those which are simply observational, whether the observation be of simultaneous or of successive phenomena, and those which are exact or which are capable (*i.e.* at least ideally capable) of a mathematical treatment.

Summing up, therefore, we may say that the sciences corresponding to Aristotle's four *causes* or methods of explanation are these: (1) The Natural History sciences, which simply investigate the constitution of things as they stand, whether at particular moments or throughout a succession of moments; (2) The Exact Sciences, which concern themselves with the analysis of concrete phenomena into their elementary principles, and thus supply us with the means of estimating the tendencies of change; (3) Metaphysical Science, which deals with the fundamental principles of knowledge and of being as known; (4) Teleological Science, which investigates the Good, the end or ideal with reference to which things exist. No doubt ideally the sphere of philosophy must be held to include that of science within it; unless we suppose the existence of an ultimate dualism, or at least of an ultimate contin-

---

[1] These two names are given here, with the view of emphasising, not their twoness, but their oneness. I add this note to obviate a misunderstanding which seems to have arisen.

gency.  For it is evident that if we knew thoroughly the
nature of knowledge and being and of the ideal for which
things are, we could hardly be ignorant of the constitution
of particular things and of the laws of their development.
But for us, at any rate, there always remains an element
of contingency in the nature of particular phenomena,
and even in the nature of particular laws; nor is it even
certain that an ultimate understanding of the meaning of
the world would exclude such an element.[1]  But the possibility of such an ultimate exclusion need not concern us
here.  For our purpose it seems clear enough that these
four distinct species of science must be recognised.  We
may distinguish them by saying that the first seeks the
attainment of *knowledge*; the second, of *understanding*;
the third, of *insight*; and the fourth, of *wisdom*.

It ought not to be supposed that each one of these
departments of science has a separate subject-matter.  On
the contrary, every concrete subject-matter involves a reference to all the four; and consequently every concrete
science[2] has in it the possibility of four different sciences.
That this is the case is a fact which is often concealed

[1] Even such a thorough-going rationalism as that of Hegel seems
still to leave a place for the contingent in nature (cf. Wallace's *Logic
of Hegel*, Translation, p. 265).  How far this view is a justifiable one,
and how far it was Hegel's, it is not our business here to inquire.

[2] The only science which is here excluded is pure Mathematics,
which is simply the abstract form of the possibility of exact science
as such.  It might be thought that the science of pure or Formal
Logic ought also to be excluded from the above statement.  But
Logic is merely a kind of applied Metaphysics—being concerned
with the ideals or regulative principles (*e.g.* the principle of consist-
ency, of systematic unity, etc.) which spring out of the nature of
knowledge as such.  It is consequently a part of Epistemology, and
falls within the sphere of philosophy proper.  And it may be added
that for every concrete science there is, in a sense, a Logic—*i.e.* in
the case of every one of them there are certain regulative principles
which have to be observed.

from us by the circumstance that in the case of most
concrete subject-matters one or other of the four elements
tends to become so prominent as to obscure the rest.
Thus Mechanics is commonly, and rightly enough, regarded
as a type of an exact science, and Geology of a Natural
History one.   But whenever it is necessary to make any
concrete application of mechanical principles, it becomes
at once necessary to consider the structure of materials
from a Natural History point of view; while in Geology,
on the other hand, the laws of the formation of strata,
and so on, contain in themselves the possibility of an
exact science.   And that Metaphysics and Teleology may
also be regarded as being concerned in the subject-matter
of each is ·sufficiently apparent.

The best instance for the illustration of this four-fold
reference in the subject-matter of the sciences will naturally
be found in those sciences in which a process of development towards an end is most distinctly traceable.   Of
these the most typical example is, of course, Biology.
Here it is easy to see that the subject-matter may be
partly treated by a simple description of observed facts
and processes, while at the same time there are in these
facts and processes certain tendencies which it is possible
to analyse and evaluate.   By pursuing the former method
of inquiry we may arrive at a *knowledge* of the processes
of vital development : by pursuing the latter, we may in
some measure arrive at an *understanding* of them.   But if
we wish to attain a complete *insight* into life, we must
carry our researches farther and investigate its relations to
existence in general ; and when this has been accomplished, we shall at the same time have gained *wisdom*,
by discovering the end towards which the development of
life is directed.

In the case of the science of Psychology also such a
four-fold process of inquiry is obviously set before us at

least as an ideal possibility. We may, in the first place, confine ourselves to the observation of the facts and processes of mental life, as we are aware of them within ourselves, or as we find them embodied in the languages and institutions of mankind, or as we see them gradually developing in the expressions and instincts of the lower animals. In the second place, we may endeavour to trace in all these processes the operation of certain general laws. Whether it is possible to express these laws, as the Herbartians have attempted, in the form of mathematical or quasi-mechanical principles, or whether, as Kant held, the series of psychological events is too simple or unilinear to be so expresssed, or whether, as some others think, that series is too complex and organic for such a reduction, it is not our place here to inquire; but in any case, it can hardly be doubted that the tendencies of mental processes may in *some* form be discovered and expressed as general laws in formulae of more or less complexity. Then, in the third place, we may endeavour to get behind even such general principles as these, and inquire into those determinations which must necessarily belong to the nature of a developing consciousness as such ; and the inquiry into these would naturally lead us also, in the fourth place, to ask what is the ideal towards which the development of consciousness points, and by the presence of which it is guided throughout the various stages of its growth.

Similarly, in the case of Ethics, or the science of conduct, we might distinguish four possible lines of inquiry; though the obvious reference which all conduct has to certain ends makes it comparatively uninteresting to consider conduct in any other than a teleological aspect. It is quite possible, however, and even useful, to examine the data of moral life in various times and circumstances, simply from the point of view of natural history, without any direct reference to the goodness or badness of particular acts or customs, as conducing to the realisation of particular ends. It is also quite possible to trace in these various acts and customs the operation of certain general laws, or the presence of certain "streams of tendency," without reference to the question whether these tendencies "make for righteousness" or the reverse. Both these investigations are evidently quite distinct from the metaphysical inquiry into the nature of the principles which underlie human conduct as such; and also from the teleological inquiry (which in this case at least is practically inseparable from the metaphysical one) into the ideal of action, or the ultimate end by reference to which our conduct is determined.

Finally, in dealing with social life generally, which is the subject that we have now more particularly to consider, there are once more these four possible 'lines of investigation. We may have a Natural History of society; we may have a Mechanics of society; we may have a Metaphysics of society; and we may have a Logic of society. The first would treat social life simply as one fact among other facts in the world, tracing its development from stage to stage, without considering either how or why it is what it is, and without analysing the tendencies which are in operation at the various stages of its growth. The second would resolve social life at particular periods into its ultimate elements, and trace the direction and estimate the force of the lines of progress which it contains. The third would investigate the meaning of social life as necessarily following from the nature of man and from the nature of the world as a whole; while the fourth would consider its meaning as having reference to an end or ideal.[1]

[1] In distinguishing these different methods of explanation, I have adopted the principle which seems to me simplest and most readily intelligible. For some purposes, however, it might be preferable to express the distinction in a different way. Thus we might say that

From this point of view, we may understand how it is that social life is capable of being studied in those various ways to which reference has already been made; and we may define more exactly the nature of these various ways, and indicate the limits within which each of them may be regarded as valuable.

/ The respective provinces of the second and third methods to which we previously referred—*i.e.* the method of induction and of deduction—are those which it is most easy to mark off; and with them, accordingly, it is most convenient to begin. These two methods are primarily concerned with what may be called the natural history of society and the mechanics of society respectively. So long as we regard the growth of social conditions simply as the evolution of one particular object which we observe, or of one particular set of objects in relation to each other, our method of study must remain at the natural history stage; and any general principles which we arrive at must be reached by induction. On the other hand, when certain general principles have been reached, we may analyse them into their elements, and work out in a rigidly deductive manner the lines of particular tendencies. These two methods have consequently an intimate connection with each other; and their results constitute to-

the particular sciences deal with objects and their relations, in so far as they can be regarded as external to each other in space and time; while philosophy is concerned with the *interpretation* of particular objects—*i.e.* with the universal principles by which their nature is determined, and by which their spatial and temporal externality to each other is transcended. Or we might say simply that philosophy reintroduces the relation of things to thought which the particular sciences omit. But either of these modes of statement seems to me more complex and difficult than that which is adopted in the text; though ultimately their meaning is the same. On the whole subject, however, compare Caird's *Critical Philosophy of Kant*, Introduction, chap. i., and *Essays in Philosophical Criticism*, p. 8 *seq.* and p. 41 *seq.*

gether the body of social science. Perhaps a glance at economic science—the branch of social science which has hitherto had most attention devoted to it—may help to make the relation between these two methods somewhat clearer.

The opposition between the historical school and the deductive school in Economics has in recent years become very sharply marked. Yet it is not difficult to see that the opposition is not one between rival economic systems, either of which might stand by itself; but only between two elements in the science of Economics, which are both essential to a thorough study of it, but to one or other of which a greater or less prominence may be given.[1] On the one hand, no competent student of economic questions will deny that it is important to have an understanding of the concrete facts with regard to the present methods of trade and industry, and even with regard to the present attitude of thought and sentiment with respect to these methods, and at the same time to have an understanding of the way in which these methods have been developed, and in which this attitude of thought and sentiment has grown up. But, on the other hand, no one who has devoted much attention to the subject can suppose that it would be possible, by such a method of inquiry alone—*i.e.* by a mere inquiry into concrete facts, present or past—to acquire a competent insight into economic questions. The economist desires not only to be a historian, but to be a prophet; and the mere "teaching of history" by itself can never furnish a basis for prophecy. History cannot even tell us that the past *must* have been as it was: much less can it enable us to predict that, amid the ever-changing stream of conditions, the future will in any particular respects resemble what

[1] Cf. Keynes' *Scope and Method of Political Economy* and Marshall's *Principles of Economics,* Book I.

the past has been. Economics without history—if we may be allowed to adapt the familiar phrase of Kant—would be *empty*; but without analysis it would be *blind*. If it is to supply us with any practical insight, it must not only fill in for us the conditions which have determined the events of the past and present, but must help us to calculate to what extent each particular element in these conditions may be expected to have weight in the future. And it is equally true, on the other hand, that if it is to supply us with any practical insight, it must not only enlighten us as to the direction and force of particular tendencies, but must also instruct us to what extent such tendencies are present, or may be expected to be present, in particular states of society—an instruction which is to be gained partly by the study of actual facts, and partly by the study of other tendencies than those which are purely economic (such as the tendencies which influence the development of moral sentiment or of political machinery). Such other tendencies must, from the point of view of Economics, be regarded as mere facts; since they are not tendencies of which economic theory as such can offer any explanation.

We have thus two elements in the science of Economics —an element which consists in the observation and arrangement of facts, and one which consists in the analysis and interpretation of tendencies. For reasons which we need not now consider, a similar distinction of elements is not so readily apparent in the other departments of social science. Still, it is evident enough that the study of political and moral development, as well as that of economic conditions, would also, in so far as it could be pursued as a pure science at all,[1] involve to some extent a two-fold reference. Both the moral life of the individual and the life of the state might, within certain limits, be

[1] But cf. *infra*, pp. 47, 48.

treated simply as given facts; and, on consideration of these facts, we might distinguish certain lines of tendency which could be traced out and made a subject of calculation. It seldom occurs to us to treat either the individual or the state quite in this way, because we habitually regard them both rather from the point of view of ends to be realised than merely as given facts. Why this is so need not at present be considered. It is sufficient to indicate that in all these cases there is at least a conceivable natural history science and a conceivable science of tendencies. We have next to note that in addition to such sciences as these, there is a possible philosophy of society.

It may seem strange, no doubt, at first sight, to speak of a metaphysic of social life. Society, we are apt to think, is simply an aggregation of individual human beings; and there are no metaphysical principles involved in its structure any more than in a heap of stones, or at any rate any more than in a herd of animals. We shall see reason, however, later on to believe that this is not the case, but that in a sense the structure of society must rather be regarded as logically prior to the existence of an individual human being. Now if this is the case, it is easy to see that there may be a metaphysic of it.[1] The principles on which such a structure rests will in all likelihood turn out to be of such a nature that they cannot simply be formulated as empirical laws, or as laws which rest on other known laws of nature. The probability is rather that the investigation of these principles

---

[1] Of course, there might be a metaphysic of society in any case, just as there might be a metaphysic of a steam-engine or of any other object in which the categories are involved. But a metaphysic of society would not be very instructive unless there were in the nature of society some intrinsic unity which such a metaphysic may disclose.

will carry us down to something which is fundamental in the nature of a thinking being, or at any rate in the nature of such a thinking being as man. If so, we shall be led into what may properly be called a philosophical inquiry.

Further, it is evident that there may be a logic of society, if we understand by a logic the consideration of a regulative ideal. For a society of human beings, in any sense in which such a society is more than a mere aggregate of individuals, is clearly not something whose existence can be accounted for without the conception of purpose. The fact that there are a number of human beings may be regarded as accidental;[1] the fact that these human beings are brought into relation to each other may also be regarded as accidental; but the particular direction in which their relations become developed is obviously due to certain .aims by which they are guided.[2]  Now these aims may to some extent be explained by reference to a number of empirical wants of which human beings, . like other animal beings, are

[1] By "accidental" in this and in other places, I mean that which cannot be explained from the point of view of the particular subject-matter under discussion.  I do not mean to imply that anything can be regarded as absolutely fortuitous.  It is only within a particular "universe of discourse" that anything is properly described as accidental.  Cf. the Platonic and Aristotelian use of ἀνάγκη and τύχη.  See the instructive discussion by Mr. D. D. Heath in the *Journal of Philology*, Vol. VII., p. 97 *seq.*, and Mr. Archer-Hind's edition of Plato's *Timaeus*, notes to pp. 162 and 166.  I suppose it is in a similar sense that Hegel speaks of "contingency" in the passage referred to above, p. 26, note 1.  It is a curious instance of "the unity of opposites" that ἀνάγκη (necessity) thus comes to correspond in meaning with contingency.  Cf. also the way in which "liberty of indifference" comes to be identical with absolute determination from without.

[2] So much may perhaps be taken for granted at this point.  For further observations upon it, cf. Chapter III.

impelled to seek the satisfaction. But to some extent also[1] these aims have an intellectual origin, and can be explained only by an examination of the nature of a self-conscious being as such. In so far as these aims depend on empirical considerations, they do not carry us beyond the region of social science. What we desire can be observed and calculated, just as it is possible to observe and calculate any other element in the conditions which constitute the nature of what we are and what we have been. But in so far as the aims in question depend on intellectual considerations, the investigation of them will have to rest on metaphysics. It will not be itself a part of metaphysics, but rather of logic; if we may be allowed to draw such a distinction between the simple inquiry into the principles which determine the nature of an object, on the one hand, and the ideal, on the other hand, to which such principles lead. But the two ν inquiries are inseparably connected, and they constitute together what may be most correctly described as Social Philosophy.[2]

While, however, it is impossible adequately to deal with our social aims except on a metaphysical basis, it is yet possible to be aware of their existence, and in some degree to realise their force, apart from any such basis. The consciousness of such aims, and the maintenance of a right balance between them, is what we describe as good sense, in the highest meaning of that phrase : and in so far as we are guided simply by this intuitive perception of their place and value, we are following the third of the methods of social inquiry to which reference was made at the beginning of this discussion—the method of common-sense. The ἔνδοξα of wise men are the intui-

---

[1] For a justification of this statement see Chapter III.

[2] On the relation between Social Philosophy and Sociology, cf. Höffding's *Ethik*, p. 182.

tions of the meaning and value of certain ideal aims, which have not yet been subjected to any ultimate analysis; and so long as metaphysics remains incomplete, the appeal to such ἔνδοξα must retain a considerable value. The common-sense method has, consequently, a certain utility as well as the other two. The other two make up social science, while the common-sense method serves as a temporary substitute for Social Philosophy.

Can we in reality get beyond that substitute? It is apt to seem at first, even to one who does not doubt the possibility of metaphysics in general, that it must at any rate be a vain hope to expect that any direct light can be gained from so abstract a pursuit on such a very concrete subject as social life. At least there is a very natural suspicion in the minds of many that no such light is reasonably to be looked for at the present stage of philosophic thought. It may be admitted that some light is to be got from metaphysics with regard to the nature of being as such, with regard to the principles of mathematical and mechanical science, perhaps even with regard to some of the most fundamental truths of physics, physiology, and psychology. But the facts of social life seem to lie at the very end of philosophical inquiry, and with regard to them we can scarcely expect for the present to receive any considerable enlightenment. Now in a sense it may be allowed that there is force in this contention : but to conclude therefore that it is vain to pursue our researches into this department of speculation, would, I think, involve a misconception of the nature of philosophic study. On this point it may be worth while to make a few remarks.

We have seen already that it is the aim of philosophy to gain insight and wisdom, rather than knowledge or understanding. Philosophy is, as Novalis expressed it, "a kind of home-sickness—a desire to be everywhere at home." It is the effort not merely to know particular objects, and to understand the modes of their connection, but to apprehend their underlying principles and meaning. It does not seek to discover new facts or even new principles under which facts may be brought, but rather to define more clearly the principles which are already assumed as true—τὸ ὁρίζεσθαι καθόλου[1]—and to see more exactly what is their place and significance in the system of truth. Now the development of such an insight as this cannot be quite similar to the growth of ordinary knowledge or of scientific understanding, in which—just because their province is limited—there is a comparatively definite beginning, middle, and end. Philosophy cannot properly begin anywhere but at its end : for its guiding principle is the ideal of a system, and its course is simply the effort to fill in that ideal. It may be compared to the children's game of fitting together the pieces of a map. The map is the end, but the idea of the map is also the beginning. Of course, this is to some extent true even of the development of the sciences; but since in their case we are dealing with a limited circle of phenomena, it is more easy to fix on a starting point and a goal. In philosophy, on the other hand, if we fix on any point and regard it as an absolute beginning, we *must* fall into error : for there cannot be any beginning except the end.[2] It is our forgetfulness of this that leads to so much prejudice against philosophy, and to so much disappointment with its results. It is often

---

[1] "The definition of universal conceptions." This, according to Aristotle (*Metaphysics*, XII. iv. 5), was the new aim which Socrates introduced into ethical speculation ; and it is chiefly on this account that he is to be regarded as the father of Philosophy.

[2] This is a somewhat paradoxical statement ; but its meaning will, I think, be sufficiently apparent. Cf. Wallace's *Logic of Hegel*, Translation, p. 4, § 1, *ad fin.*

thought—especially by men who come to the study of philosophy from that of the particular sciences—that philosophy ought to be able to offer us certain conclusions which can be set down and tabulated; and men who come to philosophy with this expectation are either disgusted because there are no such conclusions, or else imagine that they have found such conclusions, and carefully mark them down—for some one else to refute. They forget that such conclusions are necessarily wrong, just because they are conclusions: for philosophy, as we have already said, is the serpent of eternity, and within its circle there can be neither beginning nor conclusion except the idea of a system, which is both; any other beginning and any other conclusion must be wrong. The true philosopher will be comparatively indifferent to the statements and counter-statements of rival disputants. He will say to them, like Goethe,

> "Ihr müsst mich nicht mit Widerspruch verwirren :
> Sobald man spricht, beginnt man schon zu irren."

He will know that the truth of philosophy is not a truth which is grasped, but a truth which is an inspiring ideal —an ideal which shines through at every point in the growth of our knowledge, but which can never be perfectly grasped till the system of the universe is seen in its completeness. Philosophy will consequently never have any results,[1] until no results are wanted; and in the meantime its work is not the accumulation of conclusions, but a constant endeavour to press down to greater depths in the understanding of principles which to some extent are already known before philosophy begins its work at all.

---

[1] *I.e.*, it cannot have any results which are not subject to modification by a deeper insight. This is not true of the particular sciences, because they voluntarily content themselves with an insight which is not complete.

The philosopher stands midway between knowledge as a ɩ-datum of experience and knowledge as completed insight. In the former aspect, he accepts his material from the particular sciences : in the latter aspect, he tries to interpret his material in the light of a conception, which he possesses not as a datum of experience, but as the ideal presupposition of the possibility of a world of knowledge. His task is partly that of patient dredging—endeavouring to deepen his view of the conceptions supplied by the sciences—and partly that of "moving about in worlds not realised," or trying to see what the particular conceptions must mean in relation to a universe of truth of which a great part is still in the dark.

It is only when we look at philosophy in this way that we are able at once to realise its incompleteness without disappointment, its dependence on the sciences without humiliation, its tentativeness without impatience, and its true value and dignity without exaggeration. Its incompleteness means simply that its ideal is too large to be fully attained until the whole of experience shall have been filled in : its dependence means simply that its work is not that of discovery, but that of interpretation ; its tentativeness means simply that so long as it remains incomplete in its totality it cannot be complete in any one point—since to know any one point truly would be to see it in the light of the totality[1]—and that consequently it cannot advance like a mathematical science, from one definite proposition to another, but must be content rather to fill in its details by degrees, at whatever point

---

[1] Of course, the idea of the totality is present from the first, and each particular point may be to some extent defined in relation to that. It is known as complete, though not completely known ; and we can partly analyse the elements which are involved in the very idea of completeness. But a complete understanding of each particular point could be reached only if the whole were filled in.

light may at any time break : while, finally, its true value and dignity must be found, not in its supplying us with a kind of cheap omniscience or empty universality, but in its enabling us gradually to reach a clearer insight into the meaning of our world. Unless we take this view of philosophy, a social philosophy must be an idle dream : and it may therefore be worth while at this stage to add a few words on each of these four points, in order that the true scope and method of a social philosophy may be rendered a little more apparent.

The incompleteness of philosophy seems at first to be a contradiction in terms. If we admit that it is incomplete, we seem to admit that it is non-existent ; for it is the very essence of philosophy to view things in the light of the whole ; and if we have not grasped the whole, how is it possible that we should view things in its light? It would appear as if we must either grant that there is no philosophy worthy of the name at all, or else hold that philosophy is nothing more than a vague effort after system, and not in any sense the attainment of it—which, again, would only be another way of granting that there is no philosophy worthy of the name. But the solution of this difficulty is to be found in the consideration of the nature of an ideal. The possession of an ideal may be said to lie midway between the attainment of an end and the mere struggle towards it. In guiding ourselves by an ideal, we are struggling towards an end to which we already possess with more or less completeness the conditions of attainment. Such an ideal is not in the full sense knowledge; but it is a kind of prophetic insight which for a developing being like man is as good as knowledge—or, in a sense, even better.[1] Now by the introduction of this conception we may be enabled to

---

[1] It is better at least than what ordinarily passes for knowledge—which is complete only because it is limited.

attach a definite meaning to philosophy, without supposing it either to involve the attainment of a complete system of knowledge or to be but a vague and hopeless effort after such a system. If we define philosophy as the effort to attain clear insight into the meaning of our concep-tions, guided by the ideal of knowledge as a completed system, we at once save ourselves from the identification of it either with omniscience or with random speculation. According to this definition, it is neither the full know-ledge of truth nor a blind search for truth : it is a search for truth with a certain prophetic understanding of what truth must be when it is found. It is incomplete, but it is not fragmentary. It is not the whole, but the idea of the whole shines through it.[1]

The dependence of philosophy on the sciences, in like manner, is apt at first to appear like a contradiction. If it takes its material from science, we naturally ask, how can it be anything higher than science? How can it at once depend and transcend? How can it go any deeper than the foundation on which it rests? The answer is— to borrow an illustration from Hegel[2]—that philosophy is dependent on the sciences in very much the same sense as that in which eating is dependent on food. In philosophising, just as in eating, we endeavour to turn the particulars with which we are supplied into elements of a system. The system is not independent of the material by which it is built up; yet in the system— which, but for the material, is merely the idea of a whole —the material becomes transformed. Without the system, our material is "hard fact" or empirical law : within the

---

[1] The meaning of this may perhaps be made more apparent by reference to such a work as Bradley's *Appearance and Reality*, where the idea of a system is sketched out, though it is, at the same time, admitted that the content cannot be given.

[2] Wallace's *Logic of Hegel*, p. 21.

system, it is a content with a meaning. But we have to begin with the particulars and not with the meaning—or at least with the meaning only as a kind of prophetic glance—and consequently philosophy must remain in a state of dependence on the particular sciences, just as eating remains dependent on food. If it is the business of philosophy to get behind the work of the sciences and see their true meaning and relations, it is clear that it must pre-suppose a certain development of the sciences and cannot easily outstrip them. We must have got the conceptions and be able to use them with some freedom, before we set ourselves to the task of investigating their significance. It is for this reason that there always seems to be less finality in the work of philosophy than in that of the sciences. In the sciences a certain stage of know-ledge is definitely reached, and the past stage is then at once left behind and ceases to have any but an antiquarian interest. In philosophy, on the other hand, there is no such definite advance. "Knowledge comes, but wisdom lingers." The sciences go, on the whole, straight forward, like conquering armies; while philosophy remains behind to take the bearing of the territories that have been won, and to bury the dead.

It is from this point of view that we are able to under-stand the tentativeness of philosophic development—a de-velopment which is apt at first to seem nothing more than the melancholy spectacle of the formation and overthrow of system after system, and the erection of new ones which cannot reasonably anticipate a better fate. All progress which is guided by an ideal must be more or less of the nature of a stumble. It is so, for instance, with the growth of our moral being. "Our very walking," as Goethe put it, "is a series of falls." Progress towards an ideal alter-nates between partial glimpses of the ideal and the partially successful effort to bring the real into conformity with it.

And so it must be even with philosophy; since even philosophy is not independent of what Hegel described as "the brutality of facts,".in which it is seldom possible to see the ideal with perfect clearness. The development of philosophy is consequently not an advance straight forward; but is rather like the growth of an individual character, in which it not uncommonly happens that in some respects an earlier stage is richer in its contents than a later one, and in which the whole increases rather in fulness of meaning than in extent of matter. Each philosopher seeks to some extent to form a system, but the important thing about the work of each philosopher is not the particular system which he forms, but the way in which he deepens our insight into conceptions, by bringing them into relation with one another within his particular system. And thus in a manner all philosophies prove inadequate, and yet through them all philosophy is gradually taking shape. It is in this sense that the epigram of Schiller has point:—

" Welche wohl bleibt von allen den Philosophien? Ich weiss nicht.
. Aber die Philosophie, hoff' ich, soll ewig bestehen."

What is important in the philosophies is their grasp of the ideal unity of knowledge, and their effort to interpret the various particular conceptions by reference to it. Each philosopher has to say of the work of his predecessors, as Green said of that of Hegel, that "it will all have to be done over again"; but each of them may at the same time add that it all had to be done. The ideal has not been reached, but our insight has been deepened.

The method of philosophy, consequently, is one which is necessarily tentative and cannot be quite rigidly defined, and yet is not one which is left entirely vague. It must depend at each stage partly on the advancement of the particular sciences, and partly on the degree of insight which has been already won into the nature of knowledge as a whole. What each thinker has to do, is not so much to add any new conceptions to those previously known, as rather to get a somewhat deeper insight into their significance and relations : and this will be gained partly by observing the errors which have been made by previous attempts at systematisation, and partly by taking account of the new light which the particular sciences afford. Such work must be to some extent a groping in the dark. We must turn the various conceptions over and view them on every side and in all possible relations. We must rub them against each other till they strike fire. We must "stand in the old ways," availing ourselves of all the insight that has been already won, and gradually feel our way forward to something new. We must neither trust to our predecessors nor despise them, but follow them first and then try to surpass them by understanding them. We must answer their questions and question their answers. In general, we must observe, on the one hand, what the particular conceptions are and how they are applied in science, and, on the other hand, what degree of insight has been attained into their relations to each other and to the universe of thought.

It may seem, no doubt, that if this is the nature and method of philosophy, it must always remain to a great extent unscientific. It must in some measure " walk by faith " rather than by sight. It assumes certain ideal relations to a system of experience as a whole, which can never be completely worked out. Now in a certain sense such an objection is probably true.[1] Philosophy is not scientific in so far as it is not science : just as, again, it is not poetic in so far as it is not poetry, and not religious in so far as it is not religion. But if this points to a defect in philosophy, it also points to a defect in science.

[1] It is also true, however, of the higher speculations of science that they rest on faith.

To make this apparent we must add a little more with respect to the relation of science to philosophy.

The motto of the sciences is *divide et impera*. Their strength consists in the fact that they attack the world in detail. Their weakness consists in their abstraction. Each science takes up a particular class of objects, or objects under a particular aspect, or in the light of a particular conception. It "stoops to conquer." It voluntarily narrows its view in order that it may get a complete grasp of some particular province of existence. Now such abstraction as this necessarily brings with it the danger that we may lose sight of the whole from which abstraction has been made. "It often happens in investigations," as Höffding puts it,[1] "as it does to children with their toys. They take them to pieces to see what is hidden in them, and then are unable to put them together again." This is a danger which appears chiefly in dealing with complicated and living things, such as human society. The view of the scientific investigator, in dealing with such questions, is apt to be at once too narrow and too wide. He limits himself to particular aspects of things, which are meaningless apart from their relation to the whole, and then he proceeds to deal with the whole as if its nature were exhausted by the treatment of these particular aspects. He first becomes a hermit and confines himself to his own particular cave: and then he mistakes the limits of his own horizon for the limits of the world. Now such abstraction as this is inevitable in the work of the particular sciences, so long as there is no more general science by which their conceptions may be criticised.

From this point of view, therefore, we are able to appreciate the value and importance of philosophic study, without giving it an exaggerated pre-eminence, as if it

[1] *Grundlage der humanen Ethik*, v.

were able to furnish us with a ready-made and absolute
system of truth. We may say briefly that it renders a
service to the particular sciences which is both negative
and positive, and which becomes more and more important as we advance higher in the degree of complexity
of the particular sciences.

The negative service of philosophy to the particular
sciences consists mainly in this, that it criticises the conceptions of which they make use, by endeavouring to
define their place in relation to a larger whole. "An
abstract term," as De Tocqueville says, "is like a box
with a false bottom: you may put in it what ideas you
please and take them out again without being observed."
The study of philosophy is important as a safeguard
against such intellectual sleight-of-hand. It is the art of
fixing the bottoms of our boxes, by giving definiteness
and clearness to our conceptions. Now such a service
as this becomes more and more important as we proceed
from the simpler sciences to the more complex, and
especially to those that are concerned with life and
thought. In Geology there may not be much danger of
misapplying conceptions: in Chemistry or Botany there
is more: while in Psychology we are almost certain, without philosophical analysis, to be continually misapplying
them: and the same is true of the science of social life.
The reason of this is partly that the conceptions which
we naturally employ first are the simplest: and such
conceptions are adequate to the material of the lower
sciences, while they are not adequate to that of the
higher. The reason, however, is also to be found to
some extent in another consideration, which we shall
shortly have occasion to notice.[1]

But the service of philosophy with reference to the
particular sciences is more than merely negative. It is

[1] See *infra*, p. 48.

positive in so far as it supplies us with a guiding principle
in the form of the idea of system, by which it enables us
to take a connected view of the objects of our experience,
and so helps to suggest the real meaning of processes in
which only a partial discovery has yet been made by the
particular sciences.    Much has been said about "the
scientific use of the imagination": and, no doubt, much
has been very well said.    The imagination is of great
assistance in scientific research; but the imagination which
is of use is not a lawless faculty which "gives to airy
nothing a local habitation and a name," but is rather a
faculty which is closely akin to philosophic insight.    It is
a kind of creative perception which foresees analogies
and relations before they have become visible to the eye
of sense—such a perception as Goethe, for instance, possessed in a unique degree.    Such a power as this, however,
will not carry us far unless the analogies which we discover
belong in reality to the essence of things; and the power
of discovering such analogies will depend on the depth
of our insight into the general relations of objects.    The
instinct of genius may to some extent supply us with
such an insight: but only in so far as that instinct supplies
us at the same time with a kind of unconscious philosophy.    In dealing with the mental sciences, in particular,
such insight is absolutely indispensable; and it is partly
for this reason that the relation of these sciences to philosophy is more apparent than that of any other department
of knowledge.

We see, then, that philosophy renders both a negative
and a positive service to the various particular sciences.
The value of philosophy, however, becomes especially
apparent when we pass to the ethical sciences.    These,
indeed, could hardly exist without philosophy at all.    For
here the whole question is one of what we mean, or what
we want to be at: it depends on the possession of wisdom

rather than of any particular kind of knowledge.. The facts are in such cases created by ourselves; and, if our meaning changes, the facts change too.   The heavenly bodies will continue to attract one another according to the same laws, whether we interpret Gravitation rightly or wrongly, or do not interpret it at all: but it is not so with conduct; this changes as our insight into its meaning deepens.   Hence an empirical science of Ethics, which considers what men actually do and what their motives actually are, or even what they actually think they ought to do and what they actually think their motives ought to be, without entering into the question what the ultimate meaning of all this is, is no science of Ethics at all: it leaves Hamlet out of the play; it omits the very circumstance on which the progress of Ethics will depend—viz. the distinction between that which is accidental in conduct, which the progress of thought will tend to remove, and that which is essential in it, which the progress of thought will only deepen and strengthen.   And this is, if possible, even more apparent in the case of Social Philosophy; since the relations of human beings in society are more obviously liable to change in accordance with the development of their thoughts than the general laws of conduct are.

The necessity of philosophy, then, is apparent.   Nor is it a legitimate objection to it that, in a sense, as we have said, it depends on a kind of faith.   For the faith which is involved in philosophy is simply the faith which is involved in all life and thought — a faith that things have a meaning, that the world is a rational system.   This faith is unconsciously presupposed in all our efforts towards knowledge and in all the judgments of our moral life; and though it is only in philosophy that a definite effort is made to see life and existence as a system of relations, yet if this effort is to be condemned, the whole of life must be condemned along with it. Into this question, however, we cannot enter further here. It is enough to have seen what philosophy aims at and the general method which it pursues. The justification of the aim and method must be left to appear in the course of the study itself.

We may now sum up what we have been saying up to the present point, as follows. Philosophy in general arises from the necessity of answering two questions with a view to the explanation of the objects of our experience. These two questions are, that with reference to the principles which underlie the existence of the objects under discussion as such, and that with reference to the ideal or ultimate end to which the existence of these objects points. These two questions are in reality inseparable, and they constitute together the problem which all philosophy sets itself to solve : just as the particular sciences are concerned with the two questions as to the material structure of objects and as to the direction and force of the tendencies which are at work within them. Philosophy, as thus understood, will fall into a number of separate departments, according to the nature of the objects with which it is concerned ; and of these departments Social Philosophy will be logically among the last, since its object is one of the most complicated in the world of our experience. But it does not therefore follow that the study of Social Philosophy ought to be postponed till the other departments of philosophy have been fully worked out ; for the growth of philosophy cannot, from the nature of the study, be expected to go straight on from point to point, but must rather consist in a gradual deepening of our insight, now at one point and now at another. We have seen reason also to believe that such a study, though tentative and though dependent on a kind of faith, is yet both a legitimate and a valuable one.

D

While, however, we need not trouble ourselves with the
reflection that Social Philosophy must belong to the end
of philosophic study, and consequently cannot be fully
understood till all the other departments of that study have
been completed; it is yet of considerable importance that
we should have a clear understanding of the exact place
which Social Philosophy occupies among philosophic and
other studies, so that we may see precisely what are its
scope and limits, and what are the other subjects on
which it is most directly dependent. We shall begin,
accordingly, by taking note of some of its more obvious
connections, and shall proceed afterwards, as far as possible, to an exact definition of its place among philosophic
studies.

It is clear at once that the subject must touch at many
points on the sphere of Ethics. The determination of what
is good for society will depend a great deal on an understanding of what is good for the human beings who
compose it; and, on the other hand, the determination of
social ideals may be expected to throw a great deal of
light on the particular virtues and obligations of individuals. Aristotle, indeed, said that Ethics are a part of
Social Philosophy [1] (or of "Politics" which, in the Greek
sense, may be taken to mean very nearly the same thing);
but this was due in part to the somewhat empirical way
in which he regarded the science of Ethics, and in part
to the fact that what he meant by "Politics" was something rather wider than what we here describe as Social
Philosophy. When we speak of Ethics we may mean two
distinct things. We may mean a classification of the virtues,
*i.e.* in general an enumeration of the qualities which in
particular conditions of society it is desirable to cultivate.
This science is clearly a part of Social Philosophy, or
rather is a part of the Philosophy of Education, which

[1] *Ethics,* I. ii. *seq.*

again is a part of Social Philosophy.[1]  But Ethics may
also be taken to mean that science which investigates the
nature of the "law of freedom" as such, which determines
the conditions under which an "ought" is possible and
the precise meaning of that imperative.[2]  This science is
not a department of Social Philosophy, but is rather a
study co-ordinate with it, both being departments of a
still larger subject.  It is true, indeed, that the determination of the ethical imperative would involve a certain
reference to the social nature of man as a rational being;
and in this sense it might be maintained that Ethics are
a part of Social Philosophy.  But it might equally well
be maintained that Social Philosophy is a part of Ethics;
since we can hardly deal with the problems of social well-
being without presupposing the ethical "ought."  Yet we
need not infer from this mutual implication · that Ethics
and Social Philosophy are the same subject; for though
they are inseparable, they are inseparable only as all departments of philosophy, and indeed of science in general, are
ultimately inseparable from each other.  It is possible, in
dealing with the Ethical imperative, to take certain social
conditions as postulates, and so to regard the determination
of these conditions as falling outside the Science of Ethics :
and, in like manner, in dealing with social conditions, it
is possible to regard the ethical imperative as a postulate.
Thus Ethics and Social Philosophy may be regarded as

[1] I may refer to Paulsen's *System der Ethik* as a very admirable
example of a treatment of Ethics mainly from this point of view.

[2] Among the best examples of treatises on Ethics in this sense are
Kant's *Critique of Practical Reason* and Green's *Prolegomena.*  On the
relation of Logic to Ethics, cf. Wundt's *Ethik*, pp. 5-6.  It is, I think,
owing to a failure to distinguish between these two senses of Ethics
that Mr. Leslie Stephen objects to the application of Metaphysics to
Ethics.  *Science of Ethics*, p. 450 *seq.*  On the other hand, in Prof.
Alexander's *Moral Order and Progress*, p. 2, the distinction is clearly
drawn.

two separate departments of a larger subject. This larger subject was probably to some extent in Aristotle's mind when he spoke of ἡ πολιτική as including Ethics. But the larger subject is, in truth, the philosophy of human nature as rational ; *i.e.* it corresponds to the main part of what Hegel called "Philosophy of Spirit."[1] This would include not merely the determination of the ethical imperative and the investigation of social conditions, but also an inquiry into those ideals which man as a rational being is forced to frame, which are expressed in art and poetry, and which finally receive their highest embodiment in religious faith—in general, those ideals by which man as a rational being is led to look beyond his social condition to some still higher unity which his moral life involves. On the whole, then, we may say that Ethics is a subject co-ordinate with Social Philosophy, but that the Philosophy of Education, which includes certain elements that are frequently dealt with in treatises on Ethics, is subordinate to Social Philosophy.

Politics is another science which is very closely related to Social Philosophy; and here also it would be unwise to "cut things in two with a hatchet," and to treat the two subjects as entirely distinct, and yet it would be equally unwise to permit them to be confused together. We have seen already that the term Politics may be interpreted in a very large sense, so as to include not only Social Philosophy but also Ethics and the Philosophy of Art and Religion. In a more restricted sense we might use the term as an equivalent for Social Philosophy. But the term is usually and most conveniently used in a

[1] Including the Philosophy of Law (Moral and Political), the Philosophy of Art, and the Philosophy of Religion. Hegel's Philosophy of Spirit includes more than is contained in these departments ; since it involves also the consideration of the process through which the rational nature of man develops—*i.e.* human Psychology.

sense somewhat narrower than this, to signify that science which deals with what we might call social machinery— *i.e.* those conditions of social life which depend on definite human organisation, as distinguished from those which depend on the culture of individual character, with which the Philosophy of Education deals, and from those which depend on the material[1] necessities of mankind, which constitute the province of economic science. Politics, in this restricted sense, is clearly one of the departments of Social Philosophy. At the same time, it must be remembered that it is only in so far as Politics can be treated as a necessary element in the rational development of mankind, that it falls within the sphere of Social Philosophy. In so far as it is merely an inductive science, or in so far as it deals with the minutiæ of governmental arrangements, the Social Philosopher will not naturally regard it as lying within his province at all.

The science, however, whose relations to Social Philosophy it is most important to consider is unquestionably that of Political Economy; not because its relations are closer to this science than to the others that have been named, but because they are less distinct and more in danger of being overlooked. In former times Ethics may

---

[1] Perhaps it would be better to say "instrumental" rather than "material." Cf. a paper on "The Relation between Ethics and Economics," in the *International Journal of Ethics*, Vol. III., No. 3, especially pp. 284-289. That the goods dealt with by the economist are all essentially *instrumental* goods (or goods "of the second order") is a point that has been well brought out by Ehrenfels in the first of his series of papers on "Werth-Theorie und Ethik" (*Vierteljahrsschrift für wissenschaftliche Philosophie*, VII. i., p. 90), where the useful distinction is drawn between *Eigenwerthe* and *Wirkungswerthe* (*intrinsic Values* and *instrumental Values*). The same distinction has subsequently been adopted by Meinong in his more elaborate *Psychologisch-ethische Untersuchungen zur Werth-Theorie.*

have been treated as a collection of underived imperatives
and Politics as a science of national aggrandizement;
but it is hardly possible for any one now to treat of
either of these subjects without a very direct reference to
social well-being. Some of the laws of Economics, on
the other hand, lend themselves so readily to a purely
abstract treatment that there is still a danger of their
relations to human well-being becoming neglected altogether. In studying Ethics and Politics we have the
largeness and manysidedness of human nature continually
before us; whereas in studying Economics it is much
more easily possible to regard human beings as a species
of machines governed by a few simple and in general
ignoble motives; and the temptation so to treat them
is great, since it leads to a very considerable simplification
of economic doctrine. Moreover, it is perhaps more
difficult in Economics than in any other subject to avoid
writing from the point of view of a class. The moralist,
indeed, may also sometimes be tempted to

"Compound for sins he is inclined to
By damning those he has no mind to,"     '

and the political philosopher may write as a radical or
as a conservative. But the economist is more directly
concerned with those conditions on which in modern
times class distinctions mainly depend, and for that
reason it is more difficult for him to get out of the
atmosphere of a particular grade of social life. Besides,
Ethics and Politics are older sciences, and there are
certain large traditions about them which cannot lightly
be overlooked; whereas Political Economy is of more
recent growth, and is concerned with conditions which
are continually undergoing variation; and though it has
been treated by writers of great vigour and acuteness, it
has yet rarely been made the main object of study by
men of quite the same breadth and compass of mind as

have been brought to bear on ethical and political speculation. It is a subject on which there is as yet—or at
least was until quite recently—less weight of authority
and more scope for individual bias. Its doctrines can be
readily turned to suit the interests or prejudices of those
who use them. *Pectus economicum facit.* The practical
value of the work of economists has hitherto depended
largely on the question whether they had sympathy with
the progress of those classes of the community who are
least capable of protecting their own interests. When
they had not this, their work, however able otherwise,
has usually done harm; and even when they had, they
have often enough been "mischief-makers,"[1] in so far as
they have opposed the interests of those classes whom
they were supporting to those of other sections of the
community. The fact is, indeed, that Political Economy
has hardly ever been treated quite as a science at all : it
is only beginning to get into scientific shape. It has
been until lately much less a subject for the study than
for the market place; and the idols of the Forum mingle
in it confusedly with those of the Theatre and the Cave.[2]
Several of those who have written on it have been men
interested in particular branches of business, who have
taken up the subject in a very empirical way, and have
treated only of those aspects of it in which their particular

[1] Cf. Dr. Cunningham's article on "Economists as Mischief-makers,"
in the *Economic Review*, Vol. IV., No. I.

[2] This would apply, no doubt, to Ethics and Politics also, as
popularly understood ; but not to quite the same extent. Private
individuals cannot so readily tamper with Ethics and Politics as with
Economics ; though it seems possible that in the near future this
may no longer be the case. With regard to Economics, cf. Mr.
Smart's Preface to Böhm-Bawerks's *Capital and Interest*, p. xiii.
One may almost say that it is only with the German Historical School
and the Austrian Analytical School that the scientific study of
Economics has definitely commenced.

interests happened to lie, omitting to notice the relations of these fragments to the whole. And indeed in
some cases it could even be wished that such writers
had confined themselves more strictly than they have
done to the treatment of those departments with which
they were really familiar; since the consciousness of their
ability to deal with these has been apt to mislead them
and their disciples into the belief that they possessed an
adequate comprehension of the whole subject. It is
therefore more necessary in the case of Political Economy
than in that of any other science to consider carefully its
relations to Social Philosophy, in order that we may see
clearly the true place and significance of its various
methods and departments.

Economists as a class have been violently attacked in
recent times by a number of influential writers; and the
deficiencies of the older economists are now so fully
acknowledged that one is tempted rather to plead in
their defence than to heap fresh insults upon them. Indeed, the popular complaints against them are often
unreasonable and even inconsistent. If economists apply
their principles directly to practical questions, they are
accused of solving concrete problems by means of inadequate abstractions: if, on the other hand, they abstain
from any such application, they are accused of indifference.[1] They are blamed for going where angels fear to
tread, and also for not going where every fool may rush
in. The faults[2] with which they are fairly chargeable

---

[1] They are, however, justly blamable in so far as they have not
made it clear to what extent their principles are directly applicable
to practice, and to what extent they are not. It may be observed
that most of the complaints against economists refer chiefly to Ricardo,
whose methods it is certainly difficult to defend. Cf. Toynbee's *Industrial Revolution*, pp. 1-26.

[2] I mean the faults of the genuine economists. Of course, there are

are due in the main to the absence of a Social Philosophy by which their science could be guided and circumscribed. A student of any one of the special sciences can hardly be expected to look much abroad into the world as a whole: his attention is necessarily directed chiefly to the details of his own particular study. To take a comprehensive view of things is the business rather of the philosopher; and it is to the lack of a carefully worked out philosophical point of view that many of the most pernicious errors of the economists must be traced. Their errors have consisted for the most part in misleading modes of statement: and these are often of such a sort that even a little philosophy would suffice to correct them. Of course, the reference here is chiefly to English economists. In Germany, and èven perhaps in France, there has been less to complain of in this respect; but the study of Economics in these countries has been until recently little more than an episode in the main current of economic thought. In our own country, indeed, Adam Smith intended to have completed his work by the addition of a general study of society; and had he done so, it is possible that the history of the science might have been different. John Stuart Mill also interspersed his treatise on Economics with a number of reflections of a more or less philosophic character; and his example has been followed by several subsequent writers. What is wanted, however, is not a mixture of the two subjects —this often adds to the confusion instead of diminishing it—but rather a careful division between them by some one who has the faculty, to use a Platonic metaphor, of always "hitting the joint." To make the meaning

many writers who have adopted the principles of the leading economists, without any adequate comprehension of them, and applied them to personal or party aims. It is such writers, chiefly, who have brought Economics into disgrace.

of this clear, a few words of explanation seem necessary.

Economics may be treated in a variety of ways and
with a variety of objects.  In the first place, it may be
treated as a purely abstract science, concerned with the
laws of the production, accumulation, and distribution of
material wealth.  These laws, of course, are based on
certain assumptions (such as that of perfectly free competition, perfectly enlightened self-interest, and so on)
which are not completely realised in the existing state of
things : and in order to make the science complete,
these hypotheses must be stated with absolute clearness—
and how difficult this is, any one who will try to define
what is meant by "perfectly free competition" may discover; and the hypotheses ought also to be varied,
somewhat in the way that was pointed out by Plato in
the *Parmenides.*  That is, we should consider what would
follow on every conceivable assumption, or at least on
every assumption which may under any circumstances be
supposed to be approximately verified.[1]  These consequences might be worked out, as to some extent they
have already been by Cournot and others, with a perfectly
mathematical rigour; and they would possess a great
deal of scientific interest, though they would have no

[1] To give any real value even to such an abstract inquiry as this,
it is evident that there must be a certain reference to experience.
We must refer to the actual conditions of life in order to see what
hypotheses are approximately verifiable ; and we must also refer to
the actual desires and wants which human beings have.  We must
not roughly assume that men are guided by any such simple principles
as "enlightened self-interest," and the like.  Hence the truth of
Schäffle's saying that "without good Psychology there can be no
good Economics." (*Bau und Leben des socialen Körpers*, III., 285.)
It might even be added that without good Biology there can be no
good Economics.  Cf. Geddes's *Analysis of the Principles of Economics*, Part I., p. 24 *seq.*

direct practical application. They would help to clear the intellect, and enable us to see precisely what each of the abstract laws of Economics means. Any one who knows how loosely economic laws are frequently interpreted is not likely to underrate the importance of such an analysis.

But again, Economics may be treated as a historical science, dealing with society as a growing organism, and showing the relations of its members at different stages in their development. As the preceding science was entirely hypothetical and *a priori*, so is this one entirely *a posteriori* and matter-of-fact. And as in the former case the important points were to make our hypotheses absolutely clear and to work out every conceivable, or at least every approximately realisable, variation of them ; so here the important points are to make our facts absolutely certain, to have as complete a collection of important facts as possible, and to ascertain accurately their relations to one another. This science also, like the preceding, is not capable of any direct practical application. It is concerned only with " the teaching of history," and history of itself cannot teach anything but that certain relations of phenomena have been. It cannot of itself give any guarantee that similar relations will occur again, though it may undoubtedly afford extremely important suggestions of probable relations.

Finally, Economics may be treated as a practical science or art for our guidance in the actual affairs of life. Such a science would necessarily in some measure combine the two preceding, since it would require to consider both the actual facts and the way in which particular tendencies are operating upon them. But, being an art, it would involve also a certain conception of an end ; and, as these ends might vary, there would be a number of distinct species of practical Economics. The following, for instance, might be enumerated: (1) *Individual Economy*, setting up as its goal the good of each individual by himself. And of this Economy there might be a number of sub-species, according as the good for the individual should be supposed to consist in the possession of material wealth, in the attainment of personal happiness, in the development of character, or whatever else the end might be thought to be. This is the species of Economy which is frequently suggested by economic writers of the *laisser-faire* school, though they seldom attempt to work it out consistently or to explain precisely what the end is which they propose. (2) *Domestic Economy*, with the good of a family· as its goal. This also might have a number of sub-species more or less similar to those of the former class. Probably most of those writers who regard the good of the individual as the end would be prepared to recognise that for a very large proportion of the human race the good of the individual is inseparable from that of the family. It was mainly from this point of view that Xenophon's *Economicus* was written.[1] (3) *Social Economy*, with a more indefinite but not less practical aim than the preceding—viz. the well-being of particular groups of human beings—such as villages, municipalities, counties, and so on. Proudhon suggested, for example, that the *workshop* ought to be taken as the unit. Of course, within this class also there would be sub-species, according to the kind of well-being that was sought, as well as according to the nature of the groups selected. (4) *National Economy*, setting up as its goal the good of a particular nation. This was what was originally understood by Political Economy, or the theory of the " Wealth of Nations," and it is still one of its most interesting phases. It is a very important

---

[1] In Marshall's *Economics of Industry* there is a constant reference to the unity of the family

branch of Political Philosophy. And, of course, of this species of Economy, as of the preceding, there might be a variety of sub-species. (5) *Universal Economy* (*Welt-Oekonomie*), setting up as the aim to be sought after the good of the world as a whole. Here also sub-species might arise.

It is sometimes said that Political Economy is not a science. On the contrary, it is two sciences and at least five arts. And I think it may safely be maintained that every one of these subjects is an important study in its own place. The exact or abstract science of Economics is important for the attainment of clear ideas on the tendencies of particular social forces, when not interfered with by other conditions. The natural history science of Economics is important for the attainment of insight into actual human nature as it displays itself under different social conditions, and into the direction in which progress is most likely to tend. Each of the arts also is important. Doubtless, if it were possible always to look at things from the point of view of the whole, and always to influence the whole, Universal Economy would be the only one of these arts which would have any real value; or rather it would include all the others as subordinate elements in itself. But this is not possible. Sometimes we cannot directly consider anything beyond the well-being of our own nation, sometimes nothing beyond the well-being of particular groups or districts, sometimes nothing but the well-being of families or individuals. It may even be doubted whether it is always possible to consider the effects of particular lines of action with reference to all the elements of well-being even of the particular units selected. Sometimes we can only consider the effects on the increase of material wealth, sometimes only on the probable multiplication of happiness, more rarely on the development of character and the higher elements of welfare. Hence all the different species and sub-species of Economics may, within certain limits, be allowed a place. But what are these limits?

It seems clear that, in the absence of a carefully reasoned Social Philosophy, there must always remain a great danger of confusion between these various species of Economics, and of the encroachment of each beyond its proper limits. Social Philosophy ought to play the part of a kind of Platonic justice among them, setting each in its proper sphere, and teaching it to recognise what it can really accomplish and what lies beyond its limits. It would have to guard against the danger, for instance, of confounding those economic laws which are dealt with by the abstract science of Economics with ethical imperatives, or even with practical maxims of prudence that are directly applicable to life. It would also have to guard against the danger of supposing that those circumstances with which abstract Economics is capable of dealing (*i.e.* in general, those which lend themselves to a mathematical mode of treatment) are the only circumstances which are of importance in social life. Again, it would have to guard against the danger of confounding history with prophecy — of supposing that that which has been is necessarily that which will be, or at any rate that when we have investigated past conditions we are in possession of a complete clue to the future. It would also be the business of Social Philosophy to consider how far it is possible or expedient to deal with the effects of particular lines of action on particular groups or classes of a community, without reference to their effects on society as a whole ; and how far particular elements of well-being may profitably be discussed, without a consideration of the ultimate ends of life. It would have to teach the particular arts how to limit themselves without becoming narrow, how to seek particular ends without forgetting that they *are* particular, how to interest themselves in means without mistaking them for the ends which they subserve. It would have to guard against fanaticisms— from that of riches at any price to that of class against country and patriotism against the world. Such a Social Philosophy as this—or rather such a department of Social Philosophy as this—is the indispensable accompaniment of the various sciences and arts into which Economics may be divided; but it should be carefully distinguished from them, just as they should be carefully distinguished from each other.

In saying all this, I do not by any means intend to imply that the various departments of economic science may not be conveniently treated as constituting a single subject. All that I mean to insist on is that within that subject there are at least three distinguishable elements— (1) The science of tendencies, represented by such writers as Cournot,[1] Walras,[2] Jevons,[3] Edgeworth,[4] Wicksteed,[5] and the mathematical[6] economists generally; (2) The natural history science, represented by the writers of the Historical School;[7] (3) The ethical science, forming the

[1] *Recherches sur les Principes Mathématiques de la Théorie des Richesses.*

[2] *Eléments d'Economie Politique pure* and *Théorie Mathématique de la Richesse Sociale.*

[3] *Theory of Political Economy.*

[4] *Mathematical Psychics* (which, however, deals with a good deal more than economic theory) and other writings.

[5] *Alphabet of Economic Science* (the best introduction, so far as I can judge, to this mode of treatment).

[6] Of course this analytical side of economics has not always been treated mathematically. But it always lends itself to this mode of treatment; and it is only by means of mathematical conceptions (which do not necessarily imply the use of symbols) that exactness can be given to it.

[7] Comte (*Philosophie Positive* and *Politique Positive*) and Schäffle (*Bau und Leben des socialen Körpers*, etc.) are chiefly responsible for

basis for the practical art of Economics, a side which has
been made prominent by such writers as Sismondi,[1] or in
a less systematic form by Carlyle [2] and Ruskin,[3] and also
by most of the economists of the Historical School.[4]
The basis of the last of these three elements in economic
science must be found in Social Philosophy; and Social
Philosophy will thus furnish the guiding principles by which
the other two elements, in so far as they bear on practical
life, must have their spheres fixed and limited. For
philosophy, paradoxical though it may seem to say so, is
ultimately the only practical science: since it is the
science which investigates the ideals by which conduct
is determined.[5]

the development of this school.  Among its most prominent adherents
are Wagner (*Lehrbuch der politischen Oekonomie*), Schmoller (Editor of
*Staats- und Socialwissenschaftliche Forschungen*, etc.), Cliffe Leslie
(*Essays Moral and Political*) and many others.  The article on
"Political Economy" in the *Encyclopaedia Britannica* (Vol. XX.) is
especially strong on the Historical School (p. 390 *seq.*), though the
other aspects are also discussed with much fairness.

[1] *Nouveaux Principes d'Economie Politique.*  In his earlier work, *De
la Richesse Commerciale*, he follows the older economists.

[2] *Past and Present*, and throughout his works *passim*.

[3] *Unto This Last*, *Munera Pulveris*, and in several parts of *Fors
Clavigera* and others of his writings.  See also Professor Geddes's
*John Ruskin, Economist*.

[4] More recently there have been some excellent discussions by some
Austrian writers on the connection between ethical and economical
principles, especially in relation to the theory of value.  The economists, Menger, Wieser, and Böhm-Bawerk, and the psychologists,
Brentano, Ehrenfels, and, above all, Meinong (*Psychologisch-ethische
Untersuchungen zur Werth-Theorie*), have all done good service in this
respect.

[5] *I.e.* philosophy is the science which investigates the ultimate
significance of the idea of value; and this is the idea which is most
fundamental in all the practical or normative sciences.  Cf. Meinong's
*Werth-Theorie*, p. 224.  For some further remarks on the relation of
philosophy to practice I may refer to my *Manual of Ethics*, Chaps. 1.

Having thus indicated the general relations of Social Philosophy to Ethics, Politics, and Economics, we may now attempt to define as precisely as is consistent with extreme brevity its place among philosophic studies. In doing so, however, it is necessary to give warning that a full understanding of the reasons for assigning to it the precise place which I am about to define can come only after the discussion of some of the following chapters with regard to the nature of the social unity. Here, as in so many other cases, our frontiers cannot be marked out until we have fought for them. Our subject-matter cannot be defined till we have investigated its nature. Still, it will be convenient to give such a definition as is now possible, referring to the subsequent parts of our argument for such justification as the definition may seem to require.

In the first place, then, we may remark that there are three large divisions of philosophic study, which have been distinguished by Hegel as *Logic*,[1] *Philosophy of Nature*, and *Philosophy of Spirit*. The first of these is concerned with thought as such, the second with the objects of thought, and the third with objects in so far as these are themselves creations of thought. A complete justification of this division would, no doubt, involve the working out of an entire system of philosophy, in which it should be shown how thought necessarily goes out of itself to a world of objects which are not thought, and how again out of this world of objects it returns into itself by the creation of a new world of objects which are themselves thoughts. But in an introduction to Social Philosophy we cannot enter into any such discussion as

and II., and notes A and B, and to the *International Journal of Ethics*, Vol. v., No, 1, pp. 98–103.

[1] *I.e.* Pure Metaphysics or Epistemology—not Logic in the sense to which it seems to me preferable to confine the term. Cf. *supra*, p. 26.

this; and the three departments of philosophic study must in the meantime be taken for granted. Even apart, however, from the working out of any system of philosophic doctrine, it must on the whole be manifest that there are these three possible divisions of the study; though the understanding of their precise relations could come only with the development of a system. For it is clear that there may be, in the first place, a theory of knowledge, concerned simply with the abstract conditions of its possibility; in the second place, a theory of the concrete objects with which knowledge is occupied; and, in the third place, a theory of those objects (such as art, religion, and the like) which thinking beings create for themselves. It may be a question, no doubt, how far the second of these divisions can be regarded as falling within the province of philosophy at all, and whether it ought not rather to be relegated entirely to the particular sciences. To this question we cannot here attempt to give any answer; but it must at least be admitted that nature is *primâ facie* a possible object of philosophic study, especially when we remember that the life of a thinking being grows up from a natural basis, so that nature can hardly be regarded as entirely alien to thought. And if there is such a possible object, it seems clear that it must be regarded as different both from abstract thought as such and from the objects which thought itself creates. Such considerations as these may help us to realise, what only a system of philosophy could perfectly demonstrate, that there are these three divisions to which reference has now been made.

Now it is evident that Social Philosophy must fall within the third of these divisions, if society is to be regarded as belonging essentially to the nature of man as a thinking being; and that it is to be so regarded I hope to be able to make clear in the course of the following discussion. If a society of human beings were simply like a herd of animals, then, no doubt, it might be regarded as falling within the sphere of natural history—though even then, it would be an aspect of the development of nature in which it comes very close to the realisation of thought. But we shall shortly[1] see reason for believing that society is actually a product of our thinking nature, and not merely a product of an element in our animal nature which is well on in the process towards the development of thought. And if this is the case, the study of society must form a department of the Philosophy of Spirit.

Now the Philosophy of Spirit also seems to fall, at least ideally, into three main divisions. It is concerned throughout with the laws of the process by which thought creates new objects for itself—or, in other words, with the laws of freedom. But what has first to be considered is the way in which thought is able to lay down a law for itself at all, and the way in which that law becomes operative in the life of thinking beings as such. This study would be what I understand by the term Logic, which is the pure Ethics of thought.[2] In the second place, there is Ethics applied to the life of a thinking being in relation to a world. And this world is, on the one hand, the world of nature, and, on the other hand, the world of thinking beings. Then, finally, we should have to consider how it is that the ideal which thought lays down for us carries us beyond any world that is actually known, and leads us into the symbolisms of art and poetry and the aspirations of religion.

It is evidently in the second of these three divisions that Social Philosophy must be placed. If it were possible to separate the relations of human beings to the material world from their relations to each other, the

---

[1] In Chap. III.     [2] Cf. Wundt's *Ethik*, pp. 5-6.

latter alone would be the province of Social Philosophy.
But as man is from the first social, his relations to the
material world are all along conditioned by the fact that
he is also related to his fellowmen. Yet man's relations
to the material world cannot be regarded as subsequent
to his relations to his fellowmen. They are rather logically
prior to the latter. Consequently, Social Philosophy can
hardly avoid dealing with the relations of men to the
material world, as well as with their relations to each
other. The questions of art and religion, on the other
hand, can to a considerable extent be postponed as the
subject-matter of a later study. Social Philosophy, then,
may be regarded as concerned with the relations of men
to each other, with their relations to the material world,
and with the development of individual character, in so
far as that is affected by these relations. It will thus
fall into three main departments :—Political Philosophy,
Economic Philosophy, and Philosophy of Education :—
though it will obviously be quite impossible to deal satisfactorily with any one of these apart from the others.
The relations of these departments to each other, however,
will become more apparent at a later stage of the present
inquiry.[1]

I have thought it important to indicate in this way at
the outset what I regard as the true place of Social
Philosophy among other studies, in order that we may
realise clearly the limitations of our inquiry, and not
expect more from it than it is able to give. At the
same time, it must be obvious that in such an investigation as the present, which is an introduction to Social
Philosophy, and not a working of it out, we cannot profitably confine ourselves to the abstract inquiry which
has now been indicated. The interest which leads us to
select Social Philosophy rather than any other department

[1] In Chapter IV.

of philosophic study, is a practical interest; and unless we to some extent succeed in indicating the bearing of philosophic principles on practical life, we shall have failed of the achievement of the main purpose of our inquiry. Yet it is clear that if the definition of our subject is correct, it can have in itself no direct bearing on practice, apart from certain other studies which supply it with its empirical content. If, indeed, we could hope to work out with a certain fulness of detail the leading principles of Social Philosophy, even as now sketched, the points at which these principles throw light on practice would become at once apparent from the very completeness with which they were investigated. But it would be possible to do this only if the other parts of a philosophic system were also worked out with a like completeness. And it must at least be evident that in such an introductory essay as this no such fulness of treatment is to be expected. Consequently it seems clear that if the bearing of our principles upon our practice is to be in any degree made apparent, it will be necessary for us to some extent to fix our attention on considerations with which Social Philosophy by itself cannot undertake to deal. Indeed, even if this essay were a much fuller investigation of the subject than it professes to be, it is almost inevitable that there should be a certain reference to things that lie outside of our sphere. Every science and every philosophy has to look beyond itself; and this is particularly true of such a subject as the present. We have seen that Social Philosophy does not consist in the attainment of certain conceptions by an *in*duction from history, nor by a *de*duction from *a priori* principles, nor by a *pro*duction of the ἔνδοξα of common-sense; but may be described rather as an *intro*-duction—*i.e.* an endeavour to get inside or behind the notions which we use, so as to become clearly aware of their true place and significance in knowledge and in conduct. Such an inquiry must have a constant reference to the concrete facts with reference to which our notions are employed. Nor need we be guilty of any real paralogism in taking such facts into our view, provided we remember always that it is not the business of philosophy to give any complete account of such facts, but only to throw a certain light upon them. The "dry light" of philosophy would not by itself be of much interest, in reference to the problems of practical life; but when we moisten it by bringing it into relation to the springs of human hope and the streams of human development, we must still try to keep it pure, and to remember that it is only a partial light.

Seeing, then, that it is our purpose to try to discover what light philosophy can throw on the practical life of society, it seems natural that now, after having described in a general way the nature of the light which is to be made use of, we should pass to a brief consideration of the nature of the practical problems on which light is to be thrown. Such a consideration must, of course, be of a very general kind, and must rest rather on a historical than on a directly philosophic basis (though it will be scarcely possible to avoid a certain colouring of our views of history by the philosophic principles which are to follow). But, unsatisfactory as it may seem to introduce such considerations into a professedly philosophic work, it yet seems an inevitable preliminary to the discussion on which we are to enter; and to it, accordingly, we shall devote our attention in the following chapter.

# CHAPTER II.

## THE SOCIAL PROBLEM.

THE practical problem of social well-being is one which belongs peculiarly to the present time. There is, no doubt, a sense in which that problem is equally present at every stage in the history of mankind. But the sense in which it is so is somewhat similar to that in which we may say that the scientific impulse is present at every stage of human development. Men have always the desire to know, and they have always the desire of bringing themselves into right relations to their world : yet there are stages in their development at which these desires become more prominent elements in life than they are at others.

The social problem has not always been the most pressing of human problems. There have been times at which the most pressing problem has rather been an individual one—as, for instance, what must I do to be saved? There have also been times at which the most pressing problem has been political rather than social; and there have been times at which the most important problem has had regard to the discovery of abstract truths or to the advance of material prosperity. But it can hardly be denied that the problem which is now most pressing is the problem of social welfare.

There are, indeed, few things more striking than the absorbing interest which social questions have acquired

within the last generation; and it does not appear as if
that interest were likely soon to decline. We might, no
doubt, evade any difficulty which the rise of such an
interest occasions, by ascribing it simply to the increasing
preponderance of democratic influences in the modern
state. But such an explanation would not be very much
superior to Molière's "soporific virtue"; and, instead of
resorting to it here, we must endeavour to analyse with
some care the actual causes which have made these particular interests so prominent. We are more likely in this
way to understand these interests than if we were merely
to take them up as they stand, without reference to the
manner in which they have grown. To describe the
genesis of a thing—especially when it is a living thing—
is often the best method of defining it; it is at least very
often the best method of beginning the search for a
definition.

Now we may be led some way towards an understanding of this point by observing that what our increased
interest in social problems means is simply that our
interest is being directed more and more to the well-
being of people generally, instead of to the well-being
merely of the nation as a whole or of favoured individuals
in it. We no longer think of history, for instance, as a
record of kings and nobles, wars and governments, but
rather as a record of the life and progress of the people.
Our interest in economics, in like manner, is no longer
an interest in "the nature and causes of the wealth of
nations," still less in the causes of the wealth of merchant
princes within these nations, but rather in the nature and
causes of the *poverty* of individuals, and in the means
whereby their condition may be gradually ameliorated.[1]
Now the most obvious explanation of this change is to be

[1] Cf. Bonar's *Malthus and his Work*, p. 5, and Marshall's *Principles
of Economics*, Book I.

found in the increasing peacefulness of modern times.
So long as nations were in a state of perennial war, the
interest necessarily centred in the struggles of the state
as a whole and in the fortunes of its chiefs. The lower
strata of society could not be regarded as much more
than "food for powder." The virtues of a warlike state
are only those of "sparing the vanquished and beating
down the proud": it is in times of peace that men turn
to the inverse problem of raising up the humble, and
teaching the victorious how to use their power—and this
is what we understand by the social problem. Still, if
we are to understand what this problem really amounts
to, we must carry our analysis of the causes that have
made it important to a somewhat greater depth.

It is reasonable to expect, in a question affecting human
life as this does, that the causes which have led to its
prominence will have their roots both within and without
—depending partly on external conditions or environment, and partly on the growth of thought and sentiment.
Man is born at once free and in subjection, and the
history of his life—whether regarded individually or
socially—is the history of himself and of his bonds or
limitations. And, from another point of view also, these
causes will naturally have a two-fold aspect—being partly
causes that tend to make the problem a difficult one, and
partly causes that afford hopes of its solution. 'Difficulty
and hope are the spurs to exertion. What cannot be
attained and what cannot but be attained are both uninteresting, and nothing stimulates us so much to action
as hope in the midst of opposition. It is natural to
expect, therefore, that when we find the social problem
engaging universal attention, there must be at once causes
that make it difficult, and causes that give ground for
hope. We may expect too, from the general relation of
the elements of human life, that all the influences in the

problem will be very largely interdependent, so that it will be almost impossible to disentangle them and treat them separately.

We might begin, then, by dividing the causes which have led to the present prominence of the social problem into two main classes—(1) those which are concerned with the external conditions or environment of life, and (2) those which are concerned with the development of thought and sentiment. It should, of course, be understood that such a division is made merely for the sake of simplicity and clearness, and that it may require afterwards to be corrected by taking account of the fact that the two things are to a great extent dependent on one another, and cannot be profitably considered apart. Again, each of these two classes might be subdivided into other two—(1) those causes that tend to make the problem harder and more complex, and (2) those that tend to create hopes of its solution. We should thus have in all four sets of causes, which it might be convenient to consider in succession.

In order, however, to reach a clear understanding of the way in which these various influences have acted, it will be well to take a brief historical survey of the general development of thought and social conditions in Europe. It will be necessary, in fact, to consider what has been the nature of the task which the civilising forces of Europe—especially Western Europe—have had to accomplish since the fall of the Roman Empire, from which modern history may most naturally be regarded as dating. The task to which I refer has been a large and complicated one, extending over a long interval of time ; and there are many different points of view from which it might be considered. One feels a certain aversion to any attempt to crush its results into an epigram —a kind of edged tool which it is always dangerous to handle.

Historical generalisations are apt to hurt the mind in somewhat the same way as glasses hurt the eye. They accustom us to look at things in a particular way, and make it difficult for us to see them in any other way. Still, I believe it is at least not very far from the truth to say that the task of civilisation in Europe, from the time when the Roman Empire was split up, has had in the main three successive phases—which may be briefly expressed by the words Subjugation, Liberation, and Organisation. These phases, no doubt, overlap each other to a considerable extent, but they are nevertheless clearly distinguishable in their broad outlines. It is not difficult to indicate some of the leading points in the work of these three stages; and such an indication will assist us towards an understanding of the problem with which we have to deal.

(1) The first part of the work of modern civilisation was initiated and very largely carried out by the centralis- ing power of the Roman Empire itself. When the *Pax Romana* had been extended round the Mediterranean, the basis was already laid down for the unification of Europe and its reduction under law and discipline. It was something more than a patriotic conceit or the blind fervour of an enthusiast which made Mazzini regard Rome as the heart of the European organism, from which in the past the best movements of its life had flowed. Roman law was the great political legacy of the ancients to the moderns, as Greek literature was the great intellectual one ; and the one is still[1] at the foundation of European order, as the other is at the foundation of European thought. And after Rome herself had fallen as a political power,[2]

[1] This point is well brought out in Bryce's *Holy Roman Empire*, chap. xxi., p. 423 *seq.*

[2] Which happened later than has frequently been supposed. Cf. Freeman's *Historical Essays*, First Series, p. 126 *seq.*

the great unifying force for a long time to come—the force to which men naturally looked as the central spring of all that was highest in the activities of life—was what has been described[1] as "the ghost of the deceased Roman Empire sitting crowned upon the grave thereof," the Roman Catholic Church.[2] The task which had to be accomplished by this latter power, and by the other forces that co-operated with it after the Roman Empire had been finally overturned, was mainly that of subjugating, taming, and educating the semi-barbarous hordes that had overrun her dominions; and in general that of gathering up the fragments and reducing them again to some sort of unity and system. Few things could have been better adapted to serve as the inspiring impulse of this organising movement than the new ideas which had been introduced by Christianity. "Patriotism and religion," says De Tocqueville, "are the only forces in the world which can permanently direct the whole of a body politic to one end." When the old nationalities had expired, a new faith was the only power which could kindle in any large body of people that enthusiastic self-devotion which is necessary for the realisation of great ideas.[3] The Christian faith, moreover, soon proved itself to have a remarkable assimilative power. The fact that it had begun in an attitude of destructive absorption towards Judaism made it comparatively easy for it to assume a similar attitude towards the other forms of religion with which it was brought in contact; most of which had, in any case, already begun to feel their limits, and seemed to be waiting for an

[1] Hobbes's *Leviathan*, IV. 47.

[2] On the relation between the Empire and the Church, and on the unifying work of the latter, see Bryce's *Holy Roman Empire*, especially chap. vii., p. 100 *seq.*

[3] I consider this to be the element of truth, which Mr. Benjamin Kidd has distorted and exaggerated in his well-known book on *Social Evolution*.

enchanter's rod to transmute them into something better.
It soon succeeded either in adapting itself to them or in
informing them with a certain measure of its own spirit,
and so shaped itself gradually into a certain rounded
completeness in which the elements of earlier systems
appeared to be sublimated and absorbed. It "threw its
silver mantle over the dark," and changed the livery of
ancient superstitions.[1]

Round it also other forms of organisation naturally
grew. A certain element of communism associated itself
with Christianity from the first, and appeared indeed to
be the inevitable outcome of its spirit. The blessedness
of poverty and the nobility of labour[2]—two things, it is
true, which tended sometimes to contradict each other—
belonged to the essence of its teaching ; and the organisation of industry owed not a little to the influence of the
Church in the first enthusiasm of its faith. The quiet
permeation of this influence makes itself prominently apparent at a later time in connection with the Craft Gilds.
It is uncertain how far the influence of Christianity was
directly responsible for the origin of these and of the
Mediaeval Gilds generally ;[3] but there can be no doubt

---

[1] For a most instructive examination of some of the chief aspects
of this assimilative process, see the late Mr. Hatch's excellent course
of *Hibbert Lectures*. Cf. also Bosanquet's *Civilization of Christendom*.

[2] In striking contrast with the old Greek spirit as seen even in
Plato and Aristotle, by whom the mechanic is regarded as incapable
of the beautiful. It is true that a different spirit is to be found in the
teaching of the Stoics, and even of the Epicureans ; but Christianity had
the advantage over these in asserting and emphasising the essential
unity of mankind. The Friendship of the Epicureans was an external
and accidental bond ; and the Philanthropy of the Stoics, though
deeper, was only a principle of community among the "wise." The
Christian idea of Charity, resting as it did on the simple humanity
of mankind, was deeper and more all-embracing.

[3] See Brentano's *History and Development of Gilds*, especially pp.
3 and 4.

that in their ultimate growth they were largely pervaded by a religious spirit, and that it was mainly on this that their strength depended.[1]   And on the whole we might, without much violence—with scarcely any violence indeed, except that which is inevitably involved in characterising a long epoch by a short phrase—describe the centuries which elapsed between the fall of the Roman Empire and the Reformation (and, of course, the time succeeding also, in so far as a similar spirit continued to work through it), as the Age of Priestly Influence, or, in other words, as the Age of Education from above.

At the same time other forms of organisation of a more distinctly secular character were growing up, though around them also the Church cast a certain halo. Some of them, indeed, did not take definite shape, or did not display their full significance, till a somewhat later period than that to which we are now referring; while others, even before the end of that period, had already worked themselves out and decayed. Of these forms of organisation the most remarkable was the feudal system, with its ideals of honour and chivalry on the one hand, and its inevitable rivalries and tyranny on the other—a source of division perhaps as much as of union, yet on the whole to be reckoned amongst the organising forces.   Less striking than this, but tending more decidedly to order and welfare, were the earlier forms of the Craft and other Gilds to which reference has just been made—unique organisations, in some respects the most perfect that have ever been formed in connection with industrial aims. Nations also were now beginning to emerge from the ruins of the older empires, and to build up for them-selves more or less definite constitutions.   It would be interesting to trace the connection of these events, and

[1] Brentano's *History and Development of Gilds*, p. 69 *seq.*  See also p. 17 *seq.*

to see the various causes which led to the preponderance
now of one and now of another influence; but for our
present purpose such an historical inquiry would be of
little importance. What is of consequence for us to note
is merely that throughout all these developments the
same general spirit manifests itself—a spirit which may
be roughly characterised as that of aristocratic organisation, or organisation from above.[1] The aristocracy in
question was sometimes one of talent, sometimes one of
culture, and sometimes only one of force; but in nearly
every case it had a more or less explicit reference to a
supernatural sanction. The epoch to which we are
referring was, in fact, the age not only of Priests, but of
Barons and Kings[2] as well, and to a certain extent even

---

[1] It may be thought that the Gilds ought to be excepted from this
characterisation. Certainly their constitution was primarily democratic. It was formed on the model of a family rather than of an
army. Indeed, one of the principal aims of the Gilds was that of
protection against aristocratic powers. Here, in fact, we see that
even from the first the conditions of industry enforce a certain
amount of freedom. Still, it is not difficult to see that even such
organisations as the Gilds belong essentially to a time when society
is becoming consolidated rather than to one in which it is acquiring
freedom. And even the Gilds soon tended to become exclusive,
and to impose very stringent regulations; so that in a certain sense
even they became ultimately aristocratic, and had to be swept away
as soon as the conditions of industry were made freer. On this,
however, we need not here specially insist. Perfect accuracy cannot be
expected from any general formula which is used to cover a large
part of history. All that can fairly be demanded of such a formula
is that it should on the whole sum up the expression of the most
dominant tendencies. Cf. Brentano, pp. 4-6, 38, 39, 44, 50-55,
43 *seq.*, 84 *seq.* The view of some writers since Brentano (*e.g.*
Cunningham and Ashley) is still more favourable to the above
characterisation.

[2] In a sense it may be held that the authority of the feudal lord was
more absolute than that of a king; and that consequently even the
transition from the feudal system to monarchical government was

of "Captains of Industry." It was, in general, the age
of *authority*—an age in which peoples were tamed and
civilised and brought into order by forces and influences
in the determination of which the peoples themselves
as such had but little concern. Might was "in the
saddle," and men were governed by the will of the
strongest. The King, the Priest, the Master, was firmly
established at the top : the Serf, the Peasant, the Appren-
tice was firmly fastened at the bottom. It was, to use
one of Carlyle's [1] expressive phrases, the "brass collar"
period.

We have been taught to describe this period as the
*military stage* of modern civilisation ; and indeed it was
from the necessity of continual warfare that many of its
most prominent characteristics were derived, either directly
or by the subtle influence of habit. Society was organised
into a solid phalanx, both on its secular and on its religious
side, and the rigid discipline of an army pervaded the
whole. The serf was hardly more absolutely under the
sway of his feudal superior than were the intellects of men
under that of Aristotle and their beliefs under that of the
Church. It is the sense of this discipline and order that
causes such men as Carlyle or Comte, though from very
different points of view, to look back to those times with
a certain regret, as to a vanished ideal. But unhappily a
chain seems different to one who is without and to one
who is within its clasp. [2]

already a movement towards liberty. For the government of a
feudal lord was the government of individual will ; whereas that of a
king is always to some extent the government of law. Cf. Hegel's
*Philosophy of History*, IV. ii. 3. (Translation, p. 416.) See also
Montesquieu's *Esprit des Lois*, II. iii.

[1] *Past and Present*, III. xiii. and IV. i.

[2] No doubt, a more minute analysis might discover, within this first
period, several subordinate periods. Thus the feudal age might be
distinguished from the monarchical, and the time of the predominance

(2) The second part of the work of modern civilisation
was a struggle for freedom, of which the beginning may
be placed about the time of the *Renaissance*—though, no
doubt, it was heralded even earlier—and which reaches its
climax in the Aufklärung and the French Revolution. It
is the negative movement in modern progress, the key-
note of which is struck in the "*de omnibus dubitandum
est*" of Descartes on the one hand, and on the other hand
in the declaration of Rousseau that "man is born free,
and yet everywhere he is in chains." It began to be felt
that both on the intellectual and on the political side the
leading-strings of discipline had been outgrown; and so
the Age of Criticism arrived, when God and the King
and everything that claimed authority over men had to be
weighed in the balance of human reason—with a certain
*a priori* conviction that they were sure to be found wanting.

This revolution may be said to have begun at the
centre. The religious unity, which was at the heart of
all the rest, was the first that was effectually assailed.
Already, indeed, in the incessant conflicts between the
spiritual and temporal powers, we may see the germs of
dissolution. "One God, one Pope, one Emperor," was
indeed a vain ideal : for both Pope and Emperor, by the
very nature of their offices, necessarily claimed supremacy.[1]
The equilibrium of Mediaeval society was consequently
unstable, and contained in itself the prophecy of its own
decay. If this had been all, indeed, the remedy might

of the family from that of the predominance of the central government.
Cf. Schäffle's *Bau und Leben des socialen Körpers*, ii. 90 *seq.* But these
minute subdivisions do not invalidate the broad truth of the above
statements. See also Comte's *Positive Polity* (English translation),
II. 97 *seq.*, and III. 353 *seq.*; and Lotze's *Microcosmus* (English translation), II. 528 *seq.*

[1] Cf. Hegel's *Philosophy of History*, IV. ii. 1. (Translation, p. 403
*seq.*) See also an article by Professor Edward Caird in the *Contemporary Review* for June, 1890, p. 824 *seq.*

F

have lain in the unification of the spiritual and temporal powers. But the root of the malady was more deeply seated. The spirit of Christianity—itself at first one of the strongest antagonists of authority—had been buried under a mass of more or less alien forms, until its meaning was almost entirely obscured. It no longer appealed to the heart with happy tidings of release from bondage, but rather seemed itself to have become a slavery to an empty form. The Teutonic nations in particular,[1] characterised as they have always been by a strong love of independence, especially in matters of thought and religious life, revolted against formalities that had lost their meaning; and, aided by the enlightenment which the diffusion of the new learning had begun to secure, claimed for themselves the right of private judgment in matters of religion. The sticks were dry; particular abuses set flame to them; and the Reformation was the result.

All this is familiar enough to us. But what is important to notice is that it was simply a single step in a general movement. The next step—one, indeed, which began almost simultaneously with the Reformation, if not even a little before it—was to secure political rights for the whole body of the people; to abolish the prerogatives of class, and make the absolute rule of any individual or collection of individuals impossible. It is true that an effort in this direction may be traced at every stage in the history of Europe. But the effort could not become a *moral* force until a certain degree of religious independence had been won; and it could not become an *effective* force until there were adequate means—which prior to the invention of printing there were not—for disseminating the ideas of the few among the many. It

[1] Cf. Hegel's *Philosophy of History*, IV. introduction. (Translation, p. 354 *seq.*), and IV. iii. I (p. 431 *seq.*). See also Montesquieu's *Esprit des Lois*, XXIV. v.

is not surprising, therefore, that the problem of political freedom did not forcibly come to the front till about the beginning of the seventeenth century, and that even then it owed its prominence in great part to accidental circumstances : while it was not till near the end of the eighteenth century that the question of universal emancipation developed into an enthusiasm, and, we might almost say, into a religion.[1] And accompanying the work of purely political emancipation there was, of course, the similar task of freeing industry (including the important industry of printing) from governmental restraints and interferences, a task which has been accomplished chiefly under the influence of the theoretical economists. In general, this whole movement was a transference of power from the government to the leaders of the opposition. Iconoclasm was the order of the day. It was a time when men worshipped the rising sun, and when the rulers of the world were not the established authorities but rather the subversive forces.

This second period has been not unfittingly characterised as the *industrial stage*,[2] as the first was the *military stage* of modern civilisation. The solid phalanx which was necessary for war, and for a state of society in which war was one of the most prominent elements, was beginning to give place to the independent pioneers of commerce and invention. Society was passing from the condition of a solid to that of a liquid. Such a change, indeed, seems to be inevitable, whenever the internal development of national life becomes more important than its defence

---

[1] A religion, be it observed, which is based on reason ; not such a religion as that with which Mr. Kidd has recently made people familiar.

[2] This term has generally been used to cover what I describe as the third period as well. But this is a point which will be noticed afterwards. See *infra*, p. 86.

against external forces—*i.e.* whenever industry becomes
more prominent than war. An army must move like
a single man; it must be controlled by an absolute
authority from above; it must appear as the simple
embodiment of the will of its commander. And what is
true of an army is also true of the whole nature of a
society in which the existence of an army is the most
prominent characteristic. But it is not so with industry.
Industrial conditions must be conditions of individual
freedom, if full scope is to be given to the progress of
invention and the improvement of methods of work.
There can be little doubt that it was largely for this
reason that, when peace began to be established as the
normal condition of European life, and when in consequence the industrial arts began to be highly developed,
the demand for freedom was so strongly felt. The cry
of *laissez faire! laissez aller!* was as natural in an
industrial state as in a military one had been the adula-
tion of the powers that be. The inevitable march of
history was from subjugation to liberty.[1]

In such a time only is it strictly true that "society
progresses from status to contract."[2] It advances from
the state in which rights are established by authority and
custom to that in which they are established by mutual
consent. Or rather, it might be truer to say that it
advances from the recognition of obligations to the recognition of rights. In a military state the emphasis is
naturally laid on that which a man is bound to do, while
in an industrial state it is on that which he is entitled
to claim.[3] The virtue of the former is service: of the

[1] Cf. Havelock Ellis, *The New Spirit*, pp. 60-2.
[2] Cf. Maine's *Ancient Law*, chap. v.
[3] It is for this reason that the teaching of such writers as Carlyle,
Mazzini, and Ruskin, who insist on duties as opposed to rights, is
apt to seem impracticable in the modern state. But cf. *infra*, p. 86.

latter, self-help. To a certain extent the difference between these two states may be observed even in the
civilised countries of the present day, by contrasting a
military régime like that of Germany with a more purely
industrial régime like that of England or the United
States.[1] In the one a man is esteemed in proportion to
his official position, *i.e.* in proportion to the place which
he occupies in a system of political service: whereas in
the other he is esteemed almost exclusively in proportion
to his wealth, *i.e.* in proportion to the claims which he
is able to make on his society. But the latter standard
is the one which the whole course of modern civilisation
has tended to bring forward. The sacredness of property
has taken the place of the divinity of kings.

(3) And now we have just begun to enter on the third
part of the work of civilisation—what Carlyle used to
describe as the " Everlasting Yea "—the work of reorganisation or *"Palingenesie,"* the building up of a new order
on the basis of the liberty that has been achieved.

Mr. Ruskin, in a note to a passage in one of his earlier
writings, in which he had referred in somewhat exaggerated terms to the benefits of liberty, remarks,[2]—" I forget
now what I meant by ' liberty ' in this passage . . . .
It is very wonderful to me, now, to see what hopes I
had once." Perhaps our whole age might make a similar
annotation on the age that went before us. " Our time,"
says Höffding,[3] " seems to be peculiarly the time of
Pessimism . . . . The great political and social
reforms of last century were greeted with expectations of
a Golden Age, which were not fulfilled—partly for the
simple reason that those who had been set free were
without that discipline which freedom alone can give."
Partly for this reason—though I believe it would be truer

[1] Cf. Bryce's *American Commonwealth*, III. 362.
[2] *Frondes Agrestes*, VIII.     [3] *Grundlage der humanen Ethik*, IV.

of the generation immediately before us than it is of our own—but partly also because freedom of itself (at least as commonly understood [1]) is not sufficient for a Golden .Age. Indeed the discipline which freedom is giving consists to a considerable extent in making us aware of . the limitations which it requires. The preceding epoch was the age of destruction and the Happy Hunting-ground of youthful zeal, summing itself up at last in the " general overturn" of the French Revolution. To men just escaping from their prison-house everything outside seemed Elysium. They were content to forego all that convention and discipline had accomplished for mankind, and to reserve for themselves, like Alexander, " Hope."

> " Bliss was it in that dawn to be alive,
> But to be young was very heaven,"

if heaven consisted in saying No : as indeed for youth it very well may, when the Yes can be implicitly taken for granted—when the destruction of the worse seems neces-sárily synonymous with the reconstruction of the better. But experience soon teaches that there is no inevitable connection between them ; and we are in consequence beginning to pass from the demand for liberty to the demand for solidarity. Society, having passed from the condition of a solid to that of a liquid, seems now to be on the point of crystallising.

There are signs, in fact, that the *industrial stage* of civilisation (in the emphatic sense of that term) is destined to pass away as the *military stage* passed away before it. And the reason why it must pass away is sufficiently apparent. The amassing of material wealth cannot, any more than the acquisition of material power, be accepted as the ultimate, or even permanently as the dominant. end for human beings. Just as it is gradually discovered

[1] Cf. what is said on Freedom in Chap. v.

that power is only a means to prosperity, so it is gradually discovered that "the only Wealth is Life,"[1] and that prosperity is only a means to welfare. It is the consciousness of this that has slowly been introducing among us what might be called the *humanitarian stage*, in which the interest shall be centred in the well-being of persons, rather than in anything external; in which, as Prof. Geddes puts it,[2] the end shall be "not the increase of Wealth, but the Ascent of Man." As the idea of obligations gives place to that of rights, so the idea of rights gives place to that of personal welfare, or self-realisation.

This change is somewhat more difficult to trace than the preceding, chiefly because it is a change which has not yet worked itself out—which, indeed, in some departments has hardly even definitely commenced. A few remarks, however, on several of its more important aspects, may help to make it apparent that there is such a movement. And in this, as in the former case, it may be most convenient to begin with the religious aspect of the movement, though this is not the aspect in which it can be most clearly observed.

For some time after the Reformation, Protestantism fairly justified its name by remaining essentially militant. It was only by a strenuous insistence on the evils from which it sought to be free that the movement could keep itself alive and grow. *Nitor in adversum* had to be the motto of each of its adherents. They were fighting against constituted authorities—I am referring here to dissent in general, as well as to Protestantism in its more special sense—and their attitude in consequence was necessarily negative. The rights of the individual conscience had to be opposed to the claims of authority. The standards

[1] Ruskin's *Unto This Last*, Essay IV.
[2] *Claims of Labour*, p. 105.

of authority had grown empty and lifeless : but in the long run it was seen that the mere negation of what is dead is dead too.     In the generation succeeding the struggle for reform, when Protestantism was beginning to have its rights secured, theological controversy began to give place to a more positive religious spirit, which was more humanitarian than dogmatic, which was rather a life than a creed.  Of course, I do not mean to deny that at all times religion has been of this character to the most deeply religious natures.  Roman Catholicism, for instance, was so to Dante, for whom theological doctrines were little more than the veil over a deeper truth.[1]   But it can hardly be questioned that for the general consciousness both the authoritative dogmas of Roman Catholicism and the negations of Protestantism—culminating in pure Agnosticism—have tended to conceal the significance of the religious life.  Religion, in these forms, was apt to be too much separated from morality.  In so far as it influenced morality at all, it influenced it rather as an emotion which tinged it than as an inspiring force by which it was transformed and lifted to a higher level. In Roman Catholicism, the religious life tended to be so abstract that it was necessary to get away from the life of ordinary duty in order to live it at all.  In Protestantism, on the other hand, the morality of ordinary life tended rather to be accepted as it stood, and religion simply to be added on as something beyond it.  It is only in comparatively recent times that the demand has been strongly felt for a religion which should be the higher meaning of morality, and which should find its best expression in an enthusiasm of humanity.[2]  At the same

[1] Cf. Professor Edward Caird's article on the " Theology and Ethics of Dante " in the *Contemporary Review* for June, 1890.

[2] What I mean by this will become more apparent in the sequel. Cf. Chap. VI.  In the meantime it may be well to state that I do not

time, the growth of such a demand can be traced through
the whole development of the Protestant movement:
indeed, that demand may even be said to have been
the main source of its life. The interest by which the
movement was carried on was never merely the negative
interest in freedom from superstitions, but the positive
interest as well in truths that might furnish a guiding
principle for the moral life. It was the immorality as well
as the superstition of the older forms of religion that stirred
men to revolt: and however destructive that revolt might
be, it was yet guided throughout by the desire for a higher
life. But it was only after the negative movement of the
Reformation had achieved its destructive aims that the
positive side could be brought quite distinctly forward.
The idea of personal welfare could not become predominant until authority had been banished and rights secured.
We see the growing influence of that idea, however, in the
interest in the improvement of the people which accompanied the religious revivals of last century; in the zeal
which led to the emancipation of slaves,[1] in the formation
of semi-socialistic communities, and in kindred efforts in
the direction of social improvement. It is natural that
many of these efforts should be efforts after emancipation ;
and it is natural also that in many cases the moral ideals
which they suggested should be antagonistic to the ordinary
life of the modern state. But more recently the demand
has been for a religious principle which should guide and
inspire mankind not merely towards emancipation, but
towards reconstruction ; not merely towards a withdrawal

mean to imply that the highest form of religion is to be found in the
so-called Religion of Humanity. On the contrary, it seems to me that
that system is an attempt to secure the benefits of religion without
religion itself.

[1] Of course, in this, as in most other cases, the actual result was
brought about by somewhat mixed motives.

from the life of the state, but towards the development of that life to a more perfect form. ✓

When we pass from the religious life to the life of speculative thought, a similar movement is traceable : though here the process is complicated by the fact that the development of speculative thought has a movement of its own, which is to a large extent independent of the spirit of any particular age. The first note of post-reformation thought was struck by the doubts of Descartes ; but both in the case of Descartes himself, and, still more decidedly, in the case of his successors, Spinoza and Leibniz, doubt led almost immediately to a dogmatic reconstruction. It can scarcely be questioned, however, that the dominant influence on the next generation is to be found rather in the sensationalism of Locke,[1] leading directly to the scepticism of Hume, and that it is only after Kant that the effort towards reconstruction becomes predominant. These facts are, no doubt, partly to be accounted for by the necessary steps that have to be gone through in the development of thought, and partly also by the influence of the particular sciences at different times.[2] But how-

---

[1] I am not forgetting the valuable work that has been done by such writers as Webb, Hertling, Volkelt, Riehl, Fraser, and others, in bringing out the more intellectual element in the teaching of Locke, and in tracing his connections with those schools of thought in which the intellectual element is more distinctly dominant. But even if we were to grant all that is claimed by these writers, it would on the whole only make my present point more emphatic ; since it would still remain true that it was the sensational (or at least presentationist) side of his teaching that caught hold of the succeeding generation, both in France and in England. It was this element also that provoked the antagonism of Leibniz, and that, at a later date, transmitted through Hume, woke Kant from his "dogmatic slumber." Besides, a man's influence in philosophy is, on the whole, to be judged by what he *adds* rather than by what he still retains of the thought of his predecessors. Locke added the "manifold of sense," just as Kant added the "categories."

[2] Cf. *infra*, p. 151.

ever objective a thinker may be, he cannot make himself entirely independent of the atmosphere in which he has grown up; and consequently the tendencies of speculation at these various epochs are largely representative of the general spirit of the times. It is significant, therefore, that while the tendencies of thought in last century were distinctly in the direction of criticism and doubt, they have since the time of Kant been rather in the direction of a systematic reconstruction; a reconstruction, moreover, in which the life of self-conscious beings is taken as the central fact.

The significance of this becomes more clearly apparent when, instead of regarding speculative thought in particular, we consider rather the general current of opinion and sentiment, as represented in literature. In this current we are aware of two successive movements; though, no doubt, the change from the one to the other has been gradual, and almost imperceptible. The first movement consists of a thinning away of everything positive and authoritative in the life of man. God vanishes away into an *Être Suprême*; duty, into a moral sense; and the state into a social contract. It is true that in many of the leading writers soon after the Reformation we see much that is positive and authoritative—just as we see it also in the philosophies of Spinoza and Leibniz. But the positive element tends to become thinner and thinner. God changes from a personality into a substance or a harmony; and in the somewhat flashy optimism of a Shaftesbury, and still more in that of a Pope, we easily discern the beginnings of a universal doubt. Even when, as in the writings of Berkeley, the course seems to be for a moment halted,[1] and sensationalism itself is made to masquerade as a kind of idealism, we still cannot but

[1] Even this appearance of a halt arises only when we interpret Berkeley's thought in the light of ideas derived from later speculations. Cf. Fraser's *Locke*, p. 288 *seq.*

feel that the inevitable march is in a different direction.
It is only after this movement has worked itself out—
*i.e.* speaking broadly, after the time of the French Revolution—that the general tendency of thought becomes
once more positive.  It is, no doubt, unfair to speak of
the eighteenth century as if it had been characterised by
the presence of nothing but "the spirit that denies."  It
would be truer to say that it was an age of conflict, in
which the head tended to find itself in opposition to the
heart.    There was a constant undercurrent .of thought
endeavouring to make for itself some outlet in a positive
direction for the highest aspirations of human life ; but
this was continually checked by the consciousness of
insuperable obstacles.    "The cease of majesty died
not alone."    The overthrow of the older authorities
had carried along with it nearly all that could serve as
an obvious basis for the higher life of mankind ; and a
long process of struggle had to be gone through before
a new foundation could be laid.   Hence arose a suspicion
of all the higher motives of human nature, a distrust of
ideals that bordered upon "enthusiasm," a disbelief in
anything that could not be definitely weighed and measured.   It can hardly be maintained, indeed, that this spirit
has been outgrown ; but it has lost something of its power.
In the literature which began about the time of the French
Revolution, and which has been the most potent factor
in creating the spiritual atmosphere of our century, in the
writings of Goethe and Wordsworth and the others who
caught their accents, the whole tendency is obviously towards reconstruction ; and it is towards a reconstruction
in which the spiritual life of man is regarded as the
centre and the key of nature.   Authority has on the whole
passed away : the rights of reason and criticism have been
sufficiently asserted : the welfare of humanity is the note
which has now to be sounded.

In political and in industrial life the positive spirit was somewhat later in making definite appearance—partly because in these departments of life, in which external conditions have to be contended with as well as the obstructions of the spirit, freedom is more tardily achieved, and partly because they are less accessible to the influence of ideas. Yet there have not been wanting signs of the growth of a movement in these regions also in the direction of reorganisation. This may be traced, no doubt, very largely to the influence of such thinkers as Saint-Simon and Comte, as well as to the earlier teaching of German Idealism, and to the various forms of Socialism to which both these lines of thought gave rise. But even prior to the writings of these theorists, and to some extent even serving as their inspiration, we find the same spirit at work in practice. The interest in the poor, which was in great measure stimulated by the revival of religious feeling, and which expressed itself at first in the form of such elaborate inquiries as that of Eden, led at last, in men like Owen and Leclaire,[1] to positive efforts in the direction of the improvement of the conditions of life. The co-operative movement owed its birth to this spirit, and it is the same spirit that we find promoting Factory Legislation or, in a more extreme form, preaching Socialism (of a poetic or philanthropic or "Christian" sort[2]). The extent to which such ideas have influenced modern thought on industrial affairs may be to some extent gauged by contrasting the attitude of Adam Smith, Malthus, or Ricardo, with that of J. S. Mill, and that of Mill again

---

[1] There is an excellent account of the work of Leclaire in Gilman's *Profit Sharing*, p. 69 *seq.* Cf. also Bosanquet's *Essays and Addresses*, p. 16 *seq.* For an account of the work of Owen, see Sargant's *Robert Owen and his Philosophy*, or Reybaud's *Études sur les réformateurs*.

[2] "Scientific Socialism," or Socialism as an economic doctrine, is, of course, a somewhat different thing.

with that of the so-called *Katheder-Socialisten* in Germany. We seem readily to trace in the development from the earliest of these to the latest the progress from the idea of individual rights to that of general welfare.   At first rights are contended for simply as rights : then they are contended for because they are the means of personal welfare : and then, finally, it begins to be seen that there is more involved in personal welfare than the attainment of anything that can be regarded as an individual right. It might even be sufficient, for the observation of this de-velopment, to notice the changes in the attitude of Mill himself, who seems to have been peculiarly sensitive to the growth of ideas in his time.   On the other hand, when we go back beyond Adam Smith to the writings of the earlier economists, we find ourselves in a world in which the idea of individual rights itself has not become decidedly prominent.   It is in that earlier period that economics are emphatically *political* economy.   The well-being of the state as a whole is still the chief good, and individuals are regarded as having obligations rather than rights.[1]   Now, on the other hand, the tendency is already that of regarding individuals as having no obligations except the obligation to realise what is highest in their nature, and no rights except the right to the means of such realisation.

It appears, then, that we can distinguish three stages in the history of modern civilisation.   They correspond in general—and it is not by a mere accident that they do correspond—to the three phases of thought which Kant

---

[1] It was of the essence of the Mercantile System, for instance, to aim at the enrichment of the *state*; and even when the Physiocrats began to insist more on the welfare of the individual, they had to treat this to a large extent as a means to the welfare of the nation as a whole— nay, even sometimes to clinch their reasoning with the argument, "pauvre royaume, pauvre roi."

has characterised as Dogmatism, Scepticism, and Criticism respectively. We have first the education of the human spirit, in all the aspects of its life, by means of positive convictions—"mystic, wonderful"—of which no explanation is sought, but which are received simply as a revelation from above; and from the hands of an authority which is externally imposed. Then we have the revolt against the convictions, the overthrow of the authority, the denial of the revelation. Finally, there is the attempt to arrive at something positive and systematic; but at the same time something which shall no longer be merely externally received or imposed from above, but rather something whose evidence and authority are to be found in our own life and experience, something which can be examined and criticised and understood—in short, an affirmation which is not in any way forced upon us from without, but to which all the deepest elements in our nature give their assent. Thus the first stage rests on what is supernatural or transcendent; the second, on what is purely natural; the third, on what is spiritual or, in the deepest sense, human. The meaning of this, however, will become clearer as we proceed.

We must not, of course, look for any sharp line of demarcation between these three stages; any more than we should look for such a division between the stages in the growth of an individual character. In the one case, as in the other, we have a general impression, from the *tout ensemble* of the thing observed, that there has been a process from one stage to another; but when we seek to analyse the process, we soon see in each case that the different stages overlap, and even that many characteristics of the latest may be traced in the earliest. For this reason it is impossible to give any cogent proof that such a process has really taken place at all.[1] One can only

[1] At least it is impossible within the limits of such a work as this.

appeal to a certain historical taste, by which the general
*feel* of the character of a period is conveyed.  The deliverances of this taste, as of other tastes, may be expected to
vary to some extent in different observers : a certain
allowance must be made for the " personal equation," and
for the equation of the point of view.  And even when
the true deliverances of the taste have been found, one
cannot but be aware that in putting them into language
one is continually in danger of giving them a certain hard-
ness and rigidity which vitiates their truth.  But on the
whole I believe most competent observers will agree that
there is a broad truth in the division of the history of
modern civilisation into these three epochs.  If, however,
any one should dispute this, it must be admitted that he
would be, in Plato's language, θαυμαστῶς δυσανάπειστος,
very hard to convince.

 Now the prominence of social questions at the present
time depends very largely on the fact that we live in a
period of transition between the second epoch and the
third.[1]  Society has become thoroughly plastic and disin-

Nor indeed would it be possible to give a proof which would be quite
satisfactory to any one who did not enter into the spirit of the successive
periods, and, so to speak, live their lives over again.

[1] There is a sense, no doubt, in which every period is a period of
transition.  Society, as such writers as Mr. Leslie Stephen and Prof.
S. Alexander have taught us to recognise, is in a constant state of
equilibration—continually moving forward from one form of equilibrium
to another ; so that there is hardly any point at which some transition
may not be observed at least in the more progressive societies.  But
there are at least nodes in the movement, points of comparative rest.
That we are not at present standing at such a node, is a point that
may, I think, be illustrated, in a somewhat ludicrous way, by the
tendency at the present time in England to discover novelty in many
phases of contemporary social life.  Thus we hear of the New Unionism,
the New Journalism, the New Woman, the New Humour, the New
Spirit, the New Religion, and so forth.  Even the citizens of Ancient
Athens could scarcely have been more eager than we seem to have

tegrated, and "organic filaments" (to use Carlyle's expression) are only beginning to form. The powers above us have grown weak : the powers within us have not yet grown strong. There is nothing to control us and we have not yet learned self-control. This is the general aspect of the social problem, and indeed of all human problems, at the present time. But in order that we may understand it more fully, it will be necessary to consider it under the four aspects which we have already had occasion to enumerate : (1) Conditions of Difficulty, (2) Conditions of Hope, (3) Developments of thought that impede us, or that cause us to despair of improvement, (4) Developments of thought that help us, or that tend to inspire us with confidence.

I. The difficulties of the social problem have grown with our growth and strengthened with our strength. The mere increase of population has made it harder than it ever was before for each to find his place. "Over-population," no doubt—like "Over-production"—may be a somewhat inaccurate expression. The capacity of the earth for yielding subsistence to human beings is, from an abstract point of view, almost indefinitely extensible, just as human wants are ; and our power of availing ourselves of the earth's capacity is continually increasing, and seems likely to go on continually increasing, by the growth of new inventions, so that practically, so far as the life of the present generation and of those in the immediate future are concerned, the possibility of expansion might be regarded as unlimited, and the prospect of over-population as a chimaera.[1] Yet, just as it is easily possible to have

become to discover some new thing. All this has its comic side : yet it may be taken to indicate a real dissatisfaction with the ideals and modes of thought and action of the preceding generation—a sense of the necessity for a new form of equilibrium, a new *social universe.*

[1] It is so regarded, for instance, by Mr. Henry George in his *Progress and Poverty.* But perhaps this ought not to be seriously treated.

G

a glut in the market by producing the wrong things, or by producing things at the wrong place or time, so too it is possible—if we may be allowed to express it in such a way—to· have a glut of human beings, if they increase more rapidly than the power of providing them with the means of subsistence, or if they increase in such a way that it is difficult for them to spread themselves over those places that are fitted for their support, or in such a way that it is practically impossible for them to be properly organised and governed.   In any case, the larger the numbers are the more complicated in general will be the problem of uniting them into a whole—even when allowance is made for the fact (which, indeed, is partly a result of this difficulty) that in a denser population there is usually a more alert intelligence.  The Greeks used to think it impossible to constitute a state of more than a few thousand citizens; and though our ideas have expanded as our powers of organisation have grown, it seems to be still true that there are limits to the possibility of a well-ordered state.[1]   Certainly, at any rate, the question of the increase of population is one of the first that must be taken into account as a difficulty in the way of the amelioration of the condition of the people; whether or not it is ultimately to be regarded as a serious or as an insuperable difficulty.[2]

Closely connected with this difficulty is that which arises from the appropriation of the earth's surface.

[1] At least, of a state whose most important affairs are carried on by means of a central government.   But cf. Chap. vi.  Cf. also Montesquieu's *Esprit des Lois*, viii. 16.

[2] Cf. Chap. vi.   The question with regard to the evils connected with an excessive increase of population is largely a biological one. Some suggestive remarks upon it will be found in the paper on "The Conditions of Progress of the Capitalist and the Labourer," by Prof. Patrick Geddes.—*Claims of Labour*, pp. 74-111.

Land, as has often been pointed out, differs from most other important forms of property in this respect, that the total amount of it is definitely limited, and that the amount which is readily available for the use of any group of persons living in close association with each other is very soon exhausted. If this fact had been distinctly realised at the time when the land of civilised countries was being appropriated, it can hardly be doubted that it would have been wise to take such steps as would have prevented it from passing into the hands of any individuals; or, at any rate, such steps as would have effectually prevented any individual from possessing more of it than he could employ for the good of the community, and at the same time would have to a considerable extent compelled him to use it for that purpose. The confused and forcible way, however, in which land was originally seized would have rendered any such regulation impossible, even if the consequences of its appropriation could have been clearly foreseen. The result is that in modern times the land question has for most of the older civilised communities become a burning one; and the difficulty which is thus occasioned is a very momentous one, since the healthy life of any nation must depend very largely on the way in which its land is managed.[1]

---

[1] This, I suppose, will hardly be disputed. To consider the reasons which make it true would carry us beyond the limits of such an essay as the present. The view which some recent reformers seem to hold, that England, for instance, might continue to be a flourishing nation even if she were converted into a purely manufacturing country, and all the land unbuilt upon were turned into pleasure-grounds, seems somewhat unpractical; and even if it were practical, it would not show that the land question is unimportant. But the pressingness of the problem is more important if we recognise (as I believe we must) that the existence of a flourishing agricultural population is almost indispensable to the welfare of a great nation.

The primary causes, then, of the increasing difficulty of social life in modern times may be said to depend on the fact that population grows indefinitely, while land is limited in amount. To the growth of population, however, we must add the growth of complexity which the development of the arts has brought. The difficulties of the present time, apart from those which are due simply to the fact that men multiply and the earth does not, are mainly those which are naturally characteristic of a highly developed industrial state. These difficulties may be conveniently arranged in four principal divisions :— (1) Multiplicity of Functions, (2) Diversity of Interests, (3) Impersonality of Relations, (4) Instability of Conditions. It may be well to consider each of these separately, though they are so intimately dependent on one another that it is almost impossible to treat them apart.

1. As the industrial arts develop, their parts become continually more and more differentiated, until it is impossible for any one individual to undertake more than a small part of one of them. And even where division of labour is not an absolute necessity, it is yet found to be extremely advantageous for the sake of efficient and steady work, as well as of the saving of material. The remarks of Adam Smith[1] on this subject are well known, and subsequent experience has rather added to than taken from their force.[2] Indeed the division of labour has in some cases even advantages that may be called moral, in addition to those that are purely economic. It tends to the promotion of persistence and thoroughness. It secures, when it is carried out within moderate limits, a certain permanence in our

[1] *Wealth of Nations*, Book I. chap. i.
[2] This subject is admirably treated in Marshall's *Economics of Industry*, p. 49 *seq.* Cf. Walker's *Political Economy*, p. 58 *seq.*

objective interests, so that we are more able than we should otherwise be to become at home with them. It makes our present surroundings familiar and our future calculable, and in that way tends to develop a certain balance of mind, and to promote many of those virtues, such as accuracy and foresight, which distinguish a civilised man from a savage. Schiller used to say, moreover, that the great happiness of life consists in the discharge of some mechanical duty; and perhaps more people than we sometimes think would be found at heart to agree with this, provided their duties are sufficiently varied to stimulate their interest, without being so complex as to cause distraction. Πλέον ἥμισυ παντός. As Goethe said, " He who would accomplish anything must learn to limit himself." It is in many cases not only better for production, but also more conducive to our own happiness and the right development of our energies, that our sphere of action should be a limited one. But there are limits to this limitation. Even from a purely economic point of view, there can be little doubt that excessive limitation, especially in the case of young apprentices, is an occasion of inefficiency and want of resource. Escher's remark on English workmen [1] is well known :—" If I have an English workman engaged in the erection of a steam-engine, he will understand that, and nothing else ; and for other circumstances or other branches of mechanics, however closely allied, he will be comparatively helpless to adapt himself to all the circumstances that may arise, to make arrangements for them, and give sound advice or write clear statements and letters on his work in the various related branches of mechanics." We are only beginning to wake to the need, from a commercial

[1] Mill's *Political Economy*, I. vii. 5. How far the above is, or was, true of English workmen in particular, we need not here inquire.

point of view, of a broader education of workmen, which shall to some extent supply the place of the old apprenticeship system.

But there are other results of the division of labour, which are of a more pervading character, and affect not so much the efficiency of labour as the nature and happiness of the labourer. One who is limited to the performance of a single kind of action is apt, as we so constantly see, to have his nature limited and stunted by it. His interests may be narrowed to a point: he may have his attention absorbed in matters which are not fitted to supply a filling for a life, and may thus be driven to fill it up with a less innocent content. Not indeed that any activity can be other than one-sided—it is largely for that reason that "all work and no play" is said to dull—but some kinds of employment are so thoroughly "part of a part" that they afford no scope for the development and health of any of our energies at all. There is a danger, under industrial conditions, that men may be made into tools for a particular purpose, at the expense of their general humanity. "The arts advance," as De Tocqueville put it, "and the artizans fall back."[1] Society sacrifices the manhood of its citizens, as Pan has been said to sacrifice the lives of poets, that they may be made into instruments. The consequences of this have already in many ways begun to make themselves felt, and are certainly not the least of the evils under which we suffer. Heine said that in England the machines have

---

[1] In fact, they *become* artizans, and cease to be artists. In these circumstances it is, of course, only partly true that "the arts advance." Cf. Mr. William Morris's *Hopes and Fears for Art*, p. 10, etc. See also Göhre's *Three Months in a Workshop*, especially pp. 44-57, where a most instructive comparison is drawn between different forms of employment, with respect to their influence on the characters of the workers.

the perfection of human beings, and the human beings are little better than machines.[1] "Wealth accumulates and men decay."

It is not this difficulty, however, on which I wish chiefly to insist in connection with the multiplicity of functions, but rather the difficulty which that multiplicity occasions in the organisation of social life, or in what the eighteenth century writers used to call the "circulation." So long as life is simple, it is comparatively easy to adjust activities to needs; but as the needs and activities multiply, it becomes continually more difficult to arrive at a satisfactory equation between demand and supply; and the adjustment is in many cases made only by a rough adaptation—a kind of "natural selection"—which does not really succeed in satisfying the most important of human wants at the time, and leads very often in the long run to violent catastrophes. The crises which so frequently disturb our industries are a matter of some difficulty to account for—though *some* of the causes seem sufficiently obvious[2]—but perhaps the wonder ought rather to be that an instrument of so many strings "should keep in tune so long." The complication of modern industrial conditions, indeed, has rendered a wise and efficient regulation so hopeless that for a long time *laisser faire* has been the recognised principle of economic policy,[3] on any exception to which the *onus probandi* is laid; and a certain optimism, which is natural to man, has inclined many of us to believe that by such a policy the best possible results will be secured.[4] But it is clear that, if the results are on the whole good, they are at least very unsteady and incalculable, and productive of a great deal

---

[1] *Florentinische Nächte,* II.
[2] Cf. *Claims of Labour,* p. 204 *seq.*
[3] Partly, no doubt, for other reasons than this.
[4] Cf. Wagner's *Lehrbuch der politischen Oekonomie,* I. 230 *seq.*

of incidental mischief. It is said that, even within the
limits of a single factory, it is extremely difficult, if not
impossible, when there are a number of separate departments that work into each other's hands, to prevent
frequent dislocations in the arrangements by which they
are connected; and what is thus hard on a small scale,
where there is a definite central control, must of necessity
be very much harder in the totality of the business world,
even when allowance is made for the greater possibilities
of adjustment where the sphere is wider. Of course, I
do not mean to deny that in the long run there *is*
such a tendency towards adjustment (of a rough sort)
throughout industries as a whole; but it will probably be
generally conceded, both by business men and by economists, that the run is apt to be a very long one, and
that the tendency beyond certain limits is feeble and in-
effective. The *vis medicatrix naturae* is not much to be
relied on in the social body, whatever may be the case
with the individual. And even if harmony did ultimately
ensue, even if the "circulation" did ultimately set itself
in order, yet it must not be forgotten that, unless the
greatest prudence were exercised uniformly by all concerned—and a high degree of prudence is hardly to be
expected in large masses of mankind—much misery would
be occasioned while the harmony was in process of production. It seems clear, moreover, that the result, as
things are, is very far from being a genuine harmony
even in the long run.[1] Even in the long run, demand

[1] It should be remembered also that in many cases there is, strictly
speaking, no "long run" at all; since, as soon as the cause has had
time to work out its effects, the conditions have changed and the
effects will no longer fit them. If I might be allowed to borrow an
illustration from an American humourist, I should say that many
cases of economic adaptation resemble the efforts of one who was
learning to plough, and who was told to move straight in the direc-

and supply are equated not by the satisfaction of all the most important wants, but partly by the stimulus of artificial wants, which are hurtful to the general well-being, and partly by the suppression of natural ones, whose gratification would be greatly to its benefit. Articles of luxury—*i.e.* articles which are not necessary either for living or for living well[1]—are produced and used to such an extent as to be positively hurtful; while, on the other hand, the highest forms of beauty and perfection of workmanship —which *are* necessities for living well—are apt to be entirely neglected. The result of this is an injury to human beings, in their capacity as consumers, by the misdirection of their wants, and in their capacity as producers, by causing an insufficient demand for the highest forms of skill.[2] These evils would right themselves only if men's real wants were uniformly stronger and more persistent than the craving for immediate pleasure; and one can hardly hope that they will become so, so long as the sources of pleasure are so fertile as to preclude an early satiety. But until they become so, a certain culture of consumption is urgently required—a discipline of desires, an education of public taste[3]—which in its turn would react on production. But it is probable rather that the two sides, production and consumption, would require to

---

tion of a cow that was standing at the other end of the field. The result did not prove satisfactory, and he complained that when he came where the cow was, the cow was not there. It is impossible for one thing to adapt itself to another by degrees, unless the other thing is constant, or at least varies in accordance with a constant rule. Cf. Mill's *Logic*, v. vii.

[1] Cf. the remarks on luxury in Chap. VI.

[2] These points have been well insisted on by Prof. Ruskin. Also, more recently, by Prof. Patrick Geddes. See, for instance, *An Analysis of the Principles of Economics*, p. 23; *Claims of Labour*, p. 110; *Industrial Exhibitions*, p. 42 *seq.*

[3] This point is referred to again in Chap. VI.

move simultaneously. In any case, it seems clear that organisation is what we lack.

2. The next point which we have to notice is the diversity of interests. "The highest good," as Spinoza tells us, "is common to all, and all may equally enjoy it"; but it is not so with those kinds of good which are most sought after in an industrial state. The community in this case is apt to be rather like that which Francis I. professed to have with Charles V.: "What my brother Charles wishes (viz. Milan) that I wish too." If the end is common to all, it is at least one which all cannot attain together; and hence it becomes increasingly difficult to secure unity of aim. "The spirit of commerce," as Montesquieu says,[1] "unites nations; but it does not, in like manner, unite individuals." In a military society there is not the same diversity of interests between the members of a single group. It is true that even in such a state there will always be some who receive the lion's share of those things which are most valued in life, and from the enjoyment of which the others are more or less excluded. But on the whole those who receive the lion's share are visibly the lions. They have borne the brunt of the struggle for the achievement of a good which is in some degree common to all; and it seems right, in consequence, that their lives should be richer in the elements of human happiness. In such a society those in a subordinate position feel themselves on the whole to be but

---

[1] *Esprit des Lois*, xx. 2. Perhaps some qualification should be made even on the statement that it unites nations. Seeley has argued, in *The Expansion of England*, that the great wars of the last century were to a large extent commercial wars. Still, commercial wars are generally wars for unity. It is important to distinguish wars which are undertaken merely for the sake of fighting or of the aggrandisement of a particular state from those which have as their inspiring force some idea of justice, some conception of enlarged social organisation or improved intercourse.

the members of their chief. They can hardly be said to have a life except in his. They flourish only in his success, and "there if they grow the harvest is his own." His superiority is perceived to be intrinsic; and his position, with its attendant happiness, to be only the expression of that superiority. In an industrial state, on the other hand, the happiness which is sought presents itself in general as peculiar to certain individuals, of whose good the others are only the unwilling instruments. In the one case the superior position of any particular individual is only the symbol of the good which he has achieved: in the other case the superior position is apt to appear as the good itself. The one is stamped because it is current coin: the other · is current coin because it is stamped. In a military state, in short, there is, in a broad sense, no merely individual good; the good for the individual consists in the fulfilment of his obligations to the state, and any other good is valued chiefly as the expression of duty done; whereas, in an industrial state, the main good is the good of the individual, and the state itself tends to be regarded as only a convention for the protection of individual rights. Thus the more purely industrial a society becomes, the more does self-interest tend to predominate, and the more widely do individual aims diverge from one another and from the common weal. An industrial state remains military, except that the war has become civil: it is a *bellum omnium contra omnes.*[1]

The separation of interests takes many forms;[2] but perhaps the most prominent at the present time is the division between the class of employers and that of hired workmen—sometimes loosely described as the con-

---

[1] Cf. however what is said *infra*, p. 120.
[2] See, for instance, for another illustration, Göhre's *Three Months in a Workshop*, p. 77.

flict between capital and labour. The differentiation of the master into the capitalist and the *entrepreneur* on the one hand, and into the *entrepreneur* and the foreman on the other, has probably tended, more than anything else, to fix an impassable gulf between employer and employed.[1] In former times, when the struggle for existence was less keen and markets less wide, and when the duties of the "undertaker" were in consequence less complex, the distinction between the working man and his employer was by no means that sharp demarcation to which we have now become accustomed. The man belonged practically to the same social grade as his master, and in many cases hoped ultimately to become a master himself.[2] He was associated with his master in the unions of his trade, not combined with others against him; and in general there existed between the whole body of masters and workmen in any occupation a certain *esprit de corps*, based on community of aim and interest. Now, on the other hand, the *entrepreneur* in a large business is hardly brought at all into contact with his workmen. His peculiar task is to look abroad into the world of industry as a whole rather than to take charge of those in his own employment. He is "a being of a large discourse," and looks rather "before and after" and around, than at that which is immediately beside him. He belongs, moreover, to a different social grade from that of his workers; and his interests and sympathies alike lead him to connect himself rather with those in his class than with those in his employment—

[1] Cf. Walker's *Political Economy*, p. 76 *seq.*, and Brentano's *History and development of Gilds*, p. 72 *seq.* See also a very instructive article, entitled *An Interpretation of the Social Movements of our Time*, by Prof. H. C. Adams, in the *International Journal of Ethics*, Vol. II., No. I.

[2] Cf. Ashley's *Economic History*, I. 42 and 93.

whose interests, indeed, both he and they are apt to regard as antagonistic to his own.

But the separation of interest between different classes of masters and different classes of workmen is hardly, if at all, less marked than that between masters and work-men as a whole. That "potter hates potter" is a saying sufficiently old ; but the titanic scale of modern compe-tition is a comparatively new phenomenon, and has been made possible only through the liquefaction of social conditions to which we have been referring. In a more primitive society nearly everything which is not regulated by government is regulated by custom. Each district has its particular *Sitten*, and is very little interfered with by the action of others; and within each district those who are employed in any occupation may hope to be allowed to carry on their occupation, in accordance with the established methods, throughout their lives. They have not much hope of advancing themselves very greatly in position; but neither have they much fear of being thrown back. In a liquid society like ours, on the other hand, the action of men in one district has an almost instantaneous effect on the conditions of every other. If one man succeeds in doing work better or more cheaply than others, it is in vain for the latter to plead that they are doing the work according to established methods. They are at once cut out by the competition of those who have learned the newer methods. Thus there is, more than ever before, a universal war between those "undertakers" who are engaged in the same kind of work, or in kinds of work of which the products may be used as alternatives. Similarly, again, there is more competition than formerly between those workmen who are employed in the same kinds of industry; because the fluid condition of society enables men to pass more readily from place to place.

Between these various contending interests there is no mediating power, and no embodiment of Justice to hold the balance.  The economic and other mechanical factors determine things, as Wagner says,[1] with the roughness of natural forces ; and there is no adjustment of claims by any rational authority whose decisions can be regarded as equitable.  Every one's hand is against every one else, and Chaos sits as umpire.

The partition of interests to which I am referring has, however, an even deeper aspect.  It makes itself felt not merely in a positive conflict of aims, but in a certain negative exclusiveness of groups of human beings with respect to each other.  No doubt there has always been, in civilised communities, a certain separation between classes of society whose interests in life are different ; and in many respects this separation has in former times been much more sharply drawn than it is at present.  But just because the separation was so sharp in former times, it was much less subtle.  Probably there was never any time in which men tended to be so unintelligible to each other as they are now, on account of the diversity of the objects with which they are engaged, and of the points of view at which they stand.[2]  It is for this reason, no less than on account of the conflicts into which they are led, that men begin to be conscious of a pressing need for the presence of some universal end in the pursuit of which all men may once more become united.

3. The impersonality of relations in an industrial community is the point that we have next to notice.  Carlyle used to say that the Epic of modern times was no longer "Arms and the man," but "Tools and the man."  But

---

[1] "Da entscheiden denn roh mechanisch die Machtfactoren."— *Lehrbuch der politischen Oekonomie,* I. 635.

[2] We are, however, beginning to see glimpses of universal principles by which such differences may be reconciled.  Cf. Chap. VI.

under the present conditions, it might rather be said that it is "Tools and *not* the man." If it be correct to say, with Schiller, that the vulgar pay with what they do and the noble with what they are, it might seem as if we had been passing gradually from the nobler to the more vulgar payment. Under an industrial régime, character hardly counts. Personal relations become evanescent. It is no longer a case of one human being acting in concert with others or in subordination to them, but a case simply of a contract entered into between capital and labour. The machinery is the agent; the persons are instruments. In this contract also "the living are more and more ruled by the dead." The results of past activities appear in the form of Capital, and assume control over the activities of the present;[1] and what is wanted in the present is not the services of a person, but the dexterities of an operator. "Our new heraldry is hands, not hearts." The result of this is that, on the one hand, "the individual withers"—he loses value as a human being, and retains it only as a machine for accumulating wealth—and, on the other hand, he becomes subordinate to the wealth which has already been accumulated. In other words, the impersonal results of labour have acquired a value in human life which they never had before. The worth of persons tends to be estimated by their power of producing wealth, and still more by their command over wealth that has already been produced. Men have ceased to be enslaved by men; but they are beginning to fall under the dominion of their own creations. They began by using "tools," and it seems sometimes as if they might end by tools using them.[2]

[1] Cf. Mr. Smart's Preface to Böhm-Bawerk's *Capital and Interest*, p. xvi.

[2] The distinction which Prof. Adams draws, in the paper above referred to (p. 97, note 2), between *tools* and *machinery*, and between

The results of this preponderance of the impersonal
over the personal, of the dead over the living, are seen
in many forms.   The sense of personal obligation has
become less, or at least it has become far more difficult
than formerly to see definitely in what directions such
obligations hold.   The employer tends to become little
more than an exploiter of labour, and at last an exploiter
of himself; while the workman in like manner is apt to
lose all consciousness of loyalty either to his employer or
to his trade, or ultimately even to his own nature.   Each
is in the hands of a blind fate—a power, not himself,
which makes for Production—and to the dictates of this
Moloch the well-being of each has to be subordinated.
As the Greeks were said, when enslaved by the Romans,
to have conquered their masters; so it might seem as
if, in a kind of inverse [1] way, mind in conquering matter
had become enslaved by it.

The world, from this point of view, is becoming a workshop, and is ceasing to be a school for character.   Of
this we see the outward sign most distinctly in that circumstance which constitutes perhaps the greatest of all
the problems of modern civilisation—the growth of large
cities.   A modern city is probably the most impersonal
combination of individuals that has ever been formed in
the world's history.[2]   People come to these centres from
the most diverse quarters and with the most diverse aims.

the forms of society that are respectively based upon the use of these,
is particularly important in this connection.

[1] I say "inverse" because, in the other case, the Greeks were the
mind.

[2] No doubt there is something similar to it in the even more strikingly amorphous character of the population that is drawn into a new
or comparatively unoccupied country, such as the United States.
But there the immigration often takes place in groups, which hold
together in some sort of unity, till the sense of citizenship in a larger
whole has become developed.

They have no sense of common interests or mutual obligations, but are drawn together simply by the magnetic
force of industrial conditions. The physical conditions of
health are absent; and the conditions of moral health
are often even more so. Men are crowded together in
dwellings which in many cases serve the purpose rather
of tool-boxes than of homes—boxes, moreover, in which
the tool corrodes away. In such places people are, as it
has been said, "born tired." They are exhausted by the
struggle of life before they begin it, and when they do
begin it they soon succumb to it. Morally, also, they
become separated from social relationships, or brought
into relationships which are worse than none. The individual is lost in the solitude of a crowd. The North
Country proverb is realised—"Friends are far when neighbours are near." East and West Ends are formed; and
in this way the two extremes of social life are each cut
off from "the ethos of their people." The poor become,
as is often said, "hopeless" from want of stimulus and
help, and the rich charityless—in any high sense of the
term—from want of the insight which personal contact
gives.[1]

Other illustrations of the way in which personal ties

---

[1] I need hardly say that most of the statements in this paragraph
are to be understood as emphasising the evils which arise in extreme
cases rather than as describing typical conditions. It would be difficult
for any one to sum up accurately the typical conditions of life in
large towns. Such a carefully worked out book as Booth's *Labour
and Life of the People* throws a vast amount of light upon it, and
much may be hoped from the application of the methods of Le Play.
Such a book as Göhre's *Three Months in a Workshop* (recently edited
in English by Prof. Ely) is also in the highest degree interesting and
instructive. It is to be hoped that many more works of this class
will be produced. On the other hand, sensational writings, like
General Booth's *In Darkest England*, must be accepted with a good
deal of caution.

tend to have their force diminished will readily occur. The family unity is apt in some cases to be prematurely broken up;[1] and perhaps even more important than this is the destruction of that artificial kind of family which used to be supplied by the old apprenticeship system. Men are thrown at an earlier age than formerly on their own resources—often before their characters are rightly formed. But into these and similar questions it is not necessary to enter here.

4. Finally, we have to mention the instability of conditions which is characteristic of an industrial state as one of the chief difficulties of modern social life. This instability is of two sorts—(*a*) the changeableness of social conditions as a whole, or of large parts of them, and (*b*) the changeableness of conditions of particular individuals. It may be well to consider each of these two separately.

(*a*) When division of labour has been carried so far that each workman has only a single mechanical operation to perform, the next step is to invent a machine which shall do it for him. When this is done, the painfully acquired dexterity of the workman is no longer of any use; and he is apt to be either entirely thrown out of employment or reduced to the position of an unskilled workman—for which probably he is not particularly well fitted. Perhaps such changes in industrial conditions are somewhat less violent now than they were near the beginning of the century, when social and political disturbances, combined with the recent introduction of machinery, agricultural disasters, and other circumstances, rendered

---

[1] " It is, above all other considerations, the fact that, under present conditions, the family life is steadily and inevitably deteriorating, that makes the so-called labour question a burning question." Dr. Adler in the *Ethical Record*, April, 1890, p. 6. This statement is, no doubt, exaggerated. But cf. Göhre's *Three Months in a Workshop*, pp. 37-40 and 190.

the whole surroundings of life so uncertain, that it was hardly an exaggeration to say :—

"Alles regt sich, als wollte die Welt, die gestaltete, rückwärts
Lösen in Chaos und Nacht sich auf, und neu sich gestalten."

The whole social order seemed then to be crumbling to pieces. We are now beginning to reconstruct; but still there is a constant danger of the recurrence of such calamities, and on a smaller scale they are continually recurring.

And, in addition to these permanent causes of instability, there are a number of smaller circumstances that occasion fluctuations from year to year. These are largely due to the great complication of industry, to which we have already referred. There is no central control, there is no fly-wheel, to keep the various parts of the industrial system in steady motion. Things are continually getting out of gear. There is capital wanting investment, men wanting work, and the community wanting goods; and yet the capital cannot be made to employ the men for the production of the goods. The "circulation" is in disorder; and, owing to its extreme complexity, it is very difficult indeed to set it right. Here again matter has the mastery over mind : the mechanism of industry is not under our control, but runs away with us. The result of all this is, that we are subjected continually to that great curse of modern social conditions—irregularity of employment.[1] And this evil is, of course, not merely economic, but moral as well. Irregularity of employment produces irregularity of habit; and these two things, once produced, tend mutually to increase each other. It is needless to add, that it is also productive of intense misery. Robert Burns used to say, that he knew of no

---

[1] See *Claims of Labour*, p. 186 *seq.*, and *Industrial Remuneration Conference*, p. 173 *seq.*

"more mortifying picture of human life than a man seeking work."[1]   Perhaps there is only one more mortifying, and that is when he ceases to seek it.

(*b*) There is also another element of uncertainty in modern industrial conditions, arising from the freedom of contract.   Engagements which were once for life are now tending to be from month to month.   The evils of the "cash nexus" were exhibited by Carlyle, with his usual emphasis;[2] though he weakened his case by the defence of slavery and older methods of organisation.   It has, however, been maintained by Socialistic writers that the condition of working men under the present arrangement is essentially one of slavery, since it is a condition of subjection enforced by the necessity of living, without on the other side any obligation enforced by social law.   This is in the main merely a rhetorical exaggeration; yet it cannot be denied that there is a certain colour of truth in it.   The essence of slavery consists in a man's being treated as a thing instead of as a person—*i.e.* being treated as an object from which something may be demanded, and to which nothing is owed.   This is not the condition of any one under present social arrangements.   Wherever services are required, the claims of those who render the service are recognised.   The evil attacked is rather, that freedom of contract has caused men to cease to recognise any obligations to each other beyond the momentary one which particular contracts imply, and that in consequence of this loosening of personal ties men are placed under the control of the mechanical conditions of social arrangement.   The slavery is no longer that of one person to another, but rather that of persons to things.   This *is* a kind of slavery,

---

[1] Cf. Göhre's *Three Months in a Workshop*, p. 72.
[2] Especially in *Past and Present*.   Cf. also Toynbee's *Industrial Revolution*, p. 193 *seq.*

however; for if a person is under the control of a thing, *i.e.* a mere mechanical necessity, he is himself reduced to the condition of a thing even more thoroughly than if he were under the absolute control of another person.[1]

We may now sum up the conditions of difficulty in our modern social problem by saying that they all reduce themselves to this, that society has become disintegrated or fluid, in the sense that men have to a large extent ceased to be bound to one another by fixed personal ties, and are now connected together only by mechanical conditions. This reduces us to a position which may be described as one of exploitation; if we remember that it is not the exploitation of some men by others, but rather of all men by things.

> " Things are in the saddle,
> And ride mankind."

In this expression the whole evil of our present condition is summed up. Mind is subject to matter; reason, to that which is accidental and incalculable.

II. I pass now to speak of those conditions of modern life which tend to make the social problem easier at the present time, or which afford ground for hoping that it may be dealt with more satisfactorily in the immediate future. These conditions are on the whole more obvious and less complex than the preceding; and it will consequently not be necessary to devote quite so much attention to them. The first among them is the very obvious fact, on which we are sometimes tempted to dilate too much, that the material prosperity of mankind has become enormously increased, and that this increase has been to a great extent an increase in those conditions which make

---

[1] This point is very well brought out in Wagner's *Lehrbuch der politischen Oekonomie,* i. 635. See also the paper by Prof. H. C. Adams previously referred to.

a life of culture and moral excellence more easy for the majority of mankind. The advance of material comfort has been in some degree shared in by nearly every class of the community;[1] and there seems every reason to believe that this will be more and more true as time goes on. Indeed an optimist may almost be pardoned for thinking that the present discontent with reference to social conditions is a result rather of prosperity than of adversity. The rapidity of our advance makes us sensitive to every hindrance. The greatness of our progress causes us to feel every drawback a grievance. So much has been accomplished that it seems as if everything were in our power, and we are intensely dissatisfied whenever we are, even in a slight degree, made conscious of our limits. In this view there is undoubtedly a certain amount of truth. Former generations were miserable if they but knew their misery; now we are happy enough to feel it.[2] It is clear, however, that our material progress has not sufficed to prevent the existence of intense misery in a large section of the people, but has, on the contrary, introduced new difficulties into their lives. Unless, therefore, there is some other ground of hope than this material progress, our position, though perhaps a hopeful one for the majority, will be very hopeless for certain classes.

Now, apart from this advance in our material prosperity,

[1] It is said that statistics can be made to prove anything; but it seems scarcely possible to doubt, in the face of the evidence that has been recently brought forward (by Mulhall, Giffen, and others), that there has not only been a great advance in the material well-being of mankind, but that that well-being has tended on the whole to be more equally distributed in recent years. On this point there are some interesting discussions in the Report of the *Industrial Remuneration Conference*, pp. 4-136. Cf. also Rae's *Contemporary Socialism*, p. 343 *seq.*, and Laveleye's *Socialism of To-day*, p. xxxvii. *seq.*

[2] Cf. Gunton's *Wealth and Progress*, pp. 1-4.

the conditions which make the social problem more hopeful at the present time may, I believe, all be brought under the head of progress towards a new integration, just as the conditions of difficulty consisted in the main in the various aspects of a process of differentiation. Or, with more direct reference to the summation of our difficulties which has been given under the preceding head, we may state the point rather in this way. Society has passed from that state in which men stand in fixed relations to one another, governed by authority and custom, to that in which they stand in fluctuating relations, governed by economic and other mechanical conditions; and the progress of society is towards a state in which, by certain new combinations, men may gain a mastery over these mechanical conditions. Men have been occupied hitherto in freeing themselves from one another; they are now beginning to try, by combining with one another, to free themselves from the iron laws of circumstance. Men were first exploited by men; then they were exploited by things; the problem now is to combine men together so that they may exploit things.[1]

Now such a recombination is to some extent involved in the very process which under the previous head we have been engaged in tracing. What we have called the liquefaction of society has not been entirely a process of disintegration, but partly of reunion as well. A liquid is a unity as well as a solid, and in some respects it may even be the more thorough unity of the two. If the parts are less fixedly combined, they are also less fixedly separated. And so it is with modern society as compared with more primitive communities. There may be a less

---

[1] This point is well brought out by Saint-Simon, in his *Système industriel.* Cf. Janet's *Saint-Simon*, p. 54, and Caird's " Moral Aspect of the Economical Problem " in *Time*, for January, 1888, p. 9 *seq.*

firm connection between particular individuals, but there
is more possibility of connection between all the individuals
of whom society is composed.   For instance, facility of
movement, which from one point of view is a great loos-
ener of connections, is from another point of view a great
means of forming new connections.   The power of moving
away is also the power of moving towards; and this power
has undoubtedly helped very much to integrate society.
Mr. Ruskin has said that "the glory of man consists not
in going but in being"; yet there can be little doubt
that the advantages which the increased power of loco-
motion has brought have been neither purely economic
nor confined to any single class.   It has helped very
largely to "make the whole world kin."   "Bleibe nicht
am Boden heften!" was the injunction with which Goethe
concluded his *Wilhelm Meister*; and certainly from this
point of view the liquefaction of society has been a gain.
It has made men more cosmopolitan, both in the sense
of being "everywhere at home," and in that of taking a
more enlarged view of the requirements of humanity.   It
has made the world more nearly like a single family.
"There's livers out of England" is a truth which we are
not so likely to forget as we once were: and on the
whole the consciousness of the *orbis terrarum* (if we may
be allowed such a conceit) is a great fly-wheel in human
thought which helps to steady us and keep us sane.   And,
apart from these somewhat imponderable gains, which lead
us rather to a consideration of the development of thought
and sentiment, there is another advantage brought about
by increased facility of movement which seems likely to
become more prominent in the immediate future—viz.
the possibility which it affords of removing important industries to country places.   This appears at present to be
the most hopeful method of withdrawing the pressure from
our large industrial centres; and its feasibility evidently

depends on the fact that the conditions of life have become more fluid.

And similarly it might be shown that nearly every circumstance that has been mentioned as an instance of
disintegration of social conditions, is, from another point
of view, an instance of a more extended combination.
The fact that local unities are more and more broken
down means simply that the entire world is becoming
more completely a whole.

Again, the separation of men's interests leads in many
cases to a more thorough organisation. The separation
of the interests of employers from those of their workmen,
for instance, has enabled the latter more completely to
assert their independence and form themselves into a
unity as a class. This has been one of the most important integrations in recent times. Among the means of
accomplishing this, probably the most influential has been
the Trades' Unions. These are, to a certain extent, a
kind of "after-glow" of the old Gilds;[1] but in the main
they must be regarded as a new phenomenon; and there
is hardly any other single force which has contributed so
much as they have, not only to the actual improvement
of the condition of the people, but also to the development of a sense of unity and power. They have accustomed men to think for themselves, to practise foresight
and self-restraint, and to act in harmony for a common
end; and it is probably by this discipline, more than by
any other, that the working classes have been prepared
—in so far as they *are* prepared—to take part in political
life.

Then, again, the diffusion of literature and culture
among the masses of the people has been an accompaniment of the growing fluidity of social conditions, and has
been one of the best fruits which that fluidity has borne.

[1] See Brentano's *History and Development of Gilds*, p. 101 *seq.*

It is true that in popular literature, as in freedom of
contract and facility of movement, we have been recently
taught by Carlyle and Ruskin and others to discover
many evils.[1] Sometimes silence is golden. Literature
may prove a Babel instead of a diapason. Even "light
from heaven" may be used to "lead astray." "Zwar
sind sie an das Beste nicht gewöhnt" may often be a
corollary to "Sie haben schrecklich viel gelesen"; and
there may even be some point in the paradox that when
there is "no end of making books" there is an end of
making good ones. But when such concessions have
been made to the satirist, we must still hold that the
spread of literature is one of the strongest of our
"organic filaments." It is more than a sufficient com-
pensation in many cases for a certain loss of personal
relationship in some of the business connections of life.
It enables men to come into personal relationship with
the choicest minds of the race. Yet the possibility of
this depends largely on the conditions of modern life
which we have called fluid. Thus these conditions are
seen, in this case also, to be a means of integration as
well as of differentiation.

Finally, the growth of popular government may be
referred to as the culmination of those integrating forces
which are the counterparts of our modern differentiation.
Facility of movement, the spread of literature, the
discipline of Trades Unions, have all contributed something to make Democracy possible, in a sense in which
it never was possible before; and it is on this possibility
that much of the hopefulness of the present generation
depends. The despair of social improvement rests largely

---

[1] The dangers of popular literature had previously been insisted
on by Goethe, Hegel, and others. Cf. Schäffle's *Bau und Leben
des socialen Körpers*, I. 461 *seq.*, and Ruskin's *Fors Clavigera*, VII.
266-7.

on the distrust of governments; that distrust which for many generations made the cry of *laissez faire* so popular and so truly necessary. But the more truly a state becomes a whole, and the more truly the entire force of government is in the hands of that whole, the less reason can there be for distrust, and the greater is the hope that social evils may be dealt with by the state. The possibility of a democratic government is consequently one of the inspiring elements in our present social condition, opening up an almost infinite prospect of improvement in the organisation of industry and of life in general. Democracy is, in fact, the ideal form of government for a perfect fluid, as Aristocracy is for a solid : and the more our society tends to liquefy, the more entirely does Democracy become at once possible and necessary. The more fluid a society becomes, the more essential is it that the peculiar needs of every atom at every moment should be represented—since all the atoms are different from each other, and becoming continually more different; and thus Democracy may be regarded as affording at once the possibility and the safeguard of a fluid state. It is the special form of integration which that condition requires. At the same time it must be allowed that if it is in some respects a safeguard, it is in itself very greatly in need of safeguards,—to some of which we shall have occasion to refer hereafter.[1]

We see, then, in general, that the fluidity of society brings with it a certain species of integration as well as differentiation, and thus supplies us with a ground of hope as well as of difficulty. Still, it remains true that a condition of fluidity is one of great fluctuation and uncertainty, and that it does not adequately provide its own remedy. Many of the forms of union to which we have referred

[1] In Chap. VI.

are only partial; others are rough and unreliable; and nearly all leave a great mass of the population comparatively unaffected by their beneficial influences. If the problems of exploitation and "social wreckage," to which our fluid condition gives rise, are to be dealt with satisfactorily, it seems clear that other forms of organisation are required than those which that fluid condition itself provides. We require that it should to a certain extent become solid.

Now there are not wanting signs of the growth of other forms of organisation; though they are, for the most part, only in an embryo state. Among these probably the most important is the development of Co-operation, including the principle of profit-sharing, which seems likely to do much in the way of elevating the working classes from the position of mere instruments of exploiting agencies.[1] Again, there is some evidence that the sense of personal obligation as involved in business relations is becoming largely extended. Masters, here and there, are beginning to realise that their position as captains of industry has a moral as well as an economic aspect;[2] and if a similar remark is not yet so obviously true in the case of landlords, one can at least say that the feeling is growing among the public that of them also something more is required than a mere business relationship; and the work of Miss Octavia Hill and others has given to this feeling a certain practical shape. When we pass to such points as these, however, we are touching rather on the growth of thought and sentiment, which belongs to the following head.

Again, there are some points at which the liquefying

---

[1] Cf. Chap. VI.

[2] Of course, the chief examples of this spirit are to be found in such men as Owen and Leclaire; but cf. also *Claims of Labour*, pp. 82-3.

process in modern social conditions seems to meet with a check, or to pass over into its opposite; and at these points some other influence must be brought to bear. Perhaps the most important of these cases is to be found in the growth of monopolies, which is brought about by the very freedom of competition itself. The natural result of the struggle for existence, when it is at its keenest, is that only the one that is fittest should survive; and when this one has gained a position of advantage, future competition becomes in many cases a practical impossibility. The result is that in many forms of industry the smaller undertakings tend to be crushed out, until ultimately only one or a few large ones are left, which are then lifted out of the region of struggle into an independent and autocratic position. Here we see that the fluid state of society cannot even sustain itself, but passes into solidity of a very hard kind. Whether this is to be regarded as a condition of difficulty or of hope it might be hard to say. Certainly in the meantime the problem of the regulation of such monopolies is one of the gravest that we have to encounter, and is one of those that indicate most clearly the need for a certain control of industry from above. At the same time it is a hopeful feature of our present state, in so far as it seems to indicate a way out of the struggle of our competitive system—to point to the fact that society is in some directions recrystallising. If these monopolies can be regulated in an efficient way, they may prove rather beneficial than otherwise.[1] But till

[1] On this point Prof. Foxwell has made valuable suggestions. Cf., for instance, his paper at the Bath meeting of the British Association, September, 1888. Several articles on the same subject have appeared also in the American economic Magazines. Some of the writers of these articles even regard the growth of monopolies as on the whole a hopeful sign. Cf., however, Baker's *Monopolies and*

this can be done the existence of such monopolies, together with the fact of exploitation, are among the chief circumstances that supply a *raison d'être* to our modern Socialism—which may be described, from this point of view, as the effort to make society once more a solid all through.

III. The development of thought and sentiment in recent generations, by which our attitude towards social questions has been affected, is in the main the counterpart of the growth of outward conditions. Yet many of the difficulties of our present social problem are due to the fact that the development of our inner nature has not kept pace with the development of our outward conditions. We have not acquired with sufficient rapidity the *Sitten* which our new circumstances demand. The conditions have grown upon us before we had time to assimilate them and make them our own. For instance, the increase of material prosperity has tended to outrun very much the growth of our insight into the true value of material things. As we have become richer, we have not become happier in an equal degree. Our riches have been, so to say, heaped upon us, instead of being absorbed into our nature and made a part of our life.[1] Production has increased more rapidly than the knowledge what it is desirable to produce, and it has become possible to consume more rapidly than it has become clear what kinds of consumption will make life larger. Again, it seems as if human nature had hardly yet adapted itself

*the People*, where the whole subject is very fully discussed, with complete recognition both of the growing difficulty of the problem and of the possibilities of dealing with it by the development of new machinery and a new spirit.

[1] Thus illustrating the truth emphasised by Simmel (*Einleitung in die Moralwissenschaft*, Vol. I., p. 172), that, in the fullest sense, we can possess nothing but what we are.

to the most prominent condition of modern life—existence in large cities. The mere physical necessities of such life constitute of themselves a great problem; but what I here mean is rather that those elements of mutual consideration of class for class and of individual for individual which such a life necessitates have not yet been adequately developed. All this, however, is merely another aspect of the general truth that material conditions have gained a certain mastery over life—not, indeed, the material conditions which nature presents (these we are more and more conquering), but the material conditions which we have ourselves created.

From this point of view, then, one great difficulty in connection with our inner development arises from the fact that it does not keep pace with the growth of our outward conditions. In the main, however, what we find is rather an exact parallelism between our inner and outer development—the one appearing as simply the reflection of the other. Just as there has been a disintegration of social conditions, so there has been a disintegration of our thoughts and sentiments. Just as our lives have tended to become enslaved by their mechanical conditions, so our thoughts have tended to become enslaved by their mechanical categories. The difficulties, then, that we have here to consider are—(1) The Individualism of our general attitude, and (2) The materialisation of our point of view.

1. Individualism is the intellectual counterpart of the process of liberation to which reference has already been made, and its growth may be traced partly to the sense of the need of independence under industrial conditions. Partly, however, it must be traced also to the sense of the infinite worth of the individual life, which was introduced by Christianity. Now this spirit of individualism was at first an element of hope and inspiration in human

life. It was the idea that animated men in the struggle against mischievous outward restraints, and, on the other hand, it taught them to seek for the highest truths in their own deepest consciousness of things rather than in any external authority. But this idea, like other half-truths, wears at last into a half-lie. "Help thyself, and Heaven will help thee" is a good doctrine when each applies it to himself, but bad when each applies it to his neighbour. When he applies it to himself, the self-help that he thinks of includes the use of every external aid that may present itself: when he applies it to others, it is apt to mean simply that no external aid is to be expected. In the former case it preaches hope; in the latter, despair. The Spirit of Independence is "Lord of the lion heart and eagle eye" only when it means the throwing away of helps that do not help and the grasping at those that do. It is the spirit of mere weakness when it comes to mean that there is no help anywhere but in ourselves. Now the war of independence in the former sense is already fought and won. It cannot be said now, even with rhetorical truth, that the banner of Freedom

"Streams like the thunderstorm *against the wind.*"

It has prejudice on its side, and is everywhere victorious in *posse* if not in *esse.* Accordingly, Individualism is now rather an element of despair than of hope. Such new independence as we are winning is independence in the bad sense—mere isolation. The real battle of our time—the advance which *is* still "against the wind"—is that rather in the direction of union and of organisation, and it is in this direction that hope now lies. The new Gospel is not that of leaving everyone to help himself, any more than it is that of helping everyone; it is that of helping everyone to help himself.[1]

It is not, however, merely in the way of preventing us

[1] Cf. Chap. VI.

from dealing adequately with our outward conditions that this spirit of individualism has done harm. It has led also to a disintegration of our thoughts and opinions, which adds not a little to the confusion of life. The duty of private judgment—the duty of getting below mere tradition and authority and seeing truth with our own eyes —which was the good side of individualism, has passed, as has been said, rather into the *right* of private judgment—the privilege of having, so to speak, a little private truth of one's own. Hence we have all the vagaries of individual caprice, separating people into innumerable parties and sects. In religion, as Swift said, many have just enough to make them hate one another, not enough to make them love one another. In politics the time-honoured oppositions of history give place to a bewildering Valhalla. In art and literature the grotesque and fantastic lead us almost to forget what is eternally beautiful. That our modern views of things tend to be conventional, that we "rub each other's angles down"[1] and lose our independence, is to some extent merely another aspect of this same truth—though it seems at first to contradict it. If everyone has a right to his own views, everyone must have a certain respect for those of everyone else, and must avoid any undue conflict with them. When individualism is strong, it is the search for truth, and the war against convention; but when it is weak, it becomes itself convention tempered by caprice. Toleration is fostered by difference of opinions; but the toleration which in this way arises is apt to amount to little else than a conviction that there is nothing but opinions to be had, that there is no objective truth.[2] The

[1] Cf. Mill, *On Liberty*, chap. iii.

[2] "When religious differences come to be, and are regarded as, mere differences of opinion, it is because the controversy is really decided in the sceptical sense." Stephen's *Liberty, Equality, and Fraternity*, chap. ii.

I

general attitude, therefore, to which individualism leads us
is that which is summed up in the saying that "there is
nothing new and there is nothing true, and it does not
much matter." Thus pure individualism in thought leads
us first to confusion, then to scepticism and despair.

There are other roads also by which individualism leads
to pessimism. When we think of mankind as a mere
collection of individuals, we necessarily regard man's life
on earth as a failure. The end of every individual life is
death ; and its history up to that consummation is largely
a record of ideals missed. The " bare, ruined choirs" of
even a Shakespeare's life might well lead us to despair
of humanity, if our hope were founded on that which any
individual can achieve. The individual life, in fact, is an
egg out of which any amount of melancholy may be sucked ;
and so long as we regard the problem of social well-being
as that of the perfect fulfilment of the wishes of a number
of separate individuals, there is no limit to the hopeless-
ness that we may find in it.

2. The statement that our main interests are material,
again, is the counterpart of the statement that we live in
an industrial age ; and for these two facts various explanations might be given. They are due, no doubt, in
great measure to the circumstance that the human race
has been moving farther and farther from its original
" habitat," and passing into regions in which less is done
for man by nature, and more has to be done by his own
exertions. We might also connect the increase of material
interests in our time with the fact that we are becoming
increasingly democratic. We have already seen that to
a certain extent democracy grows out of industrialism ;
but it would be equally true to say that the industrial
conditions are favoured by the growth of democracy.
The spread of a spirit of individual independence re-
moves the stigma from labour, and at the same time

makes it more and more necessary that each one should labour for himself. The material rewards of labour also tend under a democracy to acquire more and more social importance. The virtue of a democracy is self-help, and its sign is wealth. Hence it is that, as De Tocqueville tells us, "to mimic virtue is of every age; but the hypocrisy of luxury belongs more particularly to ages of Democracy." Respectability, as Carlyle used to be fond of reminding us, tends to be identified with "keeping a gig." In this way men are reduced more and more under the dominion of things, and the realisation of their ends is made to depend more and more on the lottery of external circumstance—in which, to use the familiar metaphor of Malthus, many must "draw a blank."

But the growth of material interests has not only had the effect of leading us into material difficulties: it has also obscured those other interests which are of a more ethereal texture, whose loss robs life of some of its chief contents. The commercial spirit has "eclipsed the gaiety of nations." It has immersed men in sordid cares and accustomed them to utilitarian standards of value, by which such elements of life as art and poetry tend to be depreciated. It has, further, elevated the mechanical categories into an undue prominence in thought, so that it has become difficult to regard human life and the world in general in any other than a mechanical way. Everything has to be conceived on the analogy of those laws of action and reaction of one thing upon another which in dealing with material conditions had seemed to afford an adequate explanation. A spiritual account of the world is thus made to appear incredible, if not inconceivable; and spiritual life itself tends rather to be accounted for as a kind of machinery. The whole atmosphere of thought which grows around the world of our material interests veils the heaven in which the higher interests of our nature have their centre. The world becomes prosaic, and seems to be ruled by an iron necessity. Where once men saw pliant divinities, they now see only inexorable laws. Thus again materialism leads to pessimism.[1]

One of the chief respects in which this pessimistic tendency of materialistic views has shown itself has been in dealing with the economic conditions of life. It was for this reason that Carlyle called Political Economy the "dismal science." When economic laws first began to be appreciated by the popular consciousness, what chiefly impressed men with regard to them was their iron necessity. Ricardo's doctrine of wages[2] and Malthus's law of population seemed alike to damp every hope of permanent improvement in the condition of the people. And even when hope was not entirely crushed, men were at any rate taught to "hope humbly." They were led to perceive that the "mills of God grind slowly," that human life is hemmed in with many mechanical limitations, from which it is impossible to escape, and against which it is vain to struggle. In these and similar ways the occupation of men's minds with the material conditions of life tends to lead to an intense despair.

IV. We pass now, finally, to those developments of thought and sentiment which tend to help us, or to make us more hopeful, in dealing with social questions. And

---

[1] The connection between the mode of thought here described and the present economic conditions seems to be especially apparent in the case of German "Social Democracy." On this point reference may be made to Schäffle's *Impossibility of Social Democracy* and Göhre's *Three Months in a Workshop*. It is probable, however, that both these books have been rendered somewhat one-sided, in the one case by antagonism to democracy, in the other case by devotion to the Church.

[2] And the doctrine of the Wage Fund generally. Cf. Walker's *Wages Question*, p. 138 *seq.*

here again we may notice a certain parallelism between our inner growth and the growth of our outward conditions. As we saw before that the outward conditions which give rise to hope in dealing with the social problem are to a great extent the very same circumstances as those that give rise to difficulties, so it may be pointed out that a similar remark holds good with respect to the development of our thought. The ideas that appear, from one point of view, as the disintegrating force of Individualism and the degrading weight of Materialism, may be seen, from another point of view, to be influences that help to give our life both elevation and power. They are clouds that have a silver side.

Individualism, for instance, if it means, on the one side the disintegration of our thoughts and sentiments, leading at last to pure Scepticism and despair, yet means also, on the other side, a breaking away from authority and tradition to a more earnest search for truth. It means that we have become Utilitarians, in the primary and best sense of the term—that we have come to have a regard rather for the real ends which things subserve than for the traditional means of their attainment. It means, in fact, that there has been a decay of *pedantry*. The Pedant, no doubt, is as difficult to catch as the Sophist was with Plato; but we may describe him as one who habitually mistakes means and instruments for ultimate ends in themselves. What I mean is, in short, that we are beginning to "swallow our formulas," to "clear our minds of cant," and to look more directly at the meaning of things as they stand actually before us. The modern inquirer no longer regards anyone as his master but at most as his παιδαγωγός, the schoolmaster that leads him to truth. *Nullius addictus jurare in verba magistri*, he tries rather to approach realities *sub persona infantis*. We have less regard for the dignity of history or philosophy or poetry, and more regard for fact and truth and reality, however they may present themselves.[1] In literature we have been passing in the main—though with many contradictory side currents—from propriety to truth ; in education, from tradition to utility ; in economics, from abstraction to observation. From this point of view, our individualism in thought, like our individualism in practical life, means rather an expansion than a narrowing of our nature. It means that we are ceasing to be provincials and making ourselves citizens of the universe.

Again, if our individualism means, on one side, that we confine our attention to the joys and sorrows of the individual life, and so inevitably land ourselves in pessimism ; it means also, on the other side, that we are ceasing to delude ourselves with ideals that lie outside of humanity, and to perceive that in some sense the highest good at which we can aim must consist in the happiness or welfare of persons. The emphasis which has been laid on human happiness as the highest end is one of the good fruits of individualism. The term "happiness," no doubt, is very ambiguous ; so much so that the assertion that the end is happiness—on which Aristotle said that nearly all men are agreed—has been held by some to be either meaningless or a mere tautology.[2] It is, however, something more than that, in so far as it implies that the end is not something purely external to us as human beings, but that we are in some sense "ends in ourselves."[3] This was undoubtedly one of the most important of all the ideas that were involved in the Christian conception of life ; and it is the emergence of this "good news" out of the dark prison-house of the creeds that has lent some of the best inspiration to the movements of modern life. It has

[1] Cf. Mr. Havelock Ellis's *New Spirit*, p. 8.
[2] Cf. Sorley's *Ethics of Naturalism*, p. 6.
[3] Cf. Chap. IV.

destroyed the slavery of man by man (except, as some
may think, within the charmed circle of the family life),
and is now engaged in destroying the slavery of man by
things.

Nor is the materialisation of our interests a circumstance that is without its "soul of goodness." If it
means partly an engrossment in sordid cares, it means
partly a rising above them. In a more primitive state of
society, men are content to keep up a kind of guerilla
warfare with nature. They are not always fighting with
material conditions, and have thus a certain leisure for
the higher interests of the spirit. But, on the other
hand, when they *are* fighting they are not always victorious, and are often entirely crushed by their outward
circumstances. Moreover, even the partial freedom which
they have from the struggle with matter is gained for
the few chiefly by the enslavement and degradation
of the many. Our modern warfare is more steady and
continuous, and is more thoroughly shared in by all. It
thus comes to be more of a burden. But for that very
reason it is more effective, and its victory is more complete. A man is never more entirely under the influence
of his surroundings than when he gives no heed to them.
He who literally "takes no thought for the morrow" is
the slave of the morrow. It is by thinking about our
conditions that we free ourselves from them.

The materialisation of our interests, in fact, is to a
very large extent merely another aspect of the truth that
we are taking as our end the well-being of persons, and
that our main concerns are consequently found in that
which is present before us and which may be used as
a means of personal happiness. "Happy men," says
Carlyle, "are full of the present, for its bounty suffices
them; and wise men also, for its duties engage them."
If so, the world is probably growing happier and wiser.

We have become more than ever impressed with the
conviction that "Here or nowhere is our America."
When Goethe wrote of the Golden Age that

> "War sie je, so war sie nur gewiss,
> Wie sie uns immer wieder werden kann,"

he gave expression to a sentiment which has been growing in men's minds. The Golden Age of the Greeks was
behind them, and that of the Hebrews before them : the
conviction of modern times is rather that there is no
Golden Age but that which we make for ourselves now.

The fact that we have learned to work more freely
with mechanical categories is also an influence for good.
It has saved us from mysticism and indefiniteness, and
has helped us to see clearly where the problems of
practical life lie. If, for instance, Political Economy has
been, in one aspect, a "dismal science," by making it
appear as if life were entirely subject to the necessity of
certain iron laws, it has yet been, in another and deeper
aspect, most beneficent, by helping us to trace the connections and causes of the external conditions with which
we have to deal.[1] Things which were once vaguely
attributed to "providence" are now seen to be governed
by conditions which are more or less under human
control. We are thus rendered more ready than formerly
to see what is evil in human circumstances, and to
recognise our responsibility for it. We are less apt to
content ourselves with the impious piety of a "God
mend all !" and more prepared to acknowledge that "we
must help Him to mend it"—or rather, in many cases,
that the mending which is required is the mending of
ourselves. We have learned, with more or less clearness,
that there is a certain continuity in experience, that there
is no such thing as chance, that everything is somehow

---

[1] Cf. Sidgwick's *Principles of Political Economy*, p. 593 *seq.*

connected with everything else, and that by regulating conditions .we may control events. We are learning, in fact, to understand how *large* a part of the ills that we suffer are such as human contrivances "can · cause or cure"; and the consciousness of this makes us both more sympathetic in dealing with those who suffer from such ills and more energetic in seeking the means of prevention or remedy.

Further, it is not entirely true that the introduction of mechanical categories has tended to obscure the higher elements of thought. On the contrary, the more clearly we understand these categories the more clearly do we see their limitations. If it is true that the thought of those who are continually engaged with such conceptions tends to be "subdued to what it works in, like the dyer's hand," it is also true that familiarity with them "breeds contempt." It is soon seen that the explanation of things as mechanism is an explanation that explains nothing.[1]  It only enables us to state somewhat more clearly the problem of which an explanation is sought, even in those cases in which it can do so much. Consequently, the more we are led to mechanical explanations, the more are we led beyond them. As soon as we "see with eye serene" the mechanical constitution of our world, so soon do we see that it is a "spirit still." And accordingly we see evidence that modern scientific conceptions, instead of destroying the religious view of the world, have been rather extending it and giving it a deeper meaning. They have destroyed the pedantries of dogma and the fairy-tales of tradition, and have thus helped us to penetrate with more clearness into the true spirit of the religious life.

[1] See Wallace's *Logic of Hegel*, p. 290 *seq.*  Cf. also Caird's *Critical Philosophy of Kant*, II. 519 *seq.*, and *Essays in Philosophical Criticism*, p. 31 *seq.*

Here, however, we are evidently led to a new point.
I have been endeavouring to show that in the case of
our thoughts, as in the case of our outward conditions,
the very circumstances which lead to difficulty lead also
to hope. But in the instance which we have been last
considering it is evident that the conceptions which
brought us into difficulty do not afford us a hope of
escape, except in so far as they lead beyond themselves.
And thus we are led to see that in the case of our
thoughts also, as well as in the case of our outward conditions, though it is partly true that the grounds of
difficulty are grounds of hope, yet these grounds are not
of themselves sufficient. And as in the case of our outward conditions we saw that there are some symptoms
of new tendencies growing up which carry us beyond
those that have given rise to our difficulties, so we may
see here that there are new conceptions arising which
carry us beyond the individualism and materialism out
of which our difficulties have grown.

That the great intellectual forces of our time are not
individualistic, we see at once when we "close our Byron
and open our Goethe," when we close our Bentham and
open our Comte, when we close our Herbert Spencer
and open our Hegel. Individualism, indeed, properly
speaking, said its last word in Hume and in the French
Revolution. The idea that has vitality now is rather that
of humanity as an organic whole—the idea that the mere
individual is an abstraction, and that his life has meaning only in so far as he shares in a larger life than his
own. And closely connected with the view of society as
an organic whole is the view of it as a whole which develops. It is the spread of such views as these, more
than of any others, that has served to give the death-
blow to pessimism. The idea of organism has enabled
us to extend our views of human good beyond that which

can be accomplished in the life of any one individual or of any collection of individuals; while the idea of development has made it scientific to hope, by exhibiting life not as a mere process of perpetual change, but as a growth towards a definite goal. Hence it is that a spirit of cautious "Meliorism" has been diffusing itself, a spirit of belief in the results of patient labour—"ohne Hast, aber ohne Rast"—and something of a growing readiness to listen to those voices of which Goethe tells us, which "bid us be hopeful."

This spirit is connected also with the advance from materialism to a more spiritual view of the world. The inadequacy of the mechanical categories has long been apparent; and the metaphysical criticism which was begun by Kant and carried on by Hegel and others of Kant's idealistic successors, has furnished us with at least a glimpse of the possibility of a more adequate account. Nor has this reconstructive effort been confined to pure thought. Already we see signs of the activity in practical life of a moral fervour which is inspired by the idea that there is something higher in human nature than its material aspect. How far such forces may carry us, is a question for the future to decide.

I may now sum up what we have ascertained with regard to the general aspect of the social problem. In separating difficulties and hopes, and in separating thoughts and outward conditions, we have been to a certain extent murdering to dissect; and it will be well for us now to try to look at the problem as a whole, and see how these various elements fit into each other. We may describe the general state of society for a number of generations back as one of tumultuous progress.[1] On the one side, our industries have made enormous advances; on the other side, our view of the world has become expanded and

[1] Cf. Morris's *Hopes and Fears for Art*, p. 86.

deepened. The result of all this growth has been in the main a very great improvement in the condition of nearly all classes of people and a very great brightening of our general outlook. But at the same time it has had the effect of shaking asunder a great number of the old forms of connection which had been formed among mankind. It has overthrown customs and authorities and broken bonds of union. It has made life in many directions more chaotic and uncertain. It has made men less dependent on narrow but definitely ascertainable and intelligible connections, and has made them more dependent on broad principles which it is very difficult to understand and obey. It has melted down all the little unities of our former mode of life and run everything into a single whole, with a great deal of jumbling and confusion in the process. What is wanted, accordingly, is some principle which will enable us to bring about a more perfect connection between the parts of our society, to form new links and ties, so that men may no longer be subject to the direction of iron laws over which they have no control. We have to overcome individualism, on the one hand, and the power of material conditions, on the other.

Such is the practical problem with which we find ourselves confronted at the present moment; and the ideas which present themselves as most likely to be of service to us in dealing with it are those of the organic nature of society and of the spiritual nature of man. How closely these are related to each other will, I think, become apparent in the sequel. If we can succeed in showing what is their true significance, and in indicating, even in a slight degree, what is their bearing on the practical life of society, we shall have accomplished all that can be reasonably expected from the present inquiry, and more than sufficient to justify us in entering upon it.

# CHAPTER III.

## THE SOCIAL ORGANISM.

THERE are certainly few points on which thinking men in modern times are more thoroughly at one than in the recognition that everything that is deepest in nature—and especially in human nature—must be regarded as a product not of manufacture, but of growth. Indeed this recognition has passed over even into popular thought, and become a part of our intellectual atmosphere. That constitutions are not made, is almost as familiar a truth as that poets are not. There is, it is true, a certain contrast in the antitheses which are usually brought forward in these two instances in which the conception of manufacture is rejected; for while we commonly say that the poet is *born*, we say rather that constitutions *grow*. But the contrast is, after all, more in word than in idea; for the notion that poets are born, in any other sense than that they develop from within, is, I suppose, as thoroughly exploded—since the time of the geniuses of the *Sturm und Drang*—as the notion that they may be constructed by a mechanical process.[1] If we disbelieve in the poet who has nothing but the *ars poetica* to appeal to, we equally distrust him who has nothing to appeal to but the intuitions of his own breast. We still think on the whole that Muses are required as well as poets—that a

[1] " Poeta nascitur *et* fit." Nichol's *Byron*, p. 36.

certain " inspiration" must be received from the great thoughts that are stirring among mankind, and that the poet must *grow* by the appropriation of these. Now the idea of development which is thus applied to poets and to constitutions alike, and which is coming to be applied more and more to everything that is fundamental in human affairs, forms part of a way of looking at the world in general, and depends for its justification on the truth of the whole attitude of mind which it represents. This way of looking at the world is perhaps best described as the *organic* point of view. What this means I must endeavour briefly to explain.

There are, *primâ facie*, three distinct ways in which the existence and nature of any object might be accounted for. It might be regarded, in the first place, as an independent being, of which in one sense no account can be given, or which contains the whole reason of its existence within itself. Secondly, it might be regarded as having no separate being of its own, but as existing only as a part of a larger system out of which its nature flows. Thirdly, it might be explained as at once independent and a portion of a system—as being, in a certain sense, a separate existence, and yet as having its nature determined by its relation to a larger whole. The first of these views, if it were taken as a theory of the world as a whole and worked out consistently as such, would lead to a doctrine of pure Monadism—*i.e.* to a view of the world as a collection of mutually independent parts, each possessing a separate nature of its own.[1] The second view would lead, similarly, to a doctrine of pure Monism—*i.e.*

---

[1] Of course, in most actual Monadisms—as, for instance, that of Leibniz—each monad is supposed to have a certain intrinsic relation to all the rest. But in so far as such a relation is supposed to exist, the system ceases to be a *mere* Monadism, and approximates to the conception of an organic whole.

to a view of the world as a single system, in which the nature of every part is predetermined by the whole. The third view, again, would be the view of the world as a systematic unity, in which neither the parts exist independently of the whole nor the whole independently of its parts.

The third of these views, however, might be accepted in three different senses. In the first place, it might be taken to mean that there are, on the one hand, a number of independent parts, and, on the other hand, certain principles of unity by which the parts are combined, as if by an after-thought, into a systematic whole whose laws are externally imposed upon it. Such a system of parts might be described as a *mechanical* unity. In the second place, it might be supposed that the parts are not merely brought together in accordance with certain laws ; but that when they are so brought together they cease altogether to have the character which they had in their separate state, and become entirely subordinate to the whole in which they are elements. Such a unity may be described as *chemical.* Finally, we may have a system in which the parts become what they are by virtue of their relations to the whole, and in which yet the parts retain a certain relative independence. It is this kind of unity that we here describe as *organic.* According to the first of these views, the world would involve an absolute dualism which is never reduced to unity, though it is reduced to order. According to the second view, the world would be reducible to unity, but only through a certain sublimation of an original diversity. According to the third view, the world would be a real unity, though it is a unity which expresses itself through difference.

There are thus five possible ways in which the totality of the world, or of any particular object in the world, may be regarded. It may be thought of as a simple unity, in which there is no real difference of parts; or as a mere collection of differences, in which there is no real unity; or as a system in which there is both unity and difference. And if it is thought of as a system, it may be regarded either as a system in which the parts have an absolutely independent existence, though they are subordinated to the whole to which they belong; or as a system in which the parts are deprived of their independence by being transformed and swallowed up in the whole; or, finally, as a system in which the parts have a certain relative independence, but an independence which is conditioned throughout by its relation to the system—an independence, in short, which is not freedom *from* the system, but freedom *in and through* it.

A totality of the first variety, if totality it can be called, might be typified [1] by a single crystal, in which there are no parts that can be distinguished as existing separately from the whole. One of the second variety might be typified by a heap of stones or by a bed of flowers, in which each stone or plant has an existence independent of the rest. One of the third variety might be typified by the Solar System, in which the several planets, though in themselves distinct, are inseparably connected in a unity whose laws they are bound to obey. One of the fourth variety might be typified by any chemical combination, in which the nature of the original parts is completely transformed in the building up of the new compound. Lastly, one of the fifth variety might be typified by the life of a single plant, in which each individual

---

[1] These systems can only be typified, because they are only limiting or regulative conceptions, to which the objects of our experience approximate, but to which no object of actual experience ever completely conforms. There is no mere unity, and consequently no mere diversity, in nature.

cell may be said to have a life of its own, and in which yet the life of each cell is inseparable from the life of the whole plant.

In the first kind of system, we might say that there is only a whole and no parts. The parts are what they are simply because the whole is what it is. In the second kind of system, we might say that there are only parts and no whole. The whole is merely a collection of separate parts. In the third kind of system, there are both a whole and parts, and these two elements are quite different from each other. In the fourth kind of system, there *were* parts and there *is* a whole in which the parts are absorbed and lost. In the fifth kind of system, there is in a sense neither a whole nor parts. The parts have no independent being; since the relative independence which they enjoy is merely that independence which belongs to the nature of their system, and not an independence *of* it.[1] The whole also has no independent being; since it is its nature to exist as a system of relatively independent parts. .

Now with reference to most of the great questions in which human nature is concerned, the tendency of thought in recent·times, among those who have been making a serious attempt to "think things together," has been very decidedly to look for an explanation in the direction of the fifth, *i.e.* the organic view. We see traces of it in writers who in other respects diverge so widely as Hegel, Comte, Herbert Spencer, Schäffle, and many others.[2]

---

[1] This sounds paradoxical; but the meaning of it may become clearer in the sequel. Cf. pp. 157-8.

[2] Compare Mr. S. Alexander's *Moral Order and Progress*, p. 6. Of course, I do not mean to affirm that the organic view of society is a *discovery* of recent times. It is to be found, in some form, not only in Butler's First Sermon (cf. also Hutcheson, *De naturali hominum socialitate*, etc.), but also as far back as Plato and Aristotle

And though it would certainly be foolish to assume that the tendency of thought in recent times is an infallible index of the direction in which truth is to be sought, yet there is a certain *primâ facie* probability that it is so. For the other four kinds of system have been already, to a large extent, tried as explanations of things; and it is mainly because they have been seen to break down, that we are beginning to turn to the fifth. A few illustrations may help to make this clear.

One of the most obvious instances of this change of attitude appears in the theories that have been held with regard to the nature and growth of thought itself. The monistic view is seen in those systems which are commonly characterised as rationalistic or dogmatic; in which all the elements of thought are conceived as flowing out of certain universal principles which can be ascertained *a priori*, without reference to the particular facts of experience. This point of view is illustrated by such a doctrine as that of Wolff. The monadistic view, again, may be seen in such a theory as that of Hume, in which thought is reduced to a mere series of disconnected impressions and ideas. Such a view begins by being sensationalistic and ends by being sceptical. Mechanical or dualistic[1] views, on the other hand, are those which attempt to steer a middle course between these two extremes of unity and difference—which re-

and the *New Testament.* But it is only in recent times that it has been explicitly taken as the fundamental conception, and connected with a view of the world as a whole.

[1] Dualism is generally understood as referring to the fundamental antitheses between subject and object, thought and extension, mind and matter. In a dualistic system these pairs of opposites are supposed to exist independently, and to be brought together in an external or mechanical way. Here, however, I am using the term in a wider sense, as applying to any idea of a whole which is constituted in this external or mechanical way.

present thought, for instance, as partly given in sensation and partly determined by *a priori* principles. Such a view is seen in thinkers of the Scottish school; and it is caught, so to speak, in the act of vanishing away in the philosophy of Kant. "Mental chemistry" also has been represented in the doctrines of those members of the Associationist school who have conceived that the original data of sense are transmuted into something entirely different when they are connected together by the laws of the mind. Finally, philosophy since Kant has been mainly occupied with the effort to see the growth of thought as an organic process, in which neither the particulars of sense nor the *a priori* principles of knowledge have any independent meaning of their own, but in which each of these acquires its significance through the other.

Human freedom is another very obvious case in which these different views may be taken. The act of volition in each particular moment of our lives may be conceived as relative to the totality of our character in any of the five ways that have just been mentioned. In the first place, we have the Monadistic or purely Libertarian view, according to which the volitional act of each individual moment is independent of all the other moments of our lives. In the second place, we have the monistic or strictly necessarian view, according to which the volitional act of each moment is simply the outcome of our previously formed character, and might have been fully predicted from the beginning if the. character and circumstances had been known. In the third place, there is the mechanical or dualistic view, by which a certain compromise is attempted, and our acts are explained as partly the result of independent volition and partly the outcome of our previously formed character. In the fourth place, there is a view which may be described as chemical,

according to which we begin with independent acts of
volition, but gradually lose our independence, till finally
nothing is possible for us but that which our character
determines.  Finally, there is the organic view, according
to which the volition of a particular moment is simply
one expression of our character, and our character is
simply a universal statement of the principle which is
found in the volitional acts of particular moments.[1]
According to this view, the volition is neither free from
the character nor determined by it, but is merely the
particular of which character is the universal—each apart
from the other being a pure abstraction.  This view,
again, is the one which naturally connects itself with the
whole philosophical development of our time.

Similarly, we might distinguish a monadistic, a monistic,
a mechanical, a chemical, and an organic attitude with
reference to Theology, *i.e.* with reference to our view of
the relation of the world to God.  The monadistic view
either leaves God out of the system altogether, or represents Him simply as one particular being among others,
who have no necessary relation to Him.  The monistic
view may be said to alternate between Atheism and Pan-
theism and to find rest in neither.  It either regards God
as the whole of which all particular things are parts, or
else it regards this whole as a unity which is entirely without life or thought, and God as a "hypothesis of which
there is no need."  The mechanical view represents God
as a World-Architect, planning and ordering a system external to Himself—a being who "lets the world run round
His finger."  And this same view becomes chemical when
the nature of the world is conceived as becoming entirely
transformed by the divine activity which reduces it to
system ; so that the world as it is for God is a world
completely transfigured.  The organic view, finally, repre-

[1] Cf. Mr. S. Alexander's *Moral Order and Progress*, p. 39.

sents God as a being without whom the world could not exist and who could not exist without the world—a God-less world and a worldless God being alike abstractions. Here again it is hardly necessary to point out that the deepest religious thought of recent times, from that of Goethe downwards, has been an effort to work out this last conception of the divine nature.

We might go on illustrating these different kinds of system throughout a great variety of instances ; but it must suffice here to refer to one other case in which the dis-tinction becomes apparent—viz., in the conception of justice. The monadistic view of Justice is that which regards every individual as possessing, from the beginning, independently of his social connections, certain "natural rights";' as having justice done him when he receives these rights in full, and as suffering injustice when he does not receive them. The monistic view, on the other hand, starts with the conception of the state, and regards the individual as owing obligations to it rather than as possessing rights against it. A mechanical view, again, is one which regards the relation of the individual to the state as an accidental one, and Justice as a con-ventional compromise between what the individual may naturally claim and what the state may naturally require. Similarly, a chemical view would be one which conceives the natural rights of the individual as being completely transformed within the social state, so that what he is entitled to claim within that state is entirely different from what he might have claimed without it.[1] Finally, the organic view is that which regards the rights of the individual as inseparable from his obligations to his

---

[1] The doctrine of Hobbes is perhaps the best illustration of this. We might also refer to Rousseau's conception of the *volonté générale*, by which the self-assertive claims of individuals are modified and transformed.

society, and his obligations as equally inseparable from his rights—each being but a different aspect of the demands of his nature from him as a being who cannot but be social.

This leads us at last to notice what these different conceptions of a system would mean with reference to a human society. In a general way this is not difficult to see. A monadistic view of society would be one which regarded all the individuals of whom the society is composed as by nature independent of each other, and as connected together only by a kind of accidental juxtaposition. Such a view would naturally lead to the conclusion that the connection of individuals in a society tends to interfere with the natural development of the individual life, and that it would be better for the individuals if they could manage to live apart.[1] A monistic view of society, on the other hand, would be one which regarded the union of human beings as the primary fact with regard to them, and the whole nature and character of individual life as a mere outcome of social conditions. The natural conclusion of this view would be that the individual has no right to any independent life of his own; that he owes all that he is and has to the society in which he is born, and that society may fairly use him as a mere means to its development. A mechanical or dualistic view, again, would regard the individual as partly dependent and partly independent; as to some extent possessing a life of his own, and yet to some extent dependent on his social surroundings. This view would naturally lead in practice to a certain effort after compromise—to a certain effort to realise our individual life, and yet so to subject ourselves to social conditions as not to miss that element of our being with which they

---

[1] I do not, of course, mean to affirm that it would *necessarily* lead to this view.

provide us. A chemical view would be similar, except
that it would regard the new life with which we are provided by society as a complete transformation of our
original or natural life ; a view which would bring with it
as its practical outcome a certain effort to free ourselves
from the life of nature and to subject ourselves entirely
to social law. Finally, an organic view of society would
be one which regarded the relation of the individual to
society as an intrinsic one ; one which recognised that the
individual has an independent life of his own, and yet
which saw that that independent life is nothing other than
his social life. These are the five possible views : and
what we have now to consider is whether the last view
is truer than the other four ; and, if truer, whether it is
or is not the ultimate truth.

Now it might be thought at first that there is a certain
*a priori* presumption against its truth, from the very way
in which men have been led to adopt it. It might be
pointed out that the prevalence of an organic view of
things in recent times is due simply to the fact that there
have been lately great advances in biological science ; and
it might be urged that there is no likelihood that the conceptions derived from that science will lead us any nearer
the truth than those derived from psychological science,
from mathematical science, from physical science, or from
chemical science. When men's minds were chiefly occupied
with mathematics, they naturally (as we see most clearly
in the case of Spinoza) attempted to frame all their systems
on the mathematical model—*i.e.* to regard them as monistic,
as being such that all their parts follow inevitably from
the very nature or definition of the whole. When they
were chiefly occupied with psychology, it was equally
natural for them (as we see in Leibniz, Herbart, Lotze
and others) to regard the whole system of things as monadistic, *i.e.* as composed of certain irreducible elements

similar to that ultimate unity which we seem to find in the consciousness of ourselves; and to think of the universe as produced by various combinations of these ultimate elements.   When they were chiefly occupied with mechanics, again, they naturally became dualistic,[1] thinking of the world as made up of atoms, on the one hand, and laws of interaction on the other.   A chemical view of things has never attained to quite the same prominence; but a monadistic view leads in general to a chemical view, since it is necessary to think of the monads as becoming in some measure transformed by their relations to each other. Finally, now that men have become interested in biology, the conception of organism is naturally introduced.   It might seem, therefore, as if it were a mere accident that made one or other idea uppermost; and we are thus led to suspect that one of these ideas is not essentially more adequate than any other, but that they are simply taken up from the particular science that happens to be most in vogue, and transferred from it to the other objects with which we have to deal.

And this suspicion is apt to be to some extent confirmed when we go on to consider the way in which the conception of organism is made use of by those who are fondest of applying it to human societies.   What we find in the writings of these authors is often little else than an elaborate attempt to trace the various respects in which a society of human beings resembles a living creature. Now it is in general very easy and very useless to work out analogies.   When Shakespeare tells us that "the world's a stage," it is not difficult to see that there are certain respects in which the resemblance holds; and one who had enough ingenuity might perhaps be able to discover that there is something in life corresponding to the curtain, something to the footlights, and something to the

---

[1] In the sense explained in the note to p. 146.

prompter's box.  But we should not be any the wiser for
such a discovery.  After we have exhausted the likenesses
we come upon the unlikenesses ; and these are apt to
form the larger class of the two.  In the case of human
society,- for instance, while it is easy to see that in many
respects it conducts itself like a living thing, it is equally
easy to see that in other respects it does not.[1]

The point at which the analogy is in particular seen to
'fail is in considering the independence of the individual
consciousness.[2]  There is a familiar passage in Wordsworth
in which he contrasts the progress of the sun and other
heavenly bodies in their courses with the course of human
conduct :

> "He cannot halt nor go astray,
> But our immortal spirits may."

Something similar might be said of the contrast between
the members of an animal organism and the members of
a "body politic."  The former are, by the very nature of
the system in which they are included, necessitated, quite

[1] I do not mean to deny that analogies may be instructive even
when they cannot be fully carried out.  I think the defence which
Schäffle has given (*Bau und Leben des socialen Körpers*, IV. 505 *seq.*)
of his use of biological analogies in dealing with human society, is
satisfactory so far as it goes.  I only mean that to say that society
is like an organism is not the deepest sense in which we may maintain that it is organic ; and that if we use the biological analogy at
all, we must be very careful in our applications of it.  On this whole
subject, cf. Prof. Jones's article on "The Social Organism" in *Essays
in Philosophical Criticism*, p. 187 *seq.*

[2] This difference is much insisted on by Mr. H. Spencer.  See, for
instance, *Principles of Sociology*, I. 475 *seq.*  For a criticism of Mr.
Spencer's view, see *Essays in Philosophical Criticism*, p. 194 *seq.*  The
real contrast between the social organism and an animal organism
seems to me to be more clearly brought out by Schäffle than by
Spencer.  See *Bau und Leben des socialen Körpers*, I. 8 *seq.* and
827 *seq.*  Cf. also Höffding's *Ethik*, p. 187.

as rigidly as the planets are, to "observe degree, priority, and place," so long as the system holds together.  If the members begin to set up any independent life of their own, and are not duly responsive to the central control, we begin to regard them as abnormal or diseased.  We consider that the system is breaking down.  Society, on the other hand, is a "discrete unity," and in some of its most perfect forms seems even to glory in its discreteness.  Each individual has the shaping of his life to a great extent in his own control; and there is no visible system in which the place of the individual is determined, and by which his acts are regulated, as the parts of an organism are regulated by the central organs.  The individual is in many ways independent of society, and he may even set himself in opposition to it; and the more perfectly developed a society is, the more does this seem to be the case.  It is the prerogative of every man to say "I"—and to write it with a capital.  Sometimes even it seems as if the more thoroughly we realise our lives, the more are we isolated from our social environment.  Goethe used to say that he had to tread the wine-press alone, and other instances will readily occur of the loneliness of those who are pursuing what is highest in human life.[1]  Indeed there is no truth that has been more emphatically brought home to us by the great writers of recent times than the dependence of each one of us on himself for the shaping of his career, if that career is to be anything more than the achievement of a conventional success.  It is the key-note of much that is generally recognised as best in the teaching of Fichte, Carlyle, and Emerson; while Ibsen has even gone so far as to conclude one of his most impressive dramas[2] with the declaration that "the strongest man on earth is he who stands most entirely alone."  It is the truth that lies in such a paradox as this which seems most

[1] Cf. Chap. IV., *ad fin.*    [2] "An Enemy of the People."

conclusively to make the analogy between a human society
and an animal organism break down.

From such considerations, we are led to see the necessity for a careful criticism of the conception of Organism,
before we venture to make use of it in dealing with the
facts of social life. If we merely take it at random from
biological science, it will only supply us with a few ingenious analogies and at last leave us in the dark. It
can hardly be denied that some of the analogies which
recent writers (especially Spencer and Schäffle) have traced
out, are truly enlightening; but they help us, I think,
chiefly in so far as they enable us to clear our minds
of other analogies which are less adequate; such as those
derived from chemistry or mechanics. If we wish to get
beyond this negative aid, we must ask, to begin with,
what it is precisely that we are to understand by an
organic whole.

Now what has been already said with regard to the five
possible kinds of unity may help us at least to a "first
approximation" to the definition which we require. By
distinguishing an organism from an aggregate, from a unit,
and from a mechanical or chemical combination, we are
enabled to see with some clearness what are the essential
features in its constitution. From the first two of them
its distinction is comparatively obvious. A whole which
is merely a collection of parts, and a whole whose parts
have absolutely no distinguishable existence of their own,
are clearly both wholes of a quite different character from
one whose essence consists in its relations to its parts,
and the essence of whose parts consists in their relations
to it. In a mere aggregate the unity is accidental.[1] The
parts have as much reality in separation as they have
together. In a mere unit, on the other hand, the separate
existence of parts is accidental. A particular monument,

[1] Cf. *supra*, p. 34.

for instance, is essentially the same whether it is made of a number of separate stones or of a single block.   In the first of these kinds of unity, nothing is of importance but the particular parts: in the second, nothing is of importance but the whole.   In a mechanical or chemical unity, however, as well as in an organic unity, the relative importance of the whole and the parts is more nearly equal; and it is accordingly not quite so easy to distinguish these three kinds of unity from each other as it is to distinguish any one of them from a mere aggregate or from a mere unit.   Still, the distinction of the three kinds of system is on the whole sufficiently clear, and a few words of explanation ought to make it obvious.

We may begin with the distinction between a mechanical and an organic unity.   To make the contrast apparent, the simplest way will be to begin with the consideration of instances in which it is broad and unmistakable, and then to proceed to the consideration of cases in which it is almost on the point of vanishing away.   The former consideration will enable us to see the main features of the contrast in a distinctly marked form; the latter will enable us to judge whether these features persist even when the contrasted objects approximate to each other. In neither case, however, will it be necessary to enter upon a lengthened discussion.   To indicate the salient points will be enough for our present purpose.

It is tolerably easy, for example, to perceive the leading points of contrast between an ordinary machine and a highly developed organic structure, when both are regarded simply as forms of unity.   A machine is a contrivance adapted to the realisation of an end outside itself, whereas the primary and most important end of a living thing lies within it.   It is true that we may regard animals and plants also as adapted to other ends beyond their own individual lives, and in particular as being

subservient to the preservation and development of their ·
species. "Grass" is as useful to "cattle" as "the mountains" to "wild goats"; aphides might be thought to
exist chiefly for the benefit of ants; oaks are valued for
their timber, and bees for their honey; and particular
dogs or pigeons may be esteemed chiefly as specimens
of a breed: and all these species of organic beings may
be cultivated, and their structures modified and changed,
with a view to such external ends, either by human contrivance or by the contrivance of nature herself. Indeed,
in some sense, a *sic vos non vobis* may be addressed to
nearly every organism that we know. But such outside
ends, however important from the point of view of the
world, must be counted only *parerga* so far as the organism itself is concerned. It does not exhaust itself upon
them, in the same way as a machine does on the work
for which it is adapted. Or if in any case it does so
exhaust itself, it is only in yielding its life for the propagation of other individuals like itself, in which its own
life may be said to be carried on. Its main end is thus
either the development of its own life or that of other
lives in which its own is reproduced. And, indeed, if we
are ever tempted to regard living things as having no
reference to an inner end, the temptation is, in general,
not so much to think of them as relative to some end
outside them, as to think of them as having no end at all.
In this way, then, an organic being seems to be very distinctly differentiated from a machine.

But another difference between an organism and a
machine may be discovered in the manner in which their
parts are related to one another and to the whole. A
part of a machine, such as a wheel or lever, is itself a
machine; and, if it is separated from the system to which
it belongs, it still remains the wheel or lever it was before.
The relation of the parts to the whole is not essential:

the parts, when taken out of the whole, retain the same character as they had in it. It is not so with the parts of an organism. When they are cut off from the whole, they die; they lose the character which they had before, as vital portions of a living being, and become mere pieces of inert matter. A hand, as Aristotle pointed out, is no longer a hand when it is separated from the body; and so it is with the other parts of which an organic structure is composed. Their relation to the whole is intrinsic. The parts of an organism are not organisms, as the parts of a machine are machines: it is their nature to be only parts of an organism, and when they cease to be parts they cease to be organic. No doubt, some parts of organisms may be said to persist and to retain an independent character when they are separated from the whole —such as hair or the limbs of a polype. But we can hardly regard hair as forming an essential part of an organic structure; and, with respect to the limbs of a polype, it is not quite true that they maintain their character when they are cut off, since they then become something which they were not before—viz. organic wholes.[1] Here, then, we seem to have found another point of difference between an organism and a machine.

Another obvious difference consists in the way in which change takes place. An organism grows, whereas a machine is altered. The latter is changed by the substitution of new parts for old ones, whereas in the former a change can be effected only by a gradual transformation. This, indeed, follows from what has just been said; for if the relation of the parts to the whole is intrinsic, it is clear that a new part—which has no intrinsic relation to the whole—cannot be suddenly inserted. It must insert

---

[1] For, I suppose, it will hardly be maintained that they were organic wholes from the first. If they were, however, then the original polype was not an organism, but rather a collection of organisms.

itself through a gradual and continuous process, by the development of a new relation. Accordingly, change in the case of an organic being takes place from within : the principle of existence of the whole structure (so to speak), the vital cord by which its parts are connected —in short, the "geistige Band"—must be brought into relation to any new part that is added, before it can become a part at all.

When, however, instead of considering a machine, on the one hand, and a fully developed organism, on the other, we compare rather such a unity as the planetary system with a rudimentary organic structure, the contrast in these various aspects is by no means so apparent. For, in the first place, the planetary system has a certain tendency to self-conservation, which seems at first quite analogous to the self-asserting activity of the lower forms of life. In this sense, therefore, the one would seem to be as truly an end to itself as the other; while, in the case of plant life, and even in the case of the lower forms of animal life, there is no sense but this in which they can be regarded as ends to themselves. Both the planetary system and the organism are self-conservative : neither is conscious of self-conservation as an end to be sought. So also it may be said, in the second place, that in both systems the relation of the parts to the whole is equally intrinsic. The earth, for instance, if removed from the Solar System, would be deprived of the character which it has in that system almost as completely as any part of an organism would. Finally, such changes as take place within the planetary system take place by a continuous inner adjustment; and, if it cannot be said that there is any definite growth within such a system, it might with almost equal reason be questioned whether there is any distinct process of development in the life of some of the lower organisms, apart from the simple process by which they are formed.

In reply to this, however, we may remark, in the first place, that there is no sharp line of separation between the various forms of unity. They are only limiting conceptions to which the objects of our experience more or less closely approximate. There is probably no actually discoverable whole in nature which can be correctly described either as a mere aggregate or as a mere unit; and in like manner it may be impossible to find any combination which is either purely mechanical or purely chemical or purely organic. Indeed, if the world is to be thought of as a developing system, it seems inevitable that we should suppose that even in the mechanism of nature there is to some extent "the promise and potency" of life. And, on the other hand, in the lowest forms of organic structure, it can scarcely be said that there is much more than such promise: they are rather on the way to become alive than actually living. But, in the second place, it may be pointed out that even such a unity as the planetary system is, after all, clearly distinguishable from an organic whole. It may simulate the life of an organism, just as an automaton may; but it does nothing more than simulate it.

In the first place, though such a system may be said to be self-conservative, yet self-conservation does not constitute its essence; nor can it be said, in any real sense, to have failed of its end if it fails to conserve itself. Now even the meanest form of organic· life, however absolutely it may be lacking in any consciousness of an end which it wants to attain, evinces a, certain effort —though it may be only a blind impulse or *Trieb*—to conserve and perpetuate its being, and without that effort would not be what it is at all. What that effort means, apart from any consciousness by which it is directed, is, no doubt, somewhat difficult to explain ; and it may even be the case that the appearance of such an effort is illusory. But *if* it is illusory, the organic nature of the being in question is also illusory. We may suppose, as certain Cartesian philosophers did, that the lives of plants and even of the lower animals are simply instances of automatic activity—*i.e.* of an activity which can be mechanically explained, though the explanation of it lies within the system itself. But, if so, plants and animals are not organic wholes. They are merely — to use Professor Huxley's phrase—"the cunningest of nature's clocks." If the idea of mechanism is sufficient to account for their lives, it is not necessary to resort to the idea of organism at all; but if the idea of organism is to be employed, it is inevitable that the idea of an inner end should be accepted along with it.

That this is the case becomes more apparent when we consider, in the second place, that in every true organism the relation of the parts to the whole must be intrinsic; whereas that relation is not intrinsic in any merely mechanical system. It is true, indeed, that in most of the organic structures which we know—and especially in the lower forms of life—we encounter many elements whose relation to the whole seems to be of an accidental character. The branch of a tree, for instance, can be made into a part of another tree; so that it would appear that the branch had no necessary connection with the tree to which it originally belonged. This fact, however, is capable of more than one interpretation. It may mean that the relation of the branch to the tree is external, or it may mean that it is an internal relation which is capable of transference. If the former is the true interpretation, the organic structure in question is of a merely mechanical nature. If the latter is the true

L

interpretation, the relation of part to whole is, after all, intrinsic. Now it is not possible for us here to inquire whether the former or the latter of these interpretations is correct. This must be left to the biologist, or to the student of the philosophical principles which are involved in biology.[1] We are not now particularly concerned with the actual nature of organic structures. Organic structures may be merely elaborate machines; and, if so, they are of no particular interest to us here. What we have to deal with is merely the *conception* of organism, whether or not there is any object which actually conforms to it. It is, consequently, sufficient for our present purpose to point out that even in the lowest forms of life there is something which at least *suggests* the applicability of this conception, *i.e.* the existence of an intrinsic relation of parts to whole; and that if there is not such an intrinsic relation, the system must be regarded as merely mechanical.

And if we suppose that in all organic structures there is an intrinsic relation and an inner end, it is clear that we must suppose also, in the third place, that the development takes place from within. For nothing can be added on from without, until it has been placed in an intrinsic relation to the organism and to its inner end. Nor can any alteration take place within the organism, except in so far as such alteration is rendered compatible with subordination to the organism as a whole and to the end towards which it is directed. In a purely mechanical system, on the other hand, since there is no genuine inner end, there can be no real inner

---

[1] For a discussion of the nature of the organic unity of plants and animals, see the paper on "The Relation of Philosophy to Science," by R. B. and J. S. Haldane, in *Essays in Philosophical Criticism*, p. 52 *seq.* Cf. also the article by the latter of these writers in *Mind*, IX. 27-47.

adaptation. If anything enters into the system from without, what enters in has from the first, so to speak, an equal right with the elements originally in the system. The system is transformed by the new elements, quite as truly as the new elements are transformed by the system.[1]

When the distinction of an organic system from a mechanical system has been explained, its distinction from a chemical system ought not to give us much trouble. If an organic system is one in which the parts are intrinsically related to the whole, in which there is a development from within, and in which there is a reference to an inner end; then in all these respects such a system is distinguished from a chemical combination no less than from a mechanical one. In a chemical combination the parts are not intrinsically related to the whole, but are rather lost in the whole. So long as they continue to exist as separable parts, they are independent of the whole; but in the whole they become transfigured. Nor can there be any development in such a system, nor any end towards which a development could be directed: the parts are swallowed up in the whole, so that nothing further can take place within the system, except by its dissolution. Any readjustment of it would imply that the parts retain a certain independent being, which in such a system they have not.[2]

---

[1] It may be thought that the distinction which is thus drawn between a mechanical and an organic system is a somewhat arbitrary and dogmatic one. But it must be remembered that we are dealing only with two limiting conceptions, and that it is consequently impossible to show in a conclusive way from any concrete examples that there is an absolute distinction between them. The real distinction is an ideal one: and concrete examples can serve only as inadequate illustrations of it.

[2] Here again it may be well to insert the caution, that in making such statements we are not to be understood as dogmatising with

We may sum up, then, in this way. A mechanical system is a collection of parts externally related; it changes by the alteration of its parts; and it has reference to an 'end which is outside of itself. A chemical system is a compound of parts which are absorbed in the whole; it does not change except by dissolution; and it has no end to which it refers. In an organism, on the other hand, the relations of the parts are intrinsic; changes take place by an internal adaptation; and its end forms an essential element in its own nature. We are thus led, by contrasting an organism with a mechanical and with a chemical unity, to see some of the most essential points in the conception of organism itself. We see, in short, that an organism is a real whole, in a sense in which no other kind of unity is so. It is *in seipso totus, teres, atque rotundus.* All its parts belong to it: they cannot be altered, so to speak, without its own consent; and the end which it seeks is also its own. It is a little universe in itself. At the same time it *is* a universe, and not a unit; it has parts, and it does grow, and it has an end. We may define it, therefore, as a whole whose parts are intrinsically related to it, which develops from within, and has reference to an end that is involved in its own nature.

A little consideration will make it evident that the various points mentioned in this definition are essentially connected with each other; and that the definition would still be adequate if it stated simply that an organism is a variable system whose parts are intrinsically related to it. For an intrinsic relation of parts within a variable system is possible only on the supposition of a development from within towards an end which is included in the idea of the system. If there were no inner development, there

regard to the actual constitution of chemical compounds, but only as explaining a limiting or regulative conception.

might be an intrinsic relationship, but there could not be any change. If there were no inner end, there might be change, but there could not be any intrinsic relationship. A statical system is conceivable in which all the inner relations should be intrinsic; and a dynamical system is conceivable in which there should be no inner end; but if a system is at once dynamical and intrinsically related within itself, it must have an inner development towards an end. An intrinsic relation, in short, in a variable system, is possible only on the supposition that the variation of the system is itself intrinsic, *i.e.* that it is not merely a change, but a development carried on from within and in accordance with an inner principle. On this point, however, it is not necessary here to insist : for though the definition may be simplified in the way which is thus suggested, yet for various reasons the longer form will be found more convenient. I have indicated the possibility of such a simplification merely to show that the three elements which are stated in the definition are not accidentally found together, but belong essentially to the nature of an organic system, as one which combines a certain freedom of movement in its growth with a necessary connection among its parts.[1]

/ This, then, is the conception which we are to endeavour to apply to human society. Now we may to some extent test its applicability to society by taking a general survey of its nature as it appears to common-sense. There is a certain advantage in Philosophy in beginning the inquiry into any subject by a superficial view of it; since in the analysis of conceptions we are inevitably led away from the surface of things, and are sometimes in danger of losing sight of it. A really profound view of any subject

---

[1] The full meaning of an organic system will become more apparent from the considerations which are adduced in the latter part of this chapter.

must include the surface as well.   There is such a thing as a bathos of profundity, which undermines itself and becomes, so to speak, superficiality on the other side. For this reason the example of Aristotle, of beginning with ἔνδοξα and gradually working inwards, is one that deserves imitation.   At any rate, if society is fundamentally organic, we may expect that this organic nature will declare itself even on a surface view; and, having by such a superficial observation discovered its more obviously organic features, we shall then be able to go deeper and see what are the most essential points.

Are there, then, any respects in which society is obviously organic, in the sense in which that term has been already defined?   As our definition involved three characteristic elements, this question involves three subordinate inquiries which it will be convenient to ask in succession : —(1) Are the parts of a society intrinsically related to the whole of which they are parts?   (2) Does society grow from within?   (3) Has society a reference to an inner end?

1. Now, in the first place, it seems sufficiently clear that human beings have an intrinsic relation to their society, in so far as their individual nature is formed and coloured by it.   Indeed, the more we study the history of different times and races, the more are we led away from a monadistic view of the relations of individuals to their societies, and the more are we tempted to adopt rather a monistic view, and to think of the nature of their individual lives as flowing simply out of their social conditions.   Each nation and tribe produces in its children its own type of character, which has grown up in it through the influence of the physical surroundings and past history of the people.   Each individual is not a new phenomenon in the world, but only one particular specimen of a race; whether he be a yeoman "whose limbs were made in England," a painter whose eyes were

developed in Italy, or a philosopher whose brain grew in Germany. And after the individual has been produced with his particular type of potential character, the direction in which that character develops is determined mainly by the habits and customs of his particular people and class. From such observations as these, we have come more and more to regard the characters of individuals neither as freaks of nature nor as the choice of the individual soul (as in the fable of Plato[1]), but rather as determined mainly by inheritance and social conditions. From this point of view, there is an obvious sense in which the relation of the individual to his society is an intrinsic one. His life is controlled both by the dead and by the living among his people. He is what his fathers have been before him, except in so far as he has breathed a different air. Nor is this influence of social environment something purely external by which the individual is affected. There is not first the individual and then the influences which mould his life. He is nothing except what he has become through the influence of that spiritual setting. There is nothing deeper in our nature than our inherited traits: there is nothing more our own than our national disposition and sentiments : there is nothing by which we are more possessed than the spirit of our time. We cannot go behind the elements of our constitution to find something deeper which we can regard as our very self, and which is prior to such impressions. They are the elements out of which our self has grown, and we can find nothing beyond them that in any deeper sense belongs to us, or that in any deeper sense is *we*.[2]

[1] *Republic*, x. 614 *seq.*

[2] This whole subject is very well stated and illustrated in chapter iii. of Mr. Leslie Stephen's *Science of Ethics*. Cf. also Clifford's *Lectures and Essays*, Vol. II., pp. 111-2.

Nor is it merely the weaker natures among mankind that are thus interpenetrated by the genius of their surroundings. It is rather in the strongest that the power of the *Zeit-Geist* becomes most impressive. Often, indeed, it is just owing to a large infusion of it that they *are* strong. It is men of an iron will like Napoleon whom we find declaring[1]—"I am not a person: I am a *thing*." It is men like Shakespeare or Milton or Cromwell or Goethe who seem to be the impersonation of all the forces that their age contained. Such men are rightly said to be *inspired*. "They build better than they know": they are carried away by forces larger than their own individuality, which yet have become for them a second nature. It is true, indeed, that those forces of inspiration which constitute what we know as *genius* are not entirely traceable to the influence of the social environment. They are partly due to what is called the "subconscious" movement of the mental structure of the individual himself;[2] and have thus to be referred to inherited impulses as well as to the atmosphere in which he lives. But the deepest kinds of inspiration, and those which are most far-reaching in their influence, seem in nearly all cases to owe their force to elements which are not peculiar to the individual, but which he has drawn from the spirit of his time. Or perhaps we should rather say that his power depends on the character which he inherits; and the use he makes of it, on the atmosphere which he breathes. Goethe rightly says of himself—

[1] Cf. Seeley's *Napoleon*, p. 269.

[2] I mean that they are due to elements in his individual consciousness of the workings of which he is only partly aware. Cf. Carlyle's saying that "the Unconscious is alone complete." See also Simmel's *Einleitung in die Moralwissenschaft*, Vol. II., p. 298 *seq.*, Ehrenfels's *Werth-Theorie und Ethik* (*Vierteljahrsschrift f. w. Phil.*, VII. II.), p. 213, *etc.*

> " Vom Vater hab ich die Statur,
> Des Lebens ernstes Führen :
> Vom Mütterchen die Frohnatur
> Und Lust zu fabuliren " :

but " Werter " and " Faust " and " Wilhelm Meister " belong neither to father nor mother, but to the spirit of the German people and of the time that followed upon the French Revolution. Such men as these are in organic relation to their spiritual environment ; and what is emphatically true of these is in some measure true of all.

But the most obvious illustration of the social determination of our thoughts and sentiments is to be found in the fact of language. The saying of Comte is familiar, that it is impossible even to give utterance to the "blasphemous" doctrine that we are independent of society, since the very expression of it involves language, which is itself dependent on society : the assertion would contradict itself. But language is not only the means of expressing thought : it is also the means of forming and preserving it. An Englishman, a Frenchman, a German, and an Italian, cannot by any means bring themselves to think quite alike, at least on subjects that involve any depth of sentiment ; they have not the verbal means. Nor can we bring ourselves to think quite as the Greeks or Romans did. It is largely for this reason that the study of language is so important an instrument of culture : it adds a new wing to our spirits ; it enables us to enter regions of thought which were before unopened and inaccessible.[1] Even provincial modifications of dialect affect, no less than they express, the modes of thought of those who use them. And the language of manners and customs and institutions—the embodiment of ideas in the sights and sounds by which we are environed

[1] For interesting illustrations of this point, see Mr. Leslie Stephen's *Science of Ethics*, p. 105 *seq.*

throughout our lives—is only less influential than that of words. The cathedrals of Italy and the factories of England must each have their influence in moulding the characters of the respective peoples. We are "suckled at the breast of the universal ethos,"[1] and made what we are by the whole society in which we participate. Our relation to it is intrinsic.

Nor is this relationship annulled or weakened even in those cases in which we seem to set ourselves in opposition to our society, or to withdraw ourselves from it and live a life of our own. The destroyer of his country, as well as its saviour, is one of the fruits which that country bears. He is one of the expressions of its life, though he is an expression of disease. The forces which

> " rend and deracinate
> The unity and married calm of states,"

are as truly a product of their constitution as those that bind the state together. Nor can the solitary remain unaffected by the pulses of his country's life; or if he ever succeeds entirely in becoming an ἰδιώτης in the Greek sense, it is only by becoming at the same time what its English derivative implies. The "self-made man" who is of no sect or school, and calls no one master, can be nothing more, as Goethe put it, than "a fool in his own right" ("ein Narr auf eigener Hand"). The aloofness which belongs to greatness is of another order than this. It is a solitude whose votaries are "never less alone than when alone," because they carry the finest essence of the world's spirit with them. Coleridge said once that "the egotism of such a man as Milton is a revelation of spirit"; because when he seems to think only of himself and to speak out of the fulness of his own inner life, he is giving utterance to thoughts and

[1] Hegel. Cf. Bradley's *Ethical Studies*, p. 156.

feelings which are not merely private, but belong to the human race; he has become in himself a microcosm, by absorbing what is deepest in the universal consciousness.[1] Such a life is not severed from its society, any more than the brain is severed from the body when it builds up for itself a world of dreams, undisturbed by any intrusions of sense. The materials have been derived from the system, though they are elaborated in retirement from it.

Even the superficial view of society which is thus indicated might be sufficient to convince us that it is not a mere aggregate of separate individuals, or a mechanical or chemical combination of them. That it is a chemical system might indeed be suggested by the consideration that the individual owes his character to some extent to inheritance and to some extent to the atmosphere in which he lives. But when we recollect that even what we inherit is inherited from a social atmosphere, we see that there is nothing in the individual nature which can be regarded as independent of society. We are led, therefore, to regard society either as a monistic or as an organic unity. Perhaps, indeed, what has been said so far might lead us to think of it as a unity rather of the former kind than of the latter.

2. Our view of the relation of the individual to his society is, however, further modified, when we consider that society itself grows, and that consequently it cannot be regarded as a definitely pre-existing thing out of which the individual life issues. If society were a monistic system, it could not grow. It could only change from one thing into another; and when it changed, its parts would be changed along with it, or else it would cease to be a system. When it became altered, the parts that

[1] The relation of great men to the spirit of their times is well brought out in Mr. S. Alexander's *Moral Order and Progress*, pp. 354-5. Cf. *Essays in Philosophical Criticism*, p. 210.

belonged to its prior state of existence would no longer be the parts that flowed out of its new nature; and if these parts remained in it unchanged, the system would become a dualistic one; the relations of its parts would no longer be intrinsic. Now it might be supposed that society is a unity of this sort. It might be supposed that it is a system by which its citizens are formed; and that when the system changes, it either makes its citizens different or ceases to be a system to which they are intrinsically related. In this case the development of society would not be from within, in the sense in which we have understood that term. The old system would give place to a new one, into which parts had to be fitted afresh, instead of gradually modifying itself by a continuous readjustment of its parts.

Now there are facts in history which might lead us to regard the life of society in this way. When one people is conquered by another, for instance, a new system of society is often introduced. The conquered people has to adapt itself to the habits and customs of its con- querors. Again, we hear of individuals, such as Solon and Lycurgus, forming constitutions for the states to which they belonged, by which a set of customs was imposed externally on the individuals of which the society was made up, so that they were forced to adapt themselves to a new whole. And even in the ordinary life of societies around us, we may easily find instances of men who have fallen out of touch with the general current of the life to which they belong, and who seem as if they were parts of a different system.

But that such facts as these do not belong to the ordinary life of societies is at once apparent. When a people is conquered and subjected to another, it ceases to be a society, except in so far as it retains a spiritual life of its own apart from that of its conquerors. Yet it does not become an integral part of the victorious people's life, until it is able to appropriate to itself the spirit of . that life. So long as the citizens of the conquered state are merely in the condition of atoms externally fitted into a system to which they do not naturally belong, they cannot be regarded as parts of the society at all. They are slaves: they are instruments of a civilisation of which they do not partake. Certainly no more melancholy fate can befall a nation than that it should be subjected to another whose life is not large enough to absorb its own. But such a subjection cannot be regarded as a form of social growth. It is only one of those catastrophes by which a society may be destroyed. In so far as there is growth in such a case, it is still a growth from within. The conquering society must be able to extend its own life outwards, so as gradually to absorb the conquered one into itself; otherwise the latter cannot be regarded as forming a real part of it at all, but at most as an instrument of its life, like cattle and trees. And similar remarks may be made of those who in any other way drop out of touch with the life of their people. In so far as they cease to share in the current of their people's life, they cease to be a part of the system to which they belong, and become only instruments of its advancement or impediments in its way. Such facts illustrate rather the disintegration than the growth of society.

Nor is the formation of artificial constitutions a fact of such importance as it might at first appear. Historical investigation has led us more and more to believe that "Constitutions are not made, but grow."[1] Solon and

[1] It is, no doubt, possible to exaggerate the extent to which the choice of a government is dependent on the inner growth of the people. Cf. Mill's *Representative Government*, chap. i. But Mill's objections do not apply to the above remarks.

Lycurgus have become for us, in a sense, almost as mythical as Pallas Athene. It is inconceivable to us now that states should have been formed simply by means of "Paper Constitutions," which did not in some way grow out of the whole previous life of the people. If we do ever believe in the possibility of men forming constitutions "out of their heads," we believe it only in the case of those who have already absorbed the life of their people into their heads, so as to be able to supply them with just those elements which that life required. And what is thus felt to be true of the development of states, is even more clearly obvious with regard to the development of language, social customs, and national character. These things, on the whole, cannot be *made*, and cannot be *altered*: they can only *grow* or *decline*. Changes take place in them only by a gradual readjustment of elements in relation to the whole nature of the system which changes.

At this point, in fact, we begin to perceive that there is a monadistic as well as a monistic element in human society. If it is true that the individual is formed by the habits and customs of his people, it is true also that the habits and customs of the people grow out of the characters of the individual citizens. The relation of the individual to society is similar in kind to the relation of the will of an individual to his character. As will is the expression of character, so is the individual the expression of his society; but as change of character takes place only through change of acts of will, so a change in society takes place only through change in its individual members. And just as our wills are free, although they are the expression of our characters, so the individual has an independent life, although he is the expression of his society.

That there is no contradiction between the independence which. is now claimed for the individual and the fact of his social determination, becomes evident when we consider the nature of that determination and of that independence. That the individual is determined by his society, means merely that his life is an expression, of the general spirit of the social atmosphere in which he lives. And that the individual is independent, means merely that the spirit which finds expression in him is a living force that may develop by degrees into something different. Now these two truths are so far from being contradictory of each other, that they are rather to be regarded as but different sides of one truth. The very fact that the life of a society has become embodied in an individual, implies that he is not simply *determined* by his society. If he were simply determined by it, it must be something which is not he. When we say, for instance, that in Goethe the spirit of his time was summed up, we say at the same time that Goethe was not simply determined by his time, but was an independent personality. He was free from the external influence of his time, in so far as he had made its inner spirit his own: and he was thus able to mould it and advance it to something better. In the same way, a man is free in an act of will just in so far as his whole character is present and expresses itself in that act: and just to that extent is it possible for such an act of will to advance and strengthen his character. On the other hand, if a man's character is in abeyance when he acts, his act is determined by momentary impulses and he is not free. The independence of his will consists just in the fact that it is the expression of his character: and the independence of his life consists just in the fact that it is the expression of his society's life. As the individual becomes an independent thinker in mathematics by mastering the work of his predecessors, so he becomes an original force in life by absorbing the ideas by which the world has been guided.

Such illustrations as these may help us to see how it is that though the individual is determined by society, yet it is through the development of individual lives that society grows. Thus, even on a surface view, it becomes more or less apparent that society develops from within.

3. That the growth of social conditions has reference to an inner end, is a point on which we need not here enlarge. That the movements of social development are purposeless, no one supposes; and that the purpose which it subserves lies within itself, is equally apparent. What the end is, it may be difficult to determine; but it is easy to perceive that it is some form of human well-being. In changing our modes of thought and speech, and the customs and institutions of our social life, we are trying to make our life in some respects more possible or more happy: we are trying to promote τὸ ζῆν or τὸ εὖ ζῆν: and there are no other ends than these which we can think of the growth of our social conditions as promoting.[1] If anything else is ever proposed as an end—such as the realisation of a divine purpose in the world—we at least think of this other end as one in which the well-being of persons is an indispensable part. Thus, from this point of view also, society is *primâ facie* organic.

So far, however, we have been dealing with the surface appearance of things, and showing how, in accordance with our ordinary ἔνδοξα or common-sense views, society may be seen to be organic, in the sense in which that term has been defined. Such considerations are sufficient to justify us in believing that society is more nearly analogous to an organic whole than to any other form of unity. But we have still to find out how it comes to

[1] Cf. what is said on this point in Chap. IV.

pass that man has this intrinsic relationship to his social
environment, and what is its ultimate meaning. It seems
strange at first sight that a human being should be thought
of as having so essential a relationship to other human
beings. Many of the lower animals are gregarious as well
as man; yet we think of each one of them as an independent being, and do not regard their herds as organic
wholes. And although it is true that an animal is a mere
type of its species to a far greater extent than a man is
of his society, yet it is clear that the animal's relation to
its herd is not one of so intrinsic a character. It is not
constituted by its social atmosphere, in the sense in which
a human being is so constituted. It is constituted much
rather by its inherited instincts, which grow up within it
almost independently of its particular environment. An
animal that has never been associated with its herd appears to be almost indistinguishable from one that has:
it shows hardly any sign of that relative barbarity which
an isolated human being has. A herd of animals, in
fact, does not appear to form an atmosphere for its com-
ponent members at all. There is nothing in it which is
not in each of them when they are separated from it.
It has no traditions which are not embodied in their
instincts: it has no institutions which these instincts do
not naturally create: it does not, so far as we can see,
supply them with a language, or with the means of higher
development. Their society, in short, is nothing—or next
to.nothing—but an aggregate of individual animals.[1] Now

[1] Of course, this can only be accepted as expressing a broad distinction. That some animals have a very close relation to the whole
to which they belong may be seen in such a case as that of bees—

> "Creatures that by a rule in nature teach
> The act of order to a peopled kingdom."

Cf. Mr. Leslie Stephen's *Science of Ethics*, p. 99 *seq.* But even in
such a case as this, there is still no evidence of an inner develop-

this difference between a herd of animals and a society of men leads us naturally to suspect that the organic nature of human society must depend on those conditions by which man is differentiated from the other animals. The inquiry whether this is so or not may lead us to a deeper view of the organic nature of society.

ment towards an end. Ehrenfels remarks (*Werth-Theorie und Ethik*, p. 266) that, just as bees and ants are directed by their natural instincts to ends of which they are themselves unconscious, so it is probable that the actions of individual human beings at the present time have a reference to important social ends, of which succeeding generations may become aware. This is, no doubt, partly true. A man may often build better than he knows. Adam Smith's idea of the way in which self-interest is turned to account for the general benefit is not without an element of truth (Cf. Bonar's *Philosophy and Political Economy*, pp. 162, 173, etc.); and the "economic harmonies" are not the only ones. The social unity may force even the wrath of men to praise it. Yet on the whole there is a distinction. In the case of the bees and ants the individual may be said, on the one hand, simply to follow its impulses, while, on the other hand, its actions are guided by the nature of a totality to which it is externally related. In the case of man neither of these statements would be quite true. He seldom follows a simple natural instinct without reflection on the way in which its gratification is likely to be regarded by the general consciousness of the group to which he belongs; and, at least in the more developed periods of human life, he tends to be affected also by the consideration of the way in which the equilibrium of the group will be affected by his action. Further, while his action is thus determined by the nature of the whole to which he belongs, it is not determined by it without a certain reaction. Determination by the group is dependent to an increasing extent on approval of the ends to which the action of the group is directed; and here again, in the more developed forms of social life, the disapproval of even the meanest individual may be an important factor in the transformation of the whole group. Thus, in a two-fold way, the social consciousness enters into the determination of the life both of the individual and of the whole of which he is a member; and, for this reason, the analogy to which Ehrenfels refers is probably not so complete as he seems to suggest.

Now the great point of difference between man and
the animals is usually said to consist in the consciousness
of self, which is present in the former and absent in the
latter. This, however, is a somewhat ambiguous statement. In one sense, there is every reason to believe
that the animals are as much conscious of a self as we
are, or at least that the consciousness of self is as prominent in them, relatively to the general distinctness of
their consciousness of things, as it is in us. An animal
is an individual being, and if it is not aware of itself as
such—in many cases keenly aware of itself—we must be
very much deceived by appearances. Nor is there any
particular reason to suppose that an animal is not dimly
conscious of a distinction between its own subjective
states and the objects which it perceives. What it is not
conscious of, so far as we can make out, is the unity of
its individual life, the connected system of its experiences
as a whole, in which each single experience has a definite
place. It is this consciousness that is referred to when
it is said that self-consciousness is the distinguishing
feature of humanity. But in order that this may be made
more clearly intelligible, a few words must be said on
the different meanings which may be attached to the term
"self-consciousness," or rather on the different forms in
which self-consciousness appears.

There are a number of distinct senses in which it is
possible to speak of a self with a definite and intelligible
meaning ; or, rather, there are a number of distinct stages
in the development of the self—stages which glide insen-
sibly into each other, but which yet it is important, as
far as possible, to discriminate. The following are the
most prominent of these stages. ▷

1. There is a sense in which any object whatever may
be said to have or to be a self, in so far as it is capable
of being regarded as an individual object at all. It is

natural to say that a river empties *itself* into the sea, that a mountain maintains *itself* unchanged from century to century, and even that a heap of stones remains during a certain period of time identical with *itself.* Each of these objects has a self, in the sense that it may be regarded as forming a whole. As, however, any object may be viewed in a number of different aspects, an object which, from one point of view, has a self in this sense, would, from another point of view, not have a self at all. This sense of the term is consequently artificial and unimportant.

2. The next sense is that in which an object is said to have a self when it not only *may* be regarded as a whole, but *must* be so regarded if it is to be truly understood. Now the necessity of being regarded as a unity may have various degrees, and even various kinds, of cogency. A house must be regarded as a whole; but the necessity which compels us so to regard it arises from the fact that it has reference to an end apart from which it has no significance. This end, however, lies outside of itself: it lies in the nature of man. Consequently, the same necessity which leads us to regard a house as a whole, leads us also to regard it as not a whole in itself, but an element in something beyond itself. Again, a picture or a poem must be regarded as a whole; and the necessity which compels us so to regard them is a deeper kind of necessity than that which compels us to regard a house as a whole. They are wholes (if they are true works of art) because they have a single meaning; or, at least, because their various parts have an essential reference to each other. This meaning or mutual reference may be said to lie within the work of art; and the work of art is consequently a whole in a deeper sense than that in which a house is a whole. Still, the necessary unity of such a whole exists only for the mind which apprehends

it. A Greek play is not a necessary unity for the mere philologist or grammarian, but only for one who recreates its passion and thought. For such a mind a book or a picture is a living thing ; so that, as Milton said, it would be as well to kill a man as to kill a good book. But without the recreative mind the book is nothing. The book, therefore, or the work of art, though it has a self in a deeper sense than a house has, is still not in the deepest sense a necessary unity. The house has no self, but is a whole for another self : the work of art has a self (*i.e.* a self-reference), but it also has a self only for another self. With an organic being the case is different. Such a being is a necessary unity apart from any other finite self to which it refers.[1] The elements of which it is composed cannot be understood except in relation to the whole to which they belong; and in referring them to that whole, we do not directly refer them to anything which lies beyond it.[2] An organic being, therefore, has a self in a deeper sense than that in which a house or a work of art has one. It has a self in the sense that, from the very nature of the unity which belongs to it, it must necessarily be regarded as a whole if it is to be understood at all.

3. A still deeper meaning of the term self is reached

---

[1] I do not mean to deny that an organic being, as well as any other being, can exist only with reference to the absolute self-consciousness for which the world is. But since this applies to all objects alike, it may be abstracted from in contrasting one object with another.

[2] *Indirectly*, no doubt, we refer them to the absolute self-consciousness. It may be well to remark that in all that we have here said, the presupposition is involved that organic beings are really organic, in the sense in which that term has been defined. As, however, we are merely explaining a sense in which the term self may be understood, it is not necessary at this point to discuss the validity of this assumption. It may be taken for granted for purposes of illustration.

when the unity of an organic being attains to consciousness, as it does in the lives of animals. It would be beyond the limits of such a book as this (even if it were otherwise possible) to consider the precise relations of consciousness to vitality; but it is clear at least that in consciousness a deeper kind of unity is attained than that which belongs merely to the organic connection of part with whole. The parts are reflected into a focus, where their relations to the external world register themselves, and where a reaction upon the external world begins. Consciousness is from the first a presentation of a manifold in unity; though, no doubt, in its more rudimentary forms the differentiation is but slight. But the most characteristic and central element in the lower forms of consciousness seems to be the simple feeling of pleasure or pain, *i.e.* the consciousness of the harmony or disharmony of the content of experience with the unity in which it is contained. It is this which determines the activity of the conscious being, *i.e.* the reaction of its unity upon the content which is presented to it; and it is in virtue of this also that such a being may be regarded as an organic whole, in a sense in which no unconscious being is organic. In the life of such a being "when one member suffers, all the members suffer with it." When there is a breach of harmony at any point within the organism, it is reported at the central office, and an effort is made towards readjustment. Such an organism has a self, not merely in the sense that it must be regarded as a unity, but in the sense that it is a unity *for itself.* The unity of its life has come to consciousness—though it is true that it has not yet come to the consciousness of itself *as a unity*, but only to the consciousness of pleasure and pain.[1]

4. The next stage is that at which an organic being

[1] Which, however, is *implicitly* a consciousness of unity.

becomes actually conscious of itself *as a unity—i.e.* the stage at which it reflects upon its own life, and recognises itself as one throughout all its changes. How the one consciousness grows out of the other, it is not our business here to trace. It is sufficient to remark that, just as the feeling of pleasure and pain is the central fact with regard to the preceding form of consciousness, so the sense [1] of happiness and misery is the central fact with regard to this form. The chief difference between pleasure and happiness consists in the fact that the former is immediate, whereas the latter involves a certain reflection on the life of the individual as a whole. Pleasure is given along with the object which is pleasant. If an experience is pleasant, it *is* pleasant; and there can be no further question. Happiness, on the other hand, depends on the point of view. *Fortunati nimium sua si bona norint* is not a paradox with respect to happiness, though it would be one with respect to pleasure. If we are asked whether an experience is pleasant or not, we can answer at once—at least we could answer at once if mere sense were capable of giving an answer. But if we are asked whether we are happy, we must reflect; and our answer will be different according to the point of view from which we regard our experience—*i.e.* according to the view which we take of the elements that ought to be contained in a happy life.[2] The view which we thus form of our lives as totalities evidently involves a

[1] I purposely call it a "sense" rather than a "feeling," because the former is a vaguer term. The consciousness of happiness and misery is not a mere feeling, since it involves reflection; but it may, quite correctly, be described as a sense.

[2] Happiness is often understood to mean simply a sum of pleasures. According to this view, the reflection referred to in the text would consist simply in a rough calculation of pleasures and pains. The chief reasons which lead me to reject this view will be stated in the next chapter.

deeper conception of the self than that in which it is nothing more than the immediate unity into which our organic experiences are reflected as pleasant or painful.

5. But there is still a further stage in the development of the self. The consciousness of man is a unity, not only in the sense that his life is for him a whole, but also in the sense that his world is a whole. He is aware of his individual life not as a microcosm in a chaos, but as a microcosm in a macrocosm, to the objective unity of which his individual life as well as everything else is referred.[1] Nor is he aware of the unity of the world of his experience as an accidental fact with regard to the nature of that world; he is aware of it rather as the necessary presupposition of a possible experience. Consequently, this unity must not be regarded as simply belonging to the objective world; it belongs also to the consciousness for which the world is, in the sense that without such a unity there could not be any such consciousness. Here, then, we have a third focus into which experience may be reflected. There is, first, the immediate unity of experience, as all occurring in a continuous consciousness. Then we have the unity of reflection, by which the permanence of the individual self is opposed to the manifold changes of its states. Finally, we have the unity of apperception, by which all objects of a possible experience are referred to a single system

---

[1] For a very clear discussion of the different interpretations of this objective unity, I may refer to Professor Dewey's article in *Mind* for January, 1890. Here I can only state the view which I regard as correct. For a fuller analysis of the various stages in the development of the consciousness of self, see Dr. Ward's article on "Psychology" in the *Encyclopaedia Britannica*, Vol. XX., p. 83 *seq.* I may also refer, for some further explication of my own view on this matter, to my article on "Mr. Bradley's View of the Self," in *Mind*, July, 1894.

or universe.[1] And just as the central characteristic
of the first unity is the sense of the pleasantness or
painfulness of particular elements within the unity of
consciousness; and as, in like manner, the central
characteristic of the second unity is the sense of the
happiness or misery of the individual life regarded as a
whole; so we may find the central characteristic of the
third unity in the sense of *blessedness* or the reverse (to
adopt Carlyle's favourite antithesis to happiness) which
results from our recognition of the harmony or disharmony of our objective experience regarded as a
system. It is not difficult to see, in a general way,
the distinction between these three forms of desirable
consciousness. It is one thing to feel that one has
been pleased; it is another thing to be conscious that
one has

> "sighed deep, laughed free,
> Starved, feasted, despaired—been happy":

and even when we have attained to this latter consciousness, we may still be aware that the highest end of life
has been missed. There is, moreover, a fundamental
difference between the recognition of harmony in the
three cases. In the first case, the recognition of harmony
is an immediate perception which comes along with the
experience in which the harmony is perceived; in the
second case, it is the result of a reflection, by which a
certain idea of life as a whole is attained; in the third
case, it is the apprehension of a pure ideal, which cannot
be completely realised within a finite experience. Pope's
line, "Man never is, but always to be blest," may consequently be accepted (though in a somewhat different
sense from that in which he intended it) as expressing
a fundamental truth; since *blessedness*, in the sense

---

[1] On the relation of this consciousness to the consciousness of the
individual self, cf. Wundt's *Ethik*, p. 386.

in which it is here understood, is an ideal which would be attained only by a consciousness to which the world could be presented in its totality as a harmonious system.[1]

These, then, are the five senses in which it seems to be intelligible to speak of any object as being, or having, a self. Now when we speak of a *consciousness* of self, we may refer to the self either in the second, the fourth, or the fifth of these senses. The first sense is, as has been already stated, trivial; since it may be applied to any object whatever. The third sense also has no *consciousness* of self corresponding to it; for, as soon as we become conscious of it, it passes into the fourth. If, therefore, we wish to distinguish between animals and men, in respect of their consciousness of self, we must consider to what extent they are aware of themselves in the second, the fourth, and the fifth senses. Now it might seem at first that an animal can hardly be supposed to be ignorant of itself in the second sense. If the ox "knows its master's crib," it must surely know itself as an organic unity; for, in addition to such a knowledge of its own organism as it has of its master's crib, it has also the consciousness of the intimate connection of that organism with its sensitive life; and this seems sufficient to give it at least a dim consciousness[2] of its organic life as a unity. But it must be remembered that a mere animal cannot, properly speaking, *know* its master's crib. To know that or any other object involves the use of conceptions; and, unless animals think, they cannot

---

[1] These distinctions are more fully explained in the following chapter. See also my *Manual of Ethics*, chaps. v. and vi., where I have endeavoured to make this point clearer by the introduction of the conception of different "universes" of reference.

[2] That kind of consciousness which is sometimes referred to as *Coenesthesis.*

apprehend objects by means of conceptions. Consequently, it cannot be supposed that animals have any definite consciousness of the organic unity of their lives;[1] though it may be allowed that they have a vague apprehension of it, as they have of other objects. The fact, however, that a man has thus a more definite consciousness of himself than a mere animal has, does not constitute a fundamental distinction : since it is only a particular instance of the wider fact that a man has a more definite consciousness of objects in general.

Nor, again, does the fundamental distinction between a man and an animal consist in the fact that the one has, and the other has not, a consciousness of self in the fourth sense. That animals have a certain sense of their individual lives as unities can scarcely be denied. The self-consciousness which they frequently display—their vanity and love of approbation—seems inconsistent with the denial of such a sense. It might, no doubt, be argued that the presence of such a self-consciousness as this in any animal is a sufficient indication that it is not a mere animal, but is in some degree a thinking being; and it might at the same time be pointed out that this is by no means the only indication which we have of the presence of thought in the higher forms of animal life. But it seems at least conceivable that a certain sense of the unity of the individual life, as well as a sense of the unity of the organism,[2] should arise

---

[1] *I.e. mere* animals if there are, or so far as there are, any such beings.

[2] Some may think that this is a distinction without a difference. The difference lies in this, that the mere consciousness of the unity of my organism is the same in kind as my consciousness of the unity of any other organism ; whereas the consciousness of the unity of the individual life is the consciousness of the *me*, the focus of inner reflection which exists for myself alone.

in an animal consciousness even prior to the growth of thought—*i.e.* prior to the formation of definite conceptions of objects. At any rate, in so far as the consciousness of the individual self involves thought, it involves it only because it at the same time involves a consciousness of the self in the fifth sense—*i.e.* a consciousness of the objective unity of our world. It is in this last form of self-consciousness that the most fundamental distinction between man and other animals is to be found; and it is to it, accordingly, that we must chiefly direct our attention.

We might illustrate .the relation of self-consciousness in this sense to the other two kinds of self-consciousness to which we have referred, by considering the aspects from which we may regard any concrete personality, such as that of Shakespeare. We say familiarly that we know Shakespeare, meaning that we are acquainted with his plays; and in this sense we may know him well, though he made no effort to reveal himself in them. In another sense we know almost nothing with regard to Shakespeare except what is to be gathered from his Sonnets; and even with respect to these it has been said by Browning that if Shakespeare revealed himself in them "the less Shakespeare he." In a third sense, again, we know nothing about Shakespeare except a few unreliable stories. We might almost say, in fact, that there were three Shakespeares. There was the Shakespeare who jested at the *Mermaid* and played at the *Globe*, who travelled from Stratford to London and from London to Stratford, and who finally died in 1616.[1] This was

---

[1] Of course, the life of a rational being, even when externally regarded, reveals the fact that he is a thinking personality, and consequently that he exists for himself and has a world in himself. Still, the significance of this inner life does not appear to one who merely regards him as an organic being.

Shakespeare as he was for his contemporaries. Then there was Shakespeare as he was for his own private consciousness, suffering pain and enjoying pleasure, now

> "all alone weeping his outcast state,
> Troubling deaf heaven with his bootless cries,
> Looking upon himself, cursing his fate,
> Wishing himself like one more rich in hope,
> Featured like him, like him with friends possessed,
> Desiring this man's art, and that man's scope,
> With what he most enjoyed contented least";

and then again "singing hymns at heaven's gate," and "scorning to change his state with kings." Shakespeare in this sense no one ever knew or can know fully but himself. Then, finally, there was Shakespeare as he is for eternity —the Shakespearian world, the cosmos of experience which he created for himself, and which he partly revealed to others. Shakespeare might, therefore, be regarded from these three different points of view; and not only so, but he might regard *himself* from each of them, and thus have the consciousness of self in three different senses. The first sense is one which he might share with a dog, in so far as a dog can have an objective consciousness at all. The second sense also is one which might, in a dim manner, belong to such a being; for a dog's heart also may "know its own bitterness" in which a stranger cannot partake. It is in the third sense chiefly that the consciousness of man rises above that of the animal—if an animal is not capable of thought.[1]

When, however, we have distinguished these three senses of self-consciousness, it becomes at once necessary

---

[1] The familiar line, "Self-reverence, self-knowledge, self-control," may be quoted as an illustration of these three senses of the term "self." The self which we control is the animal self: the self which we know is the individual self; the self which we reverence is the ideal or universal self.

to add, so as to prevent misconception, that after all it is not possible to have any one of them fully without having all three. The consciousness of the organism as a unity is a consciousness of a definite object distinguished from and related to other objects; and such a consciousness contains in itself implicitly the consciousness of the world as a systematic whole in which objects are embraced.[1] Further, the consciousness of the organism as a real unity is possible only through the recognition of the focus into which it is reflected, *i.e.* of the fact that all its parts are organically related to a single consciousness. But a being who is capable of realising this, is already aware of the unity of his individual life. Consequently, it is not possible to be fully conscious of the unity of the organism, without being at the same time conscious both of the unity of the individual life and of the unity of the objective world. In like manner, the consciousness of the unity of the individual life may be shown to involve the other two. Indeed, it is evident that it must do so; for the unity of the individual life is recognised by reflection on the unity into which our organic being is reflected, and presupposes the consciousness of that being as a unity. Hence, if the consciousness of the unity of the organic being involves the other two, the consciousness of the unity of the individual life must *a fortiori* involve all three.[2] Not only so, but the reflection by which the unity of the individual life is discovered, is implicitly identical with that by which the

---

[1] For a fuller discussion of this and kindred points, I may refer to Caird's *Critical Philosophy of Immanuel Kant, passim.* (See, for instance, Vol. I., p. 313.)

[2] It is not necessary here to discuss the possibility of an individual consciousness which should not be connected with an animal organism at all; since we are here dealing only with animals and men, in both of which there is such a connection.

ideal of an objective unity is set up. So soon as we learn to regard our individual life as a system, we become conscious also of the demand that everything which enters into that life (and the knowledge of the world enters into it) must be capable of being regarded as an element in a system. We become aware of the unity of the individual life in distinction from, and in relation to, a world of objects; and the consciousness of such a world is consequently an essential element in the consciousness of the individual life. And if that objective world could not be regarded as a system, the individual life also, which is determined in relation to that world, could not be ultimately regarded as a system. Hence, whenever we regard the individual life as a system, we implicitly set up the ideal of a systematic world. Finally, it is evident that the ideal of a systematic world can exist only for a being who is conscious of the unity of his individual life as connected with an organism which is a unity. A systematic world exists only for a being who is at the same time an individual. The Shakespearian world, for instance, although it may be regarded as an objective system which not merely was for Shakespeare, but is for any one who can appropriate it for himself, is yet not an objective system except for some individual consciousness. In itself, it is merely a collection of details, which, without a combining intelligence, would at once become disintegrated and dissolve away into nothingness, and "leave not a rack behind." And the same applies to any system of which we can form a conception. We speak of our physical world, for instance, as a system. We refer to the planets as revolving in their courses, and so on. But it is clear that the world forms such a system as this only for a being who can regard the various parts as separate and yet as existing together. The courses of the planets, so to speak, do not exist for the planets themselves. The planet is at any moment here and not there, now and not then. It exists but from moment to moment and from spot to spot: and its course forms a system only for a being to whom the fact that it *was* there is as real as the fact that it *is* here, and who can thus connect the stages of its being, and see them as a whole. Now such a being is clearly distinct from the system which exists for him. He is a being who is present to all the parts, and who can at once discriminate and synthesise them. Such a being is not merely a system of experiences, but an individual for whom a system is, and apart from whom (or from some similar unity) the system itself would fall to pieces. And that such a consciousness cannot be conceived by us except as connected with an organic life could, I think, without much difficulty be shown.[1]

These reflections lead us to a new difficulty. We have distinguished three different senses of self-consciousness, and have stated that while animals may possess—at least in germ—the first and second kinds, they can hardly be supposed to attain to any degree of the third. But now it begins to appear that the three kinds of self-consciousness imply each other, and cannot be found apart. A little consideration, however, shows that the opposition between these statements is not so great as it at first appears. It seems to be undoubtedly true that self-consciousness in either the first or the second sense is,

---

[1] It is not necessary here to discuss the possibility of an absolute self-consciousness which should not have any individual form of reference. It is enough to point out that, so far as our experience goes, the objective unity of experience is always connected with the subjective unity of an individual consciousness and with the unity of an organic life. For a discussion of the nature of the totality of possible experience as an individual whole, I may refer to Mr. Bradley's *Appearance and Reality*, and to the article on "Mr. Bradley's View of the Self" previously mentioned.

in its full realisation, inconceivable without self-consciousness in the third sense; and it is also true that self-
consciousness in the third sense does not exist apart
from the first and second. But that a certain degree of
the first and second may be realised without the third
seems clear from the fact that, even in the human consciousness, the conception of the world as a system
remains to a great extent latent, whereas self-consciousness in the other two senses is much more frequently
present. This fact, however, appears at first only to
raise another difficulty. For if it be true that self-consciousness in the third sense may remain latent in man,
how can it constitute the distinction between man and
animals—in which also it must be supposed to be, in
some sense, latent? The answer to this question ought
to make the distinction quite clear.

When we consider what is implied in that thoroughly
systematic knowledge in which we can be fairly described
as having formed to ourselves a universe, it is evident
that nothing less is involved in it than the possession of
a completed philosophy. Not only so, but if the distinction between science and philosophy to which we
referred in Chapter I. is a valid one, such a systematic
knowledge would involve not only a completed philosophy, but a completed science also. It would involve
at once a clear understanding of the conceptions which
are involved in knowledge and in the ideal by which
knowledge is necessarily guided, and a clear insight into
the application of these conceptions to all the particular
facts in the world of our experience. Such a systematic
knowledge as this is evidently only an ideal for the
philosophic and scientific intelligence; and indeed we
can scarcely say that it is always clearly present even to
the philosophic and scientific consciousness. For even
to have it clearly present as an ideal involves, if not a

completed science,[1] yet in a sense a completed philosophy. It involves at least a distinct conception of what is to be understood by a systematic unity—a conception which it is by no means easy to reach. It is obvious, therefore, that such knowledge as this, which is only an ideal even for the most advanced philosophic and scientific intelligence, cannot *a fortiori* be regarded as characteristic of the human mind in general, and consequently cannot be that which distinguishes a man from an animal. In ordinary knowledge we neither have our conceptions quite clearly defined with reference to their place within a systematic unity, nor do we work them out into the details of their application to particular kinds of facts. We use them roughly, as suits our practical wants at any given moment. Still, this does not make it any the less true, that the ideal of systematic unity is the characteristic feature of human knowledge. Even such knowledge as we possess in the ordinary conduct of our lives may be fairly said to be *on the way* towards systematic completeness. We think things together, in so far as we bring them under conceptions at all. When we think of one thing as before and another as after, of one as cause and another as effect, or when we think of one thing as plant and another as animal, of one set of things as three and another as four, and so on, we have already introduced a certain degree of system into our world; and every increase which we make in such knowledge as this, is a step towards the development of science which again inevitably leads on to philosophy. But we can easily think of a state of experience which is much lower than the ordinary knowledge that we have now de-

---

[1] Whether a completed philosophy does not presuppose a completed science is a question which we need not here discuss. Cf. *supra*, p. 24.

scribed.[1]   A savage who can only count up to three,
may have a glimmering sense of the difference between
a collection of four things and a collection of five things,
though he cannot describe the difference by means of
any definite conception.   Such a sense as this can
hardly be called knowledge, and yet it is not an intellectual blank.   It is experience without a conception
to give it definiteness.   In such experience the possibility
of conceptions is, no doubt, implied.   That four things
make a different impression from that which five things
make, involves already the potentiality of a definite distinction between the two.   But this definite distinction
remains latent until the conception has become developed.   Now it is such a consciousness as this that we
may suppose to exist in the case of the lower animals.
Impressions group themselves together in their consciousness, so as to have a certain coherence and, to some
extent, to suggest each other, and yet do not form
themselves into objects that can be clearly distinguished
and related.   In such experience, definite systematisation
has not even begun.   It is not even on the way towards
a view of objects as a universe or system; for it has
not even got the length of a view of *objects* at all.

Now if we interpret the animal consciousness in this
way—and it is in some such way that we seem bound
to interpret it—then what we should say is not so much
that animals have the consciousness of self in the first
two senses and are destitute of it in the third sense;
but rather that they have dim impressions and groups
of impressions, which, if they could be made clear, would
be a consciousness of self in the first sense, and that
they have dim senses of agreeableness and disagreeable-

---

[1] At least we can easily form a *negative* conception of such a
state.  To form a positive idea of the content of such an experience
is, no doubt, very difficult.

ness which, if they could be made clear, would amount
to a consciousness of self in the second sense; but that
of the self in the third sense they have not even attained
to a glimpse, since they have not attained to even the
beginnings of systematic knowledge.  In short, what we
ought to say is not so much that animals are unable to
say " I," as that they are unable to say " God ";[1] or, in
other words, that they are not in any degree guided, as
all human intelligence in some degree is, by the consciousness that their universe is a whole.

We thus see in what sense it may be maintained that
man is distinguished from all other animals by the
possession of self-consciousness.  The meaning of this
possession can hardly be better summed up than in the
familiar lines of Goethe—

> " Nur allein der Mensch
> Vermag das Unmögliche;
> Er unterscheidet,
> Wählet und richtet ;
> Er kann dem Augenblick
> Dauer verleihen." [2]

It furnishes us with that kind of knowledge which "is
power," which enables us to stand above the blind
impulses of nature, to master its laws by obeying them,
and so to perform what, from the point of view of mere
nature, would be impossible.  It is the faculty of distinction, choice, and judgment; since it is the faculty
of forming conceptions under which the particulars of
experience are brought.  And it gives eternity to the
moment; since it enables us to connect every moment

[1] Interpreting this term in its philosophical sense of a unity in
which the antithesis between subject and object is reconciled.  Cf.
the opening chapters of Caird's *Evolution of Religion.*

[2] " Man alone can perform the impossible ; he discriminates,
chooses and judges ; he can give to a moment endurance."

with every other, as parts of an abiding system. The importance of this element in human consciousness is thus sufficiently apparent; but what we have now to ask is, whether the possession of it will throw any light on the organic nature of human society. Now I think a very little consideration will suffice to show that it does throw a great deal of light upon it; but in order to make this clear, it will be necessary to indicate the peculiar position which man occupies among other creatures in virtue of this possession.

But, in truth, the main thing to notice about it is, that it is *not* a possession. Γνῶθι σεαυτόν remains, after all, an impossible maxim. One cannot, even after the utmost effort, attain to such a thorough discrimination of the content of consciousness, as to be able to see the universe clearly as a systematic whole; and for the majority of mankind this ideal is so far from being attained, that it is not even consciously aimed at. It is the distinguishing feature of mankind to be progressive; and this fact constitutes, to a great extent, the "open secret" of human life. We are moving upwards—to state it generally—from the simplest form of consciousness to a completely discriminated and systematic experience; from that attitude of mind in which we see ourselves and the rest of the world only as particular things and accidental events, to that in which we see the world as a whole and our own lives as elements in a system. It is chiefly on account of this progressive character of our consciousness that there is, in the full sense, a *history* of human life, whereas of the animals there is only description. The music of humanity is dramatic, while that of the other creatures is idyllic.

> "With Nature never do *they* wage
> A foolish strife."

They have attained the only goal which there is for them

to attain,[1] and are at rest; whereas we have to press towards the mark of a higher calling.[2] Man is, in short, the only creature that has an *ideal—i.e.* the idea of an end. He has caught a glimpse of a kind of consciousness which he has not attained, and which he is bound to strive to attain, just because he has caught a glimpse of it.[3] Having begun to make his knowledge systematic and so to relate one thing to another, he has entered on a process of advancement which cannot stop until he has gone through the whole of science and philosophy, and so made himself completely at home in his world.

[1] *I.e.* the only goal that exists *for them.* If we are entitled in any sense (*e.g.* in that recognised by Mr. H. Spencer) to take a teleological view of the process of animal development, we may say that Nature has in view for animals (as she has for plants) a goal which they have not yet attained. But of this goal they are at least not conscious (or, at any rate, we have no reason to suppose that they are). They may be guided by an *end*, but they are not guided by the *idea of an end.*

[2] Cf. the note on civilisation near the beginning of Chap. VI.

[3] This seems to be the element of truth in the point emphasised so forcibly by Professor Huxley in his recent *Romanes Lecture.* The presence of a conscious ideal in the human mind raises man, in a sense, above the mere cosmic processes of nature. It enables him to pass judgment on these processes, and to estimate their value with reference to the end which he has in view. Thus he may even be led to oppose himself to the process of natural development. But Professor Huxley seems to exaggerate this opposition, for, after all, it can hardly be denied that there is, *in some sense,* the presence of an end, even in unconscious or half conscious natural processes. If Nature is "careless of the single life," she seems at least to be somewhat "careful of the type"; and the care which is exercised in the moral life of mankind differs from this chiefly in the fact that the definite consciousness of his end enables him to give a more precise definition to the type, and to discriminate in the choice of means to its realisation. This is, no doubt, a most important distinction, but one need not, therefore, lose sight of the continuity.

Now in this fact we already begin to see the general ground for the necessity of social life.[1] In the first place, it is tolerably apparent that the mere formation of conceptions could not be carried on without names, and that the use of language is a product of society. But this is a somewhat superficial aspect of the matter; since we might suppose conception to receive objectification in some other way than by the development of signs through the communications of one person to another. A deeper reason is to be found in the mere fact that man is a developing being, rising from sense to thought. He begins with vague impressions and animal impulses, and his whole life is a struggle towards clearness—clearness in the conceptions which he applies to things in knowledge, clearness in the conception of ends which he makes use of in conduct. Such a struggle implies a certain "divine discontent" with the stage which he has at any moment reached, and a straining towards an ideal which is not present.

> "Unless above himself he can
> Exalt himself, how mean a thing is man!"

In this phrase we have the whole gist of his peculiar position expressed. He is the only creature that is "fallen"—fallen from his own ideal—and the history of his life is the history of a struggle to place himself on a

[1] It may perhaps seem that there is something preposterous in this way of approaching the subject; since it makes it appear as if the individual, with his conceptions and ideals, first existed, and then invented society to help him in the formation and retention of these conceptions and ideals. The reason of this apparent inversion is that we are not here pursuing the historical or psychological order of investigation. We start with the finished product—the nature of man as a being guided by conceptions and ideals—and then go on to inquire what are the presuppositions of such a mode of existence.

higher level than that on which he stands. He is conscious, on the one hand, of "thoughts that wander through eternity," of a power which makes the whole world his, and, on the other hand, of feelings and passions which are purely individual and even animal in their origin and nature; and the drama of his life consists in the effort to conquer the latter and turn them into the instruments of his higher life. And thus his existence is "no resting but a moving." "Half dust, half deity," he seems to oscillate between earth and heaven. He is "in doubt to deem himself a god or beast," and cannot in reality deem himself either. He is fighting his way up from the form of a brute to some semblance of divinity. He is growing from consciousness to self-consciousness.

From this we see the need of man for society much more clearly than from the mere use of words. If man were ἢ θεός ἢ θηρίον, his life would have a certain completeness in itself: but an individual human being is not self-sufficient, because he is continually divided against himself. His nature has two sides, which are in a state of internecine war. On the one hand, there is the immediate experience of what is present in sense, the false emphasis of particular facts, the besieging of Eyegate and Eargate by the phenomena of the outer world, together with the ever-pressing requirements of the animal life. On the other hand, there is the "still small voice" of the ideal, which bids us have regard for the Universal; which tells of the True, the Beautiful, and the Good; which urges the mind to "reject the eyes" and view things rather "under the form of eternity"—

"Sich vom Halben zu entwöhnen
Und im Ganzen, Guten, Schönen,
Resolut zu leben."

Now this contrast between the particular and the universal elements within us must always be an unequal one,
so long as the ideal is only an inner voice in the conscience or in the intellectual ambition of the individual,
while the allurements of sense and the confusions of
external impressions are everywhere around. Accordingly,
the microcosm of the individual has to "call in a new
world to redress the balance of the old." It has to
project its ideal into the macrocosm. It has to create
for itself a certain objective embodiment of its own
universality. In short, if man is to become rational, he
must make for himself, or find for himself, a rational
environment.

Now this rational environment he finds ready to his
hand in society; and it is in this way that his vital
relationship to society becomes apparent. "It is certain,"
said Novalis, "that my belief gains infinitely the moment
I can convince another of its truth." This infinite gain
is secured for the more ideal elements in human nature
by the formation of states and communities, in whose
constitutions these elements are more or less distinctly
embodied. The thoughts of an individual are evanescent;
but the laws of a society have a certain endurance.
Ideas come and go, but *litera scripta manet;* and in the
laws and customs which a community establishes, in the
institutions of every sort which societies frame, but most
of all in the great literatures of the world, there is a kind
of insurance for the spiritual treasures of the race. In
them are embalmed our dead selves, which we can thus
both keep with us and use as stepping-stones to higher
things. "One swallow does not make a spring," nor
could the motion of a single ideal principle within an
individual afford the means for the development of a
rational nature. Ideas must be gathered from a thousand
sources; they must be repeated and reverberated from

generation to generation; they must be preserved and mellowed through the course of ages; they must be sifted and refined and moulded into shape, before they can become portions of the wisdom of mankind. "The individual is an abstraction : Humanity is the only reality." It is only through the development of the whole race that any one man can develop.

Such considerations as these may help us to see in some measure how it is that the relation of man to society is intrinsic. "Man is by nature a social animal"—φύσει πολιτικὸν ζῷον—partly, of course, for the same reason that makes cattle gregarious, for the simple preservation of life itself; but chiefly because man is a progressive being, struggling upwards to a higher life than that of sense, and cannot secure the means for such a progress except by a certain objective embodiment of his ideal.[1]

And how easy it is thus to objectify his ideal must be apparent from its universal character. The microcosm of our inner life, which each of us seeks to make clear for himself, is ultimately nothing other than the great world which is for all ; though it unfolds itself for each of us under a somewhat different guise. Our lives are all different, yet they are in essence the same. In our Particular Selves we are external to each other ; in our Individual Selves we live alone ; but in that form of self-realisation which consists in the clearing up and·perfecting of the system of our experience, we are realising what is common to all. Shakespeare's world, Homer's world, Dante's world, Goethe's world, all these have certain individual differences as they stand ; yet they are not entirely external to each other ; they continually intersect and overlap, and he who appreciates any one of them is well on the way towards the appreciation of all. The Nature

---

[1] Cf. Steinthal's *Allgemeine Ethik*, p. 133.

to which they hold up the mirror—the great world which each reproduces within him—is the same for every one; and every one's effort to work himself out to clearness makes clearness easier for every other. In "thinking God's thoughts after •Him," one of us catches one idea and another another; but when we have pieced them all together, the totality which they make will be a single world. Thus every attempt which human beings make to render their ideal clear and to give it an objective embodiment, is a help, not only for their own lives, but for the lives of all other human beings. There is no private property in ideals.[1]

In this way we have reached a somewhat deeper view of the organic nature of society than that from which we started. At the same time, it cannot be said that we have yet made out the fact that its nature is thoroughly organic. We have seen that it is a very indispensable means to the development of our higher life, but we have not seen that it is itself involved in the realisation of our end. In fact, the view which has been, so far, suggested, is rather the reverse of this. The need for society has been based on the imperfection of man's nature; and we have been ready to assent to the Aristotelian *dictum* that, if man were "either a god or a beast" the need for society would not exist. Hence we might expect that, as man approached more nearly to the divine nature, the need for society would become less and less. If this were so, the relation of man to society could not be said to be ultimately an intrinsic one. Now in order that we may see whether it is so or not, we must inquire more fully into the nature of the end which we seek. This, however, is a large subject, and will demand a separate chapter.

[1] Cf. Steinthal's *Allgemeine Ethik*, pp. 452-3.

# CHAPTER IV.

## THE SOCIAL AIM.

THE familiar remark of Aristotle,[1] that society was formed τοῦ ζῆν ἕνεκεν, and that it is continued τοῦ εὖ ζῆν ἕνεκεν, expresses very happily the twofold aim which our social life subserves. It enables us to exist, in opposition to those forces of nature which—as Spinoza tells us—"in-finitely surpass" the individual in power; and it secures for us the highest possible kind of existence. Now on the first of these points there is neither doubt nor diffi-culty; but the second requires both explanation and de-fence. That Life is in some sense a good and Death an evil, even a Pessimist—at least in his unguarded moments—will grant; and that society helps us to sustain life is clear to all. It is, at the lowest, a great co-opera-tive store. But what it is to live well, and whether society makes it more possible, admits of question. Even if we do not believe—as some have believed—that the state of man was better in the days when he was com-paratively free from social bonds—

"When wild in woods the noble savage ran"—

we may still think that social conditions have been only a convenient scaffolding which we must withdraw as we advance. If it is the ladder by which we climb to

[1] *Politics*, I. ii. 8, III. ix. 6, etc.

civilisation, it may yet be a ladder that we ought to remove as soon as we have climbed it. At any rate, the value which we attach to life in society will naturally depend very much on the end at which we suppose mankind to aim. Even Aristotle's firm conviction[1] of the intrinsically social nature of mankind has not prevented him from finding the highest form of life in the exercise of a speculative activity which is comparatively independent of society.[2] Now for a complete discussion of our ultimate end, reference ought to be made to treatises on the subject of Ethics generally.[3] But as it is a subject on which there is still considerable divergence of opinion, it is necessary to indicate at this point the view which I regard as correct, and to state shortly the process by which I am led to it. Let us begin, therefore, by asking what are the different opinions that may be held with regard to the end at which we ought to aim, and what are the arguments by which each of these may be supported.

There are always at least two views possible with respect to any question in Philosophy. We may believe that it cannot be answered, or we may believe that it can. Each of these views is represented in current thought with reference to the nature of that conduct and that condition which constitute *living well*. The view, indeed, that no ultimate account can be given of the

---

[1] *Ethics*, I. ii. 8, IX. ix. 3 ; *Politics*, I. ii. 8 *seq.*, etc.

[2] *Ethics*, X. vii. and viii. ; *Politics*, VII. (IV.) iii. 8, xv. I *seq.* Cf. Newman's edition of the *Politics*, Vol. II., p. 396.

[3] I might refer, for instance, to Green's *Prolegomena to Ethics*, where the point of view adopted is substantially the same as that stated in the present chapter. But it seems necessary to give some justification for the adoption of his point of view rather than any other. Moreover, I am not at all points prepared to accept his mode of statement.

nature of human good, is one that very few are inclined
unflinchingly to hold. The progress of science has led
most of us to believe that everything—*except just everything*—can be explained. All particular facts seem ex-
plicable, and only the totality unaccountable. The veriest
Agnostic thinks that he knows quite well what he wants
to be at in his social life. Yet there are still a few who
believe that the principles by which we are guided in
conduct, and by which human progress is determined, are
by their nature for us inexplicable. Some refer them to
an arbitrary will of God, and a much larger number
would be disposed to trace them back, in a purely empirical way, to certain results of a process of evolution,
of which a complete explanation is not attainable, and
which, from the point of view of human knowledge, is
entirely accidental. On the other hand, the more common opinion is that these principles can be in some way
explained by a reference to human nature, that they may
be accounted for by means of the effort after happiness
or perfection, or some other equally intelligible aim, whose
meaning can be precisely defined.

Now, as man is by his very nature a rational being,
"we divine"—as Aristotle would have said—that the end
which he seeks is likely to be an intelligible one ; and we
are inclined to revert to the contrary opinion only on
condition that every intelligible explanation can be shown
to break down. Yet before we proceed to examine these
intelligible explanations, it may be well to cast a glance
in passing at the opinions of those who think that no
such explanation is possible. Of these *ethical Agnostics*,
as we may call them, there are, broadly speaking, two
kinds. When the moral life is conceived as inexplicable,
it is of course not thought of as something spectral which
starts into being no one can guess how, but is referred to
the direction of some power, though a power that is for

us unintelligible. And that power may be supposed to be either intelligent or unintelligent. That is to say, we may refer the origin of our moral being either to the will of God or to what may be called the unconscious will of nature. It will be most convenient to look at the latter opinion first.

In considering this view, we have to deal rather with certain ἔνδοξα, which have been generated in men's minds by the prevalent theory of evolution, than with any precisely formulated doctrine. Still, the existence of such ἔνδοξα deserves at least to be noticed. The idea of the "struggle for existence" has given rise to a view of moral and social life—as of life in general—which refers it simply to the predominance of certain forces which have happened at particular times to be the strongest. According to this view, there is nothing in the inherent nature of man by which his social and moral aims can be rationally explained. They are merely the resultants of tendencies which for him are accidental; tendencies which have been fostered by his particular environment, and which with a different environment would have been developed in a different way. Those who support this view point, in illustration of its truth, to the diversity of moral sentiments among different races of mankind, to the apparent absence of such sentiments among primitive peoples, and to the changes which they undergo in correspondence with the changes of outward circumstances and social conditions. There can be no doubt that some such conception is at the present time very pre-valent in popular thought; and it ought not to be over-looked in any consideration of the subject. But there are two reasons which make it unnecessary to discuss it at any length. In the first place, it has never—so far as I am aware—been worked out in any scientific form that can lay claim to serious attention. If, indeed, one could attribute it to Mr. Herbert Spencer, it would be worth while to examine it with some thoroughness. The opinions of so ingenious a speculator are always worth considering. But though Mr. Spencer is probably responsible, more than any other single individual, for the spread of the opinion to which I am referring, yet he has himself given in his allegiance to a distinctly teleological theory, and considers the development of life or the realisation of pleasure—which, indeed, he regards as ultimately identical[1]—to be the final end. In the second place, as the essence of the present doctrine consists in its assertion of the intrinsic unreasonableness of the moral life of humanity, the best refutation of it will be found in the working out of a doctrine which shall establish the reasonableness of that life. In the meantime, therefore, it may be sufficient to remark that its plausibility is due to the fact that superficial variations are apt to attract more attention than fundamental agreements. One who looked merely at the external aspect of the lives of individuals, who saw merely the diversities of their circumstances and occupations, the various vicissitudes of their fortunes, the diseases and accidents of all sorts, by which they are visited, and by the wear and tear of which they eventually die, might be disposed to conclude that the lives of men are very dissimilar. Yet the physiologist knows that the conditions of life and death are quite definitely ascertainable. So, too, it may be shown that the conditions of moral life

[1] The precise relation between these two ends is not very obvious in Mr. Spencer's doctrine. It is, I think, more clearly brought out in Mr. Leslie Stephen's *Science of Ethics*, and in Mr. S. Alexander's *Moral Order and Progress*, where the latter of the two ends—pleasure—is definitely subordinated to the former—life (of which the perfection is conceived under the idea of health or equilibrium).

are fundamentally determinable, and capable of 'a rational justification, in spite of the superficial variations which it is possible for them to undergo. The establishment of this, however—in so far as it can be undertaken at all in such an Essay as this—belongs to the sequel.

The view, again, that the nature of the moral life is determined by what for us is an arbitrary will of God, would at no very distant past have been deserving of more attention, since it has been held by a large and influential school of moralists. According to these thinkers, there are certain ultimate principles involved in our moral life, with respect to which it is in vain to inquire farther. We "must not look a gift horse in the mouth." Our constitution has been made for us by the will of our Creator, and all that we are entitled to do is to fulfil those requirements which we find plainly imprinted within it, asking no questions for conscience' sake. This view could quite well be maintained in conjunction with that previously mentioned; since it might easily be supposed that the course of evolution has been so engineered by an over-ruling Providence as to produce a predetermined result. And this modification frees it from some of the objections which have been urged; since it does, as so interpreted, recognise a kind of teleology. It is not so obviously at variance with any reasonableness that may be shown to exist in the moral consciousness. Divine reason may be used to explain what human reason has no concern in. This whole way of thinking, however, is steadily losing its hold on men's minds; and that not only in the case of those who are deserting the theological attitude which it implies, but even of those who cling to their religious convictions most firmly. And for this there is good reason. For it seems clear that there are *some* kinds of moral obligation

O

which are derived, not from any inborn moral sense, but from the consideration of an end to be attained. Thus, such duties as that of self-culture, or of promoting the happiness of others, are understood with varying limitations, and are insisted on with varying degrees of force, just in proportion to the desirableness of the end which they subserve. But if it be allowed that the idea of an End or Good to be achieved gives rise to any moral obligations—however few—it can hardly be denied that a *system of obligations* must spring out of the idea of the *Summum Bonum*, or what is best upon the whole. Otherwise, if there were only a number of particular ends, and no system of ends, we should have an infinity of possibly conflicting obligations springing out of the infinite varieties of possible good.[1]   Now, if we had a code of duties springing from the idea of a *Summum Bonum* and also a code of duties given by the moral sense independently of this idea, we should have two distinct codes of duty which, except on the elaborate assumption of some " Pre-established Harmony " between them, might be expected at any moment to come into conflict.   We should thus be in continual danger of being reduced, not indeed to Dr. Reid's "miserable dilemma whether it is better to be a fool or a knave," but to the still more miserable one whether it is better to be a knave or a scoundrel—whether it is better to act contrary to our perception of what is good or contrary to our sense of

---

[1] Thus—to illustrate from only a single kind of end—if it were allowed that the happiness of others is a good to be sought, there are some thousand millions of human beings in the world whose happiness we might seek to promote ; and there is, moreover, an almost infinite variety of ways in which the happiness of any one of them might be promoted.   Such an end, therefore, leaves us with a great number of possible alternatives, and we require some *highest* end—such as "the greatest happiness of the greatest number "—to guide us in our choice.

what is right. Such a dilemma might, indeed, be avoided on the supposition that, in cases of conflict, one of the two codes must always yield to the other. It might be said, for instance, that it is our duty to seek the highest good only in case the pursuit of this end does not interfere with the fulfilment of those moral obligations which are otherwise made known to us. But it is evident that such a complex conception of duty hardly corresponds to that simplicity and directness of moral insight which this view, above all others, is bound to provide for us. If it has to be hedged in with a number of minute qualifications, it loses that *primâ facie* plausibility which is almost its only merit. It is partly for such reasons as these that this theory has now become discredited; though more is due to the fact that the possibility of working out other theories, which rest on a rational basis, has become more apparent. Accordingly, we may proceed without further preamble, to examine these more rational theories.

Certainly, whatever may be the case with respect to Ethics in general, it can hardly be doubted that, in the case of our social aims, what we seek is some definitely ascertainable end, which we recognise as good, and not something that we are impelled to by unintelligible impulses. Hence we find Utilitarian writers informing us with a certain air of triumph that "whatever may be thought of the principle of Utility, when considered as the foundation of morals, no one now-a-days will undertake to deny that it is the only safe rule of legislation"; and if we understand by the "principle of Utility" nothing more than what the words would naturally imply—*i.e.* the principle that our rule of conduct must be to do that, and that only, which is *useful* as a means towards the attainment of some end recognised as good—the truth of the above statement would have to be at once acknowledged not only with reference to legislation, but to the whole of our conduct in social life.  It seems clear that in endeavouring to contribute to the progress of society, we seek, and ought to seek, some definite good, whose nature is capable of being clearly stated, and which commends itself to us as something that it is worth while to aim at realising.  We have now to ask, therefore, what this definite good is which we ought to pursue.

Aristotle tells us, as we saw already,[1] that in his time nearly every one agreed that the good is happiness (εὐδαιμονία); and in our time also there would probably be a general consensus of opinion on this point, 'if by happiness we mean—as Aristotle meant—nothing more than the well-being of persons, including their well-doing. And for such a consensus there is clearly good ground. For if the end is not the well-being of persons, what other alternatives are there?  The only alternatives are to suppose either that the end is something entirely different from the well-being of persons, or that it is something which includes that well-being as one of its constituent elements, but includes also something more. Let us examine each of these in turn.

Is it conceivable that the good for such a being as man should be a purely objective one—*i.e.* that it should lie entirely outside of the conscious nature of human beings themselves?  Certainly there is only one end that has ever been thought to constitute such a good, and that is the realisation of a divine purpose in the world; and even in that good the well-being of persons has usually been supposed to form an indispensable part. Let us assume, however, that the fulfilment of a divine purpose is the real good which we ought to seek, and that in that good human well-being is only accidentally

---

[1] p. 134.

involved. We have then to ask—What is the motive which induces us to regard the realisation of that divine purpose as the highest good? Now we might answer that we are led to seek it because we see it to be / reasonable, or because we believe that by such a pursuit ∿ we shall reach our own truest happiness, or escape ⸚ certain penalties which are attached to its neglect. But it is clear that such answers as these are inconsistent with the view that the realisation of the divine purpose is the end *primarily* or *in its own right.* According to the view which such answers express, the real good is the realisation of what is reasonable, or the attainment of happiness, or the escape from punishment; and the fulfilment of the divine purpose is regarded as a good only in so far as it is a means to these, or in so far as it is the particular content which satisfies their require-ments. If this fulfilment is to be taken as itself the end, we must be able to show, not merely that it is a means to something else which we recognise as good, but that it is in itself that which our nature craves as its highest end. But this, again, it is clear that we could show only by showing that the realisation of such a purpose is in some sense involved in our own nature, as the complement of our energies, or the ideal after which we strive; and thus the end would not be a purely objective one after all. If not something actually in our nature, it is at least something which is implied in our nature; and the realisation of it would be in a sense our happiness. It can, in short, be shown to be the good for us only by being shown to be that which would satisfy the demands of our nature; and what satisfies the demands of our nature is what we under-stand by happiness.

It is clear, also, that similar remarks would apply in the case of the other alternative that we have suggested

—viz., that the good is something which includes personal well-being, but includes something more. The
" something · more " which is included would require also
to be somehow involved in our nature, or it could not
be for us an end. Consequently it would not, in reality,
be something more at all : it would be a necessary part
of our well-being. A few examples may suffice to make
this clear.

Let us suppose, for instance, that the good consisted
in the realisation of Reason or Order in the world, including its realisation in ourselves. This is the most
purely objective end that we could well propose for
ourselves; and certainly it is one that has, *primâ facie*,
a good deal to be said for it. Now, under what conditions could this be regarded as our end? Let us first
understand precisely what it would be that on this
supposition we seek to attain. It is clear that the Order
or Reason which we sought to impose on the world
could not be the same as the Order or Reason which
we already *find* in it. . In a sense it may be said that
Order is already realised in the world. Everything is
disposed in accordance with certain definite laws, and
forms part of a determined totality or rational system.

> " The world was made in order,
>   And the atoms march in tune."

In this sense we might maintain, as some have mis-
takenly thought that Hegel did, that "the Actual is the
Rational." But it is evident that *this* rational cannot be
the rational which we seek to realise by our conduct.
That rational is not something that we find in the actual, ✓
but something that we want to impose on it. It belongs to the category of the " Sollen," and not of the
" Seyn." It is not something which our mind perceives,
but something which our nature craves. It is, therefore,

in a manner subjective. It is true that it may not be
a want which we as individuals feel; it may not be a
present *wish*, and in that sense may not be subjective;
but it is at least a want of our rational nature, or we
could not regard it as a good for us. Now it is conceivable that the rational in this sense might be taken
as our end, *i.e.* we might take it as our end to conform
the world to our own image as reasonable beings, endeavouring at the same time to complete our own
conformation to that image. As it has sometimes been
held that God created the world in order to reveal
Himself through it, so it might be held that the good
for us is to take the world as we find it actually created,
and so to use it as to render it, as far as possible, a
revelation of *ourselves*, *i.e.* of our rational nature. It
might be thought that Nature had ushered us into the
world with an injunction like that which Goethe gave to
his readers at the commencement of *Wilhelm Meister's
Travels*[1]—"Stamp it like thyself, my Son!"—taking
care at the same time to make *our own* stamp a distinct
one. But it is clear that the good could not, on this
supposition, be regarded as a purely objective one. We
should seek to impose Reason on the world, only on
the ground that the realisation of *our own* rational
nature demands such an imposition. In this case also
the end would, in reality, lie within us. And it is
evident that the same line of reasoning would apply to
the attempt to realise Beauty, or any similar end, in the
external world. We cannot take any interest in the
external world unless it in a manner comes home to
us—unless we see, in some way, that its good is what
our own nature wants.

The same remarks apply, *mutatis mutandis*, to the realisation of Life as an end. Of all objective ends this is

[1] As translated by Carlyle.

the one which most naturally suggests itself, and it is the one which has been actually adopted by many writers of the evolutionist school. If all evolution is tending in the direction of the development of the highest kind of life, it would seem that such a development is the end which nature seeks; and it is natural to infer that it is also the end which we ought to seek. It is true that it is not very easy to define precisely what the end in question is.[1] But if we adopt, for example, such a definition as that of Mr. Spencer, that Life consists in a "continuous adjustment of internal relations to external relations," it is evident that we might take it as our end to make the adjustment more and more perfect. But in that case we have still to ask—What is the *motive* that leads us to take this as our end? For, of course, we are not now dealing with the doctrine that we are unconsciously driven towards it. The *fact* that Life realises itself in the world, that adjustments *do actually* become continually more and more perfect, cannot of itself supply us with a motive to seek its realisation,[2] any more than the fact that there is Order or Reason in the world gives us a motive to seek the realisation of them. The endeavour to make our lives more perfect is certainly at least a part of our aim; but what urges us to seek this perfection cannot be the mere objective fact[3] that there is a tendency in nature towards a continually more perfect adjustment. What urges us to it is rather a demand of our own nature itself—"More life and fuller, that I *want*." And to explain this want we must look within.

We see then that there is good ground for the common

---

[1] Cf. Sidgwick's *Methods of Ethics*, p. 395 (3rd Edition).

[2] Cf. *Mind*, Vol. I., pp. 56-7, and Sidgwick's *Methods of Ethics*, p. 76. See also Professor Huxley's *Romanes Lecture*.

[3] It may be that fact *as it comes to self-consciousness in us;* but with this view we are not now concerned.

opinion that the ultimate end is the happiness or well-being of persons. It must be found in something which lies within us, or which can be brought into relation to our consciousness of self so as to satisfy the demands of our nature.[1] But this conclusion is a very indefinite one. We are still very far from having reached a clear conception of the nature of that happiness which constitutes our ultimate end; and we must, accordingly, again set out with the question—What are the various views? Our nature is complex; and even if our end must be something which satisfies its demands, it still seems as if it might conceivably be one or other of a great variety of things.

But though our nature is complex, we can analyse it into a reasonably small number of separate aspects. It is clear, to begin with, that as the good of which we are in search is one that we recognise in our conscious activities, it must be something that is involved in our conscious, and not merely in our physiological, being. The latter kind of end would still be what we have called an objective end; and such an end we have already rejected. Now our conscious nature has three main aspects or elements. Knowledge, Will, and Feeling are commonly taken as exhausting the possible attitudes of our mind; and, though this division is undoubtedly open to some criticism, it may still be accepted as sufficiently accurate for our present purpose.[2] We occupy a receptive attitude towards the external world; or we react upon it;

---

[1] Cf. Sidgwick's *Methods of Ethics*, p. 394 *seq.*, and Green's *Prolegomena*, p. 407.

[2] Cf. Art. "Psychology" in *Encyclopaedia Britannica*, Vol. XX., p. 39; Dewey's *Psychology*, pp. 15-21; Lotze's *Microcosmus* (English Translation), Vol. I., pp. 177-181; Lipps, *Grundtatsachen des Seelenlebens*, p. 19 *seq.*, etc. See also Bradley's *Appearance and Reality*, pp. 459-482, and cf. *Mind*, New Series, Vol. III., No. 11, pp. 328-9.

or we are simply aware of a certain harmony or disharmony in our own inner being, in its relations to an
external world. We never, it is true, stand exclusively in
any one of these attitudes towards our world. Our re-
ception is partly creation; our reactions are stimulated
by our feeling; and feeling cannot exist without our per-
ceiving or willing. The various elements of our mental
life do not occur apart; they cannot be separated, as two
pieces of matter may be cut away from each other, or
even as two parts of a living body may be taken as independent members. Still, they are different aspects of
the totality of our conscious nature, and as such may be,
for such purposes as the present, regarded as distinguishable elements. It might be supposed, then, that one or
other of these elements involves within it the end which
our nature seeks : or it might be supposed that to get a
complete view of our end we must take two or more of
these elements together : or it might be supposed, finally,
that when we dissect our nature into these elements, we
are in reality murdering it; and that the end is to be
discovered rather by a consideration of our nature as a
whole, of which these elements are only particular and
inseparable aspects. There are thus, broadly speaking,
five possible alternatives—(1) The end may be some form
of Knowledge; (2) it may be some form of Will; (3)
it may be some form of Feeling; (4) it may be some
combination of these; (5) it may be some realisation of
our conscious nature as a whole. We will now endeavour to deal with each of these in succession.

I. It is plain, on a very slight consideration, that the
end cannot be found in the cognitive element of our
nature as such. It is true that in the acquisition of knowledge, and still more in the acquisition of clearness of insight, there is a certain satisfaction of our nature. We
speak of "knowledge for its own sake," and there are

few ambitions that are capable of exciting in us a more ardent devotion than the pursuit of truth. We feel that we can go with Solomon when he tells us—"Happy is the man that findeth wisdom, and the man that getteth understanding." But we are aware at the same time that the statement requires some justification; it is not quite one of those things that "go without saying"; and we are glad, therefore, to find him immediately adding—"Length of days is in her right hand, and in her left hand riches and honour. Her ways are ways of pleasantness." And when we are told in another passage that—"In much wisdom is much grief; and he that increaseth knowledge increaseth sorrow"—or when we are informed by Burns that—

> " It's no' in books, it's no' in lear,
>   To make us truly blest.
> If happiness have not her seat
>   And centre in the breast,
> We may be wise or rich or great,
>   But never can be blest"—

we become conscious at once that *if* wisdom did not make us blest, *if* the increase of knowledge merely increased our sorrow, such an advancement could not be the achievement of our good.[1] Indeed Milton and others have represented that being who is supposed, more than any other, to have failed in the attainment of any worthy end, as by no means destitute of knowledge, or even of a kind of wisdom. And even if it be maintained that a deeper insight would have enabled such a being to attain his end, still the very fact that we separate these two things—insight and the attainment of the end —the very fact that we say that wisdom is the infallible *means* to the end, shows at once that we do not regard wisdom as of itself *constituting* the end. Wisdom cannot

[1] Cf. Sidgwick's *Methods of Ethics*, p. 396.

be the same thing as happiness, or the question would not be possible—which yet obviously is possible—Does wisdom necessarily bring happiness with it? Even if it be true that we must ultimately answer this question in the affirmative, yet the very fact that the question can be put—the fact that it is not manifest nonsense to state it—shows that we do not, and indeed cannot, regard wisdom, apart from the other elements of our nature, as in itself the good.

II. Again, Will of itself cannot contain the end. There is even a certain absurdity in setting up Will as an end: for to will is to seek an end, and it seems preposterous to say that the end is to seek an end. In that case we should still have to ask—What is this other end that we seek? and *that*, and not the seeking of it, would be the ultimate end. Otherwise we land ourselves either in a palpable absurdity or in a *circulus in definiendo*. Green, indeed, while recognising the difficulty in any theory which regards the good will as the end, yet holds that the difficulty is not fatal to the theory; and as this opinion seems contrary to what we have just been saying, it may be well to quote the passage in which the statement is made. "It is as well," he says,[1] "to confess at once that, when we are giving an account of an agent whose development is governed by an ideal of his own perfection, we cannot avoid speaking of one and the same condition of will alternately as means and as end. The goodness of the will or man as a means must be described as lying in direction to that same goodness as an end. For the end is that full self-conscious realisation of capabilities to which the means lies in the self-conscious exercise of the same capabilities—an exercise of them in imperfect realisation, but under the governing idea of the desirability of their fuller realisation. If we

[1] *Prolegomena to Ethics*, III. ii., § 195 (p. 205).

had knowledge of what this fuller realisation would be, we might so describe it as to distinguish it from that exercise of them in less complete development which is the means to that full realisation. We might thus distinguish the perfection of man as end from his goodness as means to that end, though the perfection would be in principle identical with the goodness, differing from it only as the complete from the incomplete. But we have no such knowledge of the full realisation. We know it only according to the measure of what we have so far done or are doing for its attainment. And this is to say that we have no knowledge of the perfection of man as the unconditional good, but that which we have of his goodness or the good will, in the form which it has assumed as a means to, or in the effort after, the unconditional good; a good which is not an object of speculative knowledge to man, but of which the idea— the conviction of there being such a thing—is the influence through which his life is directed to its attainment." I quote this passage at length chiefly in order to make it apparent that though the charge of "moving in a circle" may be obviated, yet it can be obviated only by the introduction of certain conceptions which, from our present point of view, would be illegitimate. For, according to the view stated by Green, the good will is to be regarded as the highest good, not because it is the good will—not because it is the most desirable thing in its own right—but because it is the only expression known to us of that which *on other grounds* must be regarded as the highest good. In this case there is not, it is true, a *circulus in definiendo*, but only because the will *as will* is not taken as the ultimate end. If it *were* taken as the end, I see no way in which the charge of "moving in a circle" could be avoided. It appears, then, that Will cannot be taken as the end, any more than Knowledge can. At the same time it must be allowed that "we divine" that it is more nearly correct to say that the end lies in Will than that it lies in Knowledge. For there is a certain apparent absurdity in asking whether a man who wills in a perfect way is realising his highest end, which there is not (at least *primâ facie*) in asking the corresponding question with reference to a man who knows in a perfect way, or who has perfect insight. But then if we are told that a man wills in a perfect way, we naturally go on to inquire— *what* does he will? and *why* does he will it? and until we have received an answer to these questions, we are conscious that we do not yet know what his end is. We feel, in fact, that the end must somehow be involved in the good will, but we feel at the same time that the good will does not of itself bring its own explanation with it, that it has reference to something beyond itself —something which *is willed*, and that we require to know something more about it. If we will perfectly, we must be on the way to what we want; but to will perfectly is not itself what we want.

III. Is our ultimate good, then, to be found in Feeling? Can we suppose that the end consists in the attainment of pleasure or the avoidance of pain?[1] It is important

[1] I follow the common practice of using the terms Pleasure and Pain to denote agreeable and disagreeable feelings, though I think it unfortunate that words so ambiguous should have come to be used in that way. Pain, in its most ordinary acceptation, means a certain kind of organic sensation, and this is clearly something quite different from disagreeable feeling, though it is certainly one of the most striking instances of a consciousness which is disagreeable. Thus, when Mr. Leslie Stephen says (*Science of Ethics*, p. 42) that "nobody who has ever had a toothache will deny that he avoids pain," he is evidently referring to a particular kind of organic sensation. See *Encyclopaedia Britannica*, Art. "Psychology," p. 40. A somewhat similar ambiguity attaches to the term Pleasure. (Cf. Alexander's *Moral Order and Progress*, p. 203.)

to consider this view of the good as carefully as possible, and that for a variety of reasons. It is a very plausible view; it has been held by a very large and influential school in England : and in particular, it has been applied with great confidence in dealing with social and political questions. I believe, moreover, that the consideration of it will lead us into the very heart of our subject. It may be as well to say at once that the view appears to me to be an entirely mistaken one, due to a confusion of thought; and I must accordingly endeavour to make my objections to it as clear as possible. But, as a preliminary step, I will endeavour to state the view in the form in which it seems to me most plausible. As Knies has well said—"In the realm of scientific inquiry, whoever wishes to be victorious must in the first place allow his antagonist to come forward with all his armour on, and in his full force." This is what we must now attempt to do, as far as it is possible within our present limits.

In the first place, then, it seems clear that if we are thoroughly satisfied we must have thoroughly attained our end : while if we are thoroughly dissatisfied we have evidently not attained it. If I am perfectly pleased it is in vain for me to protest that I have not attained what my nature craves; if there were any craving left within me, however faint, it is impossible that I could be perfectly satisfied. Similarly, if another person is perfectly pleased, it is in vain for me to try to persuade him that he has not attained what his nature craves, unless I can at the same time succeed in displeasing him. On the other hand, if anyone is thoroughly displeased, it is plain that he has not got what his nature demands; if he had even in a slight degree got that, he would at least in a slight degree be satisfied. To be thoroughly satisfied is to realise everything which we are conscious of as a want : to be thoroughly dissatisfied is to fail entirely to realise our conscious wants. Now, the good for such a being as man must surely be something at which he, with more or less clear consciousness, aims. Consequently, a man who is thoroughly satisfied must have attained his good, and a man who is thoroughly dissatisfied must have failed to attain it. So far, all seems clear.

Again, life does not consist of a single moment; and if its end is to be thoroughly realised, it must be realised throughout the whole of it. Hence, if we are thoroughly to realise our end, we ought to be thoroughly satisfied at every moment of our existence. And since mankind may be regarded as constituting a single whole—indeed, on reflection, *must* be so regarded—it follows that if mankind is to completely attain its end, all human beings must be thoroughly satisfied during every moment of their lives.

As a matter of fact, however, such an ideal as this is clearly unattainable. No one is at any moment thoroughly pleased or thoroughly displeased : our satisfaction varies from moment to moment : and while one man is happy, another is miserable. Hence, if we know only that to attain our end is to attain a perfect and lasting satisfaction for all, we know only that our end is unattainable. If the ideal is to be of any use for practical guidance, therefore, we require some criterion by which we can distinguish between a more and less complete realisation of it. Now, such a criterion seems to be easily got. Instead of the complete satisfaction of a moment, let us say the greatest satisfaction which is at that moment attainable : instead of the satisfaction of every moment, let us say the satisfaction of as many moments as possible : and instead of the satisfaction of everyone, let us say the satisfaction of the largest number within our reach. We thus arrive at the conception of "the greatest happiness of the greatest number" as the end—that happiness being measured with respect both to its intensity and to its duration. This conception supplies us with the basis of a Hedonistic calculus, which can then be worked out with any required degree of refinement.

This is, broadly, what modern Utilitarians have to say —"Nur mit ein bischen andern Worten"—and it must be allowed that it is a very pretty piece of theorising, and looks on the surface as sound as could be wished. Also, if theories are to be judged by their fruits, there is surely none which has so much to show. The Utilitarian principle is supposed to have revolutionised the theory of legislation, and to be slowly influencing the practice of it; and the doctrine of "Final Utilities" in Economics, and of "Utilities" in general, which has been a source of so much clearness and suggestiveness, has—as commonly stated—an obviously hedonistic reference. A theory with so good credentials cannot be lightly thrown aside.

Yet, if it be true that the Utilitarian theory "admits of no answer," it seems clear at the same time that it "produces no conviction." From the first day when the doctrine was propounded down to the present, the moral consciousness of unsophisticated men has steadfastly rebelled against it: and such a general dissatisfaction as this can hardly be disregarded by a theory which considers satisfaction to be the end. It is true that this dissatisfaction may turn out to be due merely to a confusion of thought; but in the meantime the fact that dissatisfaction exists is one that deserves attention. Now it may be observed, to begin with, that the dissatisfaction, as commonly expressed, does not consist in an utter repudiation of a certain element of happiness (in

P

the sense of pleasure or enjoyment) in the attainment of the ultimate good. Even such a writer as Carlyle, who was so intensely scandalised by what he called "the Pig Philosophy," was quite willing to allow that what seemed to him the highest good for man might fairly be characterised as "blessedness."[1] But there are two points in the Utilitarian theory which have always provoked the antagonism of the ordinary moral sense—(1) the idea that pleasure *alone* constitutes the good, and (2) the idea that mere *quantity* of pleasure is the measure of our attainment of the good.[2] Men in whom the moral con- ✔

---

[1] Cf. also Bradley's *Ethical Studies*, p. 83, *International Journal of Ethics*, Vol. iv., No. 3, pp. 381 and 386, and Vol. v., No. 2, p. 221. I may remark here that it is open to doubt whether Carlyle intended his "blessedness" to imply a state of pleasant feeling at all. He seems on the whole to have meant nothing more than the consciousness of doing right, and it is not certain that this is always a state of pleasure. At anyrate, the use which Mill makes in his *Utilitarianism* of this expression of Carlyle, as involving the admission that the highest good is some sort of pleasant feeling, seems to me to contain a total perversion of Carlyle's meaning. At the best (*i.e.* assuming even that Carlyle did intend his "blessedness" to imply some sort of pleasure) it is as if some one were to take the Stoical assertion that "the wise man alone is rich," and interpret it as implying that riches are, in some sense, the chief good. Similarly, I cannot regard the statement of Professor Marshall (*Elements of Economics*, p. 37, Note), to the effect that Carlyle "used the word pain in a narrow sense, in which it excludes moral and æsthetic pain," as a correct representation of Carlyle's meaning. I think he made it abundantly evident, in various parts of his writings, that he entirely rejected pleasure and pain, *in any sense*, as either the constituents or the criteria of good and evil; even if it be the case (which is doubtful) that he admitted a certain kind of pleasure to be a necessary element in the supreme good.

[2] Of course, I do not add the common notion that the Utilitarian theory involves *selfishness*, because that objection—when applied to most of the more recent developments of the doctrine—is due to an obvious misunderstanding. Yet it must be admitted that the transition from the pleasure of the individual to that of mankind remains still a very obscure point in the Utilitarian theory. Cf. *infra*, p. 234 *seq.*

sciousness is strong, are in general willing to allow that if any one has attained his highest end he must, at least under normal conditions, have a certain happiness, *i.e.* a certain sense of enjoyment, and that of an intense order; but they are seldom ready to believe that the mere fact of one's being happy constitutes the attainment of a worthy end; they think that one must not only be happy, but *deserve* to be happy. Kant's two-fold end—that of meriting happiness and receiving it—would be at once accepted by the moral consciousness as satisfactory; but not the Utilitarian single one—that of receiving it merely. A perfectly virtuous man in Hell could scarcely be supposed to have attained to the supreme good; but neither could one who enjoyed the Beatific Vision and yet remained selfish in the midst of it (if such a combination were conceivable). Again, the ordinary moral consciousness recognises different *qualities* of satisfaction, as well as different degrees; and believes that a man may have attained to a very high degree of enjoyment of a particular kind, and yet be very far off from the realisation of his highest end. Mill, with his usual sympathetic insight, perceived this difficulty in the way of the Utilitarian theory, and, with his usual facility in making compromises, introduced the notion of qualitative differences between pleasures: but in this departure he has had few followers; and his position may now be regarded as an "überwundener Standpunkt," since it is now generally admitted that such a distinction is entirely inconsistent with Utilitarian principles.[1] Such, then, are the ἔνδοξα with which Utilitarianism conflicts. I have thought it the more desirable to refer to them here, because it seems to me that it is precisely on these

[1] Cf. Sidgwick's *Methods of Ethics*, p. 89; Green's *Prolegomena*, p. 168 *seq.*; Bradley's *Ethical Studies*, p. 106 *seq.*; Edgeworth's *New and Old Methods of Ethics*, pp. 25-6.

points that the Utilitarian doctrine is most weak theoretically as well as most unsatisfactory morally. I will now proceed to state what appear to me to be the most fatal objections against it.

The objections to the Utilitarian theory may be conveniently arranged under the following heads :—(1) Even if the attainment of the end consists in perfect pleasure, it does not follow that the *greatest* pleasure is the nearest approximation to the attainment of the end; (2) It is not clear that pleasure admits of quantitative measurement at all with reference to its intensity; (3) It *is* clear that pleasure cannot be summed with reference to its duration; (4) If pleasure is the end, the pleasure of others cannot be an end for us; (5) The Utilitarian standard is not of any practical use; (6) The idea that pleasure is the end at all appears to be due to a confusion of thought.

1. On the first point it is unnecessary to insist at any length, since it is tolerably apparent on the surface. Suppose we have 100 balls, 90 black and 10 white. If we put them all into a box, it is clear that the 10 white balls must be included in the number. If we put 99 into the box, it is clear that at least 9 of the white balls must be included. In the same way, if we put in 98, there must be at least 8 white balls in the number; and so on, until we come down to the number 90, after which the white balls may or may not be included. After this point, also, *any number* of the white balls may be included among those that are placed in the box, until we bring the total number down to 9, at which point it is clear that there cannot be more than 9 white balls included. So too, if we put only 8 balls in, there cannot evidently be more than 8 white; and so on. Between the numbers 1 and 9, therefore, we know that there cannot be *more* than certain definite numbers of

the white balls included; between the numbers 91 and
100, we know that there cannot be *less* than certain
definite numbers; while between the numbers 10 and
90, it is quite uncertain how many, or whether any, of
the white balls are present.   The only points of absolute
certainty are the numbers 0 and 100.   If we put no
balls in, we know that none of the white balls has been
put in: if we put all the balls in, we know that all the
white balls have been put in.   The case of our satisfactions is similar.   If all our wants are satisfied, we
know that those wants which constitute our ultimate end
must have been satisfied among the rest: if none of our
wants is satisfied, we know that the wants which constitute our ultimate end cannot have been satisfied: but
between these extremes all is left in uncertainty.   A man
may be very much satisfied, and yet his balls may all
be black: the satisfactions may all belong to the lower
parts of his nature.   A man may be very little satisfied,
and yet he may have got all the white, or a very
considerable number of them; most of the really important needs, which constitute the ultimate demands
of his nature, may be included among those that he
has satisfied.   Hence it does not appear that a quantitative estimate of pleasure would necessarily give any
real clue to the extent to which we have achieved our
end, even if it be granted that the achievement of our
end implies the attainment of pleasure, and that the
attainment of perfect pleasure implies the perfect achievement of our end.

2. But, in the second place, there is no evidence that
pleasures are commensurable at all.   The evidence
seems all to point rather in the opposite direction.   We
are aware, it is true, that some pleasures are more intense
than others; just as we are aware that some tempera-
tures are higher than others, or that some colours are

brighter than others. But to suppose that when a pleasure is more intense than another there must be something present in it which is double the amount of that in the other, or which bears some quantitative ratio to it, seems as crude a notion in Psychology as the old notion in Chemistry that degrees of heat depended on the quantity of "caloric" that was present.[1] We sometimes say that one thing is twice as hot as another, and it is easy enough to find a sense in which such a statement may be explained;[2] but in the obvious and natural sense of the words it appears to be meaningless, since degrees of temperature are not commensurable. In the same way, we may say that one pleasure is twice as intense as another,[3] but there is no evidence that such a saying has any scientific meaning. Similarly, one object may be more beautiful than another; but it would be difficult to attach any meaning to the statement that it is twice as beautiful. So too one animal may have a higher form of life than another; but can it have one twice as high? One poet may be greater than another; but would there be any conceivable meaning in saying that he is twice as great?[4] In

[1] When, for instance, Professor Edgeworth speaks of "atoms of pleasure" (*Mathematical Psychics*, p. 8) he seems to imply a misconception of the nature of pleasant feeling. From such a mode of speaking, one would suppose that pleasures are like lumps of sugar.

[2] Heat regarded as *energy* may be measured. So may pleasure regarded as *preferability*. Cf. *infra*, pp. 251-2.

[3] I do not think we very commonly make use of such expressions, even in ordinary discourse. The only instance I remember in popular literature is from a well-known Scotch song:—

"But a' the pleasures e'er I saw,
　Though *three times doubled* fairly,
　That happy night was worth them a'."

[4] Perhaps there would. We might mean, for instance, that he

general, is it possible to attach any meaning to a quantitative estimate of things which are by their nature not quantities but qualities — *i.e.* which differ not in amount, but in degree? There may be some meaning in such an estimate; but, if so, it has yet to be discovered and explained.[1]

3. But, it may be said, we can surely estimate pleasures at least with reference to their duration. I may be aware that at each of two successive moments I have a pleasure of approximately the same degree; and I may thus be entitled to say that the pleasures of these two moments taken together are twice as great as the pleasure of one of them alone would have been. Surely $1 + 1 = 2$. Now, to this the obvious answer is that it is indeed true that $1 + 1 = 2$, but it is also true that $1 + 1 - 1 = 1$. When the second pleasure is added the first is taken away, and there is only one left. If I have only one pleasure now, I am none the richer for the fact that I had another before. It is true that I may survey my life as a whole, and perceive that I was pleased at so many different moments; and it might be an amiable hobby on my part to try to make the number of pleasant moments as large as possible. But

displayed all those poetic qualities which the other displayed, and, in addition, a number of other qualities of about equal merit. And there are several other possible ways in which the statement might be explained. But clearly it does not mean precisely what it seems to say. Of course, it is hardly necessary to add, that I do not mean to affirm that any one of the above instances is quite parallel to the case of pleasure. I mention these examples only for the purpose of showing that there may be a higher degree of a quality without the possibility of direct quantitative measurement.

[1] On the difficulty of expressing intensive magnitudes in terms of extensive (with special reference to psychical intensities), I may refer to Münsterberg's *Beiträge*, III., pp. 4-5.

I should not be any the better off for such an effort.[1] At the present moment I am just as happy as I am, and no happier: I am not also as happy as I was, or as happy as I shall be. In the past, on the other hand, I was as happy as I was; and in the future I shall be as happy as I shall be. Every moment stands on its own basis; and the number of moments makes no difference to the happiness of life as a whole, because, according to such a view, life is *not* a whole. " A short life and a merry one " is as happy as a long one. A moment of blessedness would be as good as an eternity, because the eternity would only go on repeating the blessedness and not increasing it. If the water runs out of the sieve as fast as the Danaïdes pour it in, it is all one whether they go on pouring for an hour or for a year. If I paint a square foot of boarding red, I shall not make it any redder by painting two square feet. The paint will not run over; and neither will the happiness of one moment run over into another, so as to make it any richer. It makes no difference to me now[2] whether I was in the Slough of Despond twenty years ago or was in the third

---

[1] Cf. Green's *Prolegomena*, p. 236, and Alexander's *Moral Order and Progress*, p. 196 *seq.* Mr. Alexander has, I think, succeeded in bringing out some defects in Green's mode of statement; but his own statements are, to my mind, somewhat vitiated by the fact that he does not (especially on pp. 200-1) sufficiently distinguish between the feeling of pleasure and the sensations by which it is accompanied, though the distinction is afterwards (p. 203) very clearly drawn. I conceive the real point of the present objection to be that pleasant feelings are, from the Hedonistic point of view, discrete, and consequently incapable of being summed up as a whole of the same kind. Cf. my *Manual of Ethics*, p. 113, and *International Journal of Ethics*, Vol. v., No. 2, p. 226.

[2] Of course it may *cause* a difference, as in the familiar saying that "sorrow's crown of sorrows is remembering happier things." Cf. next paragraph.

heaven, if it is all quite past and forgotten. It made a difference to me twenty years ago, but that does not concern me now—if pleasure is my end.

> "The present moment is our own—
> The next we never saw";

and the last we shall never see again. "Sufficient unto the day is the evil thereof."

It is true that there seems to be a certain absurdity in all this. We feel that the past and the future do make a very real difference to us now. We believe that it is sometimes right to feel remorse, and that it is always wise to give some consideration to the coming years. But why is it that the past and the future make a difference for us? Surely it is because life is a whole, and not merely a series of moments. What affects us with regard to the past is not that it was sweet or sour when it was present, but that it has left a pleasant or a bitter taste in our mouths. In estimating our happiness we count in the past, because it colours the present. And often we are pleased at a past unhappiness or pained at a past joy, because we perceive that we are the better or the worse for it. We count in the future also, because we perceive that the value of the present depends on its reference to what is to come. In estimating the happiness of Job, we consider both the time of his original prosperity, the time of his affliction, and his "latter state"; because we know that all these conditions must have given a colouring to his consciousness as a whole. But if we regarded them merely as successive moments, what we should have to say would rather be, that there were three distinct persons, of whom one was happy, the second miserable, and the third more happy than the first; and that it did not matter in the least to any one of them what the state of the other was. A benevolent person might wish that all three had been happy; but this triple happiness would not be the happiness of any one of them, and could not naturally be regarded by any one of them as his good—if the good is pleasure.

4. This leads us directly to the fourth point—viz. that the pleasure of others cannot be the good for us, if the good is pleasure. If the evidence of having accomplished the end is to be satisfied, it is clear that I cannot have accomplished my end unless *I* am satisfied. The fact that someone else is satisfied—even if that someone else should be myself at a past or future time—is altogether beside the question. I cannot realise my end by proxy. If pleasure is the good, the good for me must be my own pleasure; and the pleasure of others can be my good only in so far as it is a means to my own. It is true, indeed, that an "impartial spectator" might judge that the good of others deserves realisation as much as my own good, just as he might judge that my own happiness in the past and in the future is as important as my happiness now; and it may be maintained that my own reason is capable of playing the part of such an impartial spectator.[1] But it is clear that for such an impartial spectator pleasure is not the complete expression of the good; and if the impartial spectator is myself, pleasure cannot be the complete expression of the good for me. For, before the impartial spectator can decide that it is good that the pleasure of each should be attained, he must have some other standard of justice by which he determines that this is good; and that standard is evidently not pleasure, but some conception of what is reasonable or fair. Hence into the conception of the good which such a being forms, it is clear that some other element than pleasure enters; and

[1] Cf. Sidgwick's *Methods of Ethics*, p. 120, Note, and p. 381.

if that being is myself, my conception of the good for
me cannot be simply the conception of pleasure.   But if
my primary conception of my good is pleasure, and if
yet I, as an impartial spectator or as a reasonable being,
am led to regard something else as good, it is clear that
I have two standards of the good, which may very possibly
come into conflict.   And when such a conflict arises, I
shall be reduced, as Dr. Reid put it, to "the miserable
dilemma whether it is better to be a fool or a knave,"
or, in the case of my own happiness, to the dilemma
whether it is better to be stupid or foolish—to sacrifice
the enjoyment of the present or that of the future.   Pro
fessor Sidgwick, with his customary candour and impar-
tiality, has frankly acknowledged the existence of this
insoluble dualism in the Utilitarian theory,[1] and has
made no attempt to conceal its importance.   But it
appears to me that the difficulty is far more fatal to
the doctrine than he seems to suppose.   For how is it
possible that there can be such a dualism in our consciousness of what is ultimately our good?[2]   It is conceivable that our consciousness should leave us in uncertainty
as to what our good is : but is it conceivable that it
should inform us positively that two things, which are
not the same, are both the good for us?   If so, we might
well despair of philosophy.   But surely this is inconceivable.   If our consciousness plainly tells us that our good
is pleasure, then the happiness of others can be a good
for us only in so far as it is a means to our own enjoyment.

---

[1] *Methods of Ethics*, pp. 379, Note, 402, 492 *seq.*

[2] It may be said, no doubt, that there is a distinction here between
the *Good* and the *Right*. (See *Methods of Ethics*, pp. 401-2.) But
this, as Dr. Sidgwick himself points out, is only another way of
saying that there is an ultimate conflict between the two ends that
are set before us.   For what is right means simply what is good for
us as rational beings. Cf. *supra*, pp. 210-1.

If, on the other hand, our consciousness tells us that the good is something which is a good not for the moment but for our life as a whole, and which is a good for all mankind as well as for ourselves, then the good is not pleasure. It is, indeed, conceivable that our consciousness may tell us that pleasure *would be* the good if we were not rational, but that since we are rational the good is the happiness of mankind. But in that case the good for us *as rational beings* is not pleasure; and it is with such a good alone that we are here concerned. It is surely inconceivable that our consciousness should say *both*— "the good for us as rational beings is our pleasure"— *and*—"the good for us as rational beings is the happiness of mankind." The art of walking on a razor's edge between two precipices may be carried far; but at such a point as this it looks as if one must tumble off on the one side or on the other.

5. We thus see that there are, to put it mildly, very serious theoretical difficulties in the way of the acceptance of the Utilitarian theory. Still, if it could be shown to be a good working hypothesis, the only one which is able to give us any practical guidance on the great questions of Ethics and Politics, we might be excused for persisting in our allegiance to it, in a sort of desperate faith that the difficulties will some day be removed.

We have, therefore, now to ask whether it is really the case that Utilitarianism affords practical guidance in dealing with ethical and social questions; and, if so, whether it is the only theory which does afford such guidance. Now the chief claims of Utilitarianism to practical value seem to rest on (*a*) the principle of "the greatest happiness of the greatest number" in legislation, and (*b*) the principle of "utilities" in Economics. The worth of these principles, and especially of the latter, I readily admit : but I believe it can be shown that so far as they are useful they are not hedonistic, and that so far as they are hedonistic they are positively prejudicial or misleading.

(*a*) It is clear that, in estimating the value of the Greatest Happiness principle, we ought not to include as one of its merits the introduction of the maxim of equity, that "every one is to count as one and nobody as more than one"; since this maxim is evidently not derived from Hedonism, and is perhaps not even quite consistent with it.[1] The real merits of the doctrine seem to be rather (1) that it insisted on the well-being of mankind as the end to be kept in view in legislation; and (2) that it furnished an easily-understood criterion for the estimation of that well-being. The first of these is a service for which its authors can hardly be too highly praised; but it is clearly an accident that the well-being of mankind should be supposed to consist in pleasure; and the supposition that it did so consist, has tended to some pernicious consequences.[2] In the first place, it is almost impossible that those who hold such a doctrine, with the exception of a few of their most enthusiastic leaders, should avoid being influenced by that dualism to which we have referred, in such a way as to be tempted, if not to prefer the satisfaction of themselves or of their class or party to those of mankind, at least to be somewhat obtuse to distant claims that would involve a considerable immediate sacrifice. To such temptations mankind is always prone, by whatever theory its actions may be regulated; but it can hardly be maintained that Utilitarianism has made the temptation less. It has tended to favour present desires

[1] Because, as I have already indicated, a consistent Hedonism seems to be necessarily egoistic. See *supra*, p. 234 *seq.*

[2] Cf. Green's *Prolegomena*, Book IV. chap. iii.

rather than ultimate ideals.[1] And, in the second place, it does not readily supply an adequate criterion of the importance even of our present desires. Whatever a large number wish strongly will naturally, on such a theory, be regarded as intrinsically desirable, without considering whether other things, that are at the moment less keenly sought after, may not be in reality more desirable. Of course, I do not deny that the theory may be so modified and refined as to get over this error. But then so may any other theory. The question is only whether Utilitarianism supplies a more sufficient practical guidance than other theories can do; and it seems to me that, as compared with other theories which accept the well-being of persons as the end, it certainly does not.

With regard to the second merit that I have mentioned, however, there can be less question. The criterion which Utilitarianism supplies, has a certain *primâ facie* simplicity which at once commends it; and it is no doubt largely for this reason that it has been so influential. Yet it is by no means so simple as it seems. For instance, so far as I am aware, it provides of itself no answer to the question whether we ought to prefer the double happiness of one to the single happiness of two, or *vice versâ*; yet this is a question which must very frequently occur in practice. It is true that this question has been answered by some Utilitarian writers, and answered in the way which seems in accordance

---

[1] I mean that it takes up our present desires as they stand, without reference to the significance which these desires have in our lives as developing beings, with an ideal before us in which our present desires may be submerged or transformed. This is essentially the same objection as that which has been raised by Mr. H. Spencer, Mr. L. Stephen, and other evolutionist writers, to the ordinary Utilitarian method, on the score of its purely empirical character. Cf. also my *Manual of Ethics*, p. 114.

with the verdict of ordinary morality—viz. that, other things being equal, a lower degree of happiness for two should be preferred to a higher degree for one—but this answer is provided by aid of the principle that "every one is to count as one," which is obviously extra-hedonistic.[1] Apart from such points as this, however, one must admit that the Utilitarian theory has not only a very decided simplicity to commend it, but also a certain "frank naturalism" which has a charm for many minds. For these reasons, one cannot but feel glad that a theory so well fitted to take hold of the popular understanding, should have been brought forward and utilised as a force for social improvement. It is one of those rough engines that clear the way for better things.[2]

(*b*) With respect to the use of the principle of "Utilities" in Economics, something more has to be said. This conception is one of the most fruitful that have ever been introduced into the study of that science. It has enabled economists to reduce the law of Demand and Supply to something like mathematical precision, and has thrown a great deal of light on the method by which the real value of different kinds of Wealth ought to be estimated. It has supplied us, in particular, with a vivid conception of the way in which increments of Wealth in any particular direction diminish in value as the total amount increases, until at last any further increment in that direction becomes rather an incumbrance than a

---

[1] Because it introduces the conception of what is equitable or reasonable. Cf. also what is said in Edgeworth's *Mathematical Psychics*, pp. 118, 122. I assume here that the principle that every one is to count as one, is intended to imply a certain effort after equality in the distribution of pleasure. Prof. Edgeworth seems (p. 117, etc.) definitely to renounce any such effort, except in so far as equality in distribution tends to increase the aggregate.

[2] Cf. Green's *Prolegomena to Ethics*, Book IV. chap. iii.

gain. Now these facts have usually been stated in a hedonistic form. It has been said that as Wealth increases, the pleasure which is derived from any further increment becomes continually less; and that after a certain point has been reached, any increase of Wealth in a particular direction ceases to be an increase of Utility, *i.e.* of Pleasure. But it is surely evident that this reference to Pleasure is not directly implicated in the doctrine, and tends rather to confuse it than to make it clear. The doctrine is not a psychological one : it could be applied to plants which have no feeling, as well as to human beings who have. The facts are simply these. Every species of Wealth is of value to us in so far as it helps us to supply some of our wants. These wants are of an almost endless variety, and differ very greatly in the degree of their importance—the supply of some of them being absolutely essential for the continuance of life from day to day, that of others for its prolongation during the normal period of time, that of others for its health and energy, that of others for culture or enjoyment. If any of these wants remain entirely unsatisfied, we are to that extent the losers; and our loss is in proportion to the importance of the wants whose satisfaction is denied. But each of our wants demands only a limited amount of the material which is appropriate for its gratification ; and when this has been granted, it demands no more. Moreover, each want can in general be supplied, in such a way as to serve its purpose moderately well, with a considerably less amount of material than that which would bring it up to the limit at which the demand would absolutely cease. Hence as Wealth increases in a particular direction, the increments in that direction become less and less valuable for the supply of our wants. In all this, there is no necessary reference to pleasure. It is true that pleasure is connected with the satisfaction

of our wants. But even if pleasure were not so connected; still, if the need of living continued,[1] and were
supplied by the same means as before, a large number of
our wants would be quite unaffected by the change, and
would continue to have the same relative importance;
and the doctrine of Utilities would still remain as applicable to them as ever.[2] A scale of Utilities might quite
well be drawn out for particular kinds of plants. Not
only so, but the theory of "Final Utilities" seems to me,
as ordinarily applied, to be faulty, just in so far as it
leaves out of account the intrinsic importance of our
wants, and considers only the intensity with which they
are felt, or the immediate pleasure of their satisfaction.
On this point, however, we cannot dwell further at
present.[3]

6. Such considerations as the foregoing may be sufficient to convince us that, notwithstanding its apparent
simplicity and applicability to practical questions, there is
no real advantage in the Utilitarian theory. No doubt,
in order to make this quite evident, it would be necessary
to go into a more detailed examination of it than is
possible in such a book as this. There is, however, one
further point on which it is necessary to touch now. The
saying of Coleridge, that until we "understand a man's
ignorance" we must assume that we are "ignorant of his
understanding," is as applicable to schools of thought as
it is to individual men; and, accordingly, if we are
thoroughly to see through the Utilitarian error, we must

---

[1] Of course some teleological conception is here involved. We
must have some conception of an end. But the point is that *any*
conception of an end would serve quite as well as that of pleasure.

[2] The calculations, for instance, given in Prof. Edgeworth's *Mathematical Psychics* seem to me to be calculations of *preferability*, not
of *pleasure*. Cf. *infra*, pp. 251-2. See also pp. 300, 341-2, etc.

[3] Cf. *infra*, pp. 346-7, and Note on Value at end of this chapter.

first get back to the πρῶτον ψεῦδος from which it springs. This it is not very difficult to do. We have seen already wherein the plausibility of the doctrine consists. Our end seems plainly to lie in the realisation of something which our nature wants. Such a realisation brings pleasure. Hence, it is very natural to identify pleasure with the realisation of our end; and this is rendered the more natural from the fact that, in dealing with our ultimate end, it is difficult to give any definite account of it, except that it would give us complete satisfaction. But further reflection makes it apparent that, though pleasure accompanies the realisation of our ultimate end, it cannot in itself be identified with that end.

In order to make this apparent, it is necessary to consider what the feeling of pleasure essentially is. There is, no doubt, a certain absurdity in attempting to give a definition of a fact of experience so ultimate as such a feeling; yet, by stating it in a different way, we may make its meaning somewhat clearer. We may say, then, that the feeling of pleasure is simply the sense of *interest* or of *value for consciousness.*[1] It is, in fact, an implicit judgment of value. Now, on this, there are two remarks which it at once occurs to us to make. The first is, that the *sense of value* presupposes *value.* The second is, that if value, or the sense of value, is to be estimated as more or less, we must have a standard of value, or a standard of the sense of value. And, in connection with this second remark, we may add that it will be important for us to determine whether it is value or the sense of value that we are seeking to estimate. On each of these points some further explanation seems to be now required.

[1] Cf. Dewey's *Psychology*, p. 16, and *International Journal of Ethics*, Vol. v., No. 2, p. 219 *seq.* See also the Note on Value at the end of this chapter.

With regard to the first point—viz. that the sense of value presupposes value—it may be noted that it is merely another way of saying that wants (needs for certain objects) are prior to the consciousness of pleasure in the attainment of these objects.[1]  That this is the case may become more apparent if we study the order of development of the elements in sentient existence.  A plant, we may say, wants air and sunlight, though it is not *aware* of its want, and consequently is not aware of having its wants satisfied—*i.e.* is not pleased.  It is true that objection may be taken to such a statement as this, on the ground that it is nonsense to speak of a want of which we are not conscious.  It may be said that to speak of a plant as wanting sunlight, is on a par with Mr. Ruskin's speaking of flowers as being " happy."  But if we believe that there is any " immanent finality " in a plant's life— if we believe that it has an end to realise which is in a sense its own, viz. the development of its own life—we may then fairly describe it as *wanting* what is necessary for the realisation of this end.  Now, such a teleological view as this is certainly at least suggested by the facts of vegetable development.  It will be seen, however, in any case, that such an objection is a merely verbal one in so far as the following argument is concerned.  For let us pass now to the consideration of animal life.  The appetite of an animal is different from the " Trieb " (or unconscious impulse) of a plant, in so far as it is not merely a want, but a want of which the being itself is conscious—a want whose satisfaction brings pleasure, and the thwarting of whose satisfaction brings pain.  Yet the wants of an animal are similar in kind to those of a

[1] Cf. Butler's *Sermons*, XI. ; Hutcheson's *Nature and Conduct of the Passions*, Sect. I. ; Green's *Hume*, Vol. II., p. 26 (*Collected Works*, Vol. I., p. 326), *Prolegomena*, pp. 167-8 ; Sidgwick's *Methods of Ethics*, pp. 43-9, *History of Ethics*, p. 189 *seq.*

plant. They are directed to those objects which are necessary for the realisation of its life. They have only this new element added, that the realisation is accompanied by a consciousness which is agreeable, and the thwarting by a consciousness which is disagreeable. Hence, if we adopt any theory of a development which proceeds upwards from vegetable to animal existence, it seems clear that wants—understanding by wants simply unconscious needs—must be regarded as by their nature prior to the consciousness of their satisfaction. What the plant wants is certain things—*e.g.* air or sunlight.[1] What the animal wants is also primarily certain things—*e.g.* food or drink[1]—and only secondarily the gratification which the attainment of these brings with it. It may be said, indeed, that it is this secondary want which for a conscious being is first presented. Still, it seems clear that, but for the existence of those other needs, this consciousness could never have arisen. Even if the pleasures are the πρότερα πρὸς ἡμᾶς, the needs are the πρότερα τῇ φύσει. Human desires, again, are different from animal appetites, in so far as there is present in them not merely a consciousness of the pleasure or pain of satisfied or unsatisfied want, but also a more or less clear view of the end at which the want aims. The plant, in short, absorbs what is necessary for the support of its life, without being in the least aware what it is doing, or why it should do it: the animal performs similar acts, driven by the uneasiness of hunger (if hunger is an uneasiness) and by the stimulus of other cravings: man, on the other hand, though also conscious of a similar uneasiness, is able to restrain his particular impulses by the thought of the objects which he seeks, and acts rather from the idea of the end which he wishes to realise—viz. the support of his life—than from the prompting of any im-

[1] More strictly, the *attainment* of air, food, etc.

mediate want.[1] And the higher the desire is, the more clearly does this difference come out. In the case of our more purely intellectual needs, there is no want that prompts us at all, until we create it by the conscious recognition of some end which it is desirable to pursue. The mathematician is pleased when he has solved his problems ; but there is no inborn want which urges him to their solution. He sets up the solution of the problem as an end, and thus for the first time creates a want, of which the satisfaction then becomes a pleasure. In this case the idea of an end is prior to the want, and the want is prior to the consciousness of pleasure that results from its satisfaction. In other words, an object is first determined as having value for our consciousness before the *sense* of its value arises.[2]

We might illustrate the difference in this respect between plants, animals, and human beings, by means of a simple image. Let us suppose a number of vessels which are filled with water and other kinds of liquid by means of pipes which communicate with cisterns above them. Let us suppose that the cisterns themselves become from time to time empty, and are from time to time refilled ; and that the vessels also are frequently emptied by human beings drinking out of them. Let us suppose, further, that of these vessels there are three different sets. In the case of one of the sets of vessels, the cisterns above are filled with water, and the water is kept constantly running so long as the cistern is full. The vessels are in consequence kept full to the brim, and overflowing, so long as there is any water in the cistern; but when

---

[1] Cf. Green's *Prolegomena*, p. 128 *seq.*

[2] Of course, the priority in such a case as this can only be a *logical* priority. A self-conscious being can hardly determine an object as having value for him without *at the same time* being aware that a sense of value will accompany its attainment.

that fails they become empty, and there is no means of refilling them, unless water is brought from elsewhere. In the case of the second set of vessels, the cisterns are filled, we may suppose, with a more valuable liquor, which is not allowed to overflow; and, for the purpose of preventing such an overflow, each vessel is provided with a valve or cock, which is automatically closed whenever the vessel is full, and opened again whenever it is empty. Finally, in the case of the third set of vessels, the cisterns above are filled with a variety of liquors of different values, which are under the care of a superintendent. All these vessels are fitted with valves or cocks, of which some are moved automatically, and others required to be regulated by the human hand. The superintendent watches all the vessels, and keeps each as full as he thinks desirable. In general he allows those that are fitted with automatic valves to regulate themselves; but occasionally he interferes even with them, by preventing the valves from either opening or closing. The first of these sets of vessels represents the life of plants, the second that of animals, and the third that of men.

Now the hedonistic theory amounts to the view that the end in each case consists not in the filling of the vessels, but in the motion of the valve. This view has a certain plausibility in the case of animal appetites, in which the motion of the valve is the invariable accompaniment—except in cases of derangement—of the gratification or baulking of the want; but it cannot be so easily applied either to the needs of plants or to human desires, in which there is no valve at all, or in which it is regulated by the conscious pursuit of an end.

But the basis of the discussion may be carried deeper. It may be urged that, even if all that has now been said be granted, it must still be allowed that pleasure is the ultimate end which we pursue. For, however true it

may be that our wants are primarily directed towards
objects, yet the only final rationale of our desire for
them is to be found in the pleasure which they bring.
If we seek, for instance, the support or development of
our life, do we not, it may be asked, seek it simply
because we know that, in the long run, the attainment
of that end is productive of the highest pleasure? And
is not pleasure, in like manner, the ultimate good that
we strive after even in our highest and most intellectual
desires? At least, "when we sit down in a cool hour,"
is not the anticipation of pleasure the only justification
that we can give to ourselves for the approval of such
desires by our reason? Do we not approve of them,
in other words, because we find that the attainment of
their objects brings with it a certain *sense of value* for
our consciousness?

In order to answer this question, it will be necessary to
bring in the second remark to which reference was made
above—viz. that for the estimation of value, or of the
sense of value, it is requisite that we should have some
definite standard. It is requisite, in short, that all the
values, or all the senses of value, should be commensurable with each other. We must be able, in other
words, to distinguish the pleasures which result from the
satisfaction of our various desires as higher or lower in
degree: otherwise we could not prefer the satisfaction of
one to the satisfaction of another, if our end is simply
pleasure. Hence it is necessary, on this view, to maintain that the pleasures which result from the satisfaction
of our various desires are all identical in quality or kind;
since it is only on that condition that their degrees can
be compared. At least, it is only on that condition that
their degrees can be taken as the only factor in the
comparison; and if there is another factor, that other
factor must be capable of being expressed in terms of

degree, or no comparison will be possible. Accordingly, almost all our leading Utilitarians, with the exception of Mill, have regarded pleasures as identical in quality. This view evidently harmonises very well with the necessities of Hedonism. But does it harmonise as well with the facts of our consciousness? Can it be reasonably maintained that the pleasure of " push-pin " is the same in kind as the pleasure of "poetry"? Both may be agreeable; but are they agreeable in the same way? Or is the pain of an uneasy conscience of quite the same sort as that of toothache? It is difficult to find anything similar in two cases such as these, except that both are disagreeable, and that both are frequently accompanied by a certain depression of spirits—which also is disagreeable, but disagreeable in a different way from that of either of the other two experiences. The pain or disagreeableness itself seems to consist simply in a consciousness of disharmony, or *sense of negative value*, within our nature; and that consciousness is of an entirely different character in these various cases. A burning heat and a jarring sound both make us uneasy; but there seems to be nothing similar in the two uneasinesses, except that both *are* uneasinesses (though of different sorts) and that they are accompanied by corresponding organic sensations—such as that, if they are sufficiently intense, both may produce a headache. Otherwise these annoyances are not only different in degree, but in kind as well.

To put it shortly, there does not appear to be any such thing as agreeableness or disagreeableness in the abstract, but only the agreeableness or disagreeableness of particular kinds of consciousness; and between two such different experiences no quantitative comparison can be made. Pleasure, in fact, is not a distinguishable element in our constitution, but, at most, only an aspect of it. It is the consciousness of a satisfied want, and its nature varies with the nature of the want which is satisfied. It has been said, indeed,[1] that though pleasure is inseparable from the total content of our consciousness, it may yet be treated as a distinguishable element in that total, just as the angles of a triangle may be distinguished from the sides. But, as it has often been pointed out, the cases are not really parallel. The angles of a triangle are not affected by the nature of the sides, whereas our pleasures derive their whole colouring and content from the objects which afford pleasure—or rather from the totality of the consciousness which we feel to be agreeable.

But, it may be said, we *do* at least distinguish pleasure from the other elements of our consciousness; and consequently it must surely be some one thing which is distinguishable from them, and which is uniform in its own nature. We do not, for instance, confound the fact that we are displeased with the fact that we are ignorant; and whether we are displeased by a bitter taste or by a bad action, we say in each case alike that we are displeased. In the first two cases, then, there must be something distinguishable, and in the last two there must be something identical. This is true. There is undeniably a common element in all pleasures; but if I may be allowed to make an Irish bull, I should say that the common element is something which is different in each case. We might illustrate this by a parallel instance. A horse and a dog are both living things, while a stone is distinguished from both by being inanimate. Life, therefore, is an element which is common to the horse and to the dog. Still, it would be rash to infer from this that there is something in the horse and in the dog which is identical in the two cases,

---

[1] Sidgwick's *Methods of Ethics*, p. 125, Note.

and differs only in amount or in degree. The life which exists in the horse or in the dog is not any *thing*; it is only a particular manner of existence; and though the manner of existence of the horse is so far of the same general class as that of the dog, yet within that class the two may differ not only in amount and in degree but in kind as well. So it seems to be with pleasure. If pleasure is to be defined as a sense of value or of harmony within our consciousness, it may be allowed that there is this element in common in all particular pleasures, and yet it may still be true that the sense of value or harmony is very different in different cases.

And that this actually is true, seems evident. What has been said in the last chapter about the different stages in the development of the self, may enable us to see that it must be so. For to each stage in that development there corresponds a different sense of value or harmony. Sense of value depends on the point of view from which value is estimated; and our point of view does not naturally remain constant throughout our conscious experience. What is pleasant to sense need not be pleasant to thought; and even what is pleasant to thought in some particular attitude, may not be pleasant to it in a different attitude.[1] We might, of course, arbitrarily select a particular standard of refer-ence. We might say that pleasures are to be judged according to the value which they have for us when we are in a particular mood of mind. But if we select such a standard, we have already pronounced judgment on our pleasures; and we have pronounced judgment upon them, not from the point of view of

[1] The conception of a "universe of desire," explained in my *Manual of Ethics*, chap. v., seems to me to be useful in this connection.

their intensity as pleasures, but from the point of view of their worth with reference to a particular standard. Not only have we gone beyond a simple pleasure-estimate by the selection of a particular standard, but even with respect to that particular standard our estimate is not an estimate of pleasure. In order to make this apparent, some further considerations must be adduced.

It is sometimes said that degree of pleasure means nothing more than degree of preference, and that by interpreting it in this way a certain meaning may be attached to the statement that pleasures differ merely in degree. When we prefer one pleasure to another, this means that the former is for us the greater;[1] and since pleasure is a purely subjective experience, what is *for us* the greater *is* the greater. Now surely we can in general tell which of two pleasures we prefer, and consequently we can tell which is the higher in degree, however different they may seem to be in quality. To this we must reply, that it certainly does seem that we can in general tell which of two pleasures we like best. It does seem also that, in the case of different kinds of pleasure, the fact that we prefer one to another is the only intelligible meaning that can be attached to the statement that the one is higher in degree than the other. Consequently, we may agree that to say that one pleasure is higher than another in degree, may be understood to mean nothing more than that we prefer the one to the other. But it is clear that *if* the fact that one pleasure is higher than another in degree *means* simply that the one is preferred to the other, then it cannot also be the *explanation* of the preference of the one to the other.

---

[1] Of course, "prefer" must be understood here to mean simply *like better:* it must not refer to a choice made on any other ground than that of liking.

We cannot say that we prefer a pleasure *because* it is higher in degree; if the fact that it is higher in degree *means* simply that we prefer it. In fact, when we interpret degree of pleasure in this way, it becomes a mere tautology to say that we choose as our ultimate good what seems to us the greatest pleasure; for this means no more than that in the last resort we like best what we like best.[1] It still remains to explain *why* we like one thing better than another; and to say that we do so *because* the former is the greater pleasure is simply to go round in a circle. The explanation of our choice must be something different from the mere fact that we choose —*i.e.* it must be something different from mere difference in the degree of pleasure.

We may put this in another way. To say that we prefer one pleasure to another, is in truth not the same thing as to say that the one pleasure is *as pleasure* higher[2] than the other in degree. When we prefer, we reflect; and what pleasure means for us *on reflection*, is not the same thing as what it is for us *prior to reflection.* Suppose we have two agreeable consciousnesses which we wish to compare. Each of these is a sense of value. One of these senses of value may be more intense than the other, and it may also differ from it in many other respects. The one may be a sense of value for us as sensitive beings; the other may be a sense of value for

---

[1] What we choose as our ultimate good must be what we like best when we are in that reflective attitude in which we think of our ultimate good at all—*i.e.* it must be what we *as rational beings* like best. Of course, this is not necessarily what appears to us the most exquisite pleasure when we are *not* in the attitude of purely rational beings. Here again the conception of Universes of Desire appears to me to be helpful.

[2] I use the term "higher" rather than "greater" advisedly. It has already (p. 229 *seq.*) been pointed out that we must not assume that pleasures can, strictly speaking, be compared as greater or less.

us as rational beings; and there may be other differences which we need not attempt to enumerate. We now compare the two together, and prefer one to the other. This preference is again a sense of value; but it is a sense of value different from either of the other two. It is a sense of value for us as reflecting. And when we prefer the one pleasure to the other, this does not mean that the one sense of value is perceived to be greater than the other sense of value, but that for us as reflecting the former sense of value has *greater value* than the latter. We must, in short, here draw the distinction to which we have already referred,[1] between a *greater sense of value* and a *sense of greater value*. Our preference is a sense of greater value, and it does not imply that the pleasure which we prefer is in itself a greater sense of value, *i.e.* a greater pleasure.[2]

The discussion of this point has led us into a somewhat lengthy argument. The idea that pleasure is our end is the most obstinate of our preconceptions; and even after all that has been above said, we cannot but foresee that there will still be some who will ask—"But, after all, could we regard anything as our end unless it gave

[1] P. 242.

[2] Cf. Alexander's *Moral Order and Progress*, p. 206, where the *preferability* of a pleasure is clearly distinguished from its *intensity*. Mr. Alexander's point, indeed, if I understand him rightly, is not quite the same as mine; since the preferability to which he refers is not preferability for any actually existing consciousness, but is used rather in an anticipatory sense with reference to consciousness in general. But it is an easy step from the recognition of a distinction between the intensity of a pleasure and its preferability in this anticipatory sense, to the recognition of a similar distinction between its intensity and its preferability even for the reflective consciousness of the individual who feels it at the moment of feeling it. See also the article on "Psychology" in the *Encyclopaedia Britannica*, p. 85, and Franz Brentano's pamphlet *Vom Ursprung sittlicher Erkenntniss*, pp. 22-24.

us pleasure ? "—and who will not be satisfied with the obvious answer—" Certainly nothing would have value for us as self-conscious beings unless it brought with it a sense of value ; but it does not follow that the value of objects is to be estimated by the intensity of the sense of value which they bring." But to the present writer, at any rate, it seems clear that this is true. We may hold, with Mr. Havelock Ellis,[1] that "whatever tastes sweet to the most perfect person, that is finally right," and yet believe that the standard of its rightness is to be found rather in the perfection of the person than in the sweetness of the taste.[2]

IV. We ought now to consider the possibility of supposing that the end consists in some combination of the three elements of our nature—*i.e.* that it consists in some sort of realisation of Knowledge and Will, or of Will and Feeling, or of Feeling and Knowledge, or of Knowledge and Will and Feeling, taken together. But the fact that no one of these can be taken to constitute an end by itself, is a sufficient proof that no combination of them can. For the three elements could be taken as forming the complete end in combination only if each of them separately could be taken as *an* end ;[3] and the same would apply to a combination of any two of them. But we have seen that no one of the three elements can be regarded as constituting an end for us at all ; and consequently no combination of them can constitute our end. If then, we have any rational end at all, it must

---

[1] *The New Spirit,* p. 110.

[2] For some further discussion on Hedonism, I may refer to some articles in the *International Journal of Ethics,* Vol. v., Nos. 1, 2, and 3.

[3] Unless we were to suppose that the fact of combination somehow transforms them ; and this would be to suppose that they are not simply combined.

consist in some kind of realisation of our nature as a whole. If we might, after the manner of Plato,[1] represent the search for the end as a prize competition, we might say that Feeling and Will have been bracketed for the second prize, and that Knowledge is deserving of honourable mention; but that either our nature as a whole (or at least some unity in our nature which is deeper than these distinctions) must secure the first prize, or the first prize must remain unawarded; since none of the other competitors has come up to the standard. Accordingly we must now examine and endeavour to define the claims of our nature as a whole.

V. The results at which we arrived in our examination of pleasure, suggest a direction in which we may look for further light. We saw that the end seemed to consist rather in the fulfilment of certain wants of our nature, than in the pleasure which ensues upon their satisfaction. It may be well, therefore, to inquire what the most fundamental wants of our nature are; since in this way we shall be pretty certain to stumble upon our end. Now the answer to the question, what our most fundamental wants are, has been already, in a rough way, provided. There are, in the first place, what may be called our vegetable wants; in the second place, there are those that arise from our organic or animal sensations; and, in the third place, there are those that are due to reason. The primary wants are those that minister directly to the support of our life, such as the want of food and air and light and warmth. The secondary wants are those that owe their origin to the fact that we are conscious, and that some kinds of consciousness are pleasant and others painful. In general, no doubt, what is pleasant is that which promotes life, and what is painful is the reverse; but, as we know only too well, the

[1] *Philebus*, 23 A, etc.

coincidence between the agreeable and the useful is by no means complete. Thus, we have cravings for pleasant tastes and smells and sounds, and so on, which are not directly, and often not at all, connected with the maintenance of our animal being. The tertiary wants, again, are those that are connected with the rational part of our nature, such as the desire for truth or beauty, the "hunger and thirst after righteousness," and the like. It would seem then as if the good for us must consist in the satisfaction of some or all of these wants.

Now it seems clear that the end for which we are seeking cannot consist in the satisfaction either of our vegetable or of our animal wants as such. This, indeed, we have already seen. It cannot consist in the satisfaction of our vegetable wants, because these wants do not, as such, belong to our conscious being; whereas, as we have seen, our good does. It cannot consist in the satisfaction of our animal wants, because these wants, as such, are directed merely towards certain sensations which are agreeable in a variety of different ways; and there would be no criterion of the desirability of such ends except the degree of their agreeableness; and such a criterion is, as we have seen reason to believe, impossible —even if pleasure as such could be for us an end. Though, therefore, it is possible that the satisfaction of our vegetable and animal wants may enter as an element into the constitution of our ultimate good—just as any objective thing may do—yet it appears that the satisfaction of these wants as such cannot itself be the good, or even any part of the good.[1] Hence we are led to look for our good in the satisfaction of our rational wants. If we cannot find it there, our plight will be indeed a desperate one.

---

[1] Though it may be a part of the objective content of that form of consciousness which is our good.

Now in order to discover what our rational wants are, we must glance again at the nature of our constitution as reasonable beings. We have already tried to indicate [1] wherein the peculiarity of man as a rational being consists. We have seen that it consists in what may be called self-consciousness or apperception; and that this means the clear discrimination of the contents of his experience, regarded as a whole. To be rational or self-conscious, in fact, means to be a microcosm or little world, and to be at home within that world. We have seen, however, that man is not in this sense rational or self-conscious, but is only developing towards such a form of existence. He has the idea of a completely discriminated content, but has not completed either the content or its discrimination. What, then, is the want which such a nature imposes? Surely that of completing what is left imperfect, that of realising the idea which is dimly present. Such an idea is clearly an ideal: it cannot but present itself to a reasonable being as an object to be realised. Let us, then, endeavour to understand more precisely what the ideal thus presented is.

We have seen, in a rough way, that the ideal consists in attaining to clearness with reference to our world, so that it may present itself as a universe or system. Our world comes to us at first as a number of external facts presented successively to our consciousness, and we proceed by degrees, by means of conceptions, to reduce this collection of presentations to definiteness and order; and the ideal to which this process tends, is evidently that of grasping clearly the conceptions of which we make use, and seeing all the particular facts in their right relation to the conceptions. But a little consideration will show that the ideal must involve even more than this. Even if we had attained to a clear view of all the

[1] P. 184 *seq.*

R

facts of our experience in relation to each other, our
world would still not be intelligible and clear to us,
unless we could see also how all the particular facts have
come to be. If, for instance, we could see the physical
world as a collection of atoms acting and reacting
on each other in accordance with certain laws, and if
these laws were clearly intelligible to us, our world would
still be dark, unless we knew what brought the atoms
themselves into being, and how they came to be controlled by such laws. In other words, we must not only
be able to *bring* our world into a certain intelligible
order, but we must also be able to see it as *issuing out*
of an intelligible order. Such an intelligible world would
exist for us if the world of our experience were not
merely presented to our intelligence, but arose from our
intelligence—*i.e.* if we created our world as well as perceived it. And such a world would equally exist for us
if we saw it as issuing from the unity of some other
intelligence than our own. It would then appear not
merely as a collection of facts which is reduced to
system, but as a collection which flows from a system,
and which is consequently intelligible from beginning to
end. Now such an intelligible world is presented to us
by the lives of our fellow-men, and in the works which
they perform. In reading a book, for instance, we are
presented with a collection of details which we, by means
of conceptions, reduce to an intelligible system ; but
when we have reduced it to such a system, we are conscious that we have merely read into the details a system
from which they themselves issued. The ideas in the
light of which the book acquires meaning for us, are the
ideas out of which the book took its rise. Thus the
book may be said to be intelligible through and through.
It is not merely something which may be reduced into
the form of an intelligible system, but something which

has itself sprung out of an intelligible system. In grasping such an object as this, our rational nature attains satisfaction and rest. The object is thoroughly clear: because it is seen not merely as a part of an intelligible system, but as issuing out of a system which is intelligible. And if we could see all the facts of our experience in this way, we should have attained completely the ideal at which our rational nature aims.

Further, a little reflection may convince us that it is only in the lives of other intelligent beings that we could find such an intellectual satisfaction. For it cannot be supposed that the ideal should be realised within our own lives. Let us imagine that any one of us could, so to speak, become God—so that the world of our experience should be seen as issuing from, as well as returning to, the system of our self-consciousness. This would amount to saying that no world exists for us at all to unify. For if the world flowed out of the unity of our own being, we should be at home in it from the first: it would from the first be for us a universe, and there would be no need for us to go through the laborious process of forming for ourselves a system. But if so, we should not be intelligent beings at all, in any sense in which that term has meaning for us: since intelligence, as we know it, consists simply in a process of coming to clearness with reference to objects which come to us at first as presentations, and not as the outflow of our own inner being. Consequently, it is only if we can see our world as flowing from the unity of some other system than our own that we can realise our ideal.

Now we might suppose that this ideal is to be attained by our reaching gradually to a knowledge of God as the intelligence from whom all things flow. But if God is to appear as an intelligible system to us, it is evident that He must not appear simply as that kind of blank unity to which we have just referred.   For in that case it would not be true that the world of particular facts flows from Him.   There would be nothing at all in existence but what is in the unity of His own being; and the differences of things would be unexplained.   Consequently, if our minds are to find satisfaction in God, He must be thought of rather on the analogy of our own intelligence, as a unity for which there is a world of differences.   And these differences, as we have already seen, cannot be supposed simply to flow out of the unity of His own being : otherwise they would not be differences.   But if God is a being for whom there is a world of differences, and if yet these differences are themselves intelligible, they also must be seen as belonging to the unity of intelligent beings.   From such considerations as these we may be led to see that no attainment of the ideal of our rational nature is conceivable, except by our being able to see the world as a system of intelligent beings who are mutually worlds for each other.

Now how far it is possible to think of the whole world in this way, is a question for the Philosophy of Religion to discuss.   It is enough for us here to observe that, in so far as we come into relations to other human beings in the world, we are attaining to a partial realisation of the ideal which our rational nature sets before us.   And there is no other way by which we come to such a realisation.   In so far as the world is merely material, it remains foreign and unintelligible to us.   It is only in the lives of other human beings that we find a world in which we can be at home.   Now in this fact we obviously find a much deeper significance for the organic nature of society than any that we have yet reached.   For we see that the society of other human beings is not merely a means of bringing our own rational nature to clearness,

but is the only object in relation to which such clearness can be attained.

It may be asked, indeed,—Why should such clearness
be taken as our end at all? May we not rest satisfied
with the mere animal life, or with some partial attainment of clearness, such as we find in the working out of
some particular science? The answer obviously is that,
from the very nature of our rational being, we cannot
possibly be so satisfied. We cannot become mere animals,
however much we may desire it : and there is no halting-
place between the pure animal conciousness and the
attainment of our highest ideal. Every step we make in
the way of seeing our world as a universe and being at
home in it, inevitably urges us on to a step beyond. It is
our nature to seek to make such advances, just as it is the
nature of an animal being to satisfy its animal wants.

Here, then, we seem at last to have found out what
the true nature of man's end is; and we see that that
end is by its very nature a social one. It is clear too
that the end which we have now defined includes everything which "we divine" as belonging to the highest
good. It includes, indeed, every one of the ends which
have been previously enumerated. It includes what we
have described as the objective ends—the realisation of
Reason, Order, and Beauty in the world : for the realisation of them is part of our work in making our world
intelligible and clear to ourselves. It includes also the realisation of Life : for it is the fulfilment of that towards which
our lives as rational beings strive : and in the fulfilment
of this for ourselves, there is involved also the realisation
of the lives of other intelligent beings; since it is only in
the fulfilment of their intelligent nature that our own can
receive fulfilment.[1] It includes the perfection of Know-

[1] On this aspect of self-realisation, cf. Sorley's *Ethics of Naturalism*, p. 289.

ledge and Wisdom; since it is the clearing up of our
world and the making it into an intelligible system.  It includes the perfection of Will: for it is the devotion of all
the energies of our nature to that end which we recognise
as our highest ideal.  It includes the perfection of Feeling :
for it is the attainment of that in which our nature as
rational beings would find full satisfaction.[1]  And, so far
as we can judge, it may also be described as the fulfilment of the divine purpose in the world : for it is the
attainment of that which is necessarily taken as an end
by every intelligent being, and which is consequently the
only end at which we can suppose a supreme Intelligence
to aim.[2]

But, it may be said, is such an ideal any more attainable than the hedonistic one of perfect satisfaction throughout every moment of every man's existence ?  If not, we
must have some criterion of the more or less perfect
attainment of it, just as such a criterion was demanded
in the case of pleasure.  To this we must answer, in the
first place, that the two cases are not quite parallel. · The
hedonistic ideal, to which we objected, had no content.
It told us merely that we must try to get perfect satisfaction ; and since this is clearly unattainable, we had
then to ask—What are we to take as a substitute for it ?
But the ideal which we have now described has the whole

---

[1] *Practically*, the end which is sought from this point of view will
differ very slightly from that which is sought by an enlightened
Utilitarian.  For, from the nature of the case, the attainment of the
highest happiness tends to bring all other real enjoyments in its
train.  Still, it is important that we should "seek *first* the Kingdom of God."

[2] This is of course subject to the qualification that perhaps the
idea of purpose, or indeed that of process at all, is not strictly
applicable to the Absolute.  Contrast the view taken on this point
in Bradley's *Appearance and Reality* with that hinted at in Caird's
*Evolution of Religion.*

world for its content. If what we are to seek is to understand our world and to be at home in it, every step
forwards in knowledge and wisdom and goodness is a
step towards our ideal. It may, indeed, be an ideal
which we can never reach; it may be a horizon

> "whose margin fades
> Forever and forever as we move":

yet every step towards it is a step in it. We never
realise it, but we are always realising it.[1] Still, it is
necessary that we should know at least in what direction
we can realise it best; and on this point some counsel
may fairly be expected.

Further, although it now seems sufficiently clear, not
only that the realisation of any one individual's highest
life is impossible without the co-operation of others, but
even that the realisation of other lives is an essential element, indeed *the* essential element, in the realisation of our
own; yet it cannot but be apparent that, in the effort towards the highest ideal, we may very well come into conflict
with others. For though our rational nature is a social
nature, yet, just in so far as it is imperfectly rational, it is
imperfectly social; and this imperfection is apt to display
itself even at the highest points of our development. It
has been said of poets, in verses which have been already
quoted,[2] that they are actuated by two opposite desires, one
of which impels them "to the world without, and one to
solitude." And what is thus true of poets is true of all
forms of the higher life. To realise what is best in us
we must live much within ourselves as well as among

---

[1] I allow that there is a certain contradiction here, which may probably be taken as showing that the moral life is not in the highest
sense real. Cf. Bradley's *Appearance and Reality*, chap. xxv. But
it is at least more real than anything else within the finite world.
See the note on Value at the end of this chapter.

[2] P. 6.

our fellows.   We must "tread the wine-press alone." [1]
Hegel said "that in nothing is one so much alone as in
philosophy"; but the same is in some measure true of
all the deeper forms of the development of our intellectual
nature.   Thus the development of the individual's life,
even in its highest form, takes him away to some extent
from the life of society.   Yet it is only through the life
of society that the attainment of the highest ideal is possible.   Thus we are led to a certain dualism, or even to
an apparent contradiction.

It might seem at first as if this dualism were the same
in kind as that which we have already encountered in
the Utilitarian theory; and it might be thought that it
pointed to a similar defect in our own ideal.   This, however, is not the case.   The dualism of the Utilitarian is
a real and insoluble one; because, according to his theory,
the good for the individual is not the same as the good
for society.   If our ideal is the true one, on the other
hand, the two goods are ultimately identical, and only
diverge to come together again more forcibly.   If we are
ever tempted to withdraw into the wilderness, it is only
in order that we may in a sense be less alone, and that
we may return with a deeper insight to the problems of
human development.   Yet it is true that the need for
such a withdrawal, and in general the fact that the development of each individual's higher nature does not quite
coincide with that of all other human beings around him,
presents us with a very real difficulty in the way of
determining what is the best way to realise our ideal at
each particular point.   Shall we try to "make giants" or
to "elevate the race"?   Shall we press on to realise our
own highest life, or shall we rather hasten gently and try
to take the world along with us?   Unless we can give
some sort of answer to such questions as these, we do

[1] Cf. *supra*, p. 154.

not seem to be much wiser, from a practical point of view, than we were before this inquiry was begun. We must, therefore, inquire a little more fully into the nature of the ideal which our theory sets before us.

If our principles are correct, however, it is evident that the question ought not to be stated in the form of an inquiry, whether the good at which we are to aim is the highest realisation of a few or a more moderate realisation of the many. For, on the principles which we have been endeavouring to expound, neither of these could be regarded as the good at all. Nor ought the question to be stated in the form of an inquiry, which of these kinds of realisation will bring us nearest to the ultimate good. For this is an inquiry to which no answer could be given without a careful consideration of the conditions of development at different times. It would be somewhat absurd, for instance, to ask whether it would have been better that the Athenians should have had a less consummate civilisation, with its benefits more equally diffused, since it seems clear that the historical conditions never permitted such an alternative. What we have to ask is rather this—What is the form of social union in which, under given conditions, the progress will be most rapid and most secure towards that good which we must regard as the ultimate end? It is to this question that we must address ourselves in the following chapter; and, in considering it, we shall naturally have regard chiefly to present conditions, as being those that most nearly concern us. And, of course, we must proceed to this discussion with the clear understanding that, whenever such particular conditions enter, we must not look for any absolute decisions from philosophical principles.

# NOTE ON THE THEORY OF VALUE.

One of the chief points that I have hoped to bring out in the foregoing chapter, is the fundamental importance of a true theory of value in the study of ethical and social problems. The chief advance that has been made in economic theory within the last generation has consisted in the gradual appreciation of the fact that the problem of value is the central problem in economics, and in the gradual clearing up of the psychological and social principles on which the determination of values rests. The pioneer work in this subject was done by such writers as Jevons, Walras, Menger, and one or two others ; and the elaboration of it is due chiefly to Wieser, Böhm-Bawerk, and other economists of the now famous Austrian school.[1] One of the chief results of the new point of view which these writers have introduced has been one which was foreseen by Jevons—viz. the placing of the theory of Consumption on a footing of at least co-ordinate importance with that of Production. When this is done, the bearing of Ethics on Economics becomes prominent ;[2] and it becomes necessary to deal with the subject of Value in a larger sense than that which is ordinarily understood by the economist. The necessity of this larger treatment has been to some extent recognised by our English Utilitarians—e.g. Edgeworth ; and it has been emphasised by such writers as Ruskin. But the most serious attempt at a scientific treatment of the subject of Value in the largest sense is to be found in the recent writings of

---

[1] For a sketch of the doctrines of this school, reference may be made to Mr. Smart's *Introduction to the Theory of Value.* It ought to be added, however, that the Austrian writers seem in general (in common, to some extent, with Jevons) to take a one-sided view of the factors by which economic value is determined—a one-sidedness from which some of our English writers, such as Marshall, are entirely free.

[2] Cf. the article on "The Relation between Ethics and Economics" in the *International Journal of Ethics*, Vol. III., No. 3.

Ehrenfels[1] and Meinong[2]—two Austrian psychologists of the school of Franz Brentano.

Those who have given most attention to the subject of Value, either from the purely economic point of view or in the broader sense, have generally approached it from the Utilitarian point of view, or at least from the point of view of Hedonism in some sense.[3] But it is now beginning to be pretty universally recognised that the theory of Value, even as ordinarily worked out by economists, has no necessary connection with Hedonism. I understand Professor Marshall, for instance, to have definitely rejected the Hedonistic theory.[4] The so-called measurement of pleasure which is involved, is merely the measurement of the degrees of preference of particular individuals for particular objects ; and in the determination of this preference the objective side is certainly as important as the subjective. And when we pass from merely economic values to moral values, the importance of the more objective side is still further increased. For if it is true that economic values are ultimately

---

[1] See his series of articles on "Werth-theorie und Ethik" in the *Vierteljahrsschrift für wissenschaftliche Philosophie,* 1893 and 1894.

[2] *Psychologisch-ethische Untersuchungen zur Werth-Theorie.*

[3] Lotze may be mentioned, however, as a prominent writer who has emphasised the idea of Value without interpreting it in a Hedonistic sense. Cf. also Professor Alexander's article on the subject (*Mind,* New Series, Vol. I., No. 1, pp. 31-56). It should be observed also that the connection of the idea of Value with the Hedonistic theory of Ethics has introduced considerable modifications into the latter. Thus when Dr. Sidgwick distinguishes between what is *desired* and what is *desirable,* and maintains that it is the latter that is ethically important, he is practically substituting the idea of Value for the idea of Pleasure as a direct object of desire. When we "sit down in a cool hour," it is Value that we try to estimate. Similarly, the Evolutionists, in taking the development of life as their end, are substituting the valued object for the mere subjective satisfaction or consciousness of value.

[4] See his manifesto on the relation between Ethics and Economics in the *Economic Journal,* Vol. III., No. 11, especially p. 388. There are, however, passages in his *Principles of Economics* which it is difficult to interpret in any other than a Hedonistic sense—*e.g.* pp. 150, 151 note 2; 153, 177-180, 181, 185, 188, etc. (These references are to the Second Edition.) Cf. also Bonar's *Philosophy and Political Economy,* pp. 224-7, 35-6.

determined simply by the subjective preferences of individuals[1]
—by the utility or disutility to the "marginal man"—it is not
so with ethical values.

Moral value—the apprehension of the Good—seems in this
respect to be precisely similar to the apprehension of Truth
or Beauty.   In all the three cases there is both a subjective
and an objective side.   Corresponding to the objective grasp
of Truth, there is the subjective feeling, of certainty ; corresponding to Beauty there is aesthetic appreciation ; and, similarly, corresponding to Value there is the sense of Value.   Now
in each case the objective side has a certain natural priority.
In the case of knowledge what is sought is, primarily, rather
Truth than Certainty : in the case of Art, Beauty has the
priority over aesthetic delight ; and so with moral Value, the
object which has Value has a certain priority in importance
over the subjective appreciation of its worth.   Of course I do
not mean to deny that, in each case, the objective side is
inseparable from its subjective reference.   But what it is most
important to observe is that, in each case, the subjective
reference is not simply a reference to the consciousness of
this or that individual at a given time.   A few words, with
the view of making this point clear, may not be out of place.

When we say that Truth is objective, we do not mean that
it is anything apart from the consciousness for which it exists.
There cannot be a truth which is not true for somebody.[2]
But Truth is not to be identified with certainty, or even with
a greatest possible sum of certainties.[3]   We mean rather by

---

[1] Even in the case of economic values it must be remembered that
individual preferences are not determined by accident, and that, in the
long run, the objective or intrinsic value of objects tends to have its due
weight.

[2] In what sense it may be legitimate to oppose Reality to Truth, as
Mr. Bradley seems to do, it is not our business here to inquire.   See
the article on "Mr. Bradley's View of the Self" in *Mind*, New Series,
Vol. III., No. 11, pp. 323-326.

[3] This seems, however, to be practically the view of Truth which is
adopted by Dr. G. Simmel, who, curiously enough, does not accept the
corresponding Utilitarian theory in Ethics.   See his *Einleitung in die
Moralwissenschaft*, Vol. I., p. 3; and compare the notice in *Mind*,
New Series, Vol. I., No. 4, p. 546, etc.

Truth that of which an individual would be certain under normal or typical conditions. We correct the point of view of the individual microcosm or universe of thought by reference to a larger and more perfectly systematised universe, which still is a universe of possible thought. Similarly, Beauty, in the objective sense, is not simply that which produces aesthetic enjoyment in a given individual; still less does it consist in a greatest sum of aesthetic enjoyments. It is rather that which normally appeals to the aesthetic appreciation of a typical individual. Here also we correct the personal equation by referring from the centre of the individual consciousness to the centre of a more complete or ideal consciousness. But still the subjective side is not lost.[1] Beauty is necessarily thought of as an object of possible aesthetic appreciation. Now the case of moral Value seems to be exactly similar to these two.

Dr. Alexius Meinong has brought out this point in a very interesting way.[2] Using E (Ego) as a symbol for the consciousness of a given individual, and A (Alter) as a symbol for that of any other, he decides that the centre to which moral values are referred is not to be denoted by either E or A, but rather by such a symbol as X, which may be taken to mean the consciousness of some entirely disinterested person, or, as Adam Smith would say, that of an "impartial spectator." It must be remembered, however, that this consciousness is not something external and indifferent to E, but is rather the standard of judgment which the latter consciousness involves. It is, in fact, the consciousness of the ideal self, or ideal universe of reference. Such an ideal standard seems to be exactly similar to those to which reference is made in the case of Truth and Beauty.

No doubt, if any one were to propound the question what the exact nature and content of this ideal consciousness is, a

[1] Mr. Bosanquet perhaps goes too far in attempting to define Beauty without reference to the subjective element of aesthetic appreciation. Contrast his statements in the *History of Aesthetic*, especially p. 6, with those in Mr. Bradley's *Appearance and Reality*, especially p. 464. Cf. also my *Manual of Ethics*, p. 298, Note 1.

[2] *Loc. cit.*, pp. 171-180.

much more difficult problem would be raised. But the corresponding problem is similarly difficult in the case of Truth and Beauty. In the case of Truth, the corresponding problem is the fundamental question of epistemology. The answer to it, in general terms, seems to be that given in Mr. Bradley's *Appearance and Reality*—viz. that Truth consists in conformity with a self-consistent system of experience. But the further analysis of its content involves great difficulties. Similarly, it is difficult to say what in the end is to be meant by Beauty as distinguished from aesthetic appreciation. But the answer seems in the end to be similar to the answer to the epistemological question. And there can be little doubt that the answer to the question, as to the ultimate significance of moral value, must also be similar. What is ultimately valuable for us, we may say, is that which belongs to a consciousness of the world as a systematic and harmonious totality. But here also it is difficult to evolve the particular content.

And indeed there is a difficulty involved in the case of moral value, which is at least not so prominently present in the case either of Truth or of Beauty—viz. the difficulty which is connected with the existence of a process. The moral life is an activity ; and it seems impossible to think of this activity as reaching its end in. a quiescent state, without thereby losing its essential nature. Perhaps there is a similar difficulty in the case of Truth, or at least of any Truth which we can regard as being attainable by man ; and it is not certain that Beauty also does not essentially belong to a process of development, and so to finitude and unreality. But at least the difficulty is most conspicuously present in the case of moral Value.

The essential difficulty is this, that our standard of value seems to refer to a consciousness which must be thought of as above process, whereas all things that actually have value for us seem to exist within a developing process. If so, it would seem that our standard is worthless as a test of any actual experience. But I believe that the way out of this difficulty will be found to be in reality similar to that adopted by Mr. Bradley in dealing with the corresponding difficulty in the theory of knowledge. Just as in the latter case we may recognise degrees of reality falling short of that which is ultimate and absolute ; so in the case of value, we may distinguish degrees in a process of realisation as more or less satisfactory approximations to that which is ultimately valuable, even if we admit that that which has a complete and final value for us cannot be attained by any process.

Anything that can here be said on such a point must of course be only a tentative suggestion of a solution. But it seems to me that we may think of human life as guided by an ideal of systematic completeness, which it continually seeks to realise ; and that we may regard the successive stages in its effort to realise this ideal, as having a certain significance and truth, and indeed as being more real than anything else that we know ; even if we have to grant in the end that the moral life is not, after all, in any ultimate sense real.[1]

[1] It may be well to note at this point that when pleasure is defined, as I have defined it, as consisting essentially in a "sense of Value," this expression must be understood in an anticipatory or proleptical sense. Value has significance only for a rational consciousness ; and if animal pleasure is described as "sense of Value," this must be taken to mean that it is a vague anticipation of what in a more developed consciousness would be a judgment of Value. Cf. the discussions already referred to in the *International Journal of Ethics.*

# CHAPTER V.

## THE SOCIAL IDEAL.

It will be well at this point to glance back and give a brief summary of the conclusions at which we have arrived, so far, with respect to the nature of the Social Organism. We have seen that if we define an Organism —and this is, at the lowest, a very natural and convenient way of defining it—as a whole whose parts are intrinsically related to it, which develops from within and has reference to an end which is involved in its own nature, then it may fairly be maintained that a human society is organic. Its parts are intrinsically related to it; for the rational nature of the beings who compose it is entirely dependent for its being and continuance on the existence of certain social relations. It develops from within; for its growth consists simply in the unfolding of the rational nature of each of its individual members—that rational nature being, moreover, always essentially relative to the nature of the whole society in which it develops. It has reference to an end which is involved in its own nature; for the end of society is to preserve the life and to secure the highest life of its individual members—this highest life, moreover, consisting not in the attainment of anything external either to the individuals or to their society, but in the perfect realisation of their own rational nature, which can be attained

only in a perfect social life. So much having been now
determined with reference to the nature of society, it is
of small consequence whether or not we see fit to retain
the term Organism as descriptive of that nature. If we
do retain it, it is not in the sense that society has a close
analogy to the various forms of living creatures in the
world, but only that it is an instance—perhaps even a
unique instance—of an incomplete whole whose com-
pletion would consist simply in its own perfect development. Now in such a growing totality as society is thus
seen to be, governed in its development by the idea of
its own perfection, there must be at every point an
ideally best arrangement for the attainment of the end
in view; and it is this ideal that it now behoves us to
consider.

In considering this ideal, it is necessary constantly to
bear in mind that man is not ἢ θηρίον ἢ θεός—that his
nature is neither purely animal nor purely rational—but
that he is rather a being who is fighting his way upward
from the one stage to the other. It would be comparatively easy to frame an ideal for "a community of swine,"
and still more easy to frame one for a community of
angels. For the former, it would be necessary only to
heap up the troughs, and to see that each received a fair
share of their contents—an ideal which it might be difficult to realise, but which it is at least very easy to define.
For the latter, again, nothing would be necessary but to
leave them alone. Man, on the other hand, is a being
who cannot stand still either in the mire or in the ether.
We are never so brutish but that "a spark disturbs our
clod"; and, if in anything we are divine, it is in a
"divine discontent." For such a being it is not so easy
to define the ideal: it is his nature rather to outgrow his
ideals periodically, and to cast them like a slough. Accordingly we can hardly expect to discover any definite

statement of what the ideal for a society of human beings is, but only a general notion of the direction in which it moves.

In order to reach even such a general notion as is here referred to, it will be necessary to consider carefully what are the chief elements that are involved in human well-being; since the ideal direction for a society of human beings to grow in, will be that which tends to realise these elements most completely. Now if human well-being is such as we have defined it to be, it is clear that it may be regarded as having in it three different aspects or elements, which are distinguishable though not separable from each other. In the first place, there is the education or culture of the individual nature, the reducing of our own nature to inner clearness—a process which culminates in the attainment of philosophic truth, *i.e.* in the view of our world as an ideally complete system of intelligible relations. But, in the second place, this clearing up of our own nature cannot be completed except by the clearing up of the world of our experience, which at first presents itself as something external and unintelligible. Now the process of clearing up our outward world is the process in which the particular sciences, on the one hand, and the particular arts, on the other, are engaged. By the former, we take up the particular facts given to us in nature and, by bringing them under conceptions, reduce them to a certain order and system, though they still remain external to us. By the latter we take up the particular facts and modify them to serve our own ends; either, as in the case of the practical arts, by making them instrumental to the development of our lives, or, as in the case of the fine arts, by making them express in some degree the principles of our own higher life. We thus conquer nature in a double sense. By means of the sciences we get to see what it is in itself, and

how its various parts are by their own laws related to
each other : while by means of the arts we reduce it under
our own law. We first understand what its own forces
are, and then we convert these forces from enemies into
friends; so that "winds" may "blow and waters roll"
"strength" "and power and deity" instead of misery,
destruction, and death. Then, finally, we have to find in
our outward world things which are by their very nature
elements of our higher life; and these we find in the lives
of other human beings. Hence we may say that in the
attainment of human well-being there are three different
elements involved—(1) individual culture, (2) the conquest of nature, and (3) right social relations. Now
although these elements are all involved in the attainment of our ideal, yet we may easily frame different
ideals for ourselves by laying a special emphasis on one
or other of the elements. A little consideration may suffice
to show in general what the nature of these different
ideals is.

Suppose we begin with the third. If we regard the
establishment of right social relations (considered in
abstraction from everything else) as the thing which is
of supreme importance in the pursuit of the highest well-
being, the view of society to which we are naturally led
is that which we have described as monistic—or at least
is one of those forms in which the part is lost in the
whole, whether it be that of pure monism or that which
we have characterised as a chemical unity.[1] We cannot
suppose that the elements of personal culture and of
the subjugation of nature are of no consequence in
human well-being; and if we suppose that they may
safely be left to take care of themselves, this can only
be because we believe that these things are bound to
follow at once from a right organisation of society. This

[1] Cf. *supra*, p. 151.

implies that we regard the individual as a simple product of his social conditions, or at least as having his nature immediately transformed by his relations to those conditions. A purely monistic view of society is no doubt scarcely possible; for on such a view it would be inexplicable that individuals should even seem to have any independence of their social environment; but a certain approximation to such a view is not only possible, but even, in some aspects, reasonable. The general view of the ideal of human life which is thus suggested is that which may be loosely described as socialistic. The extreme type of such a point of view would be that which finds its ideal in a definitely established mechanical arrangement of social conditions, into which particular individuals have simply to be afterwards fitted. Those ideals which are called communistic approach most nearly to pure monism; while socialism, in the narrower sense, corresponds rather to what we have called a chemical unity.

If, on the other hand, we lay the emphasis rather on the conquest of nature as the important element in human welfare, the ideal to which we are led is a monadistic one. If we suppose that personal culture comes by nature, or may be left to take care of itself, and that social organisation is equally unimportant, we practically suppose the individual to be by nature independent of his society. In conquering nature, indeed, whether in the sense of getting to understand it, or in that of converting it into an instrument of our purposes, the individual will naturally be greatly helped by the co-operation of others. But such help is accidental. His life could quite well be supposed to be carried on without it. The great end to which he is devoted is not one in which the lives of others are essentially involved. Accordingly, the ideal to which we are in this case led is one in which the individual is primarily free to follow out his own purposes, and forms social ties only in so far as he finds them convenient for the accomplishment of his own private ends.

Finally, if we suppose the most important end to be the culture of the individual, we are naturally led to take a dualistic view of the social ideal. For, while we may admit that in the attainment of individual culture, social relations are directly involved, as forming the rational environment in which alone a rational individual can grow; yet so long as we are thinking of the culture of the individual merely as such, we regard these social relations only as a means of the individual development, not as themselves a portion of the end. Consequently, we are led to think of the individual as subjected to certain social conditions to which he is only accidentally related. And within these conditions we naturally think of him as advancing to a state of greater and greater freedom, in proportion to the growth of his culture. Thus the ideal comes to be that of an aristocracy of talent, sloping gradually down from the wisest man, who is also the freest, to the most foolish, who is most under subjection to the laws of his society.

Three different ideals are thus suggested :—(1) the socialistic ideal, or that of the determination of each individual by society as a whole, (2) the individualistic ideal,[1] or that of the freedom of everyone from all bonds except those into which he himself enters by a voluntary contract, and (3) the aristocratic ideal, with freedom at the top and determination at the bottom. This third ideal, as is usually the case with dualistic systems, combines the other two by a kind of compromise. These three ideals are, as we see, suggested by different views with respect to the elements of human welfare to which

[1] Cf., however, what is said *infra*, p. 285, note 2.

it is important to devote attention.  At the same time, it is quite possible that they may be adopted as ideals without any direct reference to these elements, or may even be adopted by men whose main interests are the reverse of those naturally implied in the particular ideal selected.  Indeed there is a certain natural paradox which sometimes appears in the formation of ideals.  Men whose eyes are fixed on any particular elements in human nature as constituting the ideal, are often apt to pre- suppose just those conditions for which in actual life provision would need to be made in order that that particular ideal may become possible.  Hence one some- times has to criticise an ideal as failing, from the neglect of those very objects to which its authors were most ardently devoted.  The intensity of their own devotion to certain aims leads them to suppose that all mankind, or a very large proportion of mankind, have them equally at heart, and that consequently an adequate attention to them may be assumed, without any special precautions, in such a state as they devise.  Thus Plato, in his eager- ness to secure a unity of interest among his citizens, like that which is to be found in a well-regulated family, begins with the abolition of the family itself, in which alone the sentiment of such a unity is naturally developed.[1]  So, too, some modern Anarchists, in their zeal for social organisation, do their best to destroy its basis.  For this, as well as for other reasons, we need not expect to find that the ideals to which we have referred are actually adopted from a consideration of those ends which seem most naturally to suggest them.  Indeed most ideals which have been actually proposed, combine to some extent the elements of more than one of the ideals that we have mentioned, and are adopted from a consideration of more than one of the ends.  At the same time, it will be

---

[1] See Aristotle's *Politics*, II. iv. 6, and cf. Chap. VI.

found in general that one or other of these three ends is
at the bottom of each ideal that is actually proposed, and
gives to it its peculiar tone.

Now as each of the three ideals connects itself naturally with only one element in human well-being, and as
human well-being necessarily involves all the three elements, we are led to expect that each of the ideals will
prove one-sided and deficient, and that a true ideal will
be reached only when provision is made for the realisation of all the three elements.

Let us, however, to begin with, look at each of these
three ideals on its own merits, and see whether it will
actually hold together, or, if not, at what point it breaks
down.    And it may be convenient to start with the
individualistic ideal, since that is the one which was the
first in recent history to be prominently brought forward.

1. Liberty is the idealist's ideal.    It is the ideal to
which we are led when we believe in the natural per-
fectibility of human nature, when it is but well left alone.
It is the ideal which we frame for ourselves in the first
enthusiasm of youth, and as we grow older we begin to
forget, like Mr. Ruskin, what we meant by it.[1]    And
indeed we probably meant more things than one.    We
meant a general release from the limitations and restraints
by which we find ourselves continually restricted in the
effort to develop the latent possibilities that lie within us.
We meant that we should have "scope and verge
enough" to expatiate and grow in all directions.    None
of us has been long in the world before he begins
to discover that "provision has been made that trees
shall not grow into the skies."    He finds himself

---

[1] The *dictum* of Godwin—"Give a state liberty enough, and vice
cannot exist in it"—seems, I suppose, to most modern readers, not
only incredible but unintelligible.    Cf. Bonar's *Malthus and his Work*,
p. 55.

hemmed in on all sides by what seem, at least from his point of view, arbitrary encumbrances; and to free himself from these is his first effort. The preliminary step towards the realisation of an ideal life is evidently to *have* a life—to be a person moulding circumstances, not a thing moulded by them; and to secure this, accordingly, is what we naturally take as our first ideal.

Now the circumstances from which we seek to free ourselves might be either our own intellectual and moral limitations or the restraints of our natural environment, as well as the bonds of social determinations. But it is not of either of the two former limitations that we at first naturally think. It is soon seen that we can conquer our physical surroundings only by submitting to them; while, on the other hand, the limitations of our own nature are chains to whose weight we are apt to be insensible just in proportion to the firmness with which we are bound by them. To free ourselves from the limitations which are imposed on us by society seems at once easier and more pleasant. To be free from ourselves, we must practise a somewhat painful self-control : to be free from nature, we must in a manner "perform the impossible" by evading what under ordinary circumstances are the inevitable results of natural laws—an evasion which can never be carried beyond certain very narrow limits : but to be free from our fellow-men, it appears as if we had only to shake ourselves clear of certain artificial and accidental customs. Accordingly, liberty in this sense is (at least under certain social conditions) a very popular ideal. And it is not very difficult to show that much of our social evil, especially in the earlier stages of social development, arises from the lack of such freedom as this. If it is true that " man is to man a God," it is also true that man is to man an incarnation of the principle of obstruction. For, while the universal

element in us—the fact that we are guided by a common
ideal—causes us to help each other forwards, yet the
fact that that element realises itself in different individuals in different ways, makes our aims in many
cases mutually exclusive; and when they are so exclusive,
the very fact of the community of our ultimate end only
serves to give point to our antagonism. To seek the
same thing in different ways occasions more collision
than to seek different things. Our knowledge that "the
highest good is common to all" embitters for us the
consciousness that some particular good of others is one
in which we do not share. For this reason, we are apt
not only to stand in each other's way, but even consciously to oppose ourselves to each other. There are
few of us who can say, like Goethe, that we are never
to be found on the path of envy.[1] It is not necessary
to take a cynical view of human nature in order to
recognise that, while it is easy to sympathise with the
sufferings of others, it is difficult to sympathise with their
successes. Misfortune "makes the whole world kin";
because we can all take our stand on the level of un-
attained ideals. But success is a chilling thing, when it
is the realisation of a good by another in which we ourselves do not partake; and for this reason it was even
said by Novalis that, if we are to love God, we must
think of Him as suffering. On this account it is often
best that each one should be left alone in the pursuit of
his own ideals, so long as he is able to pursue them
successfully. This applies, of course, with special emphasis to those who are endeavouring to advance in
some direction beyond the limits which human civilisation

---

[1] "Was ich auch für Wege geloffen,
  Auf'm Neidpfad habt ihr mich nie betroffen."

Compare Paulsen's *System der Ethik*, II. 470. See also Mr.
Alexander's *Moral Order and Progress*, p. 13.

has already attained.  Those by whom any
gress of this sort is made,

> "Hat man von je gekreuzigt und verbrannt

and consequently the friends of progress
been also apostles of Freedom.  Even if
agree with Fichte that "to form habits is
with Rousseau that "the only habit whic
acquire is that of acquiring none," yet w
thing distinctly new is to be done, we are a
keenly conscious that the chains of custom

> "lie upon us with a weight,
> Heavy as frost, and deep almost as life."

The great enemy of the better is the goo
achievements of the human race stand ir
progress.  We are prevented from followir
by the fact that other men's ideals are alr
and embodied in our social conditions;
thus frequently tempted to imagine that
better for us if we were not encumbered
connections, if we were left to develop ours
his own way, and if others would simply le
    But if there is any truth in what we
pointed out with regard to the organic natu
such a complete letting alone must be imp
being like man; since it is only by con
fellows that he can live and grow as a hur
all.  And even apart from this considerat
easily convince ourselves that such an idea
freedom could not be carried out.  If p
interfere with one another directly, they v
Since the means of supplying human want
it is impossible, without mutual restraint,
certain collision of interests.  If men

against each other, they are bound at least to enter into competition with each other; and this is often a more bitter, because a colder, struggle than that of sheer antagonism. In the battle of life more execution is often done with the elbows than with the fists; and pure *laisser faire*, instead of freeing us from the interference of one another, leads simply to the most intense of all struggles, in which the less capable are overcome and subjected by the more capable—or rather the less fit, who in a higher sense are sometimes in reality the most capable, by those who are more fit for the struggle of life in that particular style. The less fit are thus driven to the effort to make themselves more fit; and, as man is an inventive animal, they are often able to accomplish this by devising new kinds of instruments. These instruments then become the weapons of war—or rather they become the warriors, and the men are converted into their attendants. The result of this is, as we had occasion to point out before,[1] the exploitation of man by things. Men, in endeavouring to free themselves from one another, become enslaved by their own inventions. For this reason, if for no other, pure liberty in this sense is an impossibility. It "passes over into its opposite," as all such abstractions tend to do.

At the same time, it would be rash to conclude that there is no sense in which it may rightly be maintained that freedom is our ideal. What we find is rather this, that freedom from our fellowmen is not in reality freedom, so long as nature remains our enemy to such an extent that we require to act together in the effort to subdue her. And not only is this the case, but even if we were entirely free from each other, and were so far masters of nature, that each of us could be independent in the struggle against her, it would still not be true that we

---

[1] P. 117. See also Mr. Hobson's recent book on *Machinery*.

were free, unless we were also free inwardly. Milton said of some of the "apostles of freedom" in his time—

> " Licence they mean when they cry liberty,
> For who seeks that must first be wise and good."

To be our own masters is the precondition of freeing ourselves from other masters. Freedom, in fact, can mean for us nothing but that, in Hegelian language, we are "determined by the absolute idea throughout."[1] " Law alone can give us liberty."[2]  If our individual natures were absolutely under the control of the universal principle in us, then, no doubt, it would be quite needless and quite unadvisable that we should be controlled by anything else.  Children, however, in whom it is recognised that the rational nature is not yet fully developed, are by general consent subjected to an external rule ; and so long as there is any truth in the saying that men are but " children of a larger growth" —so long as there remain in them elements of an individual nature unsubdued—they cannot be freed from a certain amount of social regulation.  As the parent is the embodiment of the universal self for the child, so is society the embodiment of it for the man.  And thus we are naturally led from the individualistic[3] to the socialistic ideal.

In calling the second ideal socialistic we are, of course, using that term somewhat loosely.  But it is a

---

[1] On the elements involved in true freedom, cf. Mr. Alexander's *Moral Order and Progress*, p. 8.  See also Lacy's *Liberty and Law*, pp. 29-118.

[2] " Das Gesetz nur kann uns Freiheit geben."  Cf. Montesquieu's definition of Liberty—"Liberty is the right of doing *whatever the laws permit*." (*Esprit des Lois*, XI. 5.)  See also Stirling's *Philosophy of Law*, p. 39, and Caird's *Critical Philosophy of Kant*, Vol. II., pp. 271 and 320.

[3] See note to next paragraph.

loose term at the best ;[1] and it may be used to describe
the ideal to which we are now referring without at least
any wide departure from its ordinary signification. This
ideal, as I understand it, is one in which the individual
is supposed to receive the whole determination of his
life, or the determination of all that is important in his
life, from the conditions of his society. The realisation
of it, carried to its extreme point, would amount to the
pre-existence of a certain social order as a fixed system
into which the individuals had simply to be fitted. Now
into such a system it is clear that the individuals might
be fitted in accordance with a variety of different
principles. Their places in it might be determined by
their abilities, or by their needs, or by a variety of
other considerations. The simplest of all principles, however, is obviously that of pure equality ;[2] and with this
we shall accordingly commence.

[1] On the difficulty of defining Socialism, see Flint's *Socialism*,
chap. i. ; I think, however, that he goes to an extreme in concluding (as Mr. Rae seems also to have done) that we cannot
define it at all except in an eulogistic or dyslogistic sense, according
to the personal attitude which we happen to adopt towards it. We
can surely at least define it, in a more objective way, as a
particular kind of tendency.

[2] It may be well to remark at this point that, in one sense, the
contrast which is commonly drawn between Individualism and
Socialism is not well founded. Socialism in many cases, as Schäffle
has trenchantly pointed out (*Aussichtslosigkeit der Socialdemokratie*,
p. 13), is little more than Individualism run mad. Lassalle too, (the
most brilliant of the Socialists,) recognised that Socialism is in
reality individualistic. Cf. also Stirling's *Philosophy of Law*, p. 59,
and Rae's *Contemporary Socialism*, p. 387. Indeed, the readiness
with which extreme Radicalism passes into Socialism (unless it be
regarded as merely an illustration of the principle that "extremes
meet") may be taken as a sufficient evidence that Socialism is not
in reality opposed to Individualism. No doubt, Socialism is really
opposed to a certain species of Individualism—viz., to the principle
of individual *liberty*. But, in like manner, the principle of individual

(*a*) An ideal of pure equality is naturally founded on the belief that all men are by nature equal and similar, and that the differences between them are produced simply by circumstances and social conditions. Such a belief is not so absurd as it might at first sight seem : and it is one to which those who regard chiefly the universal element in human nature are very easily led.[1] The powers that lead to the discoveries of a Newton or the creations of a Shakespeare are contained implicitly in every conscious intelligence, requiring only to be evolved ; and it might seem as if nothing could account for the fact that they are evolved in one case and not in another but the circumstances that different intelligences have to work under different outward conditions. Now those who hold this belief in the natural equality of men, usually infer from it that the ideal arrangement for society would be one in which all should be restored to that equality in which they were originally born—that as all are naturally equal, they should also have equal advantages and opportunities. Such doctrinaires must be handed over in the first place to the biologists and anthropologists, who will tell them that, in accordance with certain laws of Heredity, and with some other principles of variation which are not so clearly understood, there are to be found among men, as among animals, all manner of individual differences both in the

liberty is opposed to *another* species of Individualism—viz., to the principle of individual *equality*. The real antithesis to Individualism would be found rather in the ideal of an aristocratic polity, established with a view to the production of the best *State*, as distinguished from the production of the happiest condition of its individual members. The most celebrated instance of such an ideal (that sketched in the *Republic* of Plato) happeus to be also to a large extent socialistic ; but this is in the main an accident.

[1] For an emphatic statement of the view, see Adam Smith's *Wealth of Nations*, chap. i.

kind and in the degree of those capabilities of which the possibilities are present in each at the time of birth. It is here, in fact, that the importance of the particular element in human nature comes out. Each one of us is an individual being, with a definite history in time—a history which may be carried back even to a time prior to our birth. And this particular history cannot be regarded as something merely external to ourselves: it is built into our character and belongs to us as truly as the universal part of our nature;[1] and the limits which this particular nature imposes upon us, though they may be partly modified, cannot be entirely removed. For this reason human beings cannot be regarded as by nature alike, though the rational nature of all is similar. But, in the second place, even if it were true, that men are by nature equal, it is by no means clear that it would be desirable to maintain that equality. If, indeed, all could be maintained at the highest level of human life, it would obviously be well that they should be so maintained. But the greatest advances in the condition of mankind have hitherto been made by a few individuals who have been enabled to develop particular kinds of ability in an exceptional degree; and even if it were true that such individuals have by nature no more ability than their fellows, it might yet be desirable among men, as among bees, that a few should be picked out from among the workers—whether by circumstances or by lot, or by some other mode of selection—to be sovereigns and leaders. And when we recognise, what after all is an undeniable fact, that men are *not* by nature either equal or similar, the desirability of distinctions in condition and opportunity becomes still more apparent. The tools ought to go to those who can use them and the sceptre to him who can wield it. Pure Equality, in the

[1] Cf. *supra*, p. 166 *seq.*

fullest sense of the term, is, therefore, not to be thought of; and we must look for some more guarded interpretation, if Equality is to be our ideal.[1]

(*b*) Now the most natural form of this ideal, after simple equality has been rejected, is to be found in the doctrine that every one should work for the good of the community in proportion to his natural capability, and that every one should be supplied with the advantages and opportunities of life in proportion to his wants. This is the ideal which socialistic writers, following the lead of Cabet, Louis Blanc, and others, have in general adopted as their ultimate aim, though they have usually recognised that it is not immediately attainable. And certainly as a pure ideal it would be difficult to devise any scheme which is more fair, though it would be equally difficult to devise one which is more entirely beyond our reach. It seems obviously just that, as man is by nature a member of a community, he should render to the community all the services which he has it in his power to give; and it seems equally just that each member of the community should be supplied, as far as possible, with everything of which he has need. Just as the various members of a living body are supplied with that proportion of blood which is necessary to sustain them at their normal vigour, and just as, having received their portion, they each render to the life of the whole body those particular services for which they are by nature fitted, it seems natural that in the social body a similar rule of justice should be observed. The duty of each would thus be to do all that he can for the good of society; and his right would be to receive

---

[1] On the conception of Equality, cf. Sorley's *Ethics of Naturalism*, p. 71, note. See also Hegel's *Philosophie des Rechts*, I. i. 49. Some useful remarks on the subject will also be found in Professor Flint's recent work on *Socialism*, pp. 315-317.

all that he needs, or, if that is not possible, to receive
of that which the body has to provide in proportion to
the degree of his requirements. Such is the ideal : let us
now see what are the difficulties in the way of its
realisation.

The first and greatest difficulty is that of supplying an
adequate motive for the performance of work in proportion to our abilities. It has been said, not without some
point, that the one quality which is innate in man is
laziness ;[1] and to overcome this natural inertia some
powerful incentive is required. One strong incentive
which has stirred men up to the performance of much of
the best work in the world, is the simple feeling that such
work is right—that the performance of it is demanded,
τοῦ καλοῦ ἕνεκα, or for the realisation of our ideal. The
power of this motive, however, depends on our having
reached such a stage of moral development that the
consciousness of the universal self influences us more
than our merely private interests ; and such a stage of
moral development cannot be presupposed in any state
of society. To call in this motive, in fact, is to invoke
that species of "enthusiasm of humanity" which is what
we commonly understand by Fraternity ; and the possibility of acting by this motive must be considered under
a following head, when we are dealing with the ideal of
Fraternity rather than with that of Equality.[2] It may be
sufficient to remark at this point that even at the highest
stage of moral development it would scarcely be wise to
rely solely upon this motive. It might suffice to prevent

---

[1] Emerson is reported to have said that ordinary human nature is
"as lazy as it dares to be." Cf. Gilman's *Profit-Sharing*, p. 18,
and Bonar's *Malthus and his Work*, p. 36. This applies, of course,
only to continuous exertion with a view to a prescribed end. See
also Mill's *Political Economy*, IV. vii. 7.

[2] See *infra*, p. 337.

a. the absolute neglect of the general good, but could not be trusted to produce the most energetic devotion to it. It is true, no doubt, that patriotic self-devotion is a comparatively common virtue—one which, under certain conditions, is expected and even actually found in every man. But this does not depend entirely on the motive which we are now considering. It depends partly on that fear of disgrace which is made possible by a military discipline, but which could scarcely be made effective within the much more complicated system of industrial life. It depends, moreover, on the vivid presentation of a great and obvious and imminent danger; and could scarcely be expected to show itself in that routine of customary tasks which is the common condition of industry. In the midst of such routine it would be apparent to every one that, though the public weal depended on each performing efficiently his appointed work, yet no great harm would result from a single instance of neglect on the part of one individual. The old maxim would apply—"What is everybody's business is nobody's business."[1] Each would be apt to think—and the less ground he had for thinking it, the more likely on the whole he would be to think it—that the world could get on well enough without his particular piece of service. This fallacy—what we might call *the fallacy of the exceptional case*[2]—is one that is very strongly operative in all departments of human life; but its force is roughly proportional to the extent of the cases from which the exception is made. When we are working for comparatively limited and definite interests, we are less likely to be misled by it than we should be if we had in view the interests of the whole. And there would be a possible

[1] Cf. Aristotle's *Politics*, II. iii. 4.

[2] It is, I suppose, simply a particular case of the fallacy of composition.

danger on the opposite side. Men of exceptional con-
scientiousness in the discharge of their social functions
might be tempted to sacrifice themselves more than is
desirable in the fulfilment of them ; or at least might be
tempted to work too eagerly for the realisation of an
obvious good, to the neglect of the due cultivation of
their powers for the sake of more distant ends. Under
the present system of things, a man's best work is often
work that has been delayed for many years ; and these
years have sometimes been spent in retirement and
apparent idleness, in order that the man's powers might
be completely matured and mellowed. Πτεροφυέω, Milton
said of himself in one of his early letters— " I am letting
my wings grow." Such delay, however, involves a certain
risk ; and even if it were permitted at all in such an
ideal society as that of which we are now speaking, it is
to be feared that the most conscientious men might
hesitate—even as it is, they do hesitate—to run the risk
of leaving their work unperformed. If it were our recognised duty to be continually washing our neighbours'
feet, there would always be some Peters among us who
would insist on washing their hands and their heads—
and, as has been suggested,[1] "drowning themselves in
addition." " So stirbt ein Held "; but the ideal society
must be one that knows how to preserve its heroes.[2] It
is for such reasons as these, drawn both from the frailty
and from the nobility of human nature, that it has

---

[1] *Essays in Philosophical Criticism*, p. 209.

[2] Even in our present society it can scarcely be doubted that
many are tempted to sacrifice their individual development to far
too great an extent to social ends. Of course this is largely due
to the fact that other people neglect these ends ; and it would not
be easy for one who is not a prophet to foresee whether under a
more socialistic régime the temptation to such self-sacrifice would be
increased or diminished.

hitherto been found best to rely on some other motive than that of public spirit—except, indeed, in the case of a few of the highest public offices, to which none but the most trustworthy is naturally appointed, and which none need accept unless he is prepared to fulfil their duties. Now the only other motive that has been found sufficiently powerful and sufficiently universal is that of self-interest [1]—including in that term the interests of our own family, and every other interest with which we are in the habit of identifying ourselves; and this motive may appear in the form of hope or fear—its incentive may be either reward or punishment. Reward, however, is definitely excluded from our present ideal; since the supply of benefits is to be in proportion to needs, and not to services. Hence the only motive which is left is that which is supplied by punishment. But the fear of punishment is justly regarded as the most ignoble of all motives which are not positively malevolent, since it fixes attention on the neglect of duty, instead of on the performance of it.[2] Moreover, in such an ideal society as we are here considering, it would be impossible to make punishment efficient. For no one could ever determine whether a man is doing all the work of which he is capable, or is doing what may be regarded as his fair share of the work that is to be done; and even to make any tolerable approximation to such an estimate, an extremely elaborate governmental machinery would be

[1] It ought to be carefully observed that self-interest in this sense is not identical with—and may even be opposed to—selfishness. For some good remarks on this point, I may refer to Flint's *Socialism*, pp. 364-6.

[2] The desire of some form of reward, on the other hand—especially of rewards which are immaterial—is rightly said to be an "infirmity of noble minds"; because in such cases the reward is inseparably associated with the actions of which it is the reward.

required, and a very large staff of officials. And the uncertainty which would always remain as to the degree in
which any individual had offended, together with the
odium which would naturally attach to the officials if
they dealt with any too harshly, would probably make it
necessary to treat offences with so much laxity as to
permit the indolent to neglect their duties to a very
much greater extent than is at present possible. The
inevitable result would be that the capable would be
pillaged by the incapable, just as under a system of
*laisser faire* the reverse would be the case. The·cushion
goes to the idle as naturally as the battle to the strong.
Further, there would, of course, remain also the old difficulty of all such schemes—*Quis custodiet custodes?* We
have only to add that in such a society there would be
no sufficient stimulus to the development of talent. The
sharpening of our intellect would increase responsibility
without adding to reward ; and as there are always some
to whom a pillow is more attractive than a crown of
thorns, or even of laurel, there would always be some
who would allow their talents to rust, and persuade
themselves and others that they did not possess them.
It would be the paradise of all the Skimpoles.

Again, how is the proportion of men's needs to be
determined? Man is by nature "as hungry as the sea."
Our wants are infinite, and it would be quite impossible
to assign their limits. It might be possible to find out
who is the greediest; but this would hardly be the same
thing as to discover who· had the greatest necessities.
The most clamorous wants are seldom the most pressing.
Moreover, there are some wants whose satisfaction is the
means of creating new ones. This is the case, for instance, with most wants for those things which are
commonly classed as luxuries, and also, though in a
different way, with those wants which lead to the propaga-

tion of the species.   Are such wants to be estimated on
the same footing as the others?   There are other wants,
again, of which the reverse is true—wants whose object,
when it is attained, ceases to appear desirable and sates
instead of satisfying.   "Was man in der Jugend wünscht,
hat man im Alter die Fülle."   Such wants also can
scarcely be classed along with most other wants, as
equally deserving to be provided for.   These considerations, and others like them, would add serious complications to a calculus of wants, even if it were otherwise
possible.   Further, it may reasonably be doubted whether,
if the supply of advantages were proportioned to the
number and intensity of our wants, the inequalities of
human condition would not be made even greater than
they are at present.   The claims which a highly toned
nature makes upon the world are probably infinitely
greater than those of a coarser appetite.   The result of
this, as things are, is in general that those more pressing
needs become for the being who has them "a spur which
the clear spirit doth raise"; a spur which constitutes one
of the most effective motives towards the advancement
of human well-being.   But to endeavour fully to satisfy our
most intense desires at once would probably be to make
the lots of different men more unequal than they are, and
very likely at the same time to destroy a great deal of the
interest of life.   Half the value[1] of most of the things
that we win for ourselves, consists in the fact that we win
them.

Some of the objections that have now been stated

---

[1] Not the *pleasure*-value, observe, but the *preference*-value.   (Cf.
*supra*, pp. 252-3.   The point is not that in winning these objects
for ourselves, we have the additional *pleasures of pursuit*: but rather
that, without that pursuit, we cannot really win the objects at all—
we cannot really make them *our own*, or become fully at home with
them.

might, no doubt, be rendered of far less force, by allowing some time for the development of new social instincts and new forms of social machinery. In so far, however, as it implies the development of new social interests, the ideal ceases to be one of mere social organisation, and becomes one of moral culture. It might, indeed, be said that a right social organisation would of itself be sufficient to supply the necessary cultivation of moral habit. But this could scarcely be maintained with any show of reason. In a being such as man, whose moral development involves a long and complicated process, any considerable change in the principles of action cannot be expected to be brought about at once by an alteration of external conditions. There are, I suppose, few who will not be prepared to grant that the ideal which we have now been considering must at least enter into any ultimate ideal that we can frame of a perfect human society; but it cannot, without modification by the introduction of other elements, be accepted as constituting in itself the whole idea at which we ought at present to aim.

(*c*) This ideal having failed, the next which presents itself—which, indeed, grows naturally out of criticisms that have been passed on the preceding—is that of proportioning rewards to labour or services rendered, instead of to needs. This is the ideal which is usually accepted by Socialistic writers as that which is to be immediately aimed at, whenever they have become convinced that the other is unattainable. It is the ideal represented by Saint-Simon, and by many other eminent authorities; and it is summed up in the saying, "To every one according to his capacity, to every capacity according to its works."[1] It is not so obviously an equitable ideal as the former:

---

[1] The limitation expressed in this last clause has, I think, been overlooked by Professor Flint. *Socialism*, p. 125.

for why, we naturally ask, should a man be rewarded for possessing more ability than another? But it has at least the great practical merit of supplying a more or less visible standard, and at the same time providing us with an adequate motive—not, indeed, the highest motive, but also not the lowest—for the cultivation and use of our abilities. It has, in fact, merits somewhat like those of Utilitarianism as an ethical system: it is rough, but it looks like common-sense. But is the standard which is supplied by it in reality a practicable one? A little reflection will, I think, convince us that it is not. For how are we to estimate the work which is done? Difficulties will arise in the effort to do this, whether we endeavour to estimate the labour from the point of view of the agent, or the services from the point of view of the community. It may be worth while to notice some of these difficulties.

The main difficulties are, in truth, simply those which must beset every effort to define what is to be understood by Labour in such a way as to make it a precise conception of a measurable quantity. Labour might be defined as the means whereby serviceable objects are produced, in so far as their production is dependent on human volition; and according to this definition the natural measure of the worth of labour would be the serviceableness of the object which it produces. But if this is to be the measure, how is the serviceableness itself to be estimated? Who is to determine the relative values of a yard of cloth and a line of poetry as means for the satisfaction of human wants?[1] And, even apart

---

[1] It is, no doubt, largely owing to the fact that Utilitarianism seems to furnish the means of instituting such a comparison as this, that that theory has seemed so attractive to many minds. If we could say, The article A supplies us so much pleasure, and the article B so much, the matter would be comparatively simple. But

from this difficulty, we must remember always that the value of articles (*i.e.* of course, their value in use) varies inversely with the quantity produced, until at last the production of any more becomes positively pernicious. Hence we cannot regard any particular articles that are produced as having definitely ascertainable values in themselves; and indeed to estimate aright the value of any given article, we should require to know precisely how much of the article is being produced, or has been produced, or is about to be produced, in every other part of the world with which we are in communication. It is thus apparent that very considerable difficulties would lie in the way of any attempt to estimate the worth of labour with reference to the serviceableness of the articles which it produces.

But, again, another definition of labour might be that it is the *effort* by which serviceable objects are produced; and, if we adopt this definition, the measure of the worth of labour would naturally be found in the degree of effort which is involved. But neither is the estimation of the degree of effort involved in any action an altogether simple matter. Are we to mean by effort the amount of energy expended? Or are we to mean the difficulty which a given individual experiences? The difficulty will obviously vary with the abilities of the workers, and will be a quite incalculable element; and if, instead of considering the difficulty for a given individual, we consider rather the difficulty for an average human being, we are still not freed from the presence of a factor which defies calculation. There are some forms of labour which have no estimable degree of difficulty for an average human being,

even on the Utilitarian theory it would be only ideally possible to do this: practically there would be insuperable difficulties. And we have already seen reason to believe that the Utilitarian theory is false.

but are strictly impossible. It is not allowed *mediocribus esse poetis*, and there is a similar prohibition on the performance of all the higher forms of artistic production in the manner in which a merely average human being could perform them. The reward of such production, therefore, if estimated by the difficulty for an average human being, would be expressible only by an infinite magnitude. The same remark would apply also to some extent to the labour of superintendence in some of the more complicated industries, and to the work of the scientific investigator. Nor could we escape from this difficulty by endeavouring to estimate the amount of energy which is on the average expended in different kinds of labour, rather than the degree of difficulty which is involved. For there is no common measure for different modes of the expenditure of human energy.

Moreover, even if it were possible to evade the difficulties in the way of the estimation of effort, it would be obviously unfair to reward labour in proportion to the effort which it involves without reference to the values of the objects that are produced by it—unless it could be assumed that all forms of labour in which human beings engage are necessary for the well-being of society. For it is easily possible to expend a great deal of effort upon objects which no sane community would ever think of encouraging ; and even on objects which are in themselves desirable it is easily possible to expend an amount of effort which is quite disproportionate to their value. It would not be wise, therefore, to proportion reward to effort, unless the direction of efforts to worthy objects were very strictly enforced ; and this would obviously involve serious difficulties.

Again, it is not at once obvious what forms of activity ought to be regarded as constituting effort at all. In our ordinary conception of labour we think chiefly of

muscular effort, with which it is comparatively easy to
deal. Whenever we go beyond this, it becomes very
hard to determine what is and what is not labour, and
still harder to determine what is and what is not the
product of any particular act of labour. The labour of
superintendence, for instance, or that of watching over
objects already produced with a view to their preservation, can scarcely be excluded from the category of
labour, and yet may not involve any muscular exertion
or even the expenditure of any estimable amount of
nervous force. Again, is the saving which results in the
accumulation of capital to be regarded as a form of
labour?[1] It is clearly a means by which something
serviceable is produced (*i.e. preserved*, which is a form of
production), and it is also an activity which may involve
some effort: it may involve the exercise of foresight and
self-denial. Yet if we class this as labour, the ordinary
meaning of the word seems to be entirely lost, and a
certain sense of confusion begins to be felt.

No doubt, it might be possible to avoid all these
difficulties if a hedonistic standard could be adopted—*i.e.*
if we could estimate the degrees of disagreeableness of
different kinds of effort to an average human being, and
also the agreeableness of the products of different kinds
of effort to the community at large.[2] But we have
already seen reason to believe that this cannot be done.
It might, however, be possible to estimate the degree of
aversion which most men have for different kinds of
effort, and also the degree of preference which they
have for the products of different kinds of labour. In

---

[1] It has been so regarded by Courcelle Seneuil, and by one or
two other economic writers. Cf. Böhm-Bawerk, *Kapitalzins Theorien*,
p. 346 (p. 300 in Mr. Smart's translation).

[2] Here again we see a reason for the prevalence of the Utilitarian
view among those who wish for some practical standard of value.

this way both elements in labour—both effort and result
—might be to some extent evaluated.[1]  This is, in fact,
in some degree what is actually accomplished by the
present competitive system.   But the estimate which is
thus arrived at is very rough and unsatisfactory.   Our
sense of justice is violated by the perception that human
effort is sometimes highly rewarded, merely on account of
its uniqueness, without any reference to the value of its
product; and that, on the other hand, a very slight effort
frequently meets with a great reward, merely because it
happens to have been directed to an object to which a
high value is attached.  Accidental circumstances also,
such as the existence of monopolies (natural or artificial),
prevent our present competitive system from working
quite fairly.  It would require, in fact, before it could be
regarded as a system of perfect justice, that there should
be no advantages conferred on any individuals, either by
human convention or by situation and other natural conditions, and that, at the same time, the estimate put on
the value of the products of labour by average human
beings should be constant and wise and easily calculable.
If these conditions could be fulfilled, the competitive
system would furnish the means for the realisation of that
ideal of social organisation with which we are at present
concerned.   But as the conditions are not fulfilled, that
system remains at the best extremely rough, and at the
worst almost intolerable.   Yet, on the other hand, what
other method can be adopted, if the ideal which we are
to seek is this particular kind of equality?

It might, indeed, be said that a certain rough estimate
could be made of the relative merits of different kinds of

[1] Here again, observe that, by substituting *preference* for *pleasure*,
we retain what is valuable in Utilitarianism, while we reject Hedonism, at least in its ordinary acceptation. We measure value instead
of sense of value.

labour, taking account both of their difficulty and of the value of their products : and it might be urged that such an estimate, though only a very wide approximation to what is perfectly fair, would be preferable to our present competitive system : that its results would be fairer, and would certainly be less deadly. I understand that Mr. Ruskin,[1] among others, regards some such estimate as this as the ideal method. It is pointed out that even at present this method is to some extent adopted in the payment of certain public servants—*e.g.* soldiers, clergymen, professors, and so on. But in reply to this there are several things to be said. In the first place, it is not true that the salaries of these public servants are fixed by any direct estimate of the value or difficulty of their services. They are fixed rather at such a sum as is considered sufficient to attract the right kind of men to the posts, and to support them in such a degree of comfort and social status as is supposed to be appropriate to their position. Now it is clear that that sum will depend on the profits of other occupations : and thus even the salaries of these somewhat exceptionally situated individuals are determined ultimately by competition. But, in the second place, even if it were true that they are determined by the estimate of the services which the receivers render, it is obvious that the position of such individuals is a peculiar one. They have in general certain definite duties to perform ; and each must be able to perform all his special work in a fairly satisfactory way. An incompetent public servant, in any of the higher offices, is as intolerable as a mediocre poet. It is not so in the ordinary work of life. One who is incompetent to perform a piece of work completely may yet be more or less competent, under proper guidance, to render some assistance in its performance. Such more or less

[1] See, for instance, *Unto this Last*, Essay I.

incompetent persons—who are perhaps the larger half of
mankind—have under the present system wages which are
fixed by a certain rough kind of competition : but, under
the system which we are now considering, they would
probably require either to receive the full wages of a
competent workman or to be dismissed altogether. Mr.
Ruskin seems to suggest the latter alternative.[1] But this
would be an ideal with a vengeance ! Further, if rewards
were determined in this way, there would be continual
dissatisfaction among the members of the community with
regard to the manner of their apportionment. Each
would be apt to think that the kind of work with which
he is least familiar is too highly paid.

> "The ploughman will despise and scoff
> The thing he is not skilful of" ;

and we are all ploughmen in some degree. This would
add very much to the difficulties, already sufficiently great,
of those who had the task of determining the values of
different kinds of labour—whoever these might be ; and
they would tend, in consequence—if they were subject to
human frailties at all—to favour those occupations at
which the largest number, or those who could most
easily make themselves heard, were employed. For all
these reasons, any such scheme as this appears to be
quite impracticable.[2]

(*d*) The next substitute for complete equality that re-

---

[1] At least, he does not seem definitely to suggest any other. Cf.
*Unto this Last*, Essay II.

[2] On the defects of a fixed wage system, cf. also what is said in
Gilman's *Profit-Sharing*, p. 45, etc. See also Flint's *Socialism*, p. 351,
note. I may remark here that the now generally recognised method
of estimating objective or social values by the balance of positive
and negative utilities—as explained, for instance, in Professor Marshall's
*Principles of Economics*—does not involve any such measurement of
the incommensurable as has been above referred to ; since it merely
gives an estimate of the desires and aversions of the "marginal man."

quires consideration, is the demand that at least a certain minimum should be fixed, beyond which the supply of wants should not be allowed to fall. In modern civilised communities a certain effort has always been made in this direction; but it has usually been made on the plea of charity rather than of justice, and the standard which it has set up has seldom been a high one. The causes of this are not far to seek. They are partly to be found in the individualistic view which has been taken of the nature of society, and partly in conditions that lie deeper. When we regard society as an organic whole, it seems a moderate and equitable claim that each individual in the society should have at least his existence secured, and secured in such a way that he might be able to the extent of his powers to contribute to the welfare of the whole to which he belongs. But the recognition of this claim to its full extent would be possible only on two conditions—(1) that society should exercise an adequate control over the increase of population, and (2) that everyone should be made to contribute in an adequate degree to the welfare of the whole. Society can scarcely undertake to support its rebellious children or those who ought never to have been its children at all. Now the difficulties in the way of enforcing the second of these conditions have been already noticed; and those in the way of enforcing the first condition are perhaps sufficiently obvious without special notice.[1] Accordingly, since the necessary conditions cannot be provided, the attitude of most modern societies towards their citizens represents a compromise between the recognition of their rights[2]

---

[1] Cf. what is said on this subject in next chapter.

[2] This must, of course, be modified by the fact that extreme individualists do not recognise any such rights, and that this individualistic view has had a powerful influence on the action of most modern societies.

and the recognition of the impossibility of granting them. Against such an attitude it may be urged that an obvious right must not be thus lightly passed over. It was towards the attainment of a definite recognition of such a "right to labour," as is well known, that the efforts of Louis Blanc were directed;[1] and though these efforts did not lead to any successful issue, yet in the opinion of some competent judges the failure of his schemes was due merely to the fact that they did not have a fair trial.[2] Some more recent philanthropists also[3] have thought that the most important economic problem of our time is to be found in the attempt to find some practical method of enforcing this right. But it cannot be denied that the difficulties to which reference has been made are serious and cannot be evaded. On the one hand, there cannot be any effective care for individuals if their numbers multiply indefinitely. Not only must there be some restriction on the natural increase of the population in a community, but care must be taken that the surplus from less civilised communities is not attracted into it.[4] And neither of these objects can be attained without certain forms of governmental interference which might prove very irksome and dangerous to the freedom

---

[1] The "right to existence" is, of course, distinguishable from the "right to labour." See Flint's *Socialism*, pp. 408-9, and Anton Menger's *Das Recht auf den vollen Arbeitsertrag*, pp. 15, 16. But practically, in the case of able-bodied citizens, the "right to existence" could not be interpreted as meaning anything else than a "right to labour." The "right to labour" (*droit au travail*) should of course also be carefully distinguished from the mere "right of labour" (*droit du travail*). Cf. Ritchie's *Natural Rights*, p. 230.

[2] Cf. *Encyclopaedia Britannica*, art. "Socialism," p. 209, and Anton Menger, *loc. cit.*, p. 118, note 5.

[3] See, for instance, the interesting book by Mr. Herbert V. Mills on *Poverty and the State*.

[4] Cf. next chapter.

of the individual, and which might also easily be carried out in an unwise and even positively detrimental way. On the other hand, precautions would have to be taken that no provision should be made for any individual who did not at the same time render some adequate service to the community. Otherwise the effect of any such regulation would merely be to place a premium upon indolence. Now it is very difficult for any central authority to provide labour of a really productive sort and to see that it is efficiently performed, and yet not performed in such a way as to overburden those who are in reality incapable of it. Such labour as a government provides is almost certain to be done with a minimum of exertion on the part of those who are employed; and the remuneration for it must also, in consequence, be very slight. And even when it is reduced to the lowest, if it is not otherwise rendered unattractive, there is always a danger that idlers may find it agreeable to keep out of more regular occupations, in which more is expected of them, and to swell the list of those servants of the public in general who have no one in particular to serve. At any rate, the more sufficient the government provision is, the less inducement must there be for those whose disposition is indolent and whose "standard of comfort" is low to look out for any fixed employment. And if this danger is prevented by very stringent regulations and by the most strict inquiry and supervision in each individual case, the employment is apt to become so irksome and disreputable that many will prefer to endure the utmost privations rather than to enter it. These difficulties are not raised here with the view of discrediting any such attempt, but only to make it apparent that even so moderate a measure of Socialism as this is not to be entered on with a light heart.[1] One cannot but hope

[1] Further remarks on this point will be found in next chapter.

U

that in the end some such measure will not be found impracticable : but it can scarcely be doubted that if it is to be efficiently carried out it must be accompanied by educational and humanising influences as well as those of mere state machinery.

(*e*) Closely connected with this "right to labour" is the duty of labour; and the effort to enforce this also may be taken as a modest socialistic ideal, when more ambitious schemes have been abandoned. The existence of an idle class is regarded by many as the chief grievance of the present state of society. And certainly the demand that everyone should be required to contribute, in proportion to his ability, to the well-being of the society to which he belongs, is, at least on a first view, a reasonable and obvious claim. If we owe all that we are to society, as in some sense we clearly do, it seems only fair that each of us should give what he can of service in return. And doubtless, as a matter of principle, it is fair. The moral obligation cannot be denied. The only question is, whether it is possible or expedient to enforce it. But, as soon as we reflect on it, we see that it would not be easy to enforce such a claim. Indeed, it could not be enforced at all without interfering with the rights of property. For, as long as men are allowed to acquire property, no inducement to labour can be brought to bear on those who have acquired it, unless some species of penalties were to be devised :[1] and, so far as one can at present judge, no system of penalties could be made to work. Nor is it clear that anything would be gained for society as a whole by compelling those who own property to take part to a greater extent than they do in the ordinary

---

[1] It is, of course, assumed here that the simple moral obligation is not of itself a sufficient motive for most men. That it is not, will, I suppose, not be disputed.

forms of productive industry. The great advantages with which they would enter into competition with the other workers might even render such participation harmful. What is desirable is rather that those who are so favourably situated should employ their opportunities—as some actually do—for the purpose of rendering to the state or to society such services as only those who are so favourably situated can render. But to enforce the performance of such services would be futile; partly because there are only a few who are capable of rendering them, and it cannot be determined beforehand who are so capable; and partly because the effectiveness of such services depends in some degree on their being entirely voluntary. It seems clear, therefore, that if the duty of labour were to be enforced, the right of private property would first require to be abolished. To abolish private property directly is, however, a proposal that would find few advocates, except among those who are prepared to go farther—*i.e.* among those who are prepared to demand such an equality as we have already referred to under previous heads. Private property serves certain ends in human society which are partly of an obvious and superficial character and partly of a character that is more subtle and profound. The hope of acquiring property is one of the main incentives to labour in our present state, and it can scarcely be doubted that to withdraw it would be a serious blow to industry. It is true that such an incentive as this is not the noblest possible motive. But it is at least a higher motive than the fear of punishment, which would in all probability require to be substituted for it, if it were abolished. Nor, indeed, is it so ignoble a motive as it is apt sometimes to be thought. It is but "a fruit of unripe wisdom" to suppose that because some forms of property—the forms that most commonly impress us—might very well be dispensed with, the desire for property in general is therefore to be regarded as folly.[1]  Property in some form is essential to the very idea of personality.  A man does not become completely human until he possesses something which he can call his own, on which he may in some measure impress his character.  This follows from the place which the subjugation of nature plays in the development of our self-conscious life.[2]  No doubt, as the moral consciousness grows, it becomes possible to find in the common good an object in which our personality can be sufficiently expressed.  The saying of Schiller—

> "Etwas muss er sein eigen nennen,
> Oder der Mensch wird morden und brennen,"

applies in its full force only to an elementary stage in human development.  Still, in every human consciousness this stage has to be in some form passed through.  To ignore this is to forget the element of particularity which enters into every individual consciousness.  Universal interests become developed in us only through and by means of those which are private.  And even in a community which has reached a high stage of development, the ideals of different personalities are worked out along different lines, and require different material for their expression.  Indeed, the richer a community becomes in the ideal interests of the personalities which compose it, the more diverse become their modes of expression, though they may all be the expression of a common spirit.  It is, in fact, by such divergence that different lines are able to complement each other, and

---

[1] For some interesting remarks on this subject, see Dr. Hutchison Stirling's *Philosophy of Law*, p. 37.  Cf. also Bonar's "Struggle for Existence" (*Essays in Philosophical Criticism*, p. 240), and Rae's *Contemporary Socialism*, p. 387.

[2] Cf. *supra*, pp. 274-5.  See also next chapter.

constitute together an organic whole rich in ideal content. It may be said that the kind of property required for such expression as this, is only a small part of what is commonly included in private property. It may be said, for instance, that it supplies no justification for the existence of property in land, nor for the surplus property of most rich men. But we are not here concerned to justify all forms of property, but only to point out the importance of the existence of private property in some shape. To consider *to what extent* private property is required is a much more complex subject.[1] No doubt, there are some forms of property which it is hard to justify. No doubt, also, as civilisation advances, the existence of private property of some kinds becomes less important or becomes important in a different way. The invention of printing for instance, and other modes of reproduction, has made private property in books, pictures, etc., less important than it once was. But so long as human personalities develop along different lines, and so long as these personalities have to express the meaning of their lives by means of a material which is limited in amount, it seems impossible that private property should be abolished without disastrous results.

Other arguments might be added. We might point out, with Aristotle,[2] that it is a more perfect discipline of virtue in individuals that they should learn to use their property for the public good than that they should never have any property of their own to use at all.[3] This is, however, not any real addition to what we have already

[1] Cf. next chapter.

[2] *Politics*, II. v. 8 *seq.*

[3] The recognition of this constitutes the main point in the important distinction drawn by Mr. Bosanquet between Economic Socialism and Moral Socialism. See *The Civilisation of Christendom*, pp. 304-357.

urged; for it is simply another way of saying that we rise to universal interests only through particular interests. We might add also that it is of some importance, for national reasons, that the leading members of a state should have interests of a material kind in its prosperity. Private property is to the life of a nation what the skeleton is to the body; it is not the life, but it helps to hold the living tissues together. Hence, to make any attempt to abolish private property would, at least at the present stage of civilisation, be a very dangerous experiment. But this is a point on which it is not of so much consequence to insist, and represents a necessity which may possibly at some time be overgrown.

We see, then, from such considerations as these, that the abolition of private property would involve serious difficulties. Consequently, the attempt to enforce the duty of labour would also involve serious difficulties. Here again it is scarcely necessary to state that these difficulties are not brought forward with the view of discrediting the effort to enforce these duties, but only to make it apparent that this effort cannot be made purely by means of social organisation. What we have to rely on is rather the development of public opinion. The force of this has already in some degree been felt with regard to this very matter. The glory of labour and the ignobility of sloth has been brought home to us by the eloquence of Carlyle and other writers, as well as by the progress of industrial life; and, at least for one who wishes to stand well in the opinion of his fellows, it is no longer so easy as it once was to spend a life of idleness. There can be no reasonable doubt that in the future this will be still more strikingly true; and there is everything to be hoped from the development of such a sentiment as a means of enforcing the duty of labour. But to enforce it merely by means of social machinery seems altogether impossible.

(*f*) Even when this is fully recognised, however, it may still be thought that something may be done by means of social machinery. It may be said, for instance, that though private property cannot very well be abolished, its ownership may at least be restricted to those who have earned it by their services to the community—*i.e.* we may prevent inheritance. But even this would be very difficult. For unless we prevented gift as well as inheritance, a man might easily alienate his property before his death, reserving only, if he chose, the use of it during his lifetime. Besides, to abolish inheritance would to a certain extent destroy one of the most effective (and by no means one of the lowest) motives that at present exists to labour—that of making a provision for one's family. And there is another consideration, directly connected with this one, which is sometimes apt to be overlooked —viz. that it is to a large extent the fact of inheritance that provides the possibility of a cultured class. Many of the foremost names in science and literature are those of men whose culture has depended to a great extent on the position in which their parents have been enabled to place them. It often takes two generations to make a great man—one to rise above the mere struggle for existence, and another to gain education. Such men as Goethe, for instance, or in our own time, Mr. Ruskin, might be named as conspicuous examples of men who could not easily have acquired their insight into life and art, or built up for themselves "the beautiful style which did them honour," or become so strong and independent influences in their generations, if they had not been from the first lifted above the common struggle.[1] There are illustrious instances, even in the regions of the highest culture, of men who have been "self-made"; but they

[1] Cf. Graham's *Social Problem*, p. 172, and Marshall's *Principles of Economics*, p. 313.

were men of altogether exceptional genius, and for the
most part they retain scars from the contest, and have
become great rather from the force of their personality
than from the perfection of their work. "Es bildet ein
Talent sich in der Stille," and it is for the sake of providing
this quiet that the existence of a leisured class is so important. A great deal of culpable idleness and misused
wealth may be tolerated for the sake of even a few men of
culture. "We must take care of the Beautiful," as Goethe
said; and the highest beauty in literature and art can
rarely be secured where there is not a certain repose.[1]
Leisure is the basis of civilisation, and culture is the child
of "idlesse."

(*g*) Many other methods might be noticed, in which it
has been proposed to bring about a more perfect equalisa-
tion of human conditions by a more or less drastic reorganisation of society. Such proposals, for instance, as
that of the nationalisation of the land or the abolition of
interest might be discussed. But any consideration of
these schemes would lead us too far into economic
details,[2] and would not after all help us much in the

[1] Cf. Professor Sidgwick's article on "Luxury" in the *International
Journal of Ethics*, for October, 1894.

[2] Some readers may think that even in what has been said in this
chapter we have encroached too much on the province of the economist. Certainly it is difficult to determine precisely where the
division ought to be drawn; but I have endeavoured not to touch
on economic questions, except in so far as they bear directly on the
general principles of social well-being. There have, in recent years,
been many discussions of Socialism from the Economic point of view.
The brief summary in Gide's *Political Economy* may be found useful.
Professors Newcomb and Nicholson have given somewhat more
elaborate discussions; but I think they are also more one-sided.
Professor Sidgwick's arguments on the subject, and on the whole
subject of State action, both in his *Principles of Political Economy*
and in his *Elements of Politics*, are full of suggestiveness. The more
historical treatment by Kirkup, Rae, and Graham, and also the hints

understanding of the subject with which we are now concerned. It is, however, necessary that some reference should be made, in conclusion, to those proposals which are now most commonly classed as socialistic in the narrower sense, and to which in recent times so much prominence has been given. The proposals of modern "scientific Socialism" are carefully guarded, and are not usually supposed by its more. thoughtful advocates to constitute a complete and final ideal for human society. They are suggested rather as the first attainable stage in the progress towards something more thorough. The modern Socialist recognises in general the necessity at present—if not always—for some degree of inequality in human conditions. He is not by any means

> "One who hath yearnings
> For equal returns to unequal earnings,"

but rather very much the reverse. He recognises in general the necessity for private property, and sometimes even is prepared to acknowledge the benefits which are conferred by the right of inheritance, or at least to acquiesce in the continuance of that right as a temporary provision. But he believes that the great evil of modern industrial life arises from the existence of private property in the instruments of production; and he holds, accordingly, that this kind of private property ought to be as speedily as possible abolished — that all the

contained in Bonar's *Philosophy and Political Economy*, are generally judicious and often mutually complementary. Mr. N. P. Gilman's interesting book on *Socialism and the American Spirit* shows great insight and good sense ; and more recently Professor Flint (*Socialism*, 1894) has treated the matter with sound learning and much incisiveness, though perhaps with a somewhat imperfect sympathy. Schäffle's *Impossibility of Social Democracy* is certainly trenchant, but must strike most English readers as extreme. Mr. Dawson's recent writings on German Socialism may also be referred to.

instruments of production ought to be placed in the hands of the community as a whole, or in the hands of sections of the community subject to central regulation.  Now the consideration of the economic basis of Socialism in this sense does not belong to our present subject.  It is no part of our business to inquire to what extent industry is dependent on capital, or even to what extent it is justifiable that interest should be paid for its use.  These questions belong to economics.[1]  It may be conceded to the scientific economist that much of what has been written by exponents of the socialistic cult has taken its colour from some unfortunate statements of Ricardo,[2] by which they have been led either to ignore or to under-estimate the parts played in production by the use of capital, by the services of the *entrepreneur*,[3] and even by the skill and intelligence of

---

[1] I may say that the best treatise on the general subject of interest which is known to me, is that of Böhm-Bawerk—*Kapitalzins Theorien.* (Recently translated by Mr. William Smart, under the title *Capital and Interest.*)  *Die positive Theorie des Kapitals* is a continuation of the same work, which has also been recently translated by Mr. Smart.  I think, however, that Professor Marshall is right in saying (*Principles of Economics*, I., p. 627, note) that Professor Böhm-Bawerk "would appear often to have exaggerated the errors of his predecessors; to have found sharp contrasts between the doctrines of successive schools, where there was really little more than a difference of emphasis; and to have represented their work generally as more fragmentary and one-sided than it really was."

[2] Cf., however, Marshall's *Principles of Economics*, I., p. 532.

[3] It is now pretty generally admitted that the earlier economists overlooked too much the special functions of the Undertaker, as distinguished from the Capitalist.  This point was first clearly brought out by Bagehot.  See his *Economic Studies*, pp. 52-4.  It has since been emphasised, among others, by General Walker (*Political Economy*, pp. 76-9, etc.) and by Professor Marshall (*Principles of Economics*, I., pp. 355-6, etc.).  The statements of the latter on this subject seem to me to be the most careful and well

particular kinds of workmen. But with this we are not here concerned. We have to regard Socialism, not as an economic theory, but only as a social ideal. When the importance of capital and skill has been fully recognised—and some Socialists do recognise this—it is still possible to maintain that it would be for the benefit of the community that all capital should belong to society as a whole,[1] and that all skill should be under its direct supervision. When the work of Karl Marx has been forgotten, except as a curiosity of economic speculation, and as a masterly exposition of some of the evils of the present competitive system, Socialism, as an ideal of political and social reform, may continue to awake as much enthusiasm as before.[2] And it cannot be denied that the ideal which such Socialism proposes—when it is stripped of the extravagances of some of its more extreme adherents—is one that has many recommendations. It is free from most of the defects that have been indicated in the preceding sections, and it seems to meet the great evil of the exploitation of man by things, which, as we have seen,[3] is at the basis of so much of our social misery. Yet even in this temperate and guarded form, Socialism is open to several grave objections; and though the task of overthrowing ideals is not a pleasant one, we must endeavour to make these objections as clear as possible.

The first objection is very obvious and very trite, but

balanced. Mr. Mallock has emphasised the same point in a more popular and one-sided way, in his recent book on *Labour and the Popular Welfare.*

[1] Society here being understood to mean either a state or a municipality.

[2] Cf. Mr. Smart's Preface to Böhm-Bawerk's *Capital and Interest,* p. xix.

[3] *Supra,* p. 117 *seq.*

is none the less weighty. "Society as a whole" is an expression which denotes a large and cumbrous body, composed of a great variety of heterogeneous elements, wisdom and folly, benevolence and selfishness, energy and indolence, mixed together in fluctuating and incalculable proportions; and if the conduct of affairs were left in the hands of such a body, there is no possibility of foreseeing what might occur. Would things be managed by the ablest, the most energetic, and the most public-spirited of the citizens? Does not experience rather show that qualities such as these, with the exception perhaps of the second, have not been found hitherto to lead with any certainty to popular favour. It is not to be expected that they should. A large community has hardly any means of judging which of its citizens are in reality most public-spirited, except by the promises and professions which they make; and if professions bear any proportion to performances, it is to be feared that it is in general an inverse one. Nor has such a community the means of judging of the ability of its citizens, except by watching the results of their conduct;[1] hence, a posthumous fame is an enviable distinction, and history becomes more just as its theme becomes more remote. Few things are more to be relied on than the popular judgment on actions *after* they are done; and consequently Socialism would be the true ideal for beings that lived backwards. But the great difficulty of conduct for us consists in the fact that we live forwards.

> "Es liesse sich Alles trefflich schlichten,
> Könnte man die Sachen zweimal verrichten."

If we could go back on our actions, the problem of life would be solved. The average human being is a respectable historian, but a miserable prophet: and it is chiefly

[1] Of course all this is to be taken only as *broadly* true. Many qualifications might be introduced.

for this reason that it is not safe to trust the conduct of large affairs in the hands of the public as a whole. Under the present system, there is a kind of rough natural selection, by which the shrewdest men—though, unhappily, not always in other respects the best—come to have the control of the chief industries of the country; and this is the best guarantee for their efficiency. Now this would be a matter of small importance if the wealth of a country were so great that the inhabitants of it could afford to dispense with half of it ; but any one who considers what the wealth of any country would amount to, if it were distributed uniformly among the inhabitants, will hardly be disposed to maintain that there is any country so rich that it may lightly allow the efficiency of its industry to fall off.

And there is much more that might be added from the same point of view. The general public is not only apt to be a bad judge of its most reliable men, but a still worse one of what it is most important to do in any complicated transaction. Now though the management of industries would, no doubt, under a socialistic régime, be in the main entrusted to those who were elected to be its overseers, yet the public would certainly try to retain to itself a voice in the determination of the larger questions. In dealing with large political questions, this is not so manifest an evil. The great problems of the state are "written in large letters," and can to a certain extent be judged by ordinary common-sense.[1] But in the complications of industry none but experts can be trusted. It is chiefly for this reason, as we pointed out already,[2]

---

[1] Compare the saying of Goethe—" Nothing can be more certain than that this great public, which is so honoured and so despised, is almost always in a state of self-delusion about details, but never or hardly ever about the broad truth." Quoted in Jowett's edition of Aristotle's *Politics*, Vol. II., p. 129.    [2] P. 84.

that in an industrial community state-interference is felt to
be so great an evil.

Again, if the state is to have charge of all the instruments of production, towards what end are these instruments to be directed? At present, each individual producer
sets himself to manufacture such things as he finds in
demand by a section of the community sufficiently large
to afford him a remuneration for his trouble. But if the
state were the producer, it is hardly to be expected that
it would be allowed to proceed on the same principle.
Things which were in demand by only a small section
of the community would be speedily tabooed by the rest.
This would lead, in all probability, to bitter disputes
with regard to those things which it is desirable to
manufacture, and would result in the suppression of all
production that does not tend directly to satisfy the wants
of the mass of the population. In this way all the
higher arts of life would be lost; and those whose talents
lie in the direction of producing articles for the satisfaction of such wants, would be thrown out of employment, or reduced to the necessity of earning a scanty
livelihood at work for which they are entirely unfitted.
Razors would be used to "cut blocks." Further, the
bulk of the community would probably object to be
employed in any work which is at all arduous or un-
pleasant, if it did not seem to yield them any result that
was immediately agreeable. And it is to be feared that a
large proportion of mankind prefer a good deal of future
discomfort to a little present exertion. Hence, it seems
highly probable that all the more difficult industries
would decline, and that mankind would relapse by slow
degrees into a condition of comparative ignorance and
weakness.

Again, it may be asked, what are the instruments of
production that are to be appropriated by the com-

munity?[1] It is a familiar truth that no absolute distinction can be drawn between things which are instruments
of production and those that are used only for consumption.[2] The distinction depends on the intention of the
possessor, and this cannot be foreseen by any authority
above him. Strictly speaking, indeed, the consumption
of wealth is simply the last stage in its production; it
is not in the full sense produced until it is applied to
use. The distinction is consequently a vanishing one;
and the proposal to appropriate the instruments of production either means that everything is to be appropriated,
or it is a statement that requires further definition. No
doubt, it would usually be understood to apply chiefly,
if not exclusively, to those objects which, by their very
nature, are manifestly intended to be used for the production of other objects—such as factories and machinery
in general. But if this is what is intended, we must still
inquire whether *all* machinery is to be appropriated by
the community. Are needles, for instance, and pens,
and the artist's brush to be included? It is hard to
see how they could be included without a vexatious
interference with private life; yet, if they are not to be
so included, where exactly is the line to be drawn
between those things that are to be appropriated by the
community and those that are not? It seems impossible,
moreover, that, in the case of the smaller kinds of
productive activity, any form of state regulation could
prevent the carrying on of a certain amount of illicit industry for individual profit, unless either there were a very
strict and irksome system of supervision, or we could pre-
suppose a somewhat high degree of moral development.

[1] "Community," of course, may mean here either state or municipality.

[2] For some suggestive remarks on this point, see Leroy-Beaulieu
*Le Collectivisme*, p. 13 *seq*. Cf. also Flint's *Socialism*, p. 242.

When a system of collective production is contemplated, however, what is meant may be merely that all the larger and more important industries should be in the hands of the community as a whole. Indeed, in some socialistic schemes all that is explicitly demanded[1] is that those industries *which can be conveniently managed* by the community should be undertaken by it. What is proposed, in fact, is simply that there should be a considerable extension of the present sphere of public undertakings. It is pointed out that the state has already proved its capacity for carrying on large industrial concerns, such as the post office and even railways. But to this it is at once replied that there are some kinds of work which can conveniently be done collectively and others which cannot. A number of men could combine to write a dictionary or an encyclopædia, or a series of more or less connected essays, but not an epic poem, and scarcely even a history. The only kind of work for which the state has hitherto proved its capacity, has been work which is, on the one hand, of a comparatively simple[2] and routine character, and which is, on the other hand, very readily open to public criticism.[3] In complicated undertakings, the state is likely to fail; and in undertakings that have to be carried on to a very large extent in private, it is almost certain that there would be mismanagement. The truth seems to be, in short, that the world as a whole, or a nation as a whole, or any large

[1] So far as I understand, for instance, this is all that is demanded by the Fabian Society.

[2] By "simple" I mean simple in *result* rather than simple in *process*—not work which it is easy to *do*, but work which is easy to *judge*.

[3] On the work actually undertaken by the modern state, see *Fabian Essays*, p. 47 *seq.* Cf. also Ely's *French and German Socialism*, p. 242.

body of men as a whole, has never shown itself a good
leader or manager. It cannot guide an army, or write a
poem, or direct a great business. But it does, in the
long run, know when it is well or ill led. It can
appreciate a general, it can crown a poet, it can regulate
a business. It is a bad poet or "maker," but a good
critic. "A small poet every true worker is," as Carlyle
said. The state would be a *very* small poet. A large
body of men could never write *Paradise Lost* or *Paradise
Regained*, though, in the long run, they might arrive at
a sounder judgment than even Milton on the relative
merits of these poems. The public is a 'bad actor,' but
a fairly good audience : its function is to judge and
regulate rather than to do.[1]

There are other difficulties which might be mentioned
in the way of the realisation of a socialistic scheme ;[2]

[1] Cf. what is said on the work of the state in Chap. VI.

[2] I have purposely abstained from any reference to the common
argument that Socialism would tend to crush out individuality, and
would thus lead to a monotonous uniformity. It does not seem to
me obvious that it would do so, any more than it is obvious that a
system of individual liberty tends to produce excessive variety. Indeed, it might even be maintained that the natural reaction of
human nature would produce an opposite effect. Cf. Bryce's *American Commonwealth*, Vol. III., p. 545, where it is pointed out that
the freedom of American life does not lead to variety. On the
other hand, however, it might be urged that American life is in
this respect the very type of what might be expected under a
socialistic régime ; for the freedom which the American citizen
enjoys is precisely that which the socialist would grant—"the right
of doing whatever the law permits." It is freedom of the people
as a whole, rather than freedom of the individual citizen. Indeed,
as Prof. Bryce has elsewhere pointed out, the American citizen is,
owing to the rigidity of the constitution under which he lives, in
many respects less free than the citizen of the more aristocratic
states of Europe. Cf. *American Commonwealth*, I. 37, 45, 476, 523,
534-8, III. 340, 358, etc. On the whole, therefore, it seems probable
that the disadvantage in question would really be found in a social-

X

but the discussion of them would belong more properly
to a treatise on practical economics or politics. It is
sufficient for our present purpose to have made it apparent that the proposed remedy of the evils of competition by social machinery is one which cannot be lightly
entertained. Many Socialists, indeed, when such difficulties are pointed out, reply that it is not their business
to be prophets. They consider that it is sufficient to
have shown the validity of their ideal ; and that the
adequate realisation of it, in spite of all obstructions, may
safely enough be trusted to time, which is not only "the
great Discoverer" but also the great Reformer. But such
an attitude will scarcely serve. A Socialist *is* bound to
be a prophet. For Socialism is an ideal : and any one
who sets up an ideal, as an object to be practically
aimed at, must be prepared to show that it is a realisable
ideal. It is easy to build castles in the air : it is easy
to plan Utopias which would be entirely beautiful if
things were altogether different from what they are : it is
easy to show that, if you had "a lever long enough and
a prop strong enough," you could move the world. But
we have a right to say to such schemers :—"Let us see
what you can move with the levers and props which you
possess : let us see you build a castle on the earth : let
us see you plan something more or less beautiful, things
being as things are." It is not only idle, it is positively
mischievous, to delude ourselves with ideals which cannot
be realised ; because they blind us to actual improvements that might be made with such means as are even
now at our disposal.[1] While we dream of a palace the
house is tumbling about our ears. The ideal for which

istic state. Still, I have thought it best not to introduce this
argument into the text, though, so far as it is true, it is of course
important.

[1] Cf. Barnett's *Practicable Socialism,* p. 194.

we are in search must be one for " Rome or London, not Fool's Paradise." It is better to patch an old coat than to cut a new one out of a rainbow. We must prefer a candle and a plain road to a meteor and a marsh.

(*h*) There is, however, another aspect of Socialism which is of more interest to the philosopher. Socialism is a term of great elasticity of meaning, and it covers a variety of proposals which are widely different from each other both in their content and in the motives by which men are led to adopt them. There is a comic side and a tragic side to Socialism, and there is also a side on which it represents very sober sense. It is comic when it is merely the expression of a petulant impatience and discontent that finds relief in the creation of fantastic visions. It is tragic when it is the expression of a revolutionary frenzy that is bred by intolerable wrongs. But sometimes also it. is the expression of a moral principle and an attempt to formulate the partially adequate means of its embodiment in life. There is a similar contrast in the motives by which men are led to the adoption of a socialistic ideal. Some people call themselves Socialists, as boys call themselves pirates and brigands, because they think it fine : some become Socialists, as men become pirates and brigands, because they are driven to it by misery and despair : some are Socialists to please the mob, and some because they *are* the mob : and some again are inspired by the consciousness of a profound moral truth. This last we must endeavour to understand.[1]

---

[1] The ethical significance of Socialism is well brought out in Steinthal's *Allgemeine Ethik,* pp. 265-280. Kirkup's *Inquiry into Socialism* may also be referred to as an admirable work from this point of view. It seems to me, however, that Mr. Kirkup puts a somewhat too broad interpretation on the socialistic principle. He appears to

The evil against which Socialism is a protest, is that
which we have already noted[1] as one of the most characteristic misfortunes of the present time—the exploitation
of human life by material conditions. This evil is due
largely to the multiplication of our material wants, and
to the lack of organisation in the efforts that are made
to gratify them. Philanthropists are consequently led to
seek for a remedy either in a simplification of life, or in
an improvement of its solidarity, or in some combination
of these two measures. Those who are prepared to
adopt a "heroic remedy" endeavour to accomplish both
objects at once by some form of state control. The
difficulties in the way of this scheme have perhaps been
sufficiently pointed out. But without resorting to any
such drastic treatment, an attempt may yet be made to
exercise an influence on society in the desired direction,
by means of legislative and educational reforms; and
such attempts are sometimes described as socialistic. We
might endeavour, for instance, to establish a well-defined
distinction between those objects of which the production
is essential to the well-being of a state, and those objects
which may be regarded as comparatively unimportant.
We might further endeavour to secure that every citizen
shall devote a reasonable amount of his attention to the
former, and to bring the method in which he devotes

regard everything as socialistic which is not individualistic. As I
have already said (pp. 285-6), I cannot regard the antithesis between
these two points of view as a quite justifiable one. For this reason,
the sketch of the socialistic principle which is given by Schäffle in
his *Quintessence of Socialism* (translated by Mr. B. Bosanquet) seems
to me fairer than that given by Mr. Kirkup. Cf. also Laveleye's
*Socialism of To-Day*, p. 15. Mr. Bosanquet's remarks, to which I
have already incidentally referred, on the contest between Moral and
Economic Socialism, in his *Civilisation of Christendom*, seem to me
to be full of suggestion and instruction.

[1] *Supra*, pp. 116-9.

himself to it under the control of the community; while we might leave those objects which are less important to the freedom of individual choice, except in so far as they are evidently pernicious.[1] Against such a scheme as this, Social Philosophy would have no objections to urge. It is to some extent a description of what is already attempted in most civilised communities; and it does not seem at all chimerical to suppose that efforts in this direction may be indefinitely extended. Their extension would, no doubt, require to be a very gradual process. It would not be possible, without serious danger, to determine all at once what objects are essential to the well-being of the community, and which of these objects can be conveniently controlled by it. Still less would it be possible to determine all at once to what extent individual citizens may be required to participate in the production of these objects. It might even be objected, from the very outset, that any such attempt presupposes more wisdom on the part of the community as a whole than can reasonably be expected of it. It might be said that if a community were once to let itself loose upon such attempts, it would not know where to stop. It would inevitably be drawn forward with ever-increasing rapidity; and there would be no halting-place short of a communistic system. Consequently it would be safer to avoid any measure of a socialistic nature, except provisionally and as a kind of medicine for severe disorders. Undoubtedly there is much force in this argument; but it can scarcely be regarded as conclusive in any civilised society which is fairly well supplied with conservative instincts and safeguards against haste.[2]

Now what modern socialism means, in the minds of many of its sanest adherents, is little more than this. It

---

[1] Cf. Mr. Havelock Ellis on *The New Spirit*, p. 18.
[2] Cf. Chap. vi.

is to this at least that it owes its moral force. For in this sense it is simply the practical assertion of the principle that we are "members one of another," that we are parts of an organic whole : and this assertion must always appeal to our moral consciousness. It is, no doubt, an attempt to turn this moral principle into a law of the state. But it is natural, and indeed inevitable, that we should seek to do this. What we believe that we and all men ought to do, we inevitably try to enforce, except in so far as we are aware that the enforcing of it would defeat its own end. It is readily perceived that we must not seek to regulate the whole life of individual citizens : no community would be wise enough to do it ; and if it did, it would crush out the spontaneity of their moral life. But it is not so with a mere attempt to enforce the essentials of social existence, leaving the rest of men's lives free. Such an enforcement leaves the spontaneity of the citizens and their power of individual development unimpaired. It is simply a law which says to them—Seek first the life of your kingdom and its welfare, and all the rest shall be added unto you. To what extent such an organisation can be realised, is a question for the political philosopher. All that we can here say is that from our present point of view it aims at a desirable end.[1]

Such a scheme as this, however, is not in reality socialistic, any more than it is individualistic.[2] If it is

---

[1] Further remarks on this point will be found in Chapter VI.

[2] It is perhaps only fair to remark that several of those who call themselves Socialists are perfectly ready to allow that their ultimate aims include an individualistic element as well (*i.e.* an element of individual *liberty*. Cf. *supra*, p. 285). They think it right to describe themselves as Socialists, because they consider that it is the socialistic side of things which at the present time requires chiefly to emphasised. This is perhaps true : but it may be doubted whether it is wise to devote ourselves to a one-sided view, merely because

apt to seem so to us at present, this is merely because
the current of our recent civilisation has had so marked
an individualistic trend, that the straightening of it
appears to be a move in the opposite direction.

3. We ought naturally now to pass to Fraternity, as
the third term in the great revolutionary watchword. But
it is evident that this is somewhat too vague a term to
constitute an ideal by itself. It is, indeed, little more
than a phrase which has been slipped in to give expression to a certain consciousness of the inadequacy of the
other two terms; and we need not yield to any such
sense of inadequacy until we have exhausted all the
possible ideals. Now Liberty and Equality, even in the
very broad sense in which these terms have been interpreted by us, cannot be regarded as exhausting the
possible ideals for a human society. Both these ideals
are democratic : we have still to consider the aristocratic
ideal. We have glanced at that ideal which is based
on the independence of the individual, and at that which
is based on the subjection of the individual to the will
of the whole society : we have still to glance at that
which is based on the subjection of the many to the few.

Now a pure tyranny can hardly be taken as an ideal.
It is true that in warlike states it is often felt to be an
advantage to have one powerful individual at the head
of affairs, with an almost absolute control of government,
even if the individual in question should be by no means
an ideally wise man.[1] But even in a military state this

---

the opposite one-sidedness happens to be prevalent. Cf. concluding
chapter.

[1] Most German political theorists are inclined to attach more
importance to this consideration than is commonly given to it in
England. They urge that, even if a monarch is not specially wise
or benevolent, the very nature of his position gives him a wider
outlook and a more impartial point of view than is possible for the

advantage is attended with fearful dangers. If the individual in question should be not only not exceptionally eminent for wisdom, but actually eminent for the absence of it—and this is always a possible contingency—the amount of mischief which he may do to the society is greater than the good which even the wisest man could hope to accomplish. And even in the case of those rulers who are in the main good, there is a constant risk of the intrusion of personal peculiarities and caprices in such a way as to interfere seriously with the public good. Pascal remarked once that "if Cleopatra's nose had been a little shorter the whole aspect of the world would have been different." So it may be said in general of autocratic rulers, that the history of their countries will be materially affected by every slight peculiarity of their individual characters. Such influence is likely to be specially noxious when the conditions of national life become very intricate, so that no one man, however wise, can foresee what is likely to be the ultimate effect of any particular move that he may make. For this reason, an autocratic rule speedily becomes intolerable in a highly developed industrial state.[1] The ideal, therefore, which we have now to consider is rather that of an Aristocracy of Talent than that of the sovereign rule of any individual.

Now the advantages of such an aristocracy of talent are not hard to discover. If we had society constructed on such a model as Carlyle suggested, with the philosopher-king at the top, and the rest of the citizens graduated downwards, so that each had an eminence in exact proportion to his ability, it seems, at least at

majority of his subjects. For some remarks on the contrast between the English and the German ideas of Monarchy, see Sidgwick's *Elements of Politics*, pp. 404-5.

[1] Cf. *supra*, p. 84.

first sight, as if everything might be expected to go well. If the wisest man were at the top he might be expected to be wise enough both to suppress his individual caprices and to allow a considerable amount of independence to his subordinates in the management of details, reserving for himself only the supervision of the whole. And if the wise man were surrounded by those of the citizens who approached most nearly to himself in ability, it might be expected that wherever his own wisdom failed, the deficiency would be sure to be supplied by some one of his councillors. At a first blush, accordingly, this seems decidedly the most desirable of all the ideals, if only it were practicable.

The first obstacle in the way of its practicability is found in the impossibility of discovering who is wisest. As a general rule, indeed, there is no one wise enough to be made an absolute ruler over others.[1] But even if there were such a man, it would not always be easy to find him. If it were the case—as Carlyle sometimes seemed to imagine—that wisdom were identical with effectiveness, the problem would soon be solved. The wisest might be trusted to struggle to the top whenever the "career" was "open for talent." But if this were the case, our ideal would have been reached long ere now. The fact is rather that minds of the highest wisdom are apt to be characterised by that kind of inertia which accompanies weight,[2] and are in many cases less likely than others to press rapidly to the front. Nor, as we have already seen,[3] are we entitled to trust that the ablest will be chosen by popular vote. How, then, are they to be selected? The only solution that I can think of to this problem, is that which is suggested by Plato in

[1] Cf. Aristotle's *Politics*, VII. (IV.) xiv. 2.
[2] Cf. Faraday's essay on "Mental Inertia."
[3] P. 316.

the *Republic*[1]—viz. that the highest positions should be made so unattractive, that no one would be willing to occupy them unless he were driven into them by the fear of being ruled by inferior men. In this way those who were conscious of a superior ability, and were sincerely devoted to the well-being of the state, might be got to choose themselves. Plato was fully convinced of the necessity of philosopher-kings, and he seems to have thought—probably with good reason—that the only way to make a philosopher a king is to crown him with thorns. Let us consider how far this ideal is a practicable one.

What must strike everyone in reading Plato's account of the matter is that his guardians seem to have very little to do; and it is in this, I believe, that the secret of his apparent solution of the difficulty will be found to lie. If the highest offices are not to be attractive to men of ambition, they must be offices to which but little power and dignity is attached. But this will be the case only if the real work of the state is otherwise carried out. According to Plato's scheme, the real work was to be accomplished by education. The citizens were to be so disciplined by the peculiar culture which they received, that law would become almost unnecessary; and thus the position of the guardians, so far as the ordinary business of the state is concerned, would become little more than that of "the dot on the i." But on such a view, it remains to be asked—What is to be done with those citizens who do not take in the culture which is provided? There can be little doubt that Plato's answer to this question, in so far as he had any answer at all, would have been, that the great majority of the people were to be in the condition of <u>slaves</u>.[2] Now it seems at

---

[1] Book I.

[2] Or, at the highest, in the condition of children.

least conceivable—though hardly practicable—that a small number of citizens might have their nature so cultured as to be practically raised above the need of law, and that this small number might rule over a race of slaves. It may even be said, that in some of the Greek states an approximation towards such an ideal as this was actually made; though it can hardly be maintained that an approximation was made to the philosopher-king. But such a state would certainly not be regarded as a high ideal by any considerable number of thoughtful men in modern times. Even if we could bring ourselves to have such an admiration for the Greek type of character, as to wish that we were not almost but altogether such as they were, we should always be forced to add—"except these bonds." And even on the assumption of slavery the ideal would remain, as Plato himself acknowledged, unrealisable. Such an aristocracy, for one thing, would be sure to become corrupt. Besides, some of the slaves would necessarily be very nearly on a level with the freemen; the sharp division between them would be felt to be arbitrary; there would be rebellions and quarrels, and the state would finally be overthrown or fall into the hands of some one who should prove himself a genuine ruler, with power instead of wisdom. Moreover, even if all these difficulties could be removed, such a society as is here supposed would not in reality be an ideal one, because it would not be for the majority of the citizens an educative one. The thinking would be done for the citizens by their rulers; and this would soon be found to tell on the citizens, in the way of destroying their sense of responsibility and weakening their original powers of thought. For this reason, it has even been maintained, with some plausibility, that a good despotism is worse than a bad one.[1] And thus this ideal, like so many

[1] Cf. Mill's *Representative Government*, chap. iii.

others, would ultimately fail through disregard of the very
object which was foremost in the minds of its promoters
—viz. the culture of the citizens.    In order to effect this
object, it would be necessary not to make the philosopher
a king, but rather to make philosophy king—*i.e.* to make
wisdom the ruling influence in the state—and to bring
this about, it would be necessary that *all* the citizens
should be trained to think.    If individual culture is our
aim, we must wish not that a philosopher should be king,
but that all the Lord's people should be prophets.[1]

4. Thus the last of our ideals which is founded on the
notion of a certain rearrangement of society, is seen to
break down; and we are driven to take refuge in Fraternity—if we understand by that, the recognition that
the true ideal must be founded rather on the notion of
a constitution of the hearts of the citizens.    But before
we proceed to any consideration of this, it may be well
to add a few general remarks on the various ideals that
we have already considered.    We must observe precisely
what the defects of these ideals have been, and then we
shall be better able to determine what are the elements
that are required in a true ideal.

In the first place, we may remark that each of these
ideals which we have mentioned, fails chiefly on account
of its neglect of some one of the three elements that
have been formerly[2] referred to as essential to the well-
being of a society.    The ideal of Liberty is particularly
strong with regard to the industrial element of social life
—*i.e.* the conquest of nature.    There can be little doubt
that a preponderance of individual Liberty favours a
vigorous industrial production.    Such a system also is at
least not incompatible with an effective condition of the
machinery of social life.    It is with reference mainly to

[1] Cf. Green's *Collected Works*, Vol. III., p. 476.
[2] P. 275 *seq.*

the third element that it fails—*i.e.* to the development
of the individual nature. Some individuals it tends to
crush out altogether, and those who are preserved are apt
to be hardened and almost brutalised, and reduced to
the condition of mere slaves of mechanical conditions.
The ideal of Equality, again, is particularly strong with
respect to social machinery, and is not incompatible with
the culture of the individual nature. It fails chiefly
from the inefficiency of industrial conditions which it
would be apt to encourage. Finally, the aristocratic
ideal is particularly strong with respect to the development of the individual nature, and is not incompatible
with industrial efficiency, but fails in so far as it makes
no adequate provision for social order.[1] Of course, in
the case of each of these ideals, all the elements of well-
being would tend ultimately to be affected by the failure
to provide for one of them; but primarily it is in each
case one of the three elements—and in each case a
different one—that is mainly affected. From this we may
learn the importance for a true ideal, that it should have
a due regard for every one of these elements.

In the second place, we may remark, as we already
pointed out at the start, that each of the three ideals
that we have mentioned is a type of one of the forms of
unity which we had occasion to refer to in Chapter III.
The ideal of Liberty, if it could be realised (*i.e.* if it
were possible for the individual to grow without taking
the world into himself), would evidently be a Monadistic
system, in which each part is independent of every other.
The Aristocratic ideal would similarly be a Dualistic
System, in which the majority of the parts are subjected
to a law external to themselves. The ideal of Equality,
again, would be a Monistic or a Chemical system, in
which the separate existence of the parts is merged

---

[1] *I.e.* for an *abiding* social order. It is in unstable equilibrium.

in the unity of the whole. The first fails from the lack of co-operation and unity; the second, from the lack of homogeneity and order; the third, from the lack of individual responsibility and independence on the part of the several members.[1] The first might be the ideal for a society of angels, if angels could be supposed to require an ideal: the third might be the ideal for beasts, if beasts could be supposed to frame an ideal: the second might be the ideal for a society which was partly of angels and partly of beasts, if angels and beasts could be supposed to form a community together. What is now wanted is an ideal for a community of beings struggling upwards from the brutal to the angelic nature; and this ideal must evidently be neither Monadistic, Dualistic, nor Monistic, but Organic.[2]

The first point that we have to note about such an

---

[1] I mean that these are the primary and most evident causes of failure in each case. But, as has been already pointed out, each ideal fails also from inner self-contradiction, which prevents it from achieving even that element of success which it has mainly in view.

[2] It is remarkable that the three most famous sociological writers of this century—Comte, Herbert Spencer, and Schäffle—express severally the three ideals to which reference has been made. Comte is an upholder of an aristocratic ideal, with the bankers and the priests of Humanity at the top: Herbert Spencer is the apostle of individual liberty: while Schäffle, at least in his earlier writings, emphasised so strongly the socialistic side, that Leroy-Beaulieu and others have been led to regard him as the chief exponent of Collectivism. (See Leroy-Beaulieu's *Le Collectivisme*, chap. vii., and *passim.*) In the case of Schäffle, however, it is right to add that he has made it sufficiently apparent in his *Aussichtslosigkeit der Social-demokratie* (and indeed in his *Bau und Leben* also) that his ideal is very different from that of ordinary Socialism—differing from it chiefly by the presence of an aristocratic element. It is, in fact, State Socialism, in the stricter sense. Comte's ideal also is not quite fairly represented as a purely aristocratic one. Taking these three writers together, however, we should have a very fair presentment of most of the merits and defects of the three ideals.

ideal is, that it must to some extent include all the elements which are represented by the other three. It must include such a degree of freedom as is necessary for the working out of the individual life. It must include such a degree of socialism as is necessary to prevent exploitation and a brutalising struggle for existence, as well as to secure to each individual such leisure as is required for the development of the higher life. It must include such a degree of aristocratic rule as is necessary for the advance of culture and for the wise conduct of social affairs. Indeed, it may be said that the necessity of in some degree combining all three elements is already recognised by all serious students of social life, however much they may be inclined to lay the main emphasis on one or other of the elements. But in addition to the elements recognised by the other three ideals, this fourth one must include also something which is not explicitly present in any of them—it must include, in fact, the principle which is necessary to combine them. This principle may perhaps be said to be that which is meant by Fraternity, understanding by that term the recognition of vital relationships. But we ought to re-member that the vital relationships in question must be relationships that are recognised not only between the various individuals of whom society is composed, but also between the various interests that are involved in its well-being.

Now with regard to the recognition of vital relation-ships between individuals, it might at first sight be thought that nothing is more simple. If men are so intrinsically related to each other, as we have already seen they are, it might appear as if a condition of Fraternity ought to be their natural state. But this is not so. We have already pointed out [2] that even in the

<hr />

[1] See next chapter.                    [2] P. 263.

pursuit of the highest aims we are apt to be for a time driven asunder; and what is true of the highest is much more true of the lowest. If our intellectual needs carry us into solitude, our animal needs lead us into strife. The very infinity of our ideal—the fact that each of us seeks in a manner to make the whole world his own—brings us into constant opposition. This has been very graphically put by Carlyle, in his statement about the happiness of the shoe-black :[1]—" Man's unhappiness, as I construe, comes of his Greatness; it is because there is an Infinite in him, which with all his cunning he cannot quite bury under the Finite. Will the whole Finance Ministers and Upholsterers and Confectioners of modern Europe undertake, in joint-stock company, to make one Shoeblack *happy?* They cannot accomplish it, above an hour or two : for the Shoeblack also has a Soul quite other than his Stomach; and would require, if you consider it, for his permanent satisfaction and saturation, simply this allotment, no more, and no less: *God's infinite Universe altogether to himself,* therein to enjoy infinitely, and fill every wish as fast as it rose. Oceans of Hochheimer, a Throat like that of Ophiuchus : speak not of them; to the infinite Shoeblack they are as nothing. No sooner is your ocean filled, than he grumbles that it might have been of better vintage. Try him with half of a Universe, of an Omnipotence, he sets to quarrelling with the proprietor of the other half, and declares himself the most maltreated of men." The only objection to this statement is, that what we want is not a Universe in which to enjoy ourselves, but a Universe that shall be interesting—*i.e.* one to which we may devote ourselves, and in devotion to which we may find the realisation of a higher life than that of our individual selves.[2] Still it is true that, though life consists

[1] *Sartor Resartus*, ii. 9.     [2] Cf. *supra*, p. 258 *seq.*

of many "elements," yet to the primitive man, as to Sir Andrew Aguecheek, "it consists rather in eating and drinking": and so long as we remain at this stage, or only a little higher, we necessarily quarrel. And if we are not to quarrel with others, we must first quarrel with ourselves. If we are to arrive at a state of Fraternity, we must practise self-restraint. We must keep our wants in check, until we develop to such a stage that our leading wants are for those things which "are common to all," and "which all may equally enjoy." Hence it is evident that Fraternity cannot be reached at a bound: it is an ideal to which we can attain only by patient progress. We cannot become unselfish except by educating and subduing our desires. Yet to aim at this is not to aim at a mirage, like the Socialistic ideal.[1] It is not a "far-off divine event" which we never come in sight of. We are always realising it, though it is never realised. We can become a little more unselfish every day, and we can make new social arrangements every year, by which there shall be fewer temptations to selfishness and more helps to brotherhood. In short, the ideal consists in constant progress.

And that this is the case, must be all the more apparent when we consider, that what we have to realise is not merely the bringing about of a recognition of vital relationships between individuals, but also of vital relationships between the various interests that are involved in their social life, and in particular between the three elements which, as we have seen, are required for social well-being. The attempt to realise any one of these by itself is almost certain to lead to the destruction of the others, if not eventually even of that one itself. But, on the other hand, to attempt to realise them all together is

[1] *I.e.* the *purely* Socialistic ideal. I do not mean that every ideal which is described as Socialistic is of this nature. Cf. *supra*, p. 326.

evidently a complicated problem, which must require patient adjustment and slow development. To consider, however, even in outline, the nature of this development, is a task of such magnitude that it seems to require a separate chapter.

# CHAPTER VI.

## THE ELEMENTS OF SOCIAL PROGRESS.

WHEN we recognise that our ideal is not anything that
can be precisely mapped out for us from the beginning,
and still less anything that can be achieved by a turn of
the hand, that, in fact, it is a growing ideal, and not a
rigidly mechanical one, it becomes evident that the
determination of its nature at each particular point must
be left, to a very considerable extent, to the student of
other sciences than Social Philosophy—in the sense in
which the latter is here conceived. We must allow the
economist and the politician and the educationist to discover for us what is at any moment necessary and
practicable, and also to investigate the means of its
realisation, though "the Good" which is determined by
Social Philosophy supplies these other sciences (as
Aristotle put it) with a definite target to shoot at. The
Social Philosopher is not independent of other thinkers,
either in the determination of the object at which we
ought to aim at any particular moment, or in the as-
certainment of the means by which that object may in
certain circumstances be attained. He cannot bake his
bread till the corn is ground; nor can he provide the
relishes with which it has to be eaten. The discussion
of the particular, indeed, scarcely enters within his province at all; still less the discussion of ways and means.

He is concerned with these only in so far as they follow immediately from the consideration of the general nature of the end at which we aim. Yet his work is none the less important. Though he cannot make himself independent of these other sciences, or even lay down any rigid rules for their direction, he may yet be able to indicate broadly the nature of their respective provinces and the general principles by which they ought to be guided. His business is primarily to show the ultimate aim to which their efforts must be directed, and secondarily to determine the limits within which they can be of use in contributing to the realisation of that aim. If we may compare the other sciences to nations, it is for philosophy to maintain a "scientific frontier" between them, to establish the principles of international law, and finally to effect their federation. And such a service, even in its initial stage, is not a slight one : for whenever a science begins either to venture beyond its province or to forget its relativity to others, it is sure to lead us into error; and indeed the more scientific it is, the more entirely is it likely to be wrong. Our business, then, now is to consider in general what are the principles on which the various practical sciences must proceed in their efforts to determine the ideal of human progress, and to contribute to its realisation.

In treating of the constituents of human progress, as in treating of most other subjects that may be looked at in a number of separate aspects, the chief danger is that we may so emphasise some one of them as to forget altogether the importance of the rest. We must remember that the well-being of mankind, as has been already pointed out, consists of three main elements—(1) the subjugation of nature, (2) the perfection of social machinery, and (3) personal development—and that a true .progress must include advancement in all. Now the consideration of the first of these elements, in its broad outlines, belongs most properly to the economist;[1] of the second, to the politician; and of the third, to the educationist. We cannot here attempt to do more than indicate, with as much generality and as little vagueness as possible, the principles by which each of these must be governed in the treatment of his special department: and on each department a very few words must suffice.

I. THE SUBJUGATION OF NATURE.—The importance of the conquest of nature, with a view to the achievement of human well-being, is a consideration which can hardly be said to be at the present time in much danger of being forgotten. In our conduct at least, if not in our theories, we are apt rather to exaggerate than to overlook it. It is, as Emerson said, "the day of the chattel." Yet the very fact that this element of human progress has become so engrossing for the generality of mankind, has in some instances led those who are naturally of a more idealistic turn to err in the opposite extreme. Men of the latter type are often ready to maintain, in a more or less explicit way, that the conquest of nature is a matter of small importance, that human beings may be approximately as well in one set of circumstances as in another; and that if the energies which are at present expended in the subjugation of outward forces and the increase of material comfort were withdrawn, life would remain for us as well worth living as before, and there

[1] *I.e.* it is the business of the economist to discuss the principles of social activity with special reference to the first of these aims. Of course the discussion of detailed methods for the attainment of this end falls outside the province of the economist as such, and belongs rather to the student of the particular technical sciences or arts. Similarly, the work of the political and educational theorist may be distinguished from that of the political and educational reformer. It is not the business of any science as such to consider the ways and means of its application in practice.

would be no appreciable loss in the essential well-being of the world.[1] And certainly something may be urged in behalf of such a view. It is not true that "private vices are public benefits," in the sense that the desire for luxury and ostentation helps on the general weal. "Plain living and high thinking" is a sounder doctrine to preach. At the same time, it must always remain true that all high civilisation has certain material conditions, of which it is vain to endeavour to make ourselves independent. The life of a Mediæval saint—or even, in more recent times, the life of such a man as Thoreau [2]—can never be taken as an ideal type of human life, except as a protest against a false civilisation. Such types are possible only as exceptions, and their significance as types depends on the fact that they are exceptions. Wheat does not grow by the wayside, unless it has first grown in the field; and the fact that it is found by the wayside also, is not an evidence that the cultivation of the field has had no effect, but rather an evidence of the reverse. There are, however, certain reasons which have led men of some thoughtfulness in recent times dangerously near to the view that the conquest of nature is a matter of small importance, and even that it is in some respects positively pernicious. The chief reasons [3] are, I think, (1) that the subjugation

[1] There are some interesting remarks on this point in Macmillan's *Promotion of General Happiness*, pp. 35-40. His results, however, are somewhat nugatory—chiefly, I think, because he confines himself to the futile effort to estimate pleasures. It is values that should be estimated, not senses of value. Cf. also Marshall's *Principles of Economics*, p. 180 *seq.*

[2] Cf. Havelock Ellis, *The New Spirit*, pp. 95-9.

[3] Before we notice the legitimate reasons which have led to a pessimistic view of modern civilisation, it may be well to remark that such a view has frequently been based on a consideration of the fate of ancient civilisations. With regard to this, it ought to

of nature is supposed to lead to forms of human life which are so artificial as to be opposed to man's true nature and inconsistent with his highest welfare; (2) that it leads indirectly to other evil consequences, inasmuch as it withdraws men from contact with reality, and so exposes them to the influence of many illusions. In both these reasons there is some force; but they are not in reality arguments against the subjugation of nature. The first is an argument against a hasty and one-sided subjugation, and the second is an argument against a subjugation whose benefits are not shared by all. The term "artificial" ought never to be taken as in itself a condemnation of any form of human life;[1] for in one sense it is the very excellence of human life to be artificial. It is the essence of man's being to rise above nature as a mechanical system, inasmuch as he guides himself by the conception of an end. When any form of life is blamed as artificial, this must be understood as meaning, either that it is arbitrarily determined without reference to any human end, or that it is determined in

be pointed out that the cases are not quite parallel. Broadly speaking, all ancient civilisations rested, not on the systematic subjection of nature by man, but rather on the subjection of certain races of mankind by others. Nations with such an aim could not endure. So soon as they had acquired dominion over others, they had nothing further to aim at, and sank inevitably into effeminacy and sloth. A civilisation, on the other hand, which rests on the subjection of nature, has an inexhaustible task before it. Conquest is the triumph of a moment, and leaves nothing behind it but a sigh for other worlds; whereas labour is the victory of a lifetime, and one world is more than enough for it to subdue. There are other reasons also which cause our modern civilisations to be very different from those of the ancient world: but a discussion of these would carry us beyond our present limits. Cf. Marshall's *Economics*, pp. 19-20.

[1] For a good remark on this point, see Bosanquet's *Logic*, Vol. II., p. 215.

so hasty and one-sided a way that some important elements of human development are arrested or crushed out. Now the subjugation of nature cannot be said to be an arbitrary end: it is, as we have already seen, involved in the very nature of human life. Hence any particular instance of such subjugation can be fairly condemned only if it is hasty or one-sided. Again, the objection that by the subjugation of nature we are withdrawn from contact with reality, cannot be accepted quite literally. The conquest of nature, in so far as it ever becomes an accomplished fact, does no doubt put an end to our struggle, and may sometimes make life easier than it is good for us to be; since it is in conflict that our energies are perfected. But the conquest of nature never *is* an accomplished fact: the farther we push our victories, the more do we find to subdue. It is true that if the fruits of our victories are enjoyed only by a few, these favoured individuals seem, relatively to the rest, to have attained their end, and to be raised above the contest in which others are still engaged. In this way they are apt to be withdrawn from sympathy with the struggles of their fellows, and to be removed from that wholesome contact with realities which is essential for human well-being. But this objection, like the preceding, is only a caution against an imperfect subjugation of nature, not an argument against the entire effort to become its master. There is, no doubt, another point which is frequently in men's mind when such objections are brought forward—viz. that the progress of civilisation tends to remove men more and more from those conditions which are most favourable to physical health, and to the sanity of mind which is its usual accompaniment. Certainly there is often, in a return to a simpler mode of life,

"ein Mittel ohne Geld
Und Arzt und Zauberei zu haben"

for the renovation of youthful vigour. But even this suggests rather a caution than a condemnation.[1]

By such objections as these, what we ought to be led
to see is the importance of a careful determination of the
directions in which it is most desirable that the conquest
of nature should be carried out. This is, in other words,
the determination of the value of wealth, or of the true

---

[1] The chief point here is, of course, the influence of modern life in
large cities. Cf. *supra*, p. 112, and Marshall's *Economics*, p. 253.
The cry of a return to nature is carried to its logical issue by such
writers as Walt Whitman, when they commend the simplicity and
harmony with self of the mere animal, as contrasted with, the
anxiety and discord of human life. There is a similar note sometimes in Wordsworth ; while the saying "Consider the lilies of the
field " carries us even farther. With reference to such ideals, we
may quote the words of Hegel on a similar point :—"The disunion
that appears throughout humanity is not a condition to rest in. But
it is a mistake to regard the natural and immediate harmony as the
right state. . . . Childlike innocence no doubt has in it much
that is sweet and attractive : *but only because it reminds us of what
the spirit must win for itself.* The harmonious existence of childhood
is a gift from the hand of nature : the second harmony must spring
from the labour and culture of the spirit. And so the words of
Christ 'except ye *become* as little children,' etc., are very far from
telling us that we must always remain children." (*Logic*, Wallace's
translation, p. 46.) The truth is, in fact, that the progress of
civilisation is a progress *towards* what is simple and natural (*i.e.*
what is in harmony with itself), though at first it seems to be a
progress away from it. The remark of Thackeray, that "we get
to understand truth better, and grow simpler as we grow older,"
applies in some measure to the age of the race. It must be allowed,
however, that this simplification is somewhat tardily won ; and in the
meantime there may be a certain *raison d'être* for the exaggerated
protests of Tolstoï, or of such books as Mr. E. Carpenter's *Civilisation,
its Cause and Cure.* But on the whole we must ask, with Mr. William
Morris (*Hopes and Fears for Art*, p. 88), "What remedy can there
be for the blunders of civilisation but further civilisation?" Cf. also
Spencer's *Education*, chap. IV. *ad fin.*, and Mahaffy's *Greek Life and
Thought*, p. 328. Also Ritchie's *Natural Rights*, chap. iii.

nature of wealth; though in a deeper sense than that in which that term is ordinarily understood in economic investigations. The meaning of the term "wealth" has undergone a process of continuous deepening throughout the history of economic science; and it may be doubted whether even now the sense in which it is commonly accepted in economic writings can be regarded as ultimate. On this point a few remarks may here be in place. The most palpable mistake on this subject is that of confounding wealth with money—a mistake by no means uncommon in popular thought;[1] and into which the whole Mercantile School tended to fall. When this error is corrected, our next idea of wealth is apt to be, in a vague way, that it consists in the sum of those material things which are serviceable to man. This view may be identified with that of the Physiocratic School; and it is one which has had considerable influence on economic thought. So long as this view prevails, wealth continues to be thought of as so much material;[2] and a prejudice remains against those things which merely satisfy human wants without visibly increasing our material sources— such as works of art. This view has been gradually overthrown by the increasing clearness of the perception of the difference in value between different kinds of material —or between different specimens of the same kind of material under different circumstances — as means of satisfying human wants; and in recent times the introduction of the conception of "utilities" in place of things, has enabled us to reach a somewhat more definite understanding of what is involved in the conception of wealth. We have learned to think of it as including all means for the satisfaction of human needs, and to estimate its value in proportion to the satisfaction which it

---

[1] For an interesting illustration, see Marshall's *Economics*, p. 252.
[2] Cf. Mummery and Hobson's *Physiology of Industry*, p. 7.

gives.  But the satisfaction of wants, again, involves a
certain ambiguity.  What we want may mean either what
we happen at the present moment to desire, or what is
an essential need of our nature.  There is evidently a
much deeper standard for judging of the ultimate value of
objects than that which is constituted by the imperative-
ness of our immediate wants—viz. that which is determined by the ultimate demands of our nature, as distinguished from passing whims and unreasonable cravings.[1]
If our wants themselves should happen to be leading us
to destruction, the means of satisfying them will hardly
in fairness be regarded as wealth.  Such objects would
be more correctly styled, in the language of Mr. Ruskin,
"illth."  We must distinguish, in fact, between what we
really want and what we only think we want, before a
true conception of what we mean by wealth can be
attained.  Now there are, no doubt, certain difficulties
in the way of such a use of the term "wealth" as is
here implied, by the pure economist.  For (1) in order
to discover what is wealth in this sense, it is necessary
to know what the true good of man is; and the investigation of this can hardly be regarded as lying within the
province of the economist—it belongs rather to that of
the philosopher: (2) the importance of different kinds of
wealth will vary with different circumstances and with
different stages of civilisation; and the inquiry into these
conditions belongs to the historian or to the sociologist,
rather than to the economist: (3) the value of different
kinds of wealth will depend not only on the nature of
the objects which furnish the means of satisfaction, but
also on the attitude of human beings towards these objects;
and the inquiry into this attitude does not belong to the
economist, but rather to the student of the education of the
human race.  Still, if the work of the economist is to

[1] Cf. *supra*, p. 244 *seq.*

have any practical value, he must bring it into relation to the work of students of these other departments.[1]

It is evident that such a treatment of the conception of wealth, as is here suggested, would amount practically to a discussion of the subject of luxury. The importance of what are called the "necessaries" and the "decencies" of life would be generally allowed, though there might be some disagreement with regard to the kinds of objects which fall within these classes. It is only when we pass to luxuries that there is any considerable difficulty in estimating the importance of the objects which we endeavour to win for ourselves. We might define necessaries as those objects which are under ordinary circumstances essential to sustain life during the normal period and at the normal degree of vigour.[2] Decencies are those

---

[1] As I have referred in the text to the teaching of Mr. Ruskin on this point, it may be well to explain here that I am not quite able to accept the substance of that teaching, if my understanding of it is correct. In *Munera Pulveris*, for instance (see especially chap. i. sect. 12), Mr. Ruskin seems to affirm that objects have in themselves a certain intrinsic value, independently of their relations to other things. But the intrinsic value of an object must surely depend on its serviceableness with a view to particular human ends; and this will vary with the circumstances in which the object occurs. Ultimate values are, consequently, not objective, in the sense of lying in the objects themselves, apart from their relations to other things. But they are also not subjective, in the sense of being dependent on mere human liking. They are dependent on the relations of objects to the realisation of the true good of mankind—which, as we have already seen in Chap. IV., is not to be estimated simply by liking. It is this point that seems to me to have been too much overlooked in economic investigations.

[2] It seems important to include all this in the conception of necessaries. But the expression "subsistence wages" and similar phrases are frequently understood to imply much less than is above stated. Cf. Marshall's *Principles of Economics*, I., p. 123. The recent discussions on the subject of a "living wage" have served to bring out some of the difficulties involved here.

objects which are regarded as essential to a particular station in society at a particular time. Now if every desirable object which does not fall within either of these two classes is to be regarded as a luxury, it is evident that that term will cover a considerable variety of objects. It will include (1) surplus requirements—*i.e.* objects similar in kind to those which are regarded as necessaries or decencies, differing from these only in the fact that they are not under ordinary circumstances essential either for the support of life or for the support of a particular station in life, (2) objects which are desirable in the sense of being commonly desired, but not desirable in the sense of contributing anything to the well-being of life, (3) objects which are desirable in the sense of contributing a certain momentary gratification, but not in any other way adding to human well-being, (4) objects which directly or indirectly help to raise life to a higher level. To determine broadly what kinds of objects fall within these various classes would be an important part of the work of the philosophic economist. The value of the first class of objects would be sufficiently obvious, though within somewhat elastic limits; since a margin of safety is always desirable in human affairs. The second class of objects would be entirely condemned; and so would the third, in every case in which the pursuit of them is inconsistent with the pursuit of objects of higher importance. But it would be round objects of the fourth class that the main interest would centre. Some objects of this class—such as books, pictures, and the like—are so essential to the higher development of mankind that it may fairly be said with regard to them that the necessaries of life could be better spared than the superfluities; and it is often not unwise to sacrifice the former for the sake of the latter. But it would be difficult to draw any precise distinction between this class and the third.

Many objects which seem at first only to yield a momentary gratification, are yet of considerable importance in so
far as they serve to oil the wheels of existence or to add
a bloom to life.    As Emerson put it, "The more piano
the less wolf."[1]    On the other hand, the ruin of most
civilisations has lain in the fact that the goods which are
first sought after, are those which yield a momentary
satisfaction, rather than those which tend to make life
richer and larger.[2]    As a rule, men begin with those
delights which are violent and intoxicating, and then
proceed to those which are soft and enervating; and
with these civilisation usually expires.    If we have any

---

[1] There are some good remarks on this point by Mr. W. L.
Sheldon in the *Ethical Record* for July, 1889 (p. 76 *seq.*).    Cf.
also Mr. William Morris's *Hopes and Fears for Art*, pp. 31-2,
107, 176, etc., and Marshall's *Principles of Economics*, I., pp. 124
and 181.

[2] The distinction which Mr. Bosanquet has drawn (*The Civilisation of Christendom*, pp. 268-303) between Luxury and Refinement
is of great value at this point, provided we remember that the
distinction between the two is one that cannot be quite rigidly drawn.
What begins as a mere Luxury may gradually develop into a
Refinement; and, on the other hand, what begins as a Refinement,
on the part of a few cultivated individuals, may gradually degenerate
into a mere Luxury.    Professor MacCunn, in his *Ethics of Citizenship*
(pp. 193-223), has made some suggestive remarks on the general
subject of Luxury, and has laid down two principles (durability and
unselfishness) for the distinction between good and bad forms of luxury.
These principles are good so far as they go; but they are applicable
only on the preliminary assumption that the object of choice is a
real good.    Otherwise, the more it is limited, and the sooner it is
destroyed the better it will be for all concerned.    Professor Sidgwick,
in his article on Luxury in the *International Journal of Ethics* for
October, 1894, considers certain forms of it to be essential for
artistic development.    But surely there are also refinements and
amenities of life which are educationally important without being,
in any ordinary sense, artistic.    It is right to add, however, that
Professor Sidgwick was specially dealing with *expensive* luxuries.

just reason to take a hopeful view of our modern
civilisation, it is mainly[1] because there are some signs of
a recognition of the distinction between the pleasant and
the useful.

Only when the value of different elements of wealth has
been in this way determined, are we in a position rightly to
estimate the importance of the conquest of nature in various
directions. It is certain that a high form of life can be
made possible for a considerable number of mankind only
after the rougher forces of nature have been mastered.
The gods cannot rest on Olympus till the Titans are
bound. But so long as we are without insight into the
true nature of our good, the warfare which we wage is apt
to be one of gods against gods or of Titans against Titans.
On the other hand, after we have gained an insight into
the nature of our good, the question becomes one of
practical detail, which does not concern us here. The
discussion of the extent to which it is desirable that
government should interfere for the promotion of important industries, or for the repression of those that are
pernicious, is a subject which, so far as it can be referred
to at all in such a treatise as this, belongs rather to the
following head. On the other hand, the discussion of
the best means of sustaining and increasing the efficiency
of the productivity of important arts, must be left to the
various branches of economic science, which again will

---

[1] Partly also, we have to remember such reasons as those that have
been pointed out in the note to p. 342. With regard to the point
referred to above, it is scarcely necessary to remark that this hopeful
element in modern civilisation is due largely to the influence of the
Christian religion, which has enabled large bodies of men to find
their highest good in another region than that of sensuous enjoyment. Whether any similar influence will be operative in the future,
is a grave question for the moralist. Cf. Kidd's *Social Evolution*,
where this is emphasised in an exaggerated and one-sided way.

have to relegate the consideration of some of them to the physical sciences and to the practical arts. Such subjects, for instance, as the best conditions of apprenticeship, the best system of Technical Education, the Promotion of Invention, as well as most of the other means whereby production may be rendered more efficient, would all involve, for their adequate discussion, a minute insight into the requirements of each particular industry at each particular time, and could not be profitably treated merely from the point of view of general principles. With reference to such points as these, the social philosopher can deal with the advancement of civilisation only in the spirit in which Bacon attempted to deal with "the advancement of learning," by "noting a defect" and pointing to the direction in which further inquiry is most urgently needed. And it must suffice, for the purpose of such a sketch as this, to have merely indicated the importance of a thorough investigation of such questions as have just been mentioned, and especially the questions of apprenticeship and technical education, which have never yet received the attention which they deserve, and which are at the present time more particularly in want of study.[1]

For our present purpose it is of more immediate importance that we should observe, not so much what it is desirable to do for the sake of the improvement of productive agencies, as the difficulties which arise in the effort to turn such improvements to the attainment of the end for which they are ultimately intended—*i.e.* the advancement of the general happiness. Mill has remarked in a well-known passage that it may be doubted whether all the improvements which have hitherto been made on machinery have lightened the toil of a single individual; and though it is possible that such a view

[1] Cf. Marshall's *Principles of Economics*, I., pp. 265-8.

as is here implied, would hardly have been borne out by facts at the time when it was put forward, and would be still further from the truth now,[1] yet it is clear that the progress towards a more complete mastery of nature is not necessarily a progress towards more complete happiness. The chief reasons which prevent the realisation of this end, have already been indicated in the chapter on the Social Problem, and may be briefly summed up as follows:—(1) As the means of material well-being increase, population also increases, and the struggle for existence becomes keener: (2) Human nature is not sufficiently plastic to adapt itself continuously to the changing conditions of existence: (3) Industrial progress brings with it an increasing freedom of competition, and this also adds to the keenness of the struggle: (4) Industrial progress tends to reduce the working classes more and more to the condition of a proletariate, and in that way militates directly against the happiness of the great mass of the population. Now each of these points involves a certain reference to social arrangements, and consequently belongs to a great extent to our second head. Yet it is necessary to say a few words here on the means by which these difficulties may be in some measure obviated, in order to complete our case with respect to the benefits of material progress. However important such progress may be, the pursuit of it can hardly be recommended if it continually defeats its own end, or brings with it evils·which compensate for its advantages.

1. The population difficulty is not one on which Social Philosophy can be expected to throw much light. Dr. Martineau has said, though in a somewhat different connection, that "one of the greatest difficulties of our crowded civilisation is due to the fact, that there is no-

[1] Cf. Marshall's *Principles of Economics*, Vol. I., p. 323.

body to eat us."[1]   It seems impossible to devise any means of weeding the human race, which shall not be open to serious moral objections.   It is for many reasons so important that human life should be regarded as sacred, that no scheme can be tolerated which might produce a disregard of human life.   Yet it seems equally impossible to devise any unobjectionable method of weeding the human race before it comes into being ; and it is consequently inevitable that any methods which are resorted to, must in the main be indirect.   It has been observed that population tends to increase most rapidly, and that the ill effects of such increase are most keenly felt, among those classes of the community who are least influenced by the desire to improve their condition, whether material, intellectual, or moral.   Hence it has come to be regarded almost as a truism, that the most satisfactory check to an undue increase of population, is to be found in the advancement of the "standard of comfort" among the poorer classes of the people. Now the great impediments in the way of such an advancement lie in the lack of fixity of condition and in the absence of any prospect of improvement.   Hence anything which tends to make the position of the working classes more permanent and to give them a more secure hope of bettering their conditions, will help to keep population within more manageable limits.   But the position of the working classes can hardly be expected to be either a secure or a hopeful one as long as they remain in the condition of mere labourers for hire, without any direct interest in the work with which they are

----

[1] *Study of Religion*, II. 95.   Cf. the familiar lines :—
>    " Denn der Grosse frisst den Kleinen,
>    Und der Grössre frisst den Grossen ;
>    Also löst in der Natur sich
>    Einfach die sociale Frage."

concerned. On the other hand, in so far as they become partners as well as labourers, they secure for themselves at once a relative permanence and a brighter outlook. And hence nothing is more likely to help us towards a solution of the population question than the spread of co-operative principles, and especially such principles as that of profit-sharing, among the working classes.

It is to be hoped, however, that it may gradually become possible to introduce somewhat more heroic methods of treatment. It is coming to be more and more recognised that the population difficulty is essentially a qualitative one.[1] The mere quantity of increase, if the increase is of the right kind, brings no harm at present, but rather the reverse. Hence if the difficulty is ever to be satisfactorily dealt with, it must be by the introduction of qualitative distinctions. The practical difficulties in the way of carrying these far are no doubt great; and even here it would probably be necessary in the end to rely on moral methods of treatment, *i.e.* on the growth of public opinion. But it might be possible at least to draw a pretty sharp distinction between the criminal classes and the rest of the community; and the former might be prevented from producing and rearing offspring. Perhaps this method of treatment might be extended also to those who are proved to be incapable of maintaining themselves at a certain minimum level of decency,[2] and to those who are known to be afflicted with serious hereditary diseases or incapacities. But possibly in the last-named cases it might be best to leave the matter to

[1] Cf. Marshall's *Principles of Economics*, Vol. 1., pp. 259-262.

[2] The idea of the "enslavement of tramps," suggested, for instance, by Prof. Giddings (*International Journal of Ethics*, Vol. III., No. 2, pp. 163-4), is of interest at this point. The more a human society protects the deserving, the more must it protect itself against the undeserving.

public opinion.  It is doubtful whether any further extension of such methods of treatment would be compatible
with that respect for individual life and liberty which is
essential to the highest form of social welfare.[1]

2. The problem which is occasioned by the want of
plasticity in human nature is one which is perhaps even
more difficult to deal with.   The attempt to solve it
might be made from two different sides.   We might try
to prevent the conditions of life from changing with too
great a rapidity, or we might try to make human beings
themselves more readily adaptable to the new circumstances in which they are placed.   The former effort
would inevitably meet with many difficulties.   Governmental interference must in general confine itself to a
plain Yes or No : it cannot regulate degrees.   It may
decide that something shall or shall not be done ; but it
cannot determine how fast or how slow a process is to
be carried on.   And even if it were otherwise possible to
effect any such regulation, the clog which it would put
upon industry would be an almost intolerable hindrance
to productive enterprise and a great discouragement to
the progress of invention : and it might cause the nation
which adopted it to fall seriously behind others in the
industrial race.   Consequently it seems a more hopeful
plan to limit ourselves mainly to the effort to make

---

[1] It would probably be undesirable, for instance, to advocate any
return to such methods as the exposure of infants, however much
justification there may have been for these in earlier stages of social
development.   The drastic methods suggested by Mr. Bradley in his
" Remarks on Punishment " (*International Journal of Ethics*, April,
1894) seem not to be intended to have any direct practical application.   To devise some means of bringing about the object that he
has there in view, is, however, one of the most pressing social
problems of the time.  Cf. Ritchie's *Natural Rights*, pp. 129-134.
Some valuable suggestions on this and kindred topics will be found
in Professor Haycraft's recent work on *Darwinism and Race Progress.*

men more adaptable to new conditions.[1] The chief means of effecting this would probably be found in securing a more efficient industrial education. Men who have acquired not merely a certain kind of dexterity, but a certain understanding of processes and a certain general intelligence, will not be so readily thrown out by slight changes of method, as those who have acquired only the first of these. It can hardly be hoped, indeed, that such an education of workmen can be carried out without a considerable loss of time, which will not be directly compensated by the increased efficiency of labour. But this is a loss that may well be borne, in view of the greater benefits by which it is accompanied. It must, however, be allowed also that, even with such an education as this, the adaptability of human beings could never be made to keep pace with their inventiveness; and new inventions might always bring with them a certain dislocation. There is a continual conflict between the energy of man's wit and the inertia of his habits : and to provide a complete remedy for such evils it seems probable that some system of labour insurance will have to be devised of a much more thorough character than any that has yet been thought of. Otherwise it may be found necessary to check to a considerable extent the rapidity with which new inventions are introduced.

3. The evils of free competition, again, are mainly three :—(1) It produces an excessive strain ; (2) it occasions rapid alterations of condition, to which it is difficult for men to adapt themselves ; (3) it is apt, whenever it becomes very keen, to be carried on by positively immoral means. It may be doubted whether there is any way of dealing with the first of these evils, except

[1] Not, I think, exclusively ; but the extent to which it is practicable to introduce governmental restraints cannot be here considered. Cf. *infra*, pp. 398-403.

by such an education of mankind as will lead them to care less than they tend to do for mere material success.[1] The second evil has already been referred to. The remedy for the third evil may to some extent be found in the development of public opinion; but it is to be feared that, in order to deal with it completely, more drastic measures will be required—viz. the introduction of a certain degree of governmental interference. For even to secure the development of a right public opinion on the matter, a very thorough publicity of business transactions would have to be enforced. Many things that are done in trade—even those that are not directly fraudulent—are possible only because they are not known. The spirits of evil cannot walk except by night; and the remedy for much of our commercial evil might be found by insisting that commerce shall be carried on by daylight.[2] In many cases, no doubt, this would be very difficult to effect; but, by securing it gradually in those cases in which it is easily possible, light would be let in by degrees, and public opinion would be slowly formed and directed into the proper channels. Governmental restraints could then be instituted in those cases in which the mere existence of a strong public opinion is not a sufficiently effective check upon transactions that are hurtful to the general well-being. The discussion of the particular cases in which publicity is at present most wanted, and the particular kinds of restraints which it would be necessary to devise, must be left to more detailed treatises. It must suffice here, as in other cases, to have indicated the general principle.[3]

[1] Cf. Graham's *Social Problem*, p. 354.

[2] Cf. Rae's *Contemporary Socialism*, p. 376 *seq.*

[3] There are other two remarks that it may be worth while to make here with reference to competition. The first is, that this evil may be rendered to a considerable extent less keen by the gradual intro-

4. Against the exploitation of labour, again, there can be little doubt that the best safeguard is to be found in some form of co-operation, or at least in some form of profit-sharing which will give the workmen a direct stake in the business in which they are employed. In the case of many kinds of business, especially those that require an energetic head, co-operation has not hitherto proved successful, and is subject to a number of obvious disadvantages: but profit-sharing, without co-operation, secures many of the benefits of the latter, and is not open to quite the same objections. It is sometimes thought, indeed, that the principle of profit-sharing, without loss-sharing, is one that is manifestly unfair. But on a closer examination this does not appear to be the case. If a business is at any time so unsuccessful as to bring a positive loss instead of profit, the probability is that there has either been some miscalculation in starting it, or some mismanagement in carrying it on, or some unexpected change in the conditions either of that particular industry or of industry as a whole; and for none of these circumstances can the workmen be held responsible. On the other hand, an increase of profits may often be directly traceable to their diligence and efficiency. Hence, even from this somewhat limited point of view, it seems perfectly fair that the workmen should have a share in profits, though not in losses. But even if it were not so, the benefits of such an arrangement are so great that they may well be allowed to override a slight appearance of abstract injustice, which is only an appearance,

duction of co-operation and by a more complete recognition of the inter-connection of interests. The second is, that in some cases it may work out its own cure by the development of monopolies, which can then be placed under state supervision (cf. *supra*, p. 125). Quite free competition, indeed, makes competition impossible. But neither of these remedies can be regarded as in itself adequate.

and which in the practical affairs of life can seldom be entirely avoided. *Fiat justitia ruat coelum* is a foolish maxim : we may bring down the skies, but we shall never get abstract justice ; because there is no such thing.[1]

It appears, then, that the remedy for the most prominent of the evils which accompany a highly developed industrial state, is to be found in a certain measure of what may, in a somewhat loose sense, be described as Socialism. The separation of interests between masters and workmen and the consequent degradation in the position of the latter (of which the excessive increase of population is merely one of many symptoms), is to be cured by effecting a certain combination of interests, through profit-sharing and other similar means.[2]    The

[1] It has, moreover, been pointed out by Mr. Sedley Taylor, that profit-sharing does to some extent involve loss-sharing as well. (See *Profit-Sharing*, p. 66.) This point is still more fully worked out in Gilman's *Profit-Sharing*, pp. 429-432. There are also some interesting remarks on the practical working of the scheme in a statement by Mr. Ivimey, Secretary of the Labour Association, published in *Trade, Finance, and Recreation*, March 19, 1890. On the subject of profit-sharing, see also Sidgwick's *Political Economy*, p. 110 *seq.*, and Mill's *Political Economy*, Book IV., chap. vii., § 5. Böhmert's *Gewinnbetheiligung* still remains one of the chief authorities on the whole subject. The method of *Profit-Sharing* has recently been subjected to somewhat searching criticisms by Mrs. Webb (Beatrice Potter) in her book on *The Co-operative Movement in Great Britain* (p. 159 *seq*), and by Mr. David F. Schloss in his *Methods of Industrial Remuneration*. These writers seem to me to have shown that the method is liable to grave dangers, and that it can hardly be accepted as an ultimate ideal. But I do not think they have shown that it may not be an important step towards a more satisfactory relationship between masters and workmen. Mrs. Webb's objections seem to rest partly on an erroneous theory of the nature of profits, and partly on the view that the ultimate ideal must be a socialistic one.

[2] It has rightly enough been pointed out (see, for instance, Mr. Sidney Webb's *Socialism in England*, p. 91) that co-operation is in

separation of interests between different employers is to
be cured chiefly by the development of public opinion
and by state-control. The separation of interests between
what may be called the liberal and conservative sides of
industry—between new inventions and old capabilities, or
in general between energy and inertia—is to be cured by
the supervision of education, and by other means which
involve a certain degree of regulation from above.

It will be observed that the element of Socialism which
is implied in such measures as these is not at all inconsistent with that kind of freedom which is essential to
an industrial state. State-control would not necessarily
be introduced to such an extent as to hinder free competition, but only to such an extent as to hinder it from
becoming lawless; nor need co-operation be carried so far
as to impede individual enterprise. It might be found
difficult in practice to introduce either the one element
or the other without bringing in a considerable measure
of the characteristic evils which are associated with them;
but they are not by their very nature inseparable from
these evils; though it would carry us beyond the limits
of our present inquiry to discuss the particular methods
by which they may be obviated.

II. SOCIAL ORGANISATION.—The next point to be considered is the progress of social machinery, or, as Carlyle
might have put it, the formation of organic tissues. The
treatment of this subject, from a historical point of view,
would form an important element in the work of the

---

itself a very partial and unsatisfactory remedy for industrial evils.
Co-operation in itself is a small thing : but the spirit of combination
is not a small thing ; and, once fairly introduced, it can hardly fail
to lead on to larger forms of union. In an organic society nothing
ought to be estimated simply by what it is in itself. A grain of
mustard seed is not a small thing. Cf. Mill's *Political Economy*,
IV. vii.

sociologist. The social philosopher, however, has only to note what the most important aspects of social organisation are, and to point out the ideal significance of each. The various forms of social unity may be regarded as modes of synthesis or combination in which the organic relation of human beings to each other assumes an objective shape. Some of these forms depend, no doubt, originally on accidental[1] circumstances—on physiological and spatial relations, on the necessity of co-operation for the satisfaction of animal wants, and for protection against the forces of nature and of other human beings, and on many other contingencies. But it is almost impossible for human beings to combine together for any object, however insignificant, without the emergence of a deeper relation ; and when the objects are not insignificant, but grow out of inevitable needs, the forms of combination to which the pursuit of them gives rise can scarcely fail to become modes of the expression of the essential unity of the human race. Such unions cease to be merely methods of organisation and become modes of organic synthesis.[2] Now the modes of such social union which it is possible to form among men are of an almost infinite variety. There are, however, some main species which are especially important ; and these we may now endeavour to indicate, with brief notes upon their most striking features.

1. *The Family.* The simple unity of family life—the primary school of character in the case of the majority of mankind—is a form of association so natural in its origin and so obvious in its benefits, that its importance would scarcely require to be insisted on, were it not that it tends to be ignored in a number of communistic schemes, from that of Plato downwards ; and also that, like most

[1] Cf. *supra*, p. 34, Note 1.
[2] Cf. Caird's *Critical Philosophy of Kant*, Vol. II., p. 402.

good things, it has, whenever it becomes exclusive, a detrimental aspect. Indeed the very excellence of the family as a form of union has suggested its annihilation, by leading on to the idea of the whole human race as a single unity on the analogy which the family supplies. And precisely those who have come most under the influence of its educative power may often be apt, just because they have thus been able to lift themselves to a more universal stage, to forget the benefits which they have derived from it. The "friend of man" forgets that he was once only a friend of men. But the unity which is founded on natural feeling must precede that which depends on acquired sympathies and thoughts. To begin with the love of humanity, would be to begin with a cold abstraction. The family is like a burning-glass which concentrates human sympathies on a point. With-in that narrow circle selfishness is gradually overcome and wider interests developed. Each one is supplied with the opportunity of knowing a few human beings thoroughly, than which nothing is more important as a first stage in the transcendence of the merely individual self. One who knows only himself inwardly and sees others only by a kind of outward observation, which in a large circle is an almost inevitable result, is apt to become for himself too entirely the centre of his world, if, indeed, he ever forms a world or cosmos for himself at all. The family[1] enables a few persons to become not

---

[1] On the ethical significance of the family, cf. Aristotle's *Politics*, II. iv. 6; Comte's *Positive Polity* (translation), II., p. 178 *seq.*; Höffding's *Ethik*, pp. 192-5, and Paulsen's *Ethik*, II., p. 577 *seq.* Devas's work on the Family is probably the best treatise on the whole subject that we have in English. See also the same writer's *Political Economy*, pp. 100-117; Marshall's *Principles of Economics*, p. 35; Janet's *La Famille*, pp. 6-15; and Kaufmann's *Socialism*, p. 226 *seq.*

merely objects for each other, but parts of a single life; and the unity thus effected may then be very readily extended as sympathies grow. At the same time, it cannot be denied that the family has the danger of all exclusive forms of association. The garden-wall hides the horizon. The selfishness of a family may be not less repellent than that of an individual; and the former kind of selfishness is much the more insidious of the two, since the evil spirit is there masquerading as an angel of light. The cure for these evils, however, is to be found not by destroying the family, but by treating it as a preparation for a more complete form of union. In this reference, it might be not uninstructive to consider the transition stage between the family life and that of the community which would be supplied by what are sometimes known as "associated homes."[1] The possibility of such a stage of transition has been suggested by the life in common which is to be found in colleges and other semi-public institutions, as well as by the more or less successful experiments of communistic societies. It must be allowed, however, that the possibility of such a form of life depends on a certain community of interests and congeniality of tastes which on a large scale it would be very difficult to secure. In the case of those communistic societies which have attained any high degree of success, it has usually depended also on some

---

[1] Miss Clapperton's book on *Scientific Meliorism* (chap. xvi.) may be found suggestive on this, as well as on several other aspects of social progress. Several recent writers have emphasised the importance of such forms of domestic association. See, for instance, Miss Gilliland's article on "Women in the Community and the Family" (*International Journal of Ethics*, October, 1894, pp. 41-42); Ritchie's *Natural Rights*, p. 63; and that curious new Utopia which has recently attracted so much popular attention, Mr. Blatchford's *Merrie England*, chaps. v. and vi.

form of religious enthusiasm,[1] which cannot be pre-supposed in societies generally. Still, the extent to which such associations might be carried, is certainly a question which deserves attention. But it is too large a question to be dealt with here. All that can now be added with respect to the family, is the admission that to some extent it benefits one part of the community at the expense of another. For it seems certain that there is a considerable number of people who are distinctly worse prepared for life within the circle of the family than they would be under a more communistic system. But it can hardly be doubted that those who are bene-fited constitute a very decided majority, and also that the benefit which they receive is very much greater in degree than the detriment which the others suffer. Moreover, their education reacts upon the rest of the community, and gives to it all a higher tone. The tone of social life is ultimately measured by the highest point which it reaches.[2]

Such considerations as these may suffice to show that, however desirable it may be that the unity of the monogamic family should become less rigid and ex-clusive as civilisation advances, it is scarcely to be wished that it should ever be superseded. There are, however, some directions in which it is desirable to temper the prominence of its influence. Of these the most important is to be found in an extension of the

[1] Cf. Nordhoff's *Communistic Societies in the United States* and Noyes's *History of American Socialism, passim.* These two books taken together seem to show that the only forms of communistic association which tend to be successful are those that rest on a religious or semi-religious basis.

[2] This is one of the elements of truth in the theory of "Heroes." To "make giants" is ultimately the best, if not the only, way to "elevate the race."

province of the school. The part which the Public School system has played in the lives of the wealthier classes in England is well known; and, though it has many obvious defects, it can scarcely be doubted that its effects have been in many respects beneficial as a half-way house between the home and the outside world. But it is evident that some such mediation[1] is very much more important in the case of those classes of the community for whom home life frequently means little more than squalor and degradation. There is no direction in which socialistic or semi-socialistic measures may be carried out with less fear of evil consequences than in the effort to supply such a want; and it is in this direction that there seems to be the most urgent demand for an escape from the limitations of the family.

So far what has been said has had reference to the family only as the sphere within which our earliest education is received. When we consider it rather in relation to the position of women in modern society, we are involved in a much more complicated question, to which we cannot pretend to offer any answer. The desire for greater freedom in the marriage relationship appears to be now somewhat widely felt. To some extent, no doubt, the discontent which has been expressed on this and kindred matters, is only an illustration of that individualistic pessimism to which reference has been made in Chapter II.;[2] but to a large extent also it must be ascribed to a rational demand for that personal independence which is indispensable to moral welfare. Such proposals as are made, however, by writers like Mr.

[1] Though, of course, it would have to be supplied in a very different way.

[2] *Supra*, p. 130.  Cf. also Lilly's *Right and Wrong*, p. 220.

Karl Pearson[1] and many others with more or less pronounced socialistic leanings, seem to be put forward without a sufficiently careful consideration of their effects on the majority of human beings as they actually are. "Heroic treatment" belongs on the whole to a past stage of social medicine, when revolutions were still in vogue. Those with whom "evolution" has become a watchword more naturally look for help to the development of public opinion. How powerful the influence of this is in such matters, is sufficiently obvious from the great differences in the "Sitten" of various peoples. We may contrast, for instance, Germany with England, or England with the United States.[2] But the whole question is one which would require for its adequate discussion the introduction of much more sociological detail than is consistent with our present plan.

Another direction in which we see at present a tendency to break through the unity of the family life, is in the relation to domestic service. It has been thought by some that the position of one who is in the family and not of it, approaches somewhat too closely to one of serfdom, and tends—except in the most favourable circumstances—to exercise a degrading influence on a free personality.[3] One who occupies such a position becomes in a manner given up body and soul to the authority of

---

[1] *Ethic of Freethought*, chap. xiii.   I refer to Prof. Pearson here, because his statements seem the most moderate and the most carefully considered.

[2] On this point there are some instructive remarks in Bryce's *American Commonwealth*, part VI., chap. cv., etc. Cf. also Spencer's *Sociology*, I., p. 791.

[3] Cf. on this point, the pamphlet by Mr. Maurice Adams on the *Ethics of Social Reform*, p. 20 *seq.*   On this point also, some of the present discontent may perhaps be traced to a false individualism; but it is in the main simply an application of the Hegelian maxim, *Be a person, and respect others as persons.*

a master or mistress, and does not, like other workers, simply enter into a contract to render certain definite services. In order to prevent any such renunciation of independence, it has been urged that an attempt ought to be made to enable such servants merely to enter into an engagement for definite hours of work, and at other times to remain entirely outside of the family life. The difficulties are obvious; but it is clear that a system of associated homes would render it much more practicable than it is at present; and indeed this fact is one of the main arguments by which the desirability of such a system is shown. It is impossible here to enter into any discussion of this scheme. It must suffice to have mentioned it in its place. To a considerable extent, it may be hoped that the evil complained of will be removed by the development of public opinion.

2. *The District.* This second form of union is in itself of considerably less importance than the family. As the association which depends on family relations is the most natural, so is that which depends merely on local contiguity the most artificial and external of human combinations. If, indeed, some such arrangement as Fourier's Phalanstère could be adopted, if the various local clusters of individuals could be rendered self-sufficient — each district having its own shoemaker, its own tailor, its own grocer, and so on, and each of these recognising a more than merely commercial relationship to the others—the union would be rendered more essential and organic. But it may well be doubted whether any such arrangement is either possible or desirable. It could not be carried out without very strict regulations, and, if it were carried out, it might tend to deprive us too thoroughly of the wholesome element in competition. The districts would stagnate. There is, however, one respect in which it is extremely desirable that there should be a certain self-

sufficiency in each local group. It ought to contain, as far as possible, representatives of all the *classes* and *grades* of social life ; and there ought to be a general recognition of mutual obligations among them. The separation of classes is, as we have seen, one of the worst features of modern life in large cities; and if a phalanstère could be devised for us which would avoid this evil, it would be an undeniable gain. It is probable, however, that nothing of this sort can be effected, except by voluntary effort and self-sacrifice on the part of the richer and more cultured part of the community. Such settlements as that at Toynbee Hall are a first step in this direction ; and there are few, if any, movements from which more is to be hoped. The isolation of classes is an evil for all ; and as those of us who have means and leisure go to the mountains or to the seaside for the health of our bodies and the relaxation of our minds, so we may ultimately find it necessary to betake ourselves to the centres of our overcrowded populations for the health of our souls. Many at least begin to feel this as a duty.[1] The possibility, however, of destroying these overcrowded centres by removing industries into country places is deserving of even more serious attention.

This leads us to touch on the general subject of charity, which is necessarily in the main an affair for each district to manage for itself, and consequently may very naturally be considered at this point. " Philanthropy," as Höffding says,[2] "is the effort to put right what social conditions have put wrong." A higher kind of philanthropy is that which endeavours to put right the social conditions themselves : but so long as this is not completely possible, there must remain a large sphere for the

---

[1] Dr. Coit's book on *Neighbourhood Guilds* contains some useful suggestions in connection with the points here touched upon.

[2] *Ethik*, p. 387.

2 A

lower kind of philanthropy. Now such philanthropic efforts are continually baffled by the discovery that in many directions it is impossible to help others without hurting them; and consequently it becomes a question of great importance to determine exactly in what directions this is the case. The general principle, no doubt, is clear. Nothing can permanently help any one, except what helps him to help himself. A gift is nothing unless the giver gives also the power of receiving it—except in those rare cases in which such a power may be presupposed. For this reason more depends on the manner in which help is given than on the actual nature of the help.[1] The philanthropist, like the philosopher, must seek to be "everywhere at home." He must not merely scatter his goods, but diffuse himself. He must live into the condition of those whom he seeks to aid, and in a manner make their lives a part of his own. It is not always true that "charity begins at home," but in a different sense it is true that charity is always at home; for until it makes itself at home it is not charity. Hence, it is not possible for charity to be mechanically organised:[2] it depends on personal influence. It follows also from these principles, that the great charity is education. But it is a question of considerable difficulty to ascertain what influences are educative and what are the reverse.[3]

One species of education which it is very important to

[1] Cf. Marshall's *Economics of Industry*, pp. 34-5. See also Caird's "Moral Aspect of the Economical Problem" in *Time* for January, 1888; Macmillan's *General Happiness*, p. 175 *seq.*; Loch's *How to help Cases of Distress*, pp. iv.-x.; Spencer's *Man* versus *State*, p. 71, etc., and Clapperton's *Scientific Meliorism*, chap. vi.

[2] Cf. Loch's *Charity Organisation*, p. 33.

[3] Cf. "Two Modern Philanthropists" in Bosanquet's *Essays and Addresses*.

diffuse throughout every district of a large community, is the *education of wants*. Lassalle used to speak of the " verdammte Bedürfnisslosigkeit" of the people, as one of the greatest hindrances to social advancement. But a misdirection of wants may be as pernicious as the absence of them, either by its demoralising influence in itself, or by its giving a wrong twist to industrial conditions; and consequently few forms of charity are more beneficial than those which are directed to the inculcation of higher standards of taste. Under this head, for instance, would be included the encouragement of artistic designs. This is important, both on account of the educative influence of the finer sorts of art, and because they afford opportunities for the employment of the highest kinds of skilled labour and check the despotism of machinery.[1]

It is hardly necessary to add, after what has been already said on the organic nature of society, that such charity as is here referred to, is not to be regarded, as it is sometimes apt to be, as a kind of *moral luxury* which may be indulged in after all other claims have been served. It is a *necessity* of the moral life : life without it is incomplete, so long at least as society remains diseased. It is true, indeed, that no definite rules can be laid down with regard to the limits within which

---

[1] The importance of the cultivation of right methods of consumption is well insisted on in Mummery and Hobson's *Physiology of Industry*. These writers, however, do not seem to me to distinguish sufficiently between different *kinds* of consumption. Their doctrine appears sometimes to approach dangerously near to that of Mandeville, that "private vices are public benefits." I think this remark applies also, to some extent, to the writings of Mr. R. S. Moffat and Mr. J. M. Robertson on the same subject. But these writers have rendered a useful service in directing attention to the importance of the study of the theory of consumption, which has been too much overlooked by the majority of economists.

this duty is to be observed. It depends too much on individual capacity and opportunity. It is true also that the best services of this kind are rendered not so much from the sense of duty as from the sense of love and pity; and that the attempt to substitute the former for the latter would in many cases destroy the very substance of the actions, or at least injure the fineness of its texture. It is in such instances as this that we are made aware that the moral life is the most subtle and exquisite of the Fine Arts, and requires a genius for its right accomplishment. Hence it is also, that in such cases we have to be content rather with the inspiration of great examples than with the inculcation of definite rules. But the duty is not on this account any the less plain and imperative.

3. *The Workshop.* This, according to Proudhon, is the real unit in modern society. It can, however, hardly be described as a *unit*; but it is certainly one of the most important forms of *unity*; and unhappily, as things are, it is still a unity of a very inorganic description. Not only is it apt to be a merely mechanical compound, but it is often a compound of repugnant elements; and if our social system, as it is at present constituted, is not entirely to break down, some means must be devised of rendering this unity one of a more close and vital character. And here again the remedy which most naturally presents itself, is that of the introduction of some form of co-operation or profit-sharing, to which we have already had occasion to refer. It is true that we might also suppose a more organic arrangement to be brought about simply by an education of masters which should lead them to regard themselves—as some are even now beginning to do—as "captains of industry," with the welfare of their men as one of their primary concerns. Indeed it is only by means of such an education

that we can hope for the introduction and success of co-operation or profit-sharing on a large scale. But with average human nature, and still more with that which falls rather below the average—and it is for this chiefly that in any form of social organisation provision must be made—it is very difficult for masters to assume any such attitude as this, so long as their material interests seem to be opposed to those of their men, or even so long as the two interests seem to be separate. Nor, indeed, even when they are ready to assume such an attitude, are they in general wise enough to assume it in a really helpful way. Hence, it is hardly to be expected that "captains of industry" will be developed much more rapidly than profit-sharing extends. At least, if the captains precede the sharing, the sharing must certainly precede the lieutenants and sergeants.

4. *The Trade.* Unions among those of the same trade have played a very important part among the associations of the past; but it may be doubted whether much more is now to be gained by the extension of them. It seems rather as if such combinations had now accomplished very nearly all which it is possible for them to do,[1] and as if the great unions of the future must be either of a narrower or of a more universal character. Trades unions are inevitably of a more or less partizan description; and the age of parties is past. While industrial conditions were still *developing*, it was necessary to bring forward and insist on the interests of particular classes as opposed to others; but now that they *are developed*, we can take a broader survey of them; and what has now to be insisted on is rather the interests of the whole. Hence it is probable that in the future trades unions will not *increase* in importance, and they may even decline. At the same time, the needs of

[1] Except, of course, in the case of women and of unskilled labour.

different kinds of industry will always remain somewhat distinct in character; and, consequently, it will always be desirable to have combinations of those belonging to the same trade, for the purpose of dealing with their peculiar wants. The age of parties is succeeded by the age of committees. Smaller unions, as well as national ones, begin with fighting and end with business.

5. *The Church.* The importance of the religious form of union need hardly be insisted on. Religion is the great moral motor or inspiring force. It has been said that "nothing great was ever done without passion"; and certainly it is under the influence of that emotional enthusiasm which we describe as religious, that men have been led to the highest forms of self-devotion and philanthropic zeal. Now the great hindrances to the work of the church hitherto have been disunion and unreason. One might have supposed that the former of these hindrances would have been gradually removed as the sense of uncertainty in theological doctrine increased; but of this there has been little sign. Indeed there seems to be some force in the saying of De Tocqueville that— "In time of great religious fervour men sometimes change their religious opinions; whereas in times of general scepticism everyone clings to his own persuasion . . . . not so much because he is assured of its excellence, as because he is not convinced of the superiority of any other. In the present age, men are not very ready to die in defence of their opinions, but they are rarely inclined to change them; and there are fewer martyrs as well as fewer apostates." This attitude, however, is an evanescent one, and must gradually lead to union. It is true that as the metals cool they cease to flow into each other; but when they are quite cold they will be found fastened together; and whenever they are reheated they will become one. Men are becoming more and more con-

vinced that everything in religion, except what is most
fundamental, is so uncertain and so insignificant that it
is not worth while to quarrel about it; and that, even
with respect to what is most fundamental, all forms of
expression are from the nature of the case inadequate;
that "as soon as the soul has *spoken*, it is not the *soul*
that speaks";[1] and that the same truth will always
present itself to different minds in a different guise. With
the growth of this conviction, religious disunion is gradually
vanishing. The unreason of the church, again, has appeared chiefly in forms of enthusiasm which have no
reference to life, and in forms of creed which are irrecon-
cilable with fact. From these two causes religion has
ceased to have that hold on modern life which it has
often had in the past. To enter into any consideration
of the remedies for these evils would carry us too far.

---

[1] " Warum kann der lebendige Geist dem Geist nicht erscheinen ?—
*Spricht* die Seele, so spricht, ach ! schon die *Seele* nicht mehr."
—Schiller.

This is, no doubt, only partly true. We may hope at some time
to see men united, not merely on the negative basis of uncertainty
and mutual tolerance, but also on that of certain positive beliefs.
But the metaphysical basis of such a union seems to be scarcely yet
prepared. In the meantime, it must be admitted that the other kind
of union reminds us a little too much of Bacon's saying (in his Essay
" Of Unity in Religion "), that " all colours will agree in the dark."
In this connection Mr. M'Taggart's remarks on " The Necessity of
Dogma," in the *International Journal of Ethics* for January, 1895,
may be found instructive. " It may be doubted," he says (pp. 160-1),
" whether you can get any unity worth preserving by the process,
immortalised by Mr. Saunders M'Kaye, of first stripping mankind of
their clothes, and then proclaiming them brothers ' on the gran'
fundamental principle o' want o' breeks.' The insides of two empty
boxes are no doubt singularly alike. But a unity of this sort may possibly be over-valued." Still, the man who first clearly recognised his
own ignorance was counted the wisest of the Greeks, and a combination
on the basis of mutual ignorance and a common desire to know may
sometimes be a useful preparation for more positive forms of union.

It may be enough to remark, that they must be found mainly in a thorough education of those who are to be the spiritual teachers of their time, in a knowledge of the main conditions of social and individual welfare,[1] and in an adequate provision for their independence of the shifting winds of popular favour. It may be doubted whether these conditions can be in any satisfactory measure secured for our churches generally, until they have in some form reunited.

It is an interesting department of sociological prophecy to consider what the significance of the church is likely to be in the future of our civilisation.[2] It seems clear that there must always be some kind of fellowship of the saints, some kind of association of those who are zealous for social improvement, and who meet together to give expression to their highest aspirations, and to receive from each other stimulus and guidance for their work; and the existence of such associations must always be of the greatest importance in the development of the national life. The ultimate greatness of a nation depends largely on the way in which it habitually thinks of duty; and this habit depends very much on the leavening influence of such communions as we have now referred to. But what form such association is now to take, it is impossible to predict. The chief difficulty will, no doubt, be to supply in any adequate degree the place of those mystic joys and terrors on which in the past the influence of religion on the majority of mankind has so largely

---

[1] Cf. *infra*, pp. 420-1.

[2] On this point there are some suggestive remarks in Gizycki's *Moral-philosophie*, p. 421. The view which he takes, however, is of a strongly radical character. For views of a somewhat different nature, see Toynbee's *Industrial Revolution*, p. 231 *seq.*, and Schäffle's *Bau und Leben des socialen Körpers*, i. 693 *seq.* Cf. also Bosanquet's *Civilisation of Christendom*, pp. 1-26.

depended. It may be doubted whether, for some time to come, it will be quite possible to dispense with what Plato describes as a γενναῖον ψεῦδος[1] in the teaching of religion. But it can scarcely be doubted that this will become less and less necessary, as education spreads and social bonds are drawn closer. Some may see the germs of the church of the future in such institutions as Toynbee Hall. Others may see it rather in those societies for Ethical Culture, which have been springing up so plentifully in the United States. Others may think that such merely humanitarian efforts cannot permanently satisfy our religious needs—that it is necessary even for the continuance of these in any enthusiastic form, that we should rest them on a faith that "morality is the essence of *things*" as well as of persons.[2] What we have

---

[1] "Noble falsehood." *Republic*, Book III. It must be confessed that this is a dangerous idea. The effort to "speak with the vulgar and think with the learned," can scarcely fail to be disastrous to the honesty and manliness of those who make it. Yet it cannot be denied that there is a stage of moral development at which the spiritual is apprehended only in the form of the supernatural. This is probably what Professor Macmillan means when he says (*Promotion of General Happiness*, p. 184), that "religion is much more teachable than morality to large masses of men." It might be truer to say that, at a certain stage, both religion and morality can hardly be taught except in the form of myth. The *Begriff* must appear in the form of the *Vorstellung*, reason in the form of emotion. How far it is justifiable to cater for this stage is a difficult question in casuistry. Probably the best attitude is one of passive acquiescence in the provision that is actually made for it, combined with the constant effort to raise men above the need of such provision. Cf. Green's *Collected Works*, Vol. III., pp. 274-6, and Mill's *Inaugural Address*.

[2] The extent to which such a religious attitude is required, is, I think, very clearly brought out in Mr. J. H. Muirhead's address on *The Position of an Ethical Society*. On religion as a social power, cf. Marshall's *Principles of Economics*, p. 1. Much of what is said by Mr. Benjamin Kidd in his *Social Evolution* on this subject is also good, though it seems to be vitiated throughout by a misconception

already said [1] with regard to the ideal involved in our self-conscious nature, would point rather to this latter view; but a discussion of it would evidently carry us beyond the limits of Social Philosophy. It is enough for our present purpose to have noted the important position which the church occupies, and seems likely to continue to occupy, as a centre of enthusiasm for social improvement.

6. *The Civic Community.*    This also, like the church, is a form of unity which has played an important part in the past, and seems likely to continue to occupy a prominent place in the future.    Indeed in the near future it seems likely to become more prominent than it has hitherto been.    The governments of the great European powers have been for some time in a sort of contradiction with the rest of their national life.    The general life of the people has had that sort of local independence which Industrialism naturally brings with it; whereas the government has continued to retain the rigid centralisation of a military régime.    This is inevitable so long as the provision for an impending war is a leading factor in the life of states.    But while the prospects of peace are comparatively secure, a considerable amount of local management may be introduced; and there can be little doubt that it is in that direction that we are now moving. Indeed, it is only by a considerable degree of local government that the spirit of liberty can be sustained. "Local assemblies of citizens," as De Tocqueville has said, "constitute the strength of free nations.    Town-meetings are to liberty what primary schools are to science; they bring it within the people's reach, they teach them how to use and how to enjoy it.    A nation

as to the nature of Reason, and by the consequent treatment of religion as essentially non-rational.

[1] *Supra*, p. 258.    Cf. also Caird's *Philosophy of Religion*, chap. iv.

may establish a system of free government, but without
the spirit of municipal institutions it cannot have the
spirit of liberty." But there is another consideration
which is even more important than this. The problem of
modern times is how to make life possible in large cities
devoted to industrial activities, and this is a problem
which cannot be dealt with except by the cities themselves. For this reason also, a great deal of local independence in the management of local affairs is a necessity
of modern life. One important question, for instance,
which will probably have to be dealt with in the near
future by most of our great cities, is that with regard to
the influx of a shiftless and degraded population either
from the country or from foreign lands. But no doubt
the great problem of the municipalities for a long time
to come, will rather be the consideration of the question
to what extent the introduction of socialistic measures is
possible and expedient. Some of the most fundamental
objections to Socialism disappear, or lose much of their
force, when it is confined within a narrow area.[1] At the
same time, it must be allowed that there are definite
limits to the possibility of local self-government. Not
only is it necessary for purposes of national defence that
the state should be a whole, but even in time of peace
and security there are large national interests which cannot be divided. Besides, it is difficult in small centres
to find men with sufficient ability and breadth of view [2]
to be able to decide wisely on important affairs. The
state as a whole must consequently remain always the

---

[1] Cf. *infra*, pp. 399-400.

[2] No doubt, in this respect the demand would, to a certain extent,
create a supply. If the state were more thoroughly decentralised,
there would be more encouragement to local talent, and less temptation for it to gravitate towards the capital. When there is no
Berlin, there may be a Weimar.

380 THE ELEMENTS OF SOCIAL PROGRESS.

most considerable, as it is the largest, of our social
unions.

7. *The Nation.* We are thus led to the great question
of the government of a state. And here we may begin
by remarking that probably few sayings are more foolish
than that of Pope:

> " For forms of government let fools contest :
> Whate'er is best administered is best";

for the whole question with reference to the best kind of
government might almost be summed up in the inquiry—
Which will be best administered?[1] It is, in one sense,
foolish to contend about forms of government : but
the reason is rather that the advantages of each form
vary with varying conditions, and that we can neither
frame any absolute ideal for a state nor realise any ideal
except by a gradual growth. A perfect state presupposes
perfect citizens, and an ideal government will never be
attained "till crowds at length be sane and crowns be
just," till all the members of the society are entirely wise
—and then there will be no government at all.[2] But it is
not therefore foolish to consider in what direction it is
best to move at any particular moment. Now, there can
be little doubt that, for such societies as exist in modern
civilised communities, the form of government must be
in the main democratic. There are so many different
forms of industrial enterprise, and it is so important to
cultivate individual independence and originality, that it
would be impossible for any aristocratic administration,
however wise, to lead to desirable results.[3] The great

---

[1] Cf. Lieber's *Political Ethics*, Vol. I., p. 312.

[2] At least, government would then exist only for the purpose of
formulating the general will ; and the particular form which it would
take would be a mere question of convenience.

[3] The educative influence of democracy is undoubtedly its main
recommendation. Cf. *infra*, pp. 406, 410. It is possible, however,

question, therefore, comes to be—What are the most essential requirements of a government which is fundamentally democratic?

Now the first thing to be secured with reference to a Democracy, is that it shall actually *be* a Democracy, *i.e.* a rule in which the interests of the whole people are represented. There is always a danger that what is called a Democracy should be merely a tyranny turned upside down. That the many should rule over the few is not any more desirable—rather less so—than that the few should rule over the many. What is wanted is not the preponderance of any one class, but an equitable regard for all. Now in order that the balance of justice may yield a fair result, there are three conditions requisite—that all the interests should be placed in the scales, and that the balance itself should be at once sensitive and true. Each form of government tends to violate one or more of these conditions. An aristocracy is from its nature one-sided, and represents only certain interests. A monarch, even if he is wise and impartial enough to survey all interests and estimate them fairly, is yet too far removed from the life of his people to be adequately sensitive to changes of condition. And the danger of a popular government is that the balance should be somewhat over-sensitive and not true.

To prevent the balance from becoming too sensitive is one of the chief uses of the Second Chamber which is so characteristic a feature of modern governments; and this

to exaggerate the extent to which democracy must be carried with a view to the attainment of its educational results. It is not necessary for this purpose that the citizens should actually carry on the government of their country, but only that they should take a lively interest in it, and give it what Dr. Sidgwick has well described as their "active consent." (*Elements of Politics*, pp. 584-590.) See also Caird's *Comte*, p. 237.

device seems to be on the whole effective:[1] but to devise a means of making the balance *true* is a much more difficult problem. To count the number of votes on each side of a question can hardly be a satisfactory way of finding out the relative importance of different interests. Such a calculus is as bad as the hedonistic one. As Schiller said, "We ought to weigh the votes rather than count them";[2] and how this is to be done,

---

[1] Another device to prevent over-sensitiveness, is to have a fixed constitution, as in the United States. See Sidgwick's *Elements of Politics*, pp. 535-543.

[2] "Man soll die Stimmen wägen und nicht zählen :
    Der Staat muss untergehen, früh oder spät,
    Wo Mehrheit siegt und Unverstand entscheidet."

On this subject reference may be made to the suggestions contained in Mill's *Representative Government*, on the representation of minorities (chap. vii.), and on plural voting (chap. viii.). See also Mr. F. Harrison's *Order and Progress*, p. 71 *seq.* But cf. Lotze's *Microcosmus* (English Translation), Vol. II., p. 547. See also Professor MacCunn's *Ethics of Citizenship* (pp. 91-129), where the arguments in favour of the simple rule of the majority are stated in a remarkably clear and temperate form. It may be noted that one small safeguard against the rule of the *mere* majority is provided by the trouble of going to vote. This ensures at least a certain minimum of interest on the part of the voters. I should, therefore, doubt the wisdom of Professor Ritchie's suggestion (made in his book on *Natural Rights*) that every one should be compelled to record a vote, or at least to appear at the voting place. Besides, it is probably desirable that the suffrage should be regarded as a privilege, not as a vexatious interference with freedom. And it would be better if people could be taught that they are not to vote unless they have first thought and understood. Hence I should be more inclined to favour such a suggestion as that the loss or temporary suspension of the privilege should be made a punishment for certain social offences (*e.g.* drunkenness). But how far it would be possible to carry out any such suggestion, is of course a question for the practical politician. The broad principle that we have here to recognise is simply, that this right, like every other, involves a

is perhaps the most weighty problem of modern government. Unless it can be solved, there can be little
doubt that it is on this rock that Democracy will split.
A mere counting of votes must in many cases give the
victory to "the drummers and trumpeters of the army."
Every kind of government must be in some way "tempered," though it should only be "with epigrams."
Tyranny is usually tempered with assassination, and
Democracy must be tempered with culture.[1] In the
absence of this, it turns into a representation of collective
folly. Now in order to discover how such a tempering
process is to be applied, we must consider for a little
what the various functions of a government are.

There are three main functions which every government must perform—(1) deliberative, (2) legislative, (3)
executive [2]—and the defect of most theories of government is that they overlook one or other of these. We
require in every government (1) a wise consideration of
the wants of the people, (2) a just provision for the
satisfaction of them, and (3) an effective carrying out of
the provisions which are made. One who looks merely
to the first of these requirements will naturally demand
*wisdom* in a government more than any other quality:
one who looks to the second will demand *justice*: one
who looks to the third will demand *power*. When
thinkers like Von Treitschke maintain emphatically that
"the state is Power" ("Der Staat Macht ist"), they are
thinking almost exclusively of the executive, whose main
requisite is that it shall be thoroughly effective in carry-

duty, and that the violation of duty may legitimately lead to its
suspension, in so far as it proves a man to be unworthy to be a
citizen of a free State.

[1] Cf. Montesquieu's *Esprit des Lois*, iv. 5.

[2] Which may be regarded, from this point of view, as including
the judicial.

ing out what it has to do.  A warlike state like Germany, seated in the heart of Europe with enemies on every side, leans most naturally to this point of view; and consequently theorists in that country will generally be found to prefer a strong monarchical government to any other.  English writers, on the other hand, with their eyes chiefly on domestic affairs, are especially eager to secure a just legislation, and consequently incline to support democracy, by which all interests are most equally represented.[1]  Finally, such writers as Carlyle[2] (or, in ancient times, Plato), whose attention is directed more to the education of the race than to the acquisition either of mights or rights, are disposed rather to advocate an aristocracy of talent, which would be the wisest of all governments in deliberation—or if they lean to monarchy, it is only because they hope to secure a king who is also a philosopher.

Now as it is with the requirements of Democracy that we are specially concerned, we have to note simply that, from such considerations as have now been indicated, it becomes at once apparent that Democracy is strongest in legislation, while it is comparatively weak in its deliberative and executive departments.[3]  What is chiefly wanted, therefore, to counterbalance its inherent defects, is that these two latter departments should be strengthened. Now the weakness of the executive leads to evils of so

[1] No doubt, these different proclivities may be traced also to other causes.

[2] In his saner moments.  Frequently he relapses into the view that the state is might.  Cf., however, *Essays in Philosophical Criticism*, p. 140.  Carlyle meant on the whole by his frequent references to "might" (which have been so much decried) that everything valuable in human life is an ἐνέργεια, not a mere δύναμις. But I admit that his applications are often questionable.

[3] Except in great emergencies, in which the whole people acts as one man.  Cf. Bryce's *American Commonwealth*, Vol. III., p. 306.

obvious and practical a character, that they have never been entirely overlooked in the governmental arrangement of modern states : and though there is undoubtedly much still left to be desired in this respect, yet it does not seem necessary here to do more than indicate the importance of the question, and hand it over for discussion to the political philosopher. The other deficiency is of so much more occult a nature, that it is not even customary to regard a state as necessarily possessing a deliberative department at all. This department has tended to be regarded merely as one of the aspects of the legislature. It is, therefore, desirable to touch on this point here with a little more fulness.[1]

That a wise consideration of the needs of the state is as important as either the formation of just laws or the effective carrying out of them, must be evident to every one. And that such a consideration of needs is a function entirely distinct from either of the others—as distinct as they are from each other—must also, on the whole, be apparent. It is true, indeed, that the legislature, in framing its enactments, must have regard to the wants of the country, just as it must also have regard to the powers which the government possesses of carrying out such laws as may be framed. But it is not the work of the legislature as such either to carry out the laws or to discover what the country needs. It is a presupposition of the legislature that the wants are known, just as it is a presupposition that there is power to supply them when the necessary provisions have been made. But if the wants are known which the laws are intended to provide for, prior to the time at which the laws are made, it remains for us still to ask, who it is that found out these wants. It is not the legislators ; for it is their

[1] Cf., on this point, Mr. F. Harrison's *Order and Progress*, p. 382 *seq.*

2 B

function rather to make provision for wants which are already supposed to be known. Now this is a function which could not well be combined with that of ascertaining what the wants actually are ; for it is impossible, in the ordinary course of affairs, that a thing can be calmly considered by the very people who are actively engaged in making a law with regard to it. The maker of laws is almost necessarily to a very considerable extent an advocate, whereas he who is to consider what laws are wanted ought rather to be a judge. It is essential that the legislator should have made up his mind; it is essential that the deliberator should not. Who, then, is the judge to whom the advocate appeals? Shall we say that it is the people as a whole? This seems to be the answer which is implied in the idea of representative government, in which it is to the people that the final appeal is made. But to say that the people are the deliberators, is only to say that there are none : for the people as a whole cannot think, any more than they can plan or execute. Is it, then, the Press that constitutes our deliberative assembly? There can be little doubt that it is, in so far as there is any such assembly at all. But it is impossible that the Press can perform such a function in an efficient way. The only kind of literature which has a very extensive influence on popular opinion, is that of the newspapers and the cheaper sorts of journals. Now one of the first requirements of such papers is that they should pay; and in order that they may pay, they must be at once acceptable to a large number of people. Hence the Press as a whole can do little else than represent the ideas of the majority, just as under a Democracy the legislature also is supposed to do. And hence to say that the Press is our deliberative assembly amounts to very little more than to say that the people are that assembly—*i.e.* that there is no such assembly.

But a Democracy cannot do without such an assembly —or at least without some kind of influence which shall fill its place. According to the familiar *dictum*, "the price of liberty is eternal vigilance." If the people is to rule, there must be an incessant outlook to ensure that the people shall be wisely guided. The people may contrive to act as captain, but it cannot act as pilot. And it is clear that such an outlook as is thus required upon the shoals and currents in front, must be made by those of the citizens who have most insight with respect to affairs of state. The actual framing of the laws may be left to those who possess particular kinds of skill and tact; and the actual execution of them, to those who possess particular kinds of practical effectiveness; but to consider what laws are required at any particular moment, is a task that requires the very highest wisdom. The question, therefore, comes to be—How are men of the highest wisdom to be secured for the work?

Now as the wise are the only judges of wisdom, it is difficult to see how there can be any answer to this question which will satisfy its requirements, except that which was suggested by Plato,[1] that the wisest men should be left to choose themselves: and that the penalty by which they are to be driven to this choice, is the fear of being governed by inferior men. But in order that this penalty may be enabled to operate, and may operate only on the proper persons, it is necessary that their work should be one which brings with it neither honour nor emolument nor power. It must have no extraneous attractions. It must, in fact, have no attractions at all. Men must be driven into it merely by the penalty that has been mentioned: otherwise there seems to be no possible guarantee that the right kind of men

[1] Cf. *supra*, p. 330.

will be selected, and that they will enter on their work with singleness of aim. Consequently, it is not desirable that there should be any such assembly as is here referred to, with so definite an organisation as to be able to influence public opinion in an authoritative way. As soon as it acquired such power, the penalty would be changed into a reward. It would become attractive to men of ambitious aims, and might soon sink into nothing better than a training-school for a parliamentary career.

We are thus led to what is perhaps the fundamental antinomy of a democratic rule. On the one hand, it is of supreme importance that the highest wisdom should be made into the sovereign power : on the other hand, if the appearance of wisdom confers power, the appearance is liable to take the place of the reality. The Comtean proposal of " Priests of Humanity" was intended as a means of meeting this difficulty; but it meets it by introducing an aristocracy,[1] and an aristocracy whose influence could not always be trusted to be in the best direction. If, again, we attempt to establish a deliberative assembly, we are met by the difficulty to which reference has just been made. In fact, if a deliberative assembly were constituted, it would almost of necessity be placed at the head of the state, just as a legislative assembly takes a certain precedence over the executive. The deliberative assembly would then come to correspond with Plato's Philosopher-king, or with a combination of Comte's Priests of Humanity. But in these circumstances it would cease to be purely deliberative, since it would have to rule as well as to think. Wisdom can hardly maintain its character as wisdom when it becomes also power. There can be little doubt that

---

[1] An aristocracy which could hardly fail to become one of power, as well as of wisdom. Cf. Caird's *Philosophy of Comte*, pp. 244-5, and Mill's *Comte*, p. 99.

Plato was right, in making the lives of his rulers a comparatively unenviable one. It is, in fact, the function of a true aristocracy to educate, and not to rule ; and he who would be chief in this higher kind of governing, must in a manner become "the servant of all." His position must be the least enviable rather than the most. His kingdom is "not of this world," and his power must be that neither of law nor of legions, but simply that which light has over darkness. What is required, in fact, is not a philosophic ruler, but rather, in Comte's phrase, "réaction du conseil sur le commandement."

We might put this difficulty in a slightly different way. Carlyle has characterised the two great influencing forces among mankind as *light* and *lightning*. On the one hand there is the force of insight, and on the other hand that of practical effectiveness. It is the great misfortune of human history that these have been so often distinct and it is the great problem of politics to combine them. So long as the government of states remained essentially despotic, this problem was an insoluble one, unless, as Plato put it, either philosophers were to become kings, or kings philosophers, *i.e.* unless either those who had insight were to become effective, or those who were effective were to gain insight. Under a Democracy the solution is similar; but as in this case those who are effective are simply the people as a whole, what is necessary is no longer that any one individual or class of individuals should acquire insight, but that insight should become generally diffused, or at least generally recognisable. It may be said that this is a matter rather of education than of state-arrangement: and this remark would no doubt be partially true. But it cannot be hoped that any amount of education will ever make wisdom accessible to all. There will always remain the two classes of good citizens referred to by Hesiod,[1] those who can discern wisdom for themselves and those who can only be persuaded by its voice.   Our problem, therefore, is not so much the educational one of diffusing wisdom as of making wisdom effective among the mass of the people.   This is a problem of organisation; and it is this problem that is the crux of Democracy.

Is there any way in which this antinomy can be solved? It seems evident at least, that there are a number of ways in which solutions are being attempted.[2]   Among these one of the most obvious and striking is to be found in the increasing eagerness of our great writers to deal with the problems of social welfare.   This feature is conspicuously apparent, for instance, in our recent English writers.[3]   Carlyle could not write histories in peace: Ruskin could not criticise art: Morris could not be content to remain "an idle singer of an empty day": even Tennyson could not dream among the Lotos-eaters.   All have had to pour out their libations to the spirit of social reform.   And many more instances might be given, both in England and in other countries.   We cannot, however, regard the influence of literary "Heroes" as a satisfactory means of solving our difficulty.   In the first place, it is too incalculable: it is a breath that blows where it listeth.

[1] Quoted in Aristotle's *Ethics*, I. iv. I :—

οὗτος μὲν πανάριστος ὃς αὐτὸς πάντα νοήσῃ·
ἐσθλὸς δ' αὖ κἀκεῖνος ὃς εὖ εἰπόντι πίθηται·
ὃς δέ κε μήτ' αὐτὸς νοέῃ μήτ' ἄλλου ἀκούων
ἐν θυμῷ βάλληται, ὁ δ' αὖτ' ἀχρήϊος ἀνήρ.

[2] One curious suggestion in contemporary English Politics may be noticed in connection with this, viz. that of converting the Upper Chamber into a purely deliberative, or almost purely deliberative, body.   But an Upper Chamber seems to be required for other purposes.   See Sidgwick's *Elements of Politics*, chap. xxiii.

[3] Cf. Graham's *Social Problem*, p. 21.   See also concluding chapter.

In the second place, the writers who are so effective in their influence on public thought as to become "uncrowned kings," are rarely the wisest. When wisdom cries in the streets, no man regards it. And, in the third place, there is as a general rule no one who is so wise as to be entitled to be effective in this way. The wisest man is wise only within his own world, and that is never quite coincident with the world of ultimate reality.

Another way in which the problem is being met, is by the influence of the various churches. We may perceive, I think, an increasing effort on the part of these to bring themselves into relation to the great social questions of the times; and doubtless much good may be effected in this way. It does not seem likely, however, that such influence as this can have a very wide and powerful effect, so long as there is so much disunion among the churches themselves. Nor perhaps is it altogether desirable that any very powerful influence on social movements should be exerted by the churches. The influence which comes through such a channel tends to be too much an influence from above, even when it is not affected by any other form of one-sidedness.[1] While, therefore, the importance of a right attitude towards social questions on the part of the churches cannot be too strongly urged, we can yet scarcely hope that such an attitude alone will suffice for the guidance of our democracy. The influence of the churches on social movements must be mainly indirect. It must consist chiefly in the diffusion of sound ethical views—a work which is undoubtedly of the utmost importance. As Mr. Ely has said,[2] "A wider diffusion of sound ethics is an *economic*

---

[1] What has been already said (p. 388) with reference to Comte's Priests of Humanity, applies here. But cf. Loch's *Charity Organisation*, p. 8, and *Enc. Brit.*, XIX., 401.

[2] *Labour Movement in America*, p. 311.

requirement of the times." It is also a political requirement.

Another hopeful sign, however, may be seen in the increasingly scientific character which is being given to the study of social and political questions. So long as political wisdom is to be found only in the *ipse dixit* of the man of genius, it cannot be trusted to have much influence on the people; nor, when it *has* such influence, can its influence be trusted to be wholesome. But so soon as the study of politics becomes a science, whose results are capable of precise formulation, its deliverances can be not only communicated but proved. Hitherto the only branch of social science which has had such exactness, has been the study of Economics; and this has been treated so much in abstraction from the other branches of the subject to which it belongs, that its influence has been in many cases[1] pernicious. We are now beginning to see the possibility of an exact science of social questions in a larger sense. Still, it must be confessed that there is not much likelihood of this larger science being reduced to a clear and generally intelligible shape for a long time to come. Consequently, even in this direction there does not seem any hope of a solution of our difficulty being reached. To a certain extent science may furnish us with useful light; and this light may gradually permeate the whole atmosphere of society; but it will at the best be flickering and uncertain.

But there is another phenomenon of our time in which perhaps we may see the *disjecta membra* of such a deliberative assembly as that for which we have been in search. I refer to the numerous voluntary associations

---

[1] Though not in so many cases as is frequently supposed. Cf. *supra*, pp. 8, 56, and 132; and see Marshall's *Principles of Economics*, Vol. I., p. 59, etc.

for social ends which are everywhere growing up. The most prominent of these associations have been those for the improvement of the condition of working-men, such as Trades Unions, the Knights of Labour in America,[1] the Labour Association for the spread of co-operative principles, the various societies for the propagation of Socialism, and the like. There are, however, other associations whose aims are broader. We might mention, for instance, the Social and Political Education League, the object of which is simply the diffusion of knowledge and insight into the leading social and political problems; and the Societies for Ethical Culture in America, which endeavour to spread sound principles of morals.[2] There are also societies for the study of specific social difficulties, such as that which was founded recently in London for the inquiry into the population question. The forming of such associations seems to be one of the most characteristic features of our time; associations in which a number of men who are animated by an enthusiasm for social well-being, or who have special means of information with regard to its requirements in particular departments, band themselves together for an investigation of some of the chief social and political questions, and for the diffusion of insight with regard to them. The prevalence of such societies has, indeed, been regarded with suspicion by some philanthropic writers. Carlyle saw in them a symptom of the mechanical tendency of our times, in which im-

---

[1] For a good account of these, see *The Labour Movement in America*, by R. T. Ely.

[2] The nature of these may be best gathered from their organ, *The Ethical Record*, and from such publications as Mr. Salter's *Ethical Religion*. See also Gizycki's *Moralphilosophie* (Coit's *Ethical Philosophy*) IX. iii., Coit's *Ethische Bewegung*, and Mrs. M'Callum's article in *Time*, August, 1888.

portant work is done less and less by individuals and more and more by combinations.[1] But the remark of Goethe seems to show more wisdom, that the individual can accomplish nothing unless he co-operates with the many at the right time. Not only so : the insight of any one individual is in general but a half-light, and requires to be complemented by combination with the light of others. Consequently, it seems difficult to over-estimate the good that may be done by such associations as are here referred to, as means for the diffusion of that light and culture which are required to temper our Democracy. What is now chiefly wanted is that such work should be still further extended and more completely organised.

Such combinations, indeed, have not in the past filled a very important rôle in the development of public opinion. But for this there are obvious reasons. It is only in a strongly democratic community that they could have any place : and even in such a community they have not a place in every age. It is only in recent times that the ages of Dogmatism and Scepticism have given place to that of Criticism. Now so long as men occupy either of the former attitudes, they are not much disposed to co-operate. Each dogmatist builds on his own foundation, and whoever is not for him is against him. The sceptic, again, simply overturns. It is only when men begin to criticise their foundations, that they discover the common earth on which they rest. It is largely for this reason that in the past thought and action have tended to remain so much apart. Thought has been individualistic, whether it was constructive or destructive, and it has retained so much of the abstractness of the individual nature that it has not been able to influence the concrete : and so, while thinkers have gone on from system to system, or from negation to

[1] See especially his Essay entitled " Signs of the Times."

negation, the world of action has taken a more or less independent course, "from precedent to precedent," or from revolution to revolution. Now that men are learning to criticise their foundations, and so to co-operate in thought and "rub each other's angles down," we may expect that their thoughts will be more practically effective. Here at least we see a reason why combinations of thinking men may be expected to prove more successful as political forces in the future than they have been in the past.

In the past, indeed, such combinations as have been formed, have been for the most part propagandist associations, either in the interest of particular parties in the state or in that of particular classes in the community, or, as in the case of the various Socialistic Leagues, in that of the upholders of a particular line of policy, independent of any state party. But now that the age of parties is past, now that all sane men are beginning to perceive that the life of a nation is too large a thing to have its essence summed up in any particular "cries," it is becoming more possible to have combinations of men, not for the purpose of advocating any particular kind of action, but for the purpose of deliberating as to what kind of action is best. If the world is not ripe for such combinations, the world is not ripe for Democracy. If men cannot combine their thoughts as well as their forces, if they cannot unite for deliberation as well as for advocacy, a true co-operation is impossible. It is well if we can run our light into lightning and make it a force in action; but if we can turn it into nothing but the heat of party spirit, our Democracy will be a scramble in the dark.

It may be thought that we have devoted a disproportionate degree of attention to this particular point. But the question how philosophy is to be made king, must always be the one in which the social philosopher is most keenly interested. Now there does not appear to be any prospect of this, except through such means as those which we have just indicated. We may hope that our great writers will more and more direct their powers to the treatment of social subjects, and will more and more influence public opinion upon them: we may hope that the churches will help to mould character in those directions which are most important for the common good: and we may hope that the scientific study of society will bring to light ideas and principles, by the diffusion of which our social progress may be guided: and, in addition to all this, it seems not chimerical to hope also, that those who are interested in social improvement, will find it more and more possible to cooperate with each other, both in their study of social difficulties, and in their efforts to remove them. The time is past when it was possible to suppose that the solution of important questions could be given in the abstract formulas of any particular creed, aristocratic or democratic, individualistic or socialistic. Most men who think seriously on social questions have long since abandoned these cheap "Morrison's Pills." We are all aristocrats: we are all democrats: we are all socialists:[1] we are all individualists. We are at least beginning to have glimpses of universal principles which are deeper than any of these abstractions, and by means of which they may be combined and not opposed. The problem of the present is to deal with particular evils which we all recognise; and in the effort to deal with these it is surely possible for all serious thinkers to combine.[2]

[1] Cf. Mr. Sidney Webb's *Socialism in England*, p. 96.

[2] As evidence of the growth in England of the attempt to provide a basis for the serious discussion of such problems, one may perhaps refer, on the economic side, to the recently formed British Economic

The work of such organisations as we have referred to, would not, of course, be entirely that of determining what action the state as a whole ought to take, but also that of directing the actions of individuals. The members of such societies would have taken it as their province to find out what is needed, in certain specified directions, for the well-being of the whole, or of that particular section with which they have undertaken to deal; and in considering this, they would necessarily be concerned with the duties of individuals as well as of governments. They would take up each question of social well-being as it arose, and would ask in what way it can best be solved, having regard to all the interests which may be implicated in it. If, on consideration, it should appear that the action of government ought to be called in, it would then be their business, either as individuals or as a society, to influence public opinion in such a way as to procure the desired governmental interference. If, on the other hand, it should appear that the particular problem in question could be better dealt with by private individuals than by the state as a whole, they would endeavour to incite private individuals to undertake the work which is required. Some kinds of work they themselves as a' society would undertake; other kinds would be undertaken by their individual members; other kinds they would endeavour to stimulate particular individuals or classes of the community to undertake. They would

Association and the Christian Social Union, with their respective organs, *The Economic Journal and The Economic Review.* The Ethical Societies, both in this country and in America, and their organ, *The International Journal of Ethics,* represent a movement which is more broadly human. No doubt the actual results of any of these are but slight; but they represent a growing spirit of inquiry and a growing effort to deal at once, in an earnest, a reasonable, and a conciliatory spirit with the intricate social problems of the time.

stand to the practical arts of social life in somewhat the same relation as philosophy stands to the particular sciences; they would criticise the principles on which these arts proceed and try to direct them into the proper channels. It is through such influence as this that we may hope that much of the best work of the future will be effected.

Having thus ascertained what are the main requirements of a good democratic state, we should next inquire what is the nature of the work which such a state as a whole ought to undertake. This question, however, is one which it must be left to writers on Politics to answer.[1] All that it is possible to do in such a treatise as the present is to indicate some of the most general principles on which this question may be decided. The most general principles seem to be these. A government must not undertake anything (1) which tends to deaden the sense of individual responsibility, or (2) what is not open to public criticism, or (3) of which the limits cannot be clearly defined. A few words must suffice on each of these points.

(1) The "administrative Nihilism" of such writers as Mr. Herbert Spencer is based chiefly on a keen consciousness of the difficulty of doing anything for a man without making him less a man by the act. As Humboldt has admirably put it,[2] "The happiness to which

---

[1] Cf. Mill's *Political Economy*, v. xi., and Sidgwick's *Political Economy*, III. iii.

[2] *Die Grenzen der Wirksamkeit des Staats*, III. Cf. Plato *Rep.*, III. 406-7, and, for illustration, Marshall's *Principles of Economics*, p. 586. Also Mill's *Political Economy*, IV. vii. 1, *A Plea for Liberty* (edited by Thomas Mackay), Donisthorpe's *Individualism*, and Spencer's *Man* versus *the State, passim*. Professor Montague's book on *The Limits of Individual Liberty* may be referred to as containing some very judicious arguments against the extreme advocates of liberty. See also Sidgwick's *Principles of Political Economy*, Book

man is destined, is none other than that which his own force makes for him; and the difficulties into which he falls when he is left to himself, are precisely the influences which sharpen his understanding and mould his character. Where the state destroys individual effort by minute interventions, similar difficulties arise; and they fall with overwhelming force on men who have become accustomed to lean on others. The struggle against difficulty lightens it; whereas the expectation of a help which never comes, adds tenfold to its weight. Consequently, even in the best circumstances, the states here referred to are apt to be like doctors who stave off death by pampering diseases. Before there were doctors, there was only health or death." There is force in this contention: but while it furnishes a sufficient reason for the exercise of the greatest care, it does not seem to give a sufficient reason for reducing ourselves to a condition of "anarchy + the constable." The cautions which it suggests, are chiefly two. In the first place, there is the point which was emphasised by Green,[1] that law can do only that in the doing of which it is not necessary that personal qualities should be displayed. For this reason charitable work cannot well be organised by government—except within certain narrow limits, or as a provisional scheme when private philanthropy has failed. For this reason also a government cannot well undertake work which requires energy and skill of any particular sort. Hence, as we have already had occasion to point out,[2] govern-

---

III.   I am not sure that the corresponding passages in *The Elements of Politics*, by the same writer, add much to the argument. Professor D. G. Ritchie's *Principles of State Interference* is an interesting collection of essays, but scarcely fulfils the promise of its title. There are also some good remarks on this subject in the same writer's more recent book on *Natural Rights*.

  [1] *Collected Works*, vol. II. p. 342 *seq.*        [2] P. 320.

ment cannot be expected to do much in the way of public undertakings, except in the case of those kinds of work which are of a comparatively simple and routine character. What these are at any particular time, is a question for practical politics. In the second place, we have to note the important principle that, as far as possible, nothing ought to be done *for* any individual which is not also in some measure done *by* him. No kind of help, as has often been said, is ultimately profitable except that which consists in helping one to help himself.[1] For this reason, as in the case of private charity, the best work that a government can do, is that which is in some sense educational.[2] It is clear, however, that in the case of a popular government this caution has less force than in the case of one which is more aristocratic; for in a democratic state every one is made in some measure to feel that he is not merely a recipient of a good but also one who is responsible for its conferment.[3] It is clear also, that

---

[1] Cf. *supra*, p. 370.

[2] This point is well brought out by Mr. Gilman in his excellent book on *Socialism and the American Spirit*. See especially chap. v., where the educational functions of the state are specially emphasised. Mr. Gilman remarks, with reference to the American democracy (p. 64), that "it would secure opportunity by education and suffrage, and then take its hands off:

> 'That's the old Amerikin idee,
> To make a man a Man, an' let him be.'"

This might be taken as admirably summing up the main part of the function of the State, provided we recognise fully all that is involved in "making a man a Man." I shall be inclined to add, however, that, in addition to this educational work, it is desirable for the state, as far as possible, to take over work that is of a comparatively mechanical and routine character, as distinguished from that in which personal qualities are involved. But the discrimination of these would of course in practice be very difficult.

[3] Cf. *supra*, p. 380.

the danger of "paternal legislation" is less in a comparatively small community, where every one can see what is being done, than in one which is large and complicated, where the incidence of responsibility ceases to be apparent.

(2) This leads us directly to our second point, viz., that everything which a government undertakes, must be of such a kind as to be readily open to public criticism. The necessity of this is so obvious that it is not necessary to enlarge upon it, though for the sake of completeness it was necessary to point it out. We may, however, take occasion to remark that, in this case also, the danger is less in a comparatively small community, or in one in which government is to a large extent decentralised.

(3) But however much force there may be in the two preceding considerations, there can be little doubt that the argument which has had most practical weight as a deterrent from state-interference, has been the difficulty of fixing any definite limits to the directions in which such interference may be introduced. The familiar terror of "the thin end of the wedge" attends every action of government. There is always the question—If this is to be undertaken, why not also that? and unless an answer can be given, which is not only quite clear in itself, but also readily acceptable by the community, it is felt to be better to abstain from interference altogether. Thus if a government undertakes the management of a Post Office, it is at once asked—Why should it not also take over the land? Why should it not also carry on the factories? and so on. The difficulty which thus arises, is one that cannot be lightly passed over; and it can scarcely be denied that there is a stage of national development at which it is so serious, that the best policy is one of *laisser faire*. This is true either when the government is

not sufficiently in the hands of the people to be above the suspicion of unfairness in its methods of action; or when the people are not sufficiently well educated to appreciate the broad principles on which their action must be conducted. In such circumstances it is practically necessary to have rigidly defined rules of action, and to guide ourselves rather by the understanding than by the reason.[1] It must be confessed also, that even with a free government and a well-educated people, the complications of a large state are so great, that it is difficult to lay down universally intelligible and acceptable principles of action; and for this reason the *onus probandi* must generally be allowed to rest with those who think that any particular form of governmental interference is desirable.[2] Here again, however, the difficulty becomes obviously less when the state is small or the government decentralised.

These considerations lead us to the perception, among other things, that the proper functions of government at any time depend largely on the stage of development which the people have reached. This is a point on which the student of the details of political evolution would doubtless have much more to say. But, without going into these details, there is one general remark which it may be convenient to insert here, viz., that the extent to which a popular government can interfere with the life of a people, depends primarily on the question— *where the centre of gravity of the people falls.* Or, to put it in the language of Rousseau, it depends on the question whether the *volonté générale* is wiser or less wise

---

[1] It may be remarked here, that most of the one-sided doctrines of economists, and other writers on social questions, are due to a similar necessity. Cf. Marshall's *Principles of Economics*, pp. ix. and 103.

[2] The chief argument for Free Trade, for instance, rests on these considerations. Cf. Sidgwick's *Political Economy*, p. 488.

than the *volonté de tous.* If the wisdom of a people is
of a specialised kind, and is to be found rather in the
actions of individuals than in a collective insight, then it
is best that individuals should be left alone. If, on the
other hand, the weight of the general wisdom falls on
the whole on a higher level than that of individual insight, it becomes possible for a wise governmental action
to begin. From all this it is evident that the sphere of
government cannot be determined *a priori* by any merely
philosophical considerations, but must to a large extent be
left to the political genius of a people and to the tact
of its leaders.[1] At any rate, the further investigation of
these points must be relegated to the student of Politics.

Having decided what kinds of work the state as a
whole may safely undertake, we should next have to ask
to what extent it should interfere with those kinds of
work which it does not undertake. To what extent, for
instance, ought it to limit competition, and in what ways
ought it to regulate monopolies ? These are among the

---

[1] This is excellently brought out by Mr. Gilman in his *Socialism
and the American Spirit.* See, for instance, p. 109, note, where the wise
remark of Professor Huxley is quoted, that "These necessary limitations are not determinable by *a priori* speculation, but only by the
results of experience; they cannot be deduced from principles of
absolute ethics, once and for all, but they vary with the state of
development of the polity to which they are applied. The settle-
ment of this question lies neither with the celestial courts of Poesy
nor with the tribunals of speculative cloudland, but with men who
are accustomed to live and work among facts instead of dreaming
amidst impracticable formulas." So indeed it is, ultimately, with all
practical questions. Speculative principles help us to take a broad
view of the questions before us, and to disentangle the various
elements in the problems which they present; but the final solution
of these problems must be left to the practical instincts and trained
good sense of those who have to deal with them, relying at once
on a wide experience of the past and on a sober appreciation of
present possibilities and prospects.

most pressing questions of the present time. Or, again, we might ask to what extent the state should regard the right of private property as an absolute one. It must sooner or later be recognised that "every right involves an obligation"; not merely in the sense that when one man has a right *other* men owe a certain duty to him, but also in the deeper sense that the possessor of a right *himself* owes certain duties on account of that possession— or rather that the very fact of such a possession *means*, among other things, a certain obligation which the possessor owes.[1] It can never be quite true that anyone has "a right to do what he likes with his own"; for there is nothing—not even our inmost self-consciousness— which is "our own" in such a sense as to exclude all reference to others. Now when this is recognised, the question must begin to be asked whether it is not desirable that certain restrictions should be placed on such rights as that of property, so as to prevent them from being enjoyed by those who are not prepared to fulfil the obligations connected with them. This is, of course, especially desirable in the case of those kinds of property which are by their nature limited in amount, so that the possession by one necessarily involves the non-possession by another. Of this class land is the most conspicuous instance. It might also be asked whether there is not, so to speak, a *maximum possessibile*, a certain amount of property which a man may reasonably own, and beyond which any addition to his possessions is not an addition either to the well-being of his life or to his power of well-doing. The putting of such questions has hitherto been prevented both by the prevalence of the idea of abstract rights and by the consciousness that any attempt to place restrictions on the rights of property

[1] Cf. Alexander's *Moral Order and Progress*, p. 146. See also Graham's *Social Problem*, p. 347 *seq.*

would be certain to lead to undesirable limitations on personal freedom. Certainly the latter of these reasons is a powerful one; and we can hardly hope that in practice anything better will be reached in the way of the solution of such questions than a compromise between the various interests at stake. The consideration, however, of these and other problems connected with the duties of the state, must be left to the student of Politics. Here it was only necessary to indicate the way in which such problems are bound up with the general problem of social well-being.

Another point in connection with the national unity to which it would be important to give a good deal of attention in any complete discussion of this subject, but to which at this point it is not possible to do much more than allude, is the consideration of the means of developing the patriotic spirit. This point, like some of the others that we have already noticed, touches closely on the subject of education; but, perhaps, the broad consideration would come most naturally in the present section, since it may be largely affected by methods of social organisation. It seems to be one of the dangers of modern democracies, that the questions in which the highest degree of interest are excited may be rather those of particular sections and classes of the community than those of the community as a whole, regarded as a national unity. This is probably one point at which the existence of an Upper Chamber, especially one constituted with considerable reference to the ownership of the land, may contribute a valuable element to the counsels of a nation. At any rate, where the Government of a country is purely representative, it seems desirable that some of the representatives should represent national rather than sectional interests; for though the good of the part is implicated in the good

406 THE ELEMENTS OF SOCIAL PROGRESS.

of the whole, this is an implication that is liable to be overlooked in the conflict of particular interests. Hence I should be inclined to suggest that if, for instance, it were ever to become a serious question of practical politics to revise the constitution of this country, so as to make both Houses of Parliament of a representative character, some effort should be made to render the one House representative in a somewhat different sense from the other; so that while the one might represent classes and sections of the community, whose interests would often be in conflict with one another, the others should represent rather those large fundamental interests in which the welfare of the nation as a whole is involved. The one might thus, in a manner, be said to represent, in the language of Rousseau, the *volonté de tous*; the other would represent rather the *volonté générale*.

So far, I have been referring only to the bearing of this particular consideration on the organisation of government. But it is clearly desirable, not merely that there should be some representation of the general spirit of patriotism in the central deliberations of the state, but also that such a spirit should be as widely diffused as possible in the nation as a whole. It is here that the problem becomes more particularly an educational one. Now, it might be thought that the mere existence of a democratic form of government, the mere fact of a universal participation, or at least of a universal "active consent," in the carrying on of all the more important national affairs, would of itself be a powerful stimulus to the patriotic spirit; and no doubt, within certain limits, it is so.[1] But it is subject to the qualification that, as

---

[1] Dr. Sidgwick, in his *Elements of Politics* (p. 363), while carefully qualifying some other educational influences, which a democratic form of government is supposed to yield, admits that in this one particular it is probably effective.

the political activity of a democracy is apt to be largely
directed to the reform of abuses, and to conflicts between
various classes, sections, and parties, the patriotic interest
as such is apt to be somewhat dissipated. Indeed, it is
doubtful whether the pomp and dignity of a more aristocratic form of government does not often stimulate a
warmer devotion than is even promoted by the conflict
of particular interests. It seems desirable, at any rate,
that this kind of educational influence should be supplemented by some more direct efforts to enlist the
sympathies of the citizens of a state in its welfare as a
whole. It can hardly be doubted that the study of
national history and literature has, when wisely pursued,
a most powerful influence in this direction. So far,
indeed, as history is concerned, this is perhaps sufficiently
recognised. I am more doubtful whether, in England at
least, the literature of the country has been as well
utilised as it might be for this purpose. In Scotland it
would, I suppose, be almost a treason to say that the
national spirit depends almost entirely on some knowledge of such writers as Burns and Scott; and something
similar would be true of Germany, and many other
countries. Another influence which is very potent in the
development of the national spirit is the existence of
interests which the members of a nation have in common.
The defence of their country, for instance, is one such
interest. There can be little doubt that the compulsory
military service in Germany, for example, however much
it may sometimes have been felt to be a hardship, has
had a very powerful influence in this direction,[1] even
among those classes of the community who are least
inclined for war and most dissatisfied with the present

[1] There are some very interesting remarks on this point in a book
to which I have already frequently referred, Göhre's *Three Months
in a Workshop*, pp. 121-122.

social conditions.    I suppose the volunteer system in this country has, though to a much slighter extent, had a somewhat similar influence.    But there are also other ways in which the members of a nation may thus be brought together with interests in common.    Few things, I should imagine, did more to foster a patriotic spirit in ancient Greece, than the celebration of the Olympic Games.    The Eisteddfod in Wales seems to have a similar effect; and even the public sports which are practised in England may not be without their value from this point of view.    I refer to these matters here, not with the view of urging the need of any greater insistence upon them than has been common among us, but merely because it seems necessary, for the sake of completeness, to mention them here in their proper place.[1]

8. *International Organisation.*    The last form of human association to which it seems necessary to refer, is that between separate nations.    The constant danger of collision between different states is one of the chief impediments in the way of an establishment of an industrial organisation within the states.    Now this danger can be obviated only by some form of international unity.    There is an argument in Hegel's *Philosophie des Rechts*,[2] in which he shows that, since there is no power to arbitrate between different states, war is a perpetual necessity.

---

[1] The importance of stimulating the spirit of national self-assertion has been emphasised in a very interesting way, though perhaps in a somewhat needlessly alarmist tone, in Mr. Bradley's paper on "The Limits of Individual and National Self-Sacrifice" in the *International Journal of Ethics* for October, 1894.

[2] III. iii., B. 333.    Cf. also III. iii., A. 324.    Among more recent political philosophers, Treitschke may be referred to as one who emphasises the perennial necessity of war—this doctrine being connected with his view that the essence of the State is Force.    Cf. *supra*, p. 383.

Dante, in the *De Monarchia*,[1] drew from the same premises the conclusion that there must be a universal empire. A universal empire, however, seems impossible; and a continually impending war makes order impossible.[2] Hence we must have some other alternative. What that other alternative is to be, it is one of the chief problems of international law and politics to determine.

Another important question of international politics is that with reference to emigration from country to country. A high civilisation is in constant danger of being ruined by the influx of people from neighbouring states which are lower in the scale, or even by the influx of the dregs of the population from a state which is itself highly civilised. This question, however, is in the main one for the civic community to deal with; and in that connection it has already been referred to.[3]

III. PERSONAL DEVELOPMENT.—Having thus referred to the main points in connection with the subjugation of nature and the perfection of social machinery, we have now only to consider the development or education of the individual. It is evident from all that has gone before, that this is not the least important, but rather the most important, of the three departments. It is, indeed, the necessary presupposition of the other two. It has been well said by Professor Seeley, that "culture is the larger half of politics." Fletcher's meaning was similar in the well-known saying, "Let me make the songs of a people, and whoever will may make the laws"; and Ibsen's, when he declares, with reference to the solution of social

---

[1] Book I., chap. x. Cf. also Bluntschli's *Theory of the State*, p. 31.

[2] "One can do anything with bayonets, except *sit* on them."—Talleyrand.

[3] Cf. also Sidgwick's *Elements of Politics*, pp. 295-297. Havelock Ellis, *The New Spirit*, p. 20, and Mummery and Hobson's *Physiology of Industry*, p. 213.

problems, "There is only one thing that avails—to revolutionise people's minds." Plato's *Republic* also, as we have already noticed, though ostensibly a treatise on political philosophy, is in reality concerned entirely with education. Certainly Pope's epigram about "forms of government" would have had more truth if instead of saying that what "is best administered is best," he had said rather that what gives the best education is best.[1] The best government is the one that makes itself most unnecessary, by rendering its citizens "a law to themselves." But in addition to that kind of education which pervades the atmosphere of a well-formed state, it is necessary that definite efforts should be made for the production of good citizens. Now education is a very large subject, and it would be quite impossible to deal with it here; but a few remarks upon its leading elements may not be without use.

In a complete education there seem to be three main stages. In the first place, there is that training which is necessary to produce a human being at all. In the second place, there is the training which is necessary to enable a man to become the particular individual into which he is by nature fitted to develop. In the third place, there is the training by which he is enabled to bring his own individuality into harmonious relationship with the rest of his world. In other words, we have first to acquire intelligence, then abilities, then wisdom. A few points may now be noticed with respect to these stages.

1. The main difficulties in the primary stage of education—apart from the practical difficulties of school management and discipline—arise from two ἀπορίαι. In the first place, there is a certain contradiction between that which is in itself immediately useful for life and that which serves as a key to further knowledge or as a hint to

[1] Cf. Mill's *Representative Government*, chap. viii.

higher progress; and here, as in so many other departments of human conduct, it is a great problem whether
it is better to use our bread or to cast it on the waters.
There will always be some on whom the hints of higher
progress in culture are sure to be lost ; and it might seem
best that these should acquire nothing but what can be
directly applied to life : whereas there will always be
others to whom it is of infinitely more importance to
develop powers for the future than to gain instruments
for the present. This is the first ἀπορία; and ordinary
education in general is a compromise between the needs of
the two classes. Where such a conflict arises, it may be
remarked that the higher elements ought on the whole
to receive the preference. In spite of the authority of
Dogberry, it is scarcely true that "reading and writing
come by nature"; but it is in the main true that those
kinds of knowledge and ability which are immediately
applicable to the affairs of life, are readily acquired
by anyone whose intelligence has been fairly well
developed. Hence it is on the whole safe to "take care
of the beautiful" and let "the useful take care of itself."
There is not much fear that the common will be neglected ; it is of more importance that we should be taught
to rise above the commonplace, by which, as Goethe tells
us, we are all in danger of being limited.[1] Moreover, it
is of some use even to those for whom there must
always hang a veil over the holiest of all in culture, that
they should see at least where the veil lies. Yet it must
be allowed, on the other hand, that nothing tends so
much to the development of *Philisterei* as a certain
advance in the elements of culture by those who are

---

[1] "Was uns alle bändigt—das Gemeine." Some of Dr. Martineau's
remarks on Comte's scheme of education may be found suggestive
at this point. *Types of Ethical Theory*, I., p. 449. But see also,
*per contra*, Spencer's *Education*, chap. I.

unable to appreciate them. The Arch-Philistine is one who, like Bunyan's Atheist, returns from the precincts of the Celestial City with the report that there is no such place; and this is a report which stupidity will always bring from the regions of the highest culture. To avoid this result, it is desirable that the highest elements of culture[1] should not at first be conveyed otherwise than by suggestion. As Goethe says again, "secrecy has many advantages; for when you tell a man at once and straightforward the purpose of any object, he fancies there is nothing in it."[2] To apply these truths is the work of the practical educationist. If he holds wisdom in his hands, he will open only his little finger. He will know that the road to wisdom is a winding ascent, and he will know at the same time that his pupils must be lured on to the summit by first climbing the lesser peaks. He will reveal clearly everything that lies on the surface, but will reserve the deeper things as an exercise for inquiry and reverence. He will explain what is useful and suggest what is beautiful. How to combine *utile dulci*, the practical and the ideal, will always remain a great problem; but it is a problem rather for the practical educator than for us. For our purpose it is sufficient to say, with the children in Plato, "give us both!" but especially do not neglect the ideal.

The second ἀπορία has reference to the diversity of aims in life. But if we are right in thinking that the primary end of education is rather to develop intelligence and power than to communicate particular kinds of information and skill, this difficulty need not be regarded

---

[1] This applies especially to religious instruction and to instruction in poetry, and in all other studies in which ideals are presented which cannot at first be appreciated. But to discuss this would take too long. Cf. *supra*, p. 377.

[2] *Wilhelm Meister's Travels*, chap. x.

as a serious one. A sympathetic teacher, no doubt, will endeavour to adapt his instructions to the peculiar apti- tudes of his pupils;[1] but it would require an omniscience to say "which grain will grow and which will not"; and in general the teacher must aim at imparting such know- ledge as will be useful in nearly all kinds of circumstances, such as will supply a key to a great variety of things, and above all such as will stimulate interest and develop character.[2]

The only other point to be observed with respect to the elements of general culture, is that they ought to be accessible without effort to every member of the com- munity. A nation is bound to provide for its children the possibility of becoming good citizens. This is the one charity which is absolutely safe.[3] There are, indeed, arguments of some force against the attempt to make education entirely free. It seems unfair that those who derive little or no benefit from it should be equally burdened with those who derive much; and it is argued that the necessity for paying for education is one of the checks upon undue increase of population. The latter argument has not so much weight as might at first sight appear; since those who are restrained by such a check as this, are on the whole not those who are most in need of such restraint.[4] Even if these two arguments together are of sufficient force to tell against the attempt to make education quite free, they are certainly not of

---

[1] Since the time of Rousseau, there has perhaps been a tendency to exaggerate the extent to which it is desirable to adapt teaching to individual needs. Goethe, in *Wilhelm Meister's Travels*, while insisting on diversity of pursuits, yet emphasises the need of rigidity of method. Hegel was even more pronounced on this point. Cf. Caird's *Hegel*, p. 72.

[2] Cf. Lange's *Apperception* and Herbart's *Science of Education.*

[3] Cf. *supra*, p. 370.

[4] Cf. Marshall's *Principles of Economics*, I., p. 256.

sufficient force to remove from the state the obligation to make a thoroughly good general education readily accessible to all its citizens. Provision ought to be made that every one shall be carried on to that stage in culture at which further advance becomes easily possible to the unaided efforts of men of average ability. It may be doubted whether so much as this is provided by the present system of elementary education in this country.[1]

2. With respect to the training of specialised abilities, the first requirement is to ensure their specialisation in the right direction. For this purpose it is important that every one should be provided, as near the outset as possible, with a broad survey of life as a whole, in order that he may be able to choose as wisely as possible the particular line in which his own tastes and capacities lead him. This fact furnishes us with an additional argument for limiting the earlier parts of education to what is most universally applicable rather than to what is most immediately useful for practical purposes.[2] A second point is, that specialisation must not be allowed to lead to narrowness. One safeguard against this is to be found in the breadth of the primary training; but it can hardly be doubted that for the majority such a safeguard will never prove sufficient. It is perhaps true that men of genius in any particular direction receive their best education in the pursuit of their favourite aims (though even they are in danger of becoming narrowed by confining themselves to these exclusively), and that they can reach a firm grasp of the universal by viewing

---

[1] The chief want in this respect seems to be that of evening classes for carrying on the work of the schools. But into this question we cannot enter further here.

[2] On this point, cf. Marshall's *Principles of Economics*, I., p. 313.

some particular object on every side. It is to them, if to any, that the saying of Goethe applies:—

> " Willst du ins Unendliche schreiten,
>   Geh' nur im Endlichen nach allen Seiten."

They " strike fire from every pebble," and can get an education out of almost every pursuit. But for the majority of mankind it is essential that particular aims should be supplemented by larger studies. Hence it is desirable that the highest parts of culture, as well as the beginnings of it, should have a decided infusion of those elements that broaden our interests in life, in addition to the special training which forms their staple. But it is desirable, at the same time, that a considerable amount of freedom should be left to those who have strongly marked aptitudes in particular directions, to follow out their favourite lines of study unrestrained. Men ought, in fact, to be wrapt in a certain atmosphere of universal interests, and yet be free to develop to the utmost their own particular abilities. To provide such an atmosphere, and to furnish such facilities, are the main functions of a University.

At this point, however, an important distinction emerges. Great as are the differences between the kinds of activity in which human beings may engage, there is one supreme difference which overshadows all the rest—the difference, namely, between those who teach and those who perform. The distinction is not one which can be drawn with any absolute rigour, but it is [one which in one form or other is continually recurring in human life. It is expressed, for instance, in the lines of Hesiod which have been already quoted:[1] it is expressed in the familiar saying of Carlyle,[2] " Two men I honour, and no third,"

[1] P. 390.   [2] *Sartor Resartus*, III. iv.

etc.: and, however widely civilisation may change, it is one which can scarcely ever be supposed to vanish. There must always be those whose work is to advance and communicate knowledge, and those whose work it is to act in accordance with it. It is for the training of the former class chiefly that Universities are designed; while the work of training the latter belongs rather to professional and technical schools. A few words ought here to be said on each of these forms of education.

With respect to University education, one whose attention is chiefly directed to the wants of England, is naturally struck most by two things—the need that the highest culture should be accessible to all, and the importance of giving encouragement to all kinds of studies. As regards the first of these defects, the consciousness of it has already led to the system of University extension and to the establishment of local colleges; but what has been done in this direction cannot be regarded as more than a temporary and very inadequate means of supplying the deficiency. As regards the second point, the deficiency is not less apparent. Outside observers, such as Wiese,[1] are even tempted to deny that there are, properly speaking, any Universities at all in England, so much struck are they with the absence of any serious study of subjects other than those of ordinary school training. What naturally concerns the social philosopher most deeply, is the absence of any adequate recognition of the study of social science, including Economics, Politics, and the Theory of Education. Perhaps it is true that, for the

---

[1] Cf. *German Letters on English Education*, pp. 66, 70, 118, etc. There have, no doubt, been considerable changes since Wiese wrote. It should be added also, that he is by no means blind to the advantages which the comparative narrowness of the English method brings with it. See pp. 109, 156, etc.

reason indicated by Aristotle,[1] such subjects can never be made profitable means of culture to those who are still comparatively young; but the example of Germany and America seems to show that it may at least be introduced to a much greater extent than it is in this country. And there are many other subjects of which the same may be said.[2]

Professional education, on the other hand, is a subject of too special a character to be profitably dealt with by the social philosopher. The most important point with regard to it is, no doubt, that such education should not be so exclusively professional as to shut out the larger interests of the world. For this reason it is usually desirable that it should be carried on in close connection with the more purely intellectual studies. Technical education, however, is a subject which seems to demand a little more notice, as its importance is only beginning to be felt.[3] So far, indeed, as technical education means only a preparatory training for the exercise of particular trades, it does not specially concern us here. In this sense the consideration of it belongs rather to the pure

---

[1] *Ethics*, I. iii. 5. Διὸ τῆς πολιτικῆς οὐκ ἔστιν οἰκεῖος ἀκροατὴς ὁ νέος· ἄπειρος γὰρ τῶν κατὰ τὸν βίον πράξεων. Perhaps, however, it is just for this reason important that they should study it, in order that they may at least be made aware of their ignorance.

[2] The comparative neglect of the higher studies in England may partly be attributed to the political and the practical interests which draw away so many of the ablest minds. But partly also it must be ascribed to the tyranny of examinations. This again is largely occasioned by the excessive competition for University rewards. The pursuit of truth and culture is scarcely compatible with the pursuit of glory, and is not at all compatible with the pursuit of gain as a primary object. The further discussion of this subject must, however, be left to the student of the Philosophy of Education. Cf. Wiese's *German Letters on English Education*, pp. 44, 130 *seq.*, etc.

[3] Cf. Marshall's *Principles of Economics*, I., p. 265.

2 D

economist.  But this is not what the term is commonly understood to mean, by those who are most keenly interested in it.  On the contrary, the purposes which it is intended to serve, are mainly these two.  In the first place, it is designed to prevent or to minimise that stunting of the individual nature which results from occupation with a part that is not understood in its relations to the whole to which it belongs.  The importance of this has been already sufficiently pointed out.[1]  But, in the second place, what is of more consequence than this, it is designed to suggest the relations of particular employments, not merely to the whole with which they are immediately connected, but to the system of life whose ends all particular employments subserve.  It is intended, in short, to stimulate that intelligent appreciation of purposes which makes almost[2] the meanest employment interesting, and thus at the same time to incite that spirit of service which makes almost the humblest action "fine."  If, however, technical education is to fulfil these ends in any adequate degree, it seems clear that it must be brought into relation to

---

[1] *Supra*, p. 92.

[2] I insert "almost" here advisedly.  It would be rash to affirm that *every* employment can be made interesting.  The maker of a pin-head or the stoker of an Atlantic Liner must perhaps always have a difficulty in "hitching their waggons to star."  It must be the aim of inventors and social reformers to reduce the necessity of such work to a minimum, or, at least, to render it impossible for it to absorb the whole energy of any individual.  Even as a means of accomplishing this, it is difficult to overestimate the importance of such education as tends to stimulate higher interests.  Necessity is the Mother of Invention, but the Father of it is Hope.  Cf. Höffding's *Ethik*, p. 272; *Essays in Philosophical Criticism*, p. 217, and Marshall's *Principles of Economics*, I., p. 250.  Some employments also it is impossible to make interesting, because by their nature they contribute only to what is immoral or foolish.  These it must be our aim to abolish.

other forms of education which are not merely technical.[1]
It is evident that if any such education is to be generally available, the hours of labour must be definitely
limited.

3. Wisdom, again, is an affair rather of character than
of capacity, and is a thing of slower growth, depending on
a large experience of life. We need hardly quote the now
almost hackneyed proverb:

> "Es bildet ein Talent sich in der Stille,
>    Sich ein Character in dem Strom der Welt."

It will be more to our purpose to notice the different
elements that go to constitute what we here describe as
wisdom. We have already endeavoured to explain that
wisdom is the faculty of being at home with our world,
of not only seeing things but seeing round them, and
correctly estimating their place in the system of our
experience. The wise man is the reverse of what Kant
used to describe as an intellectual Cyclops.[2] He has
eyes on every side, and "looks at all things as they
are." If he has not taken "all knowledge to his province," he has at least sympathies with all the aspects
of things, and correctly evaluates their respective worths.

---

[1] If it were part of our business in this essay to enter with any
detail into educational questions, it would be desirable at this point
to insist on the importance of certain preliminary forms of manual
training at a comparatively early stage of education. The *Sloyd*
system, for instance, which has been introduced with so much success
in Sweden and elsewhere, and which has the advantage of supplying
a certain training in artistic perception as well as in manual
dexterity, might be profitably discussed. Cf. on this subject, Urban's
*Die Knaben-Handarbeit* (especially pp. 6-12); and Rauscher's *Der
Handfertigkeitsunterricht, seine Theorie und Praxis*. There is also
an interesting account of some teaching of a similar character in
Mrs. M'Callum's article on "Ethical Societies" in *Time* for August,
1888.

[2] *Reflexionen Kant's* (ed. Benno Erdmann), II., p. 60.

He is a citizen of the intellectual world and gives nothing a false accent. He "sees himself as others see him," and, what is still more important, he sees others as they see themselves; or rather he sees everything "under a certain form of eternity." Now this faculty may display itself in each of the three aspects of intellectual life—as knowledge, feeling, or will. In the first of these aspects it is wisdom, in the narrower sense; in the second it is taste; in the third it is goodness. Ultimately no doubt, these three forms of wisdom are identical, when they are fully realised;[1] yet in their development they are quite distinct; and it may be well here to say a few words on each.

(a) The last comes first in general estimation; for, as Matthew Arnold taught us, "Conduct is three-fourths of life"; and especially with respect to our fellowmen we are in general more concerned with their actions than with their thoughts or sympathies. Now the inculcation of right rules of conduct among us has been made the work chiefly of the Christian churches; and it is to them, no doubt, that we must look in the future also for the larger part of our education in this respect.[2] In this reference we have already remarked that, if our practical ethics are to be taught from the pulpit, it is of the utmost importance that those who occupy it should themselves be well instructed with respect not only to the principles of morals, but also to the conditions of

---

[1] Hence the element of truth in the saying of Socrates that "Virtue is Knowledge," in Carlyle's identification of intellectual capacity with moral excellence, and in the doctrine of Ruskin that morality is fundamentally the same thing as good taste.

[2] Not, of course, exclusively. As Wiese says (*German Letters on English Education*, Preface), "the problem of education is to purify and to strengthen the will"; and this is an aim which must be kept constantly in view at every stage.

modern life. One who undertakes such an office of practical guidance, ought certainly in the present age to have a considerable degree of insight into the main truths of Political Economy, History, and Social Philosophy.[1] How to secure a body of teachers thoroughly trained in these respects, it is not our present business to inquire: the question may be handed over to the student of Ecclesiastical Economy—if there is any such science. In the meantime we have only, as Bacon might have said, "to note a defect," and to remark that there is likely for a long time to come to be abundant scope for the labours of men outside the churches, who endeavour to supply this want, whether they do it as private individuals or in combination with others, as members of ethical societies and similar organisations.

The rules of conduct, however, cannot, even by the wisest teachers, be profitably inculcated without a certain reference to the rest of life. The will cannot be treated as a faculty by itself. As Fichte said,[2] "Man can will nothing but what he loves"; and he can love nothing but what he can know. Hence rectitude of action must depend ultimately on a right disposition of the heart and sympathies and on an enlarged intelligence. When goodness is divorced from these, it sinks into that dull and negative and unlovely thing, which misses its own mark by want of insight, and tempts observers like von Hartmann to exclaim—"Would that people were more wicked if only they were less stupid." Morality cannot become a power in life so long as it is simply a collection of imperatives. It must be seen also as "the *beauty* of holiness," and apprehended as the deepest *truth* of things.

[1] Cf. Seeley's *Lectures and Essays*, p. 245 *seq.*, and Kaufmann's *Socialism*, p. 282.

[2] *Reden an die deutsche Nation*, II.

Partly from a recognition of this truth, ethical teaching has seldom been communicated simply as a set of moral rules, but has commonly been associated with an attempt to take a large view of the Universe as a whole, and with a certain emotional stimulus of religious feeling connected with that view of the Universe. The element of religious reverence, in particular, has always been felt to be essential to give force and colour to the highest kind of moral training. The importance of this has been well brought out by Goethe in his account of the method of training practised by "the Three" in *Wilhelm Meister's Travels*, where the first requirement of all is the inculcation of Reverence. Now Reverence may be said to lie on the border-line between aesthetic feeling and the direction of the will. What we reverence we regard as to some extent lifted above the sphere of our sympathies, as something which we may recognise as excellent, but which we cannot entirely appreciate or comprehend; and to have esteem for such an object, to which our natural inclinations do not draw us out, involves a certain act of will. Hence it is rightly said by Goethe, that reverence is not natural to man. Naturally we esteem only that which we are able to appreciate; and the faculty of reverence, by which we are raised to higher objects, requires a certain cultivation. Now we cannot esteem what is unknown until we have first learned to sympathise with what we know; and it is only through glimpses of appreciation that reverence can become developed. All true reverence is like that of Socrates for Heraclitus—What we understand is excellent, and we suppose that what we do not understand is excellent too. Reverence is simply the prophetic projection of sympathetic insight. Consequently, it presupposes a certain development of our interests and sympathies; and for this reason, if for no other, it is manifest that the

cultivation of a certain wisdom of feeling is essential to
wisdom in act. Thus we are led to consider the education
of taste.

(*b*) In a sense, indeed, it may be maintained that taste
is the most important element of all in the development
of wisdom. What we like is what we are, though what
we will is what we are struggling to become. So long
as we only "do with disgust what the law enjoins," we
have not attained the highest virtue. A completed character involves a perfected inclination, a direction of our
interests in the proper channel, a cultivated taste, or in
general what we have described as wisdom of feeling.
To have taught us the importance of this, is one of the
chief elements of what is great in the work of Mr. Ruskin.
It was seen also by Plato,[1] who placed the discipline of
the taste before the culture of the understanding: and
it has been accepted in practice by most of those who in
recent times have made successful efforts to elevate the
lives of the masses of our city populations, with whom
art and music have always been among the most potent
instruments.[2] We may know rightly and will rightly,
but until we feel rightly we are not masters of our
world. Our feeling is the consciousness of what is in
harmony or in disharmony with the central principles of
our being; and unless this consciousness is right, our being

---

[1] *Republic*, Book III.

[2] Cf. the saying of Kant—"Taste makes possible a transition,
without any violent leap, from the allurements of sense to a
habitual interest in what is morally good, as it shows us that the
imagination in its freedom is capable of being determined in adaptation to the understanding, and teaches us, even in the objects of
sense, to find a free satisfaction which is irrespective of sensuous
pleasure." *Kritik der Urtheilskraft*, I. ii., § 58. Cf. also Caird's
*Critical Philosophy of Kant*, II., p. 475, and Lilly's *Right and Wrong*,
p. 227 *seq.*

itself must be in some way disordered. "Who will teach us how to feel?" is, therefore, a great problem in moral culture.

Still, mere aesthetic culture will not lead us to the highest wisdom. To enjoy rightly is only a preliminary step towards that attitude of reverence in which our joys are "three parts pain." The ideals of a developing humanity do not at first present themselves in the guise of beauty, or as that which appeals to our natural inclinations: and if we rest merely in the delights of art, we shall miss the very key-note of the moral life—renunciation, which is "not joyous, but grievous." Life requires a certain bracing of the will, for which the "too musical man" is apt to be somewhat disqualified. In practice we have often to choose what we cannot like—at least till *after* it is chosen; and to do this we must have learnt to withstand our immediate feeling, and to think as well. "The heart is deceitful," and we must appeal from it to reason.

(*c*) The ultimate basis of wisdom can, in fact, be found nowhere but in Philosophy. Our wills must be stimulated by our interests, and must be guided by our thoughts. Wisdom of thought, therefore, must be at the foundation of wisdom of feeling and act. In recent times this truth, which is an old one, has been forgotten by many, on account of the sceptical attitude by which much of our recent Philosophy has been characterised. One set of teachers tells us that thought can lead us only to doubt and indecision: let us therefore act:—"The end of man is an action and not a thought." Another set tells us that thought will lead us only to dead and distracting puzzles: let us therefore feel:—"Art still has truth— take refuge there." Certainly if thought is to help us, it must be a kind of thought that leads to faith and not to distrust. After thinking, we must still be able, like

Margaret Fuller, to "believe in the Universe." We must
be able to believe that good is more fundamental than
evil, that beauty is deeper than deformity; that, in the
last resort, "the soul of the world is just." It is, and
has always been, the great problem of all Philosophy to
prove this, or to give good grounds for believing it: and
assuredly if we did not believe that this is the outcome
of philosophic thought, neither conduct nor art could save
us from the despair that would ensue. The only conclusion
then would be, that life is not worth living, nor death
worth dying. We are reasonable beings, and we cannot
ultimately build our lives upon unreason. To despair of
Philosophy would be a case of "Muth verloren, Alles
verloren." As Hegel says,[1] the time when a people loses
its Metaphysic, is at least as significant as that at which it
loses its statesmanship, or its moral habits and virtues. It
is also a significant time when, as seems to be now the
case in England, it begins for the first time to have a
Metaphysic.

Now as to the methods whereby these various kinds of
wisdom may become harmoniously developed, we must
leave this as a problem for the student of the theory of
education. We can here only observe that the development of it must be made a portion of the aim of education throughout its entire course: for wisdom cannot be
communicated at one moment; it can only be helped to
grow. Probably more hints with respect to this element
of culture might be derived from the *Republic* of Plato
than from any other single treatise; but the scheme of
Education, leading up to the highest philosophic wisdom,
which is there sketched out, would require to be considerably modified before it could be adapted to modern
life. On this point, as well as on the question of the
arrangement of studies generally, not much definite guid-

[1] *Wissenschaft der Logik*, Vorrede.

ance can be expected of the social philosopher.[1] It would be foolish, for instance, for any one in our generation to attempt, as Comte attempted, to draw up a scheme for the subordination of the various branches of study to the highest social ends. "The kingdom of heaven cometh not with observation." We cannot forecast the dawning of light in any particular direction, or of the sweetness which it brings with it. Yet it is not foolish to attempt to analyse the ends which we seek and to see their connection with each other. The actual working out of their relations with any fulness of detail, would require a careful consideration of the whole circumstances of a nation's life.

We have begun with industrial problems : we have ended with education. Education, however, must react on industry, as well as on social organisation. With the development of character and of insight into the meaning of life, much of the evil in our present civilisation will become more and more intolerable both to those who suffer it and to those who see it. The discontent of which education is thus the spring, is, indeed, frequently a source of disquiet to those who see in it only the addition of a new sensitiveness to our inevitable ills.[2] But it requires no excessive stretch of

[1] On the general subject of education from a philosophical point of view, I may take this opportunity of referring to the admirable work of Mrs. Bryant on *Educational Ends*.

[2] It is sometimes thought also, that education has a tendency to unfit men for the ordinary work of life. This applies, however, only to a wrong kind of education—education which consists in the heaping on of information, instead of in the development of power. It was to such education that Wellington referred in his celebrated saying, "You are over-educated for your intellect." Cf. Wiese's *German Letters on English Education*, p. 38, Marshall's *Principles of Economics*, I., p. 362 note, and Preface to Price's *Industrial Peace*, p. xxv.

optimistic faith to believe, that the forces of human invention and of human helpfulness which a deeper insight calls to life, are more than a match for all the ills which it discloses. Not only, however, does education bring with it new ideals of life and a consequent discontent with what has been already attained : it also brings with it a new sense of duty. Of education, more emphatically than of any other good, is it true that it is or may be " common to all." Some of the best results which it brings are seen at once to be universally communicable, and to be of the utmost importance for the regulation of the lives of all. Hence, there comes to be a continually deepening sense of the significance of the " Vocation of the Scholar," as one who is not merely a searcher for truth, but one who, when he has in some measure attained it, is bound, as in Plato's image,[1] to " return into the Cave" and help those who are still in darkness. With this increasing sense of the duties which knowledge and insight bring, we may expect that the spread of education will to a greater and greater extent react upon all the aspects of our social life.

. With these remarks, we must close our account of the particular problems of the present on which Social Philosophy has to endeavour to cast light. On no one of these questions can philosophy by itself afford us any complete guidance ; and even in throwing out such scanty hints as have now been offered, it must be allowed that we are in constant danger of turning ourselves into vendors of quack medicines for the body social. " Philosophy, like religion, must seek to view human life in relation to those principles which are at the making and unmaking of states; it cannot 'sit on a hill remote' to reason about abstractions; it cannot but attempt to comprehend that greatest of organisms, the State, which,

---

[1] *Republic*, Book VII.

in the 'architectonic of its rationality,' is the highest result of the conscious and unconscious working of reason in the life of man ; but, like religion, it must suffer loss when it is drawn down into the region of immediate practical politics and confounded with the attack and defence of special measures and institutions."[1]   If at any point we have seemed to touch too closely on such special measures and institutions, we can only plead in our defence that general principles without some practical application are apt to be dull and unenlightening.[2]   Moreover, if philosophy cannot help us without the scientific investigation of particular facts, what is to be said of such scientific investigation without philosophy?   Certainly the danger of our time is not that of an over-estimate of pure philosophic study.   What we have to fear is rather, on the one hand, the setting up of abstract ideals, without adequate analysis of the conditions of their fulfilment, and, on the other hand, the deadening of all ideals and the crushing out of all our higher aspirations, through the mere examination of the condition of things as they stand.   He who shall have at once a firm grasp of the concrete ideal of social well-being, and a clear insight into the conditions of its realisation, and the difficulties by which in the actual world it is beset, will

---

[1] Caird's *Hegel*, p. 95.

[2] Professor Alexander, in reviewing the first edition of this book for *Mind*, seemed to think that the introduction of practical details was just the point on which no apology was needed.   I am not so sure of this.   I am more and more convinced that philosophical considerations are enlightening in practical affairs ; but I am less and less inclined to think that any particular practical question can be solved by philosophical considerations alone ; and I am afraid that, even in the slight references that I have made to some of the weightier of the practical problems of our time, I have occasionally outstepped the limits of a strictly philosophical treatment.   Hence I still think that the apology here given was called for.

be the true social reformer of the future. It is the business of the philosopher to try to define the ideal, and to bring it into relation to those conditions of actual existence which other sciences enable us to discover. To give a general indication of the way in which this is to be done, has been the object of the present work.

# CHAPTER VII.

## SUMMARY AND CONCLUSION.

A FEW words will suffice to bring together the main points with which I have been endeavouring to deal.

In the first chapter, it was my object to explain what I regard as the scope and limits of a philosophy of society, and to indicate the relations of such a study to other departments of science. It would be useless to attempt to recapitulate the line of thought which was there pursued; but it may be well to try to meet a possible objection with regard to the relation of what is there said to the contents of the following chapters. It may be thought that in these chapters, and especially in Chapters II. and VI., we have gone entirely beyond the limits of such an investigation as is suggested in Chapter I. For in these chapters we have made some attempt to deal with the concrete phenomena of social life, and even with these phenomena as they appear at a particular time and place; whereas these phenomena, according to what is stated in Chapter I., can be dealt with satisfactorily only by social science, and would indeed involve, for their adequate treatment, the co-operation of several different departments of that science. This is, I think, true. But it must be remembered that Social Philosophy is a study whose ultimate aim is, in the highest sense, practical. It seeks to supply us with principles for our guidance in the conduct of social life; and these principles can scarcely be clearly stated without reference to particular illustrations drawn from the circumstances of actually existing societies. The introduction of such illustrations can do us no harm, if we are careful to remember that any light which Social Philosophy may be able to throw upon the problems involved in them, must be supplemented by the light which is supplied by the various departments of social science.[1] That this is the case, I have endeavoured at every step to keep steadily in view. This is perhaps all that it is now necessary to add with regard to the general scope of our inquiry.

In the second chapter, we proceeded to consider what are the main problems with which at the present time a Social Philosophy has to endeavour to deal. The chief points in the view which is there set forth, may now be made a little clearer by a reference to the contents of Chapter v. It was pointed out in that chapter, that there are four different ideals of social unity which naturally present themselves to us, according to the different points of view from which society is regarded. Now the gist of Chapter ii. may be said to consist in the statement, that in the history of modern Europe two of these ideals have already been adopted, and to a large extent embodied in

---

[1] There is, no doubt, a constant temptation, among students of social questions, to apply scientific principles too hastily to the solution of practical problems. It is partly for this reason that the study of such questions has been so slow in attaining a truly scientific character. It may often be said of the students of social problems that, in the language of Bacon, " Like Atalanta, they go aside to pick up the golden apple; but meanwhile they interrupt their course, and let the victory escape them." (Cf. Hearn's *Plutology*, p. 11, and Mr. Smart's Preface to Böhm-Bawerk's *Capital and Interest*, p. xiii.) But this is almost inevitable. We cannot avoid seeking to apply even our partial lights to the clearing up of social difficulties. The important thing is only that we recognise how partial they are.

the structure of society; and that we are now presented with the alternative of adopting one or other of the two ideals which remain. The first ideal which was adopted, was that which we have described as aristocratic. The second was that of individual liberty. At the present time the movement is on the whole in the socialistic direction. But there is also the possibility that we may, instead of passing (as hitherto) from one imperfect ideal to another, make an effort rather to work towards what in Chapter v. we have described as the organic ideal, which may be said in a manner to combine the excellences of the other three. This is substantially the argument of Chapter ii. All the statements which are made in it must, of course, be regarded as subject to correction by the investigation of students of history and social science.[1]

In the third chapter, we passed on to the question which lies at the root of our whole inquiry—the question with regard to the nature and meaning of the social unity. Here, again, it would be idle to attempt to summarise a line of thought which has perhaps already been stated with as much brevity as is consistent with clearness. It may be worth while, however, to remind the reader—a point which is continually in danger of being forgotten—that the conception of organic unity which is there introduced, is a purely metaphysical conception, and is not dependent on any facts that may be ascertained with

[1] It occurs to me at this point that, in giving a reference to Adam Smith on p. 100, I ought to have added that, while he has clearly brought out the economic advantages of Divisions of Labour, he has by no means overlooked the disadvantages, intellectual, moral, and political, by which they are apt to be accompanied. See *Wealth of Nations*, Book v., chap. i., Art. 2. The fact, however, that these qualifications are introduced so near the end of his work, and in a section dealing specially with the subject of education, has caused them to be somewhat neglected.

regard to the nature of organic life, on which it would be presumptuous for a mere student of philosophy to express an opinion.

In the fourth chapter, we were concerned with the ultimate aim of social life; and in dealing with this, it was necessary to enter into some inquiries which would fall more naturally within the province of a writer on Ethics. It was especially important, in this connection, to settle our account with Hedonism, which is so great a snare to the student of social science. Though the superficiality and emptiness of the Benthamite position are now pretty universally acknowledged, yet in more refined and emasculated forms Utilitarianism has still a considerable hold on English thought.[1] Consequently, it was necessary to indicate the defects of that theory with somewhat greater fulness than would otherwise have been desirable in such a treatise as this. What we have said on this subject would, no doubt, require to be considerably enlarged before it could be regarded as a satisfactory discussion of the question, either from a metaphysical or from a psychological point of view. But the line of argument which would have to be pursued was indicated, so far as that seemed necessary for our present purpose. After having thus criticised the hedonistic and other one-sided views of the social aim, we were able to define that aim from the organic point of view, and thus to complete the line of thought which was opened up in the preceding chapter.

In the fifth chapter, we entered upon the consideration of the guidance which our principles are capable of affording us, in supplying us with a practical ideal of social

---

[1] It has perhaps ceased to have much hold on English *ethical* thought; but it is certainly still the dominant view among writers on *Economics.* On the element of truth in Hedonism, see Hegel's *Werke*, i., p. S.

life. The four most prominent ideals of social unity were
seen to arise out of the different aspects from which the
individual life may be regarded, as standing in relation at
once to nature and to human society. In the examination of these ideals, however, and in the exhibition of
the one-sidedness of three of them, it was necessary to
a certain extent to encroach on the sphere of the sociologist, and especially upon the province of the economist.
A mere statement of the grounds of their inadequacy,
from purely philosophical principles, would have been too
empty and unenlightening, without some illustration of the
way in which their inadequacy comes out in the concrete
phenomena of social life. The degree of attention which
we have devoted to the different ideals, has also been
influenced by the facts of their presentation in the concrete. Just as in the preceding chapter, Hedonism
naturally attracted more attention than the other possible
theories of our ultimate aim, so it seemed desirable to treat
the socialistic ideal with a little more fulness than the
rest. The reason of this is, of course, to be found in
the fact that the movement towards Socialism is one of
the most characteristic tendencies of the present time;
and that it is, consequently, of more importance to guard
against the one-sidedness of this ideal than against that
of the others.[1]  "It is the temptation of writers on social
subjects to be least just to the tendencies of the time

[1] It is curious that advocates of Socialism frequently allege the
increasing prevalence of socialistic principles as an argument in
favour of its adoption. However optimistic we may be with regard
to the course of history—however firmly we may hold that *Die
Welt-Geschichte ist das Welt-Gericht*—we can scarcely deny that the
most prominent tendency at any time is usually a tendency towards
some one-sided extreme. Hence, to say that any tendency is becoming
prominent, carries with it, on the whole, not the injunction to
identify ourselves with it, but rather the injunction to be careful
how we yield to it. In what sense, and to what extent, it actually

which precedes their own, and against the errors of which they have immediately to contend."[1] The individualistic ideal is,[2] indeed, still the one which is actually dominant : but it can scarcely be doubted that it has ceased to be that which governs the thought of those who are "under five and twenty"; and there is some danger now that we may begin to forget the element of truth which was contained in it. Enthusiasm is on the other side.

Finally, in the sixth chapter, we proceeded to specify the main points of application of the true ideal in dealing with the actual problems of society as it is. The true ideal is at a disadvantage in comparison with the three imperfect ones. It cannot supply us, as they can, with edifying formulas and sweeping generalities. It has, indeed, the counterbalancing advantage, that it is able to accept the formulas of the other three, and turn them against each other : but when they are thus combined and modified, it is not so easy to adopt them as the watchwords of an enthusiasm or the inspiration of a life. Whole truths are seldom so good to fight with as half-truths; because the latter can oppose themselves more sharply to the half-lies against which we have most often to contend.[3] But whole truths are better to build with : they are more serviceable when we pass from the work

is true that recent development has been in a strictly socialistic direction is a point that is, no doubt, open to dispute. See, for instance, Kidd's *Social Evolution*, chap. viii., and Gilman's *Socialism and the American Spirit, passim.* But, in the somewhat general sense in which I have been using the term in this book, I believe that the strength of the socialistic tendency can hardly be denied.

[1] Caird's *Social Philosophy of Comte*, p. 230.

[2] *I.e.* the ideal of individual liberty. Cf. *supra*, .p. 250.

[3] This statement is itself only half-true : for, after all, there is nothing which can so thoroughly overcome a half-lie as a whole truth which absorbs the little germ of vitality that enabled it to exist.

of overturning to that of reconstructing. In this reconstructing work, however, we cannot content ourselves with the general principles which furnish the definition of our ideal: we must combine these with the facts of the actual world, which the application of the ideal is to transform. To indicate the way in which such a combination may be effected, was the work of our concluding chapter.

It is natural to ask, after reading such an essay as this—What, then, is the net result to which it leads? In what respects are we made wiser? In what respects are we helped to deal with our practical problems? It is apt to seem sometimes as if philosophy were little more than an elaborate artifice for the killing of faiths and the crushing out of enthusiasms. It may, indeed, appear to furnish us with a new light and a new law; but its light is so "dry" and its commandment is so "very broad" that the interest seems to be taken out of both. It lacks colour, and it lacks moving power.

The answer to this is, that it would be as foolish to substitute philosophy for everything else as it is to substitute any other aspect of things for the whole. Such a substitution is an error to which the students of every particular subject are liable. The physicist is apt to say —"I understand matter and motion—what is there else to know?" or "Tell me what electricity is, and I will tell you everything."[1] The economist is apt to say— "Here are the results that will follow from certain courses of action under certain presupposed conditions— Can wisdom go any farther?" The sociologist is apt to say—"I find that certain events take place in certain connections—Here be truths, and all else is vanity."

---

[1] A saying which is attributed to Lord Kelvin. There is, of course, a sense in which it is true—the sense of Tennyson's "Flower in the crannied wall."

If the philosopher is ever tempted to yield to a similar illusion of mistaking his watch-tower for the world, it may be well to remind him that "the painting of grey in grey"[1] cannot recreate the hues of life; that to discern the meaning of things cannot supply us with the things that mean; that wisdom and insight presuppose ends that are worthy to be achieved and objects that are capable of being understood. Philosophy cannot afford to despise the world : it is well if the world knows that it cannot afford to despise *it*.

What, then, is the special good that Social Philosophy yields us? It is, I think, chiefly this : It teaches us to place the various ends of life in their right relations to each other. It teaches us to regard the pursuit of wealth, the pursuit of virtue, the pursuit of knowledge and wisdom, the pursuit of culture, the pursuit of political organisation, the pursuit of æsthetic satisfaction, the pursuit of religious truth; not as a number of separate ambitions which one man may choose and another may neglect, but as all essentially parts of a single aim which no one can renounce without in some degree ceasing to be human. In the actual history of mankind, no doubt, it is inevitable that the various aspects of our life should become distinguished and separated from each other. Nor, indeed, is it desirable that the demarcation between them should ever become blurred. To turn our commercial life into a religion would be to give it a false importance. To treat art as a mere element in morality would be to destroy that playfulness which is at once its charm and its justification.[2] Knowledge, too, is best pursued for its own sake, rather than with any direct reference to the practical ends which it assists. But in all such separations there

---

[1] Hegel's *Philosophie des Rechts*, Vorrede, *ad fin.*
[2] "Ernst ist das Leben : heiter ist die Kunst."—Schiller.

is a constant danger of a wrong abstraction—a danger
which is probably greater in our own time than in any
other, with our excessive specialisation and division of
labour.    If we forget altogether, for instance, that the
pursuit of wealth is essentially a part of the same aim
as that which expresses itself in our moral and religious
aspirations, commerce at once becomes degraded ; until
at length those who are interested in the higher life, are
forced to withdraw entirely from the life of trade as
from something unworthy of a freeman or of a saint.[1]
Art also, "chartered libertine" though it is, loses its
highest significance, and even its deepest beauty, when in
the midst of its sportful ideals and capricious fancies the
earnestness of life ceases to shine through.    Nor is it
less true that religion becomes narrow and morality
empty when their relations to art, or even to the pursuit
of material well-being, are forgotten.    To place all these
aims in their right relations, to exhibit their significance
as elements in the effort to see the true meaning and
attain the true happiness of life, is one of the main
functions of philosophic study.

To understand, indeed, is not everything.    Not only
is philosophy empty without the content which the
particular sciences supply ; but even all the sciences and
philosophy taken together cannot of themselves furnish
us with a solution of our social difficulties.    There can
be no ideal society without ideal men : and for the
production of these we require not only insight, but a
motive power ; fire as well as light.    Perhaps a philosophic understanding of our social problems is not even
the chief want of our time.    We need prophets as well
as teachers, men like Carlyle or Ruskin or Tolstoï, who

---

[1] The prevalence of some such view as this has been one of the
main hindrances in the way of the development of economic science.
Cf. Marshall's *Principles of Economics*, I., pp. 4 and 19.

are able to add for us a new severity to conscience or a new breadth to duty. Perhaps we want a new Christ.[1] We want at least an accession of the Christlike spirit— the spirit of self-devotion to ideal ends—applying itself persistently in all the departments of life, and in the midst of all the complexities of our modern civilisation. It has been well said that the prophet of our time must be a man of the world, and not merely a voice in the wilderness. For, indeed, the wilderness of the present is in the streets of our crowded cities, and in the midst of the incessant war by which we are trying to make our way upwards. It is there that the prophets must be.

Or perhaps our chief want is rather for the poet of the new age than for its prophet—or for one who should be poet and prophet in one. Our poets of recent generations have taught us the love of nature, and enabled us to see in it the revelation of the divine. We still look for one who shall show us with the same clearness the presence of the divine in the human. Some glimpses, indeed, of this we have had. We have just lost one who struggled stoutly with this very problem—

---

[1] Talleyrand's advice to one about to start a new religion, that he should first get himself crucified and rise the third day, has some point. We may say, at any rate, that the inspiration required for the spread of the social religion of the future (without which it seems clear that there can be no true regeneration of society), must be expected to come, not from any mere philosophical theory, but from a living personality. Such personalities have not been entirely wanting in recent times. We have had, for instance, the late T. H. Green, Arnold Toynbee, and several others; and the influence which such men have exerted has been a quite incalculable force. In comparison with such powers as these, any theory, however excellent, is only the finite beside the infinite. At the basis of such person- alities, however, there is nearly always, if not a philosophic theory, at least a philosophic faith. Their lives, indeed, might almost be said to be philosophy in the concrete: they embody the ideals which philosophic theory seeks to analyse.

> "One who never turned his back, but marched breast forward,
>   Never doubted clouds would break."

But even he gave us rather "incidents in the development of a soul" than studies in social relations. We still need one who shall be fully and in all seriousness what Heine playfully called himself, a "Ritter Von dem Heiligen Geist," one who shall teach us to see the working out of our highest ideals in the everyday life of the world, and to find in devotion to the advancement of that life, not merely a sphere for an ascetic self-sacrifice, but a supreme object in the pursuit of which "all thoughts, all passions, all delights," may receive their highest development and satisfaction.

The philosopher, as such, cannot become either the prophet[1] or the poet, any more than he can become the man of science. He can only await their coming, appreciate them, and assign their places.

[1] On the contrast in this respect between the attitude of modern philosophy and that of ancient philosophy, there are some instructive remarks in Wundt's *System der Philosophie*, pp. 3-10. It seems to me, however, that Wundt has drawn the line between philosophic truth and moral inspiration much too sharply. It is, no doubt, true, as Hegel says (*Phenomenologie des Geistes*, Vorrede), that "Philosophy must guard itself against seeking to be edifying." Still, if it is true Philosophy, it cannot help being edifying, whether it seeks it or not. Cf. preceding note, and *supra*, pp. 4, 59, and 369.

# INDEX.

GLASGOW: PRINTED AT THE UNIVERSITY PRESS BY ROBERT MACLEHOSE AND CO.